Crime and Psychology

Clear and accessible in style, this book offers a comprehensive introduction to criminal justice and forensic mental health and the ways in which they intersect.

Assuming no prior exposure to the field of criminal forensic psychology, the book reviews ten areas where mental health professionals contribute regularly to the due process of law: comprehension of rights, competency to stand trial, transfer of juveniles to adult court, risk assessment, mitigation, sentencing, sexually violent predators, insanity, and capital punishment of persons with mental illness and with intellectual disability. The book also explores the major categories of mental disorders, how they contribute to criminal behavior, and what problems they present in courts and corrections. Landmark cases from the United States and United Kingdom are also reviewed in detail to develop a thorough understanding of the court's decision-making process. Bridging the gap between abstraction and practice through its narrative presentation of case material, emphasis on controversy, and illumination of the historical roots of problems and ideas, the book helps the forensic practitioner transition from novice to knowledgeable professional in the courtroom.

Drawing on the author's extensive experience in forensic psychology, this book is the ideal resource for the early-career forensic mental health practitioner, as well as graduate students in forensic mental health and forensic psychology, and mental health professionals seeking to enter the field of forensics.

Jonathan Venn, Ph.D., ABPP, earned his doctoral degree in Clinical Psychology at Northwestern University in 1977. He has been providing psychological services since 1971 and has evaluated thousands of criminal defendants, convicted felons, and juvenile delinquents. He has testified as an expert witness in hundreds of litigated proceedings.

Crime and Psychology
Foundations of Forensic Practice

Jonathan Venn

Routledge
Taylor & Francis Group

NEW YORK AND LONDON

Designed cover image: © Getty

First published 2024
by Routledge
605 Third Avenue, New York, NY 10158

and by Routledge
4 Park Square, Milton Park, Abingdon, Oxon, OX14 4RN

Routledge is an imprint of the Taylor & Francis Group, an informa business

© 2024 Jonathan Venn

The right of Jonathan Venn to be identified as author of this work has been asserted in accordance with sections 77 and 78 of the Copyright, Designs and Patents Act 1988.

ISBN: 978-1-032-47196-9 (hbk)
ISBN: 978-1-032-47191-4 (pbk)
ISBN: 978-1-003-38502-8 (ebk)

DOI: 10.4324/9781003385028

Typeset in Sabon
by MPS Limited, Dehradun

Access the Support Material: www.routledge.com/9781032471914

For Mary Ann, whose constant reassurance saw me through many long hours.

In memoriam: Saleem A. Shah, Ph.D. (1931–1992), one of my many teachers, who inspired a generation of mental health professionals and did more than any other individual to create the field of forensic psychology in the United States.

In memoriam: Sarah Anne Munson, J.D. (1939–1990), gone too soon like a flickering light, with your bold and gentle spirit you taught me what I know about mental health and the law.

Contents

Online support material

 www.routledge.com/9781032471914

As part of the online support material, you will find comprehensive material on the following topics:

Appendix A Specialty guidelines for forensic psychology
Appendix B U.S. Department of Justice: Code of Professional Responsibility for the Practice of Forensic Science (September 6, 2016)
Appendix C Aristotle on the question of personal responsibility
Appendix D The history of due process
Appendix E Henry de Bracton (1210–1268) and the "wild beast test"
Appendix F Native Americans encounter Anglo-American justice
Appendix G Sir William Blackstone (1723–1780) and the doctrine of mens rea
Appendix H *Rex v. Bellingham* (1812)
Appendix I *Regina v. Oxford* (1840)
Appendix J Incorporation of the U.S. Bill of Rights and the Fourteenth Amendment
Appendix K Race and the death penalty: *McCleskey v. Kemp* (U.S. 1987)
Appendix L Incapacitation: the "three strikes" laws in California
Appendix M The insanity defense and the abolitionist states
Appendix N Lawyers do not think like mental health professionals
Appendix O The statistical properties of psychometric tests
Appendix P Jamie Wilson's MMPI profile

Figures

Tables

Foreword

Even as a teenager, I was always fascinated by crime. I wondered why people would do horrible things to each other, often for no material gain. Eventually, that fascination would lead me to a career as a forensic psychologist. Prior to graduate school, I served for two years as a volunteer for the U.S. Peace Corps in Senegal. Among the many things I learned in West Africa was that "changing the world" is a massive task that would be vastly beyond my capabilities, especially when the world was not asking to be changed. I decided that helping one person at a time (often the work of a clinical psychologist) was a much more realistic goal, so I applied to graduate schools in psychology. During my graduate studies in clinical psychology, it became clear to me that few things affected the well-being of Americans more than the criminal justice system; however, at the time, psychology did not appear to be paying much attention to this incredibly powerful force in people's lives. Putting those two fields together appealed to me, so I decided to seek and eventually achieved a doctoral minor from the University of Arizona College of Law.

Having had a healthy dose of legal education, I had more preparation for forensic psychology than most of my peers. I was lucky enough to become an intern at McLean Hospital, which had recently decided to dive into the provision of clinical services to the previously infamous Bridgewater State (Forensic) Hospital. There, I had access to a group of extremely talented and experienced forensic psychologists, psychiatrists, and social workers. At least as important, for better and for worse, were the correctional officers (Bridgewater's equivalent of psychiatric technicians). While some of them were brutal and others were seemingly incompetent, there was a small subset of experienced, decent, empathic, and talented direct care staff who mentored me. Since they spent by far the most time with the patients, they knew and were able to teach me how to listen to the patients and work with them without getting hurt. Keep in mind, the patient population of Bridgewater was comprised predominantly of people with psychotic disorders and histories of very serious violent offenses.

It was around that time that I was first called as an expert witness. I had been "prepped" by the attorney who called me for about five minutes. The preparation consisted of the attorney reading my carefully written report, which said that the defendant was psychotic at the time of the offense and was therefore unable to appreciate the nature and quality of his act, which was to kill someone. Since I had been very well trained by forensic psychologists and psychiatrists, I felt very confident on the stand. The attorney had asked me each and every question we discussed during my brief preparation, except one: "Is your opinion true to a *reasonable degree of medical certainty?*" I was literally speechless, because I did not understand what he had just said. Was it a trick question intended to trap me in a lie? After all, I was not a physician, so how could I claim medical certainty? (Imagine a sudden acute attack of the "imposter syndrome.") If this book had been available at the time, I would have known exactly how to respond. (See Chapter 3 for a discussion of the history and meaning of this rather odd phrase.)

Despite the advantages that law school and supervision provided me, what I did not have and would have loved is a book like this one. While I had read many of the cases that are cited in this volume, nowhere had they been placed in context. What was not available at the time was a place where I could read about the profession I was hoping to enter, in a comprehensive, practical way. I had read a few books about forensic mental health, but there was nothing about *being* a forensic psychologist. I was given very specific instructions about how to do certain kinds of evaluations, but nowhere could I find a reliable guide to the role I was seeking to fill within the American criminal justice system, especially from a man who had filled that role for more than four decades.

Jonathan Venn has been a practicing forensic psychologist for 40 years. In this volume, instead of trying to impress people with his career or telling "war stories," he decided to humbly share some of the lessons he has learned; lessons that helped him to do his work with integrity, excellence, and the respect of his peers. His story is based on his decades of experience across the spectrum of forensic mental health, from pre-trial issues such as competency to stand trial, to at-trial issues like mental state at the time of the offense (e.g., insanity), to post-trial issues of sentencing including the death penalty, to appellate issues of competency to be executed.

This is not a book for someone looking for a sophisticated treatise on mental health law. To be sure, many of the landmark cases affecting forensic psychology are explained, often with the added benefit of helping us to get to know a bit about the people involved. There is also a comprehensive list of complex terms such as "burden of proof," "reasonable degree ... ," and "standards of evidence," each of which is explained in clear, simple language. These legal concepts and landmark cases are placed in historical context, allowing readers to know where this field comes from and perhaps where it's going.

To accommodate those who are seeking deep, scholarly explanations of law or science, the author generously provides extensive references regarding many of the legal, clinical, and controversial topics that define our field. But this book is specifically aimed at people who are contemplating or beginning careers in forensic psychology. The topics covered are comprehensive and practical; and useful because they are explained in straightforward language. This book would have been a godsend to me in my first years of forensic practice.

Like many of my peers, I am frequently asked for a description of what I do for a living. "What is a forensic psychologist?" "What do they do?" "What does mental disability have to do with crime and punishment?" "Where did this tradition of psychology and law come from and where is it going?" Experienced forensic mental health providers will enjoy this book, but they are not its target audience. Jonathan Venn has successfully created an excellent first book that answers these questions and many more for people with more interest than knowledge of forensic psychology.

This book is part of a tradition of which many readers may be unaware. In 1975, the American Psychiatric Association established the Manfred Guttmacher Award to recognize an outstanding contribution to the literature of forensic psychiatry and awarded it to Alan Stone for *Mental Health and Law, a System in Transition*. In 1980, the award was presented to Jonas Robitcher for *The Powers of Psychiatry*. In 1981, the same award was presented to psychologist John Monahan and his colleagues for *The Clinical Prediction of Violent Behavior*. In 1987, Gary Melton, John Petrila, Christopher Slobogin, and Norman Poythress produced *Psychological Evaluations for the Courts: A Handbook for Mental Health Professionals and Lawyers* (now in its 4th edition), which quickly reached status as the "must-have" volume for any forensic psychologist or psychiatrist. Stone and Robitcher wrote scholarly books about the law and psychiatry, while Monahan's book provided and explained statistical and research findings that have revolutionized our field. Melton et al. wrote four incredibly comprehensive volumes, each of which provided forensic psychologists with a plethora of information that they would need in order to competently conduct various kinds of criminal, civil, and juvenile forensic evaluations, including research findings, legal rules and processes, important cases, and even-handed explanations of the most controversial issues in the field.

Each of these was a wonderful book, albeit in different ways. However, none of them tried to explain what it is like to perform this work. Jonathan Venn understands and explains what it is like to do the work he has done for the last 40 years and to be the person who does it.

This book gives one a realistic sense of the pressures we face and the biases that can stand in the way of our aspirations toward objective, honest, and unbiased opinions. It is written with a great deal of humility, both in style and content. The author pays as much attention to what we do not know as to what we do. Like any well-written memoir, there is no effort to exaggerate or aggrandize the role of the forensic psychologist, whose job is really quite simple and humble. We write reports that express opinions and the evidence and logic upon which they are based. In court, we answer the questions that we are asked on direct and cross-examination unless there is a successful objection. Our duty is to explain what we believe to be true and the evidence and logic upon which our opinions rest.

Jonathan Venn understands some of the most fundamental and humble truths of forensic psychology. Early and often, he explains that all forensic psychological opinion testimony is based on inference. After all, we don't know what happened because we were not there and we are not privy to people's thoughts or feelings, now or in the past. Therefore, expert testimony always involves inferential leaps – the trick is to make the leaps as short as possible. With humility and experience to back him up, he provides the reader with an honest account of how we try to complete this difficult assignment, and with integrity, fairness, objectivity, and honor. As expert witnesses testifying under oath, our intention must never be the result of the trial. Simply put, our real clients are the courts, and we are not to take sides.

There is a great deal of humanity in this book. Dr. Venn discusses the major players in the history of forensic mental health, whether they were judges, attorneys, victims, suspects, or convicted perpetrators in the fullness of their personhood, avoiding the danger of shrinking them into last names and stereotypes. He tells inspiring stories of courageous judges who essentially wrote the case laws that guide us. Other stories are heartbreaking and humanize the people who perpetrated or suffered violent harm.

The author never loses sight of the enormity of the consequences that are determined by criminal trials, which often result in taking away the two most precious values in our constitution: life and liberty. Despite his humble view of his own role in the process, Dr. Venn understands that taking away someone's life or freedom is a profoundly serious job. Experienced forensic psychologists often learn these lessons through their own hard experience. Personally, I would have liked to read about it through Dr. Venn's.

The book, while staying at a "first book" level of detail, is extremely comprehensive and covers nearly every important aspect of forensic psychology, including direct and collateral evidence, psychological testing, and how statistics should and should not be used to make decisions about individual cases. I particularly appreciated the discussion of the statistical properties of psychometric tests like "degree of error" and "normative groups." These often complicated and sophisticated concepts are explained in readable, simple language.

Perhaps the greatest compliment I could give a book such as this is that it does exactly what the author set out to do. It provides an honest picture of the career of a forensic psychologist. Case studies give life to legal principles and processes, and complex questions are explained in clear, thoughtful language that is easily digested. The list of topics covered is comprehensive, and the resulting discussions are practical.

Perhaps you are someone who has wondered about the practice of forensic psychology. Or maybe you have contemplated a career in this field or started down the path that Jonathan Venn has described so well. In either case, this book is for you. I hope you enjoy reading it and learning about this fascinating profession.

Joel A. Dvoskin, Ph.D., ABPP
Board Certified in Forensic Psychology
University of Arizona College of Medicine
Co-Founder, Heroes Active Bystandership Training
Former President, American Psychology-Law Society

Preface

The year was 1968 and I was sitting in the first lecture of my first psychology course in my first year of college. Professor Robert Nicolay defined "psychology" for us as "the science of behavior." If I had known what I knew ten years later when I testified for the first time as an expert witness in a criminal trial, I would have told the professor that psychology is the science of the invisible and the obscure. The art and science of forensic psychology lies in translating these obscurities into words that have significant consequences for the life and liberty of individual defendants.

To be a forensic psychologist is to labor within multiple levels of obscurity that are laid each upon the other. First, I did not witness the crime. I must rely on a collection of physical evidence, photographs, surveillance videos, and the testimony of others to develop my mental images of the crime. These mental images are always my own and they are never going to be perfect.

Second, each person involved in the process – defendants, witnesses, victims, family members, and law enforcement personnel – has their own limited perspective and their own personal agenda. Their reports may not be fully reliable due to a combination of factors that includes forgetting, repression, denial, manipulation, and deceit. Forensic examiners must decide who and what they are going to believe, and why.

Repression can be so complete that a defendant may have no recollection of significant events in their lives – including childhood victimization – even though these events may have had profound effects on them and may have inclined them toward criminal behavior. The forensic examiner can find themselves in a situation where they believe a collateral witness – perhaps a family member – over the protests of the defendant themselves. (For an illustration of this, please see the case of Alfonse in Chapter 29.)

Third, our system of justice is based not only on what a defendant did but also on what they were thinking at the time. This is the doctrine of mens rea and is the subject of Chapters 7 and 8. In the Anglo-American system of criminal justice, we are bold enough to think that we can know what another person was thinking and that we can infer it from their actions. The doctrine of mens rea and its assumptions add another level of obscurity.

A fourth level of obscurity is contributed by a set of challenges that are inherent to the realities of communication between two human beings. Interviewees may have speech disorders. They may mumble or whisper. Their understanding of words and gestures may be idiosyncratic. They may be intoxicated at the time we are trying to interview them. They may be hearing voices, and these voices may tell them not to talk to us. They may contradict themselves, and they may or may not be aware of it when they do. Defendants often have learning disorders, aphasias, communication problems, disorganized thinking, and other symptoms that make communication difficult. (Indeed, factors including mental illness, learning disorders, and communication problems are over-represented in the offender population and help to explain why so many defendants do not fit into the mainstream economy and fall instead into the underground economy of crime.) Defendants might not speak English, and examiners may have to rely on translators. (My experience with forensic translators has been very positive. Not only have they been adept at translation, but they also have been sensitive to symptoms like disorganized thinking. Nevertheless, translation from another language inevitably adds another level of obscurity to the evaluation.)

A fifth level of obscurity is added by the psychometric tests designed by mental health professionals. Tests are tangible objects, but the constructs they measure, like intelligence and personality, are intangibles. And not only are the constructs intangible, but so are their impairments. Furthermore, tests are never perfect but are always subject to a degree of error (which is the topic of Appendix O).

Written records add a sixth level of obscurity. Records may be sketchy, imprecise, vague, enigmatic, ambiguous, inconsistent, self-contradictory, or missing. It is not uncommon to find that written records contradict each other, and the authors of old records may no longer be available to explain them. Tests and procedures identified in old records may be outdated, obsolete, unfathomable, and undiscoverable.

A seventh level of obscurity lies in the cultural differences between examiner and subject. Forensic examiners are likely to be middle-class adults with graduate degrees, and most defendants are not. Differences in race and culture can be profound. Informants may not understand our questions, and examiners may not understand their answers.

Expert testimony adds an eighth level of obscurity. We may assume that jurors have a different understanding of human behavior than the expert witness. Jurors are silent and they do not tell us what they are thinking. A forensic expert testifies about complex subjects like mental illness, intellectual developmental disorder, psychometric testing, and psychological research to a jury of untrained citizens. These concepts are difficult and took us years or even decades to master. Then we try to explain them in a few minutes to a juror with a sixth-grade education (the minimum standard in some jurisdictions). And not only did it take us years or decades to master these concepts, but the concepts themselves keep changing, as does the terminology used to describe them. Furthermore, experts disagree with each other. Not only might the testimony be difficult to understand, but the hapless juror may face the formidable task of deciding which expert to believe.

A ninth level of obscurity is added by a set of internal and external pressures that are very real in the life of the defendant but which the examiner might not even perceive. These pressures can include the realities of family dynamics, early childhood experiences, peer pressure, gang rules, and prison "politics" that are central to their own existence but which to the examiner may be a set of unknowns.

In the midst of this invisibility, intangibility, and obscurity, forensic examiners are bold enough to think that we can understand another person, know something about what it is like to be them, and know what they were thinking at the time of a crime. Then we present our opinions to silent jurors, where the words we speak about these intangibilities have serious consequences for the defendant's life and liberty in the real world.

The book you are holding in your hands is something that I began to write after I had spent 49 years in the psychological assessment and treatment of human beings. In that period of time I have seen more than 10,000 patients. I have been a military officer, an adjunct professor, a state employee, and a small business owner. I served on the staff of a Fortune 500 corporation and retired from the correctional systems of two states. I have submitted written opinions on thousands of criminal defendants and juvenile delinquents, and I have testified under oath in hundreds of litigated proceedings, including cases that raise fundamental questions about the law and mental health. I have collected some of these cases for this book, including cases of automatism (see Chapter 8), settled insanity (Chapter 8), strict liability (Chapter 12), homicide (Chapters 8, 10, 11, 19, 23, 26, 28, and 29), and capital punishment (Chapters 11, 23, and 29), including school shooter Jamie Wilson, who is, to my knowledge, the only person in the United States who has been condemned to death even though the judge at his trial found him to be so mentally ill that he could not control his behavior.

At the request of an attorney, I am not allowed to discuss a trial that is currently being litigated in Georgia, regarding intellectual developmental disorder (IDD) and murder. However, the question of IDD and murder in the state of Georgia is a unique situation that is discussed in Chapter 17 and illustrates some of the topics that are covered in this book, including the standards of evidence (see Chapter 5).

I also have collected for this book the most important landmark cases of Anglo-American law that have shaped judicial reasoning about crime and mental disorders for the past several centuries. These are the cases that define the practice of forensic mental health. The topics covered are foundational in nature and introduce the reader to the core concepts of due process, the four levels of mens rea, the three standards of evidence, the four goals of sentencing, the three incapacities of insanity, and the admissibility of expert testimony. To my way of thinking, the complete forensic mental health professional is someone who understands the science of mental disorders; their biological, sociological, and cultural aspects; the therapies; the applicable mathematics; the relevant law – both case law and statutory law; politics; and the history of this wide-ranging field. This book addresses large themes, and it lies beyond its scope to provide exhaustive reviews of these many areas. My goal is to point the reader to good sources of information where they can begin their own study. My hope is that this book will help to stem the flow of experts who ascend the steps of our witness stands (and of the attorneys who examine them) without understanding the law, the tools of their science, or their own place in history.

A courthouse is a place where disputes are litigated, and the topics chosen for this book revolve around controversies. The controversies covered in this book include:

- whether medical doctors are the only professionals who can testify as experts on mental disorders; *Jenkins v. United States* (1962) (see Chapter 2)
- how judges can determine what expert testimony should be allowed in court (see Chapter 3)
- whether expert witnesses can be allowed to testify regarding new knowledge that has not yet been generally accepted by the scientific community; *Daubert v. Merrell Dow Pharmaceuticals, Inc.* (1993) (see Chapter 3)
- whether mental health experts can be allowed to testify to the ultimate issue (e.g., regarding insanity) (see Chapters 19 and 22)
- whether mental health professionals are able to predict who will commit future acts of violence; *Baxstrom v. Herold* (1966) (see Chapter 12)
- the contest between clinical and statistical prediction (see Chapter 12)

- whether all defendants – including indigents – are entitled to receive forensic mental health services; *Ake v. Oklahoma* (1986) (see Chapter 2)
- whether all defendants are entitled to an assessment of their competency to stand trial; *Drope v. Missouri* (1975) (see Chapter 10)
- whether the content of mitigation testimony can be restricted when a defendant's life is at stake; *Lockett v. Ohio* (1978) (see Chapter 14)
- whether mental health diagnosis is scientific or political in nature, which includes the question of whether a personality disorder can be considered a mental illness (see Chapter 16)
- whether the liberties that are guaranteed in the Bill of Rights and the Fourteenth Amendment apply only to the federal government or apply also to the states (see Appendix J)
- whether a juvenile offender can be transferred to adult court without a hearing; *Kent v. United States* (1966) (see Chapter 11)
- whether juvenile offenders can be sentenced to life in prison (without the possibility of parole) without first considering their individual circumstances (*Miller v. Alabama,* 2012) and the question of their incorrigibility (*Jones v. Mississippi,* 2021) (see Chapter 15)
- whether it will be state governments or the mental health professions who define "intellectual developmental disorder (IDD)"; *Moore v. Texas* (2017, 2019) (see Chapter 17)
- whether "beyond a reasonable doubt" is an acceptable standard of evidence for claims of intellectual developmental disorder (IDD) in criminal trials, or whether this will lead inevitably to the unlawful execution of persons who have IDD; *Hill v. Humphrey* (2011) (see Chapter 17)
- whether intoxication with a psychoactive substance must be considered when a defendant is accused of murder; *Montana v. Egelhoff* (1996) (see Chapter 8)
- whether dissociative identity disorder (DID) can be considered a form of insanity (see Chapter 30)
- whether insanity can be defined as the product of a mental illness; *Durham v. United States* (1954) (see Chapter 19)
- whether defendants are entitled to the defense of diminished capacity (see Chapter 21)
- whether defendants are entitled to the defense of volitional incapacity, and whether it is even possible to assess volitional incapacity (see Chapter 19)
- whether defendants who are found to have volitional incapacity can be condemned to death; *State v. Wilson* (1992) (see Chapter 23)
- whether defendants who have intellectual developmental disorder can be condemned to death; *Atkins v. Virginia* (2002) (see Chapter 17)

- whether persons who have severe mental illness can be executed; *Ford v. Wainwright* (1986) (see Chapter 18)
- whether there is racial bias in the death penalty; *McCleskey v. Kemp* (1987) (see Appendix K)
- whether the states can be required to have the insanity defense; *Kahler v. Kansas* (2020) (see Chapter 24).

The final landmark case reviewed in Part IV is *Kahler v. Kansas* (2020), and this provides a fitting climax. Eight centuries of tradition in Anglo-American law came to an end on March 23, 2020, when the U.S. Supreme Court ruled that the states are not required to have an insanity defense. Defendants who have mental illness are no longer entitled to the insanity defense, depending on the laws of their jurisdiction.

A subtext of this book is the manner in which Anglo-American justice has been made richer by the judges who recognized the reality of mental disorders and who stood up for the idea that persons who have mental disorders require special treatment by the courts. Some of these judges were (and are) courageous souls who stood in the minority or even stood alone against their peers as they wrote well-reasoned dissents. This list includes:

- Henry de Bracton (1210–1268), an early promulgator of the insanity defense (see Appendix E)
- Judge Sir James Fitzjames Stephen (1829–1894), who recognized the reality of volitional impairment (see Chapter 19) and who admonished his colleagues on the bench for their "sarcasm and ridicule" of mental health professionals (see Chapter 22)
- Judge David Bazelon (1909–1993) of the Court of Appeals for the District of Columbia, who advocated for the product test of insanity (see Chapter 19) and who ruled that medical doctors are not the only experts who can testify in court regarding mental illness (*Jenkins v. United States,* 1962; see Chapter 2)
- Justice Ernest Adolphus Finney (1931–2017) of the South Carolina Supreme Court, who was the sole dissenting voice when that court approved the death penalty for Jamie Wilson – a defendant who was so severely mentally ill that he could not control his behavior at the time of his crime (*State v. Wilson,* 1992; see Chapter 23)
- the three-judge panel in the U.S. Court of Appeals, Tenth Circuit, who held that dissociative identity disorder (DID) is a severe mental illness that entails insanity even when the "parts" or "alters" who commit crimes are not insane within themselves (*United States v. Denny-Shaffer,* 1993; see Chapter 30)

- Justice Rosemary Barkett (1939–) of the Eleventh U.S. Circuit Court of Appeals, who argued that the State of Georgia inevitably will execute persons who have intellectual developmental disorder (IDD) because it requires that IDD be established beyond a reasonable doubt (*Hill v. Humphrey*, 2011; see Chapter 17); Justice Barkett's keen understanding of the difficulties involved in the retrospective assessment of intellectual developmental disorder was quite on point, but it was not enough to save the life of Warren Lee Hill, who was executed by lethal injection in the state of Georgia on January 27, 2015 (see Chapter 17)
- the majority of the U.S. Supreme Court in *Moore v. Texas* (2019) who were flexible enough to disregard their own rule about abstaining from "factfinding" when they declared defendant Bobby James Moore to have intellectual developmental disorder (IDD) thereby rendering him ineligible for execution (see Chapter 17)
- Supreme Court Justice Stephen Breyer (1938–), who, in a dissenting opinion, articulated the nature of moral incapacity and argued that it is a necessary part of criminal law (*Kahler v. Kansas*, 2020; see Chapter 24).

People who have mental illness are among the most powerless in our society. The job of defending their civil rights has never been easy, and with decisions like *Kahler v. Kansas* (2020) it has become harder still.

A few comments about usage:

1 I have chosen the epicene "they" as the generic singular pronoun. I accept the wisdom of the American Psychological Association (2020) and the American Dialect Society (who made "they" the "Word of the Decade" for the 2010s). I embrace their vision that this four-letter word has the potential to end centuries of sexist language and decades of awkward usage.

2 I use person-first language when referring to people who have mental disorders. Therefore, I do not refer to people as "schizophrenics," "alcoholics," "bipolars," "borderlines," or "psychopaths," but rather as "people who have schizophrenia," "people who are addicted to alcohol," "people with bipolar disorder," "people who have been diagnosed with borderline personality disorder," or "people who meet the criteria for psychopathy," for example. People who have mental disorders are human beings first and are not the equivalents of their disorders.

3 In keeping with *The bluebook: A uniform system of citation* (Columbia Law Review et al., 2020, pp. 90–91), long Latin phrases are italicized but Latin words and short phrases that have become part of the English vocabulary – including such terms as mens rea, stare decisis, and

certiorari – are no longer italicized. When quoting documents, including court documents, I have retained the italicized versions of Latin words if those were used in the original.

4 Also in keeping with the *The bluebook* (p. 89), numbers zero through ninety-nine are spelled out in letters, whereas numbers above ninety-nine are expressed in numerals.

5 The past tense of "plead" is "pleaded," even though "pled" is more pleasing to the ear.

6 Color words that refer to race (i.e., "Black" and "White") are capitalized except when quoting authors who did not capitalize those words themselves.

7 I generally use the word "defendant" when referring to persons who have committed crimes or who are suspected of committing crimes, regardless of their status within the criminal justice system. Such a person might otherwise be called a "suspect," "accused," "respondent," "detainee," "perpetrator," "offender," "prisoner," "inmate," "appellant," "claimant," "parolee," "probationer," or "tortfeasor" depending on their age and the nature and status of the proceedings against them. For example, juveniles in court are generally called "respondents" and not "defendants," in order to distinguish the more rehabilitative mission of the juvenile court from the more punitive mission of adult court. A single individual may carry many labels in the course of the proceedings against them. For example, O. J. Simpson was a suspect in 1994, then an accused, an escapee, an inmate, a defendant, an acquittee, a tortfeasor, and then a defendant again, an accused again, a defendant again, a convicted offender, a prison inmate, and finally a parolee. For simplicity's sake, I will use the word "defendant" as a generic term even in situations where other terms might be more accurate. I beg the reader's indulgence as I try to spare you some of these complexities. What I lose in precision I hope to gain in readability.

In reporting my own cases I have disguised the identities and jurisdictions beyond recognition, with the exceptions of school shooter Jamie Wilson, and Mitchell Sims, the "Domino Pizza killer." An abundance of relevant information about those two men is already before the public. Both have been the subject of numerous publications, and Sims has been the subject of three television productions. Also, Wilson's guardian has given me written permission to share the details of his mental health evaluation.

In reporting landmark cases, I have done my best to base my narratives on court records exclusively and to avoid the swirl of rumor that surrounds sensational crimes.

In reporting the utility of psychometric tests, I use the error matrix and receiver operating characteristics (ROCs) wherever possible (see Appendix O for an explanation of these statistical methods). The profession has shifted toward using ROCs, which are useful because they avoid the base rate problem (see Appendix O), and because their statistical significance can be expressed qualitatively in words like "small," "moderate," and "large." The error matrix, however, is easier to conceptualize: The quantity in each cell represents a number of individual human beings. Error matrices allow us to answer a straightforward examination question about error: "Doctor, how often are you wrong?" For this reason I have included error matrices wherever possible.

Getting back to my own story, I graduated from college in 1972 with a Bachelor's degree with Honors in Psychology and a strong minor in Philosophy. I was elected to Phi Sigma Tau, the Honor Fraternity in Philosophy. I won an award in Latin. After getting my Ph.D. in clinical psychology at Northwestern University, I taught statistics courses for the University of Maryland. My mother wanted me to be a lawyer like my cousin Bob. (Sorry, Mom.)

My hope is that this will be a good "first book" for readers who are interested in questions about crime and mental illness. I have written it in simple and straightforward language, assuming that the reader has no prior background in this area. It is designed to get beginning professionals "over the hump" from being novices to being knowledgeable professionals in the courtroom. This is the book that I wish someone could have handed to me in 1978, when I first testified as an expert witness in a criminal trial. I think of it as a mentoring conversation between the 2023 and 1978 versions of myself, in which I tell myself the things I have learned and the things I want myself to know, in words that my 1978 self would have understood. It is my retirement book and also my COVID-19 book, written during these years of social distancing and shelter-in-place. I entertain the thought that a person who spends more than four decades studying a single topic bears a responsibility to share what they have learned with the next generation. This book is intended for the mental health professionals (and the attorneys who examine them) who can regard their participation in the criminal and juvenile justice systems as something worthwhile and not as something to be dismissed, avoided, or ignored.

A second subtext of the book is personal in nature: I hope to convey a little about what it is like to work as a forensic mental health professional. A third subtext draws attention to the work of women and minorities who brought their unique perspectives on justice to our understanding of mental health and the law. These include: Justices Finney and Barkett (mentioned above) and also Saleem Shah, Ph.D., of the National Institute of Mental Health (one of my many teachers), who inspired the next generation of psychologists and did more than any other individual to create the new field of forensic psychology in the United States; and Dr. Mary Alice Conroy of the Federal Correctional Institution in Lexington, Kentucky (another of my many teachers), whose testimony in *United States v. Denny-Shaffer* (1993) clarified the issues surrounding dissociative identity disorder and the insanity defense (see Chapter 30). These men and women were pioneers in their field, representing women and racial minorities, and advocating – sometimes in the face of strong opposition – for the reality of mental disorders and the need for their special handling by the courts.

A fourth subtext is my hope that this book will do its part to keep the past alive and carry its wisdom forward. In the words of Marcus Tullius Cicero (106 BCE–46 BCE), "To be ignorant of what occurred before you were born is to remain always a child. For what is the worth of human life, unless it is woven into the life of our ancestors by the records of history?" Each professional person bears a duty to be independent and not let other people tell them what to think, but I have watched with dismay (as did my professor at Northwestern University, Donald Campbell [1975], another of my many teachers) as my culture has disappeared around me. Personally I am fascinated by the culture of the present, but time does not permit balance: When my generation has "shuffled off this mortal coil," it will be no great loss to our future if we did not understand the culture of the present, but if the present generation loses the wisdom of the past, then that wisdom is lost forever.

A fifth subtext of the book concerns the manner in which our society deals with those powerless people who get into trouble with the law. No minority in our country has less political power than the groups who are discussed in this book: defendants, prisoners, indigents, juveniles, persons with mental disorders (including substance use disorders), and our racial, sexual, and political minorities. This discussion goes beyond science, beyond mental health, and goes to the very heart of who we are as human beings and who we are as a nation.

Clifford Whittingham Beers – whose autobiography, *A Mind That Found Itself*, inspired the mental hygiene movement of the early 20th century – wrote that people who have mental illness are "those afflicted thousands least able to fight for themselves" (Beers, 1908/2007, p. 90). When Beers wrote that, more than a century ago, the population of the United States was 90 million. Today, those "afflicted" souls number in the millions. Let us please help them when we can!

Jonathan Venn, Ph.D., ABPP
Gold River, CA
March 31, 2023

References

Ake v. Oklahoma, 470 U.S. 68 (1986).

American Psychological Association. (2020). *Publication manual of the American Psychological Association. Seventh edition.* Washington, D.C.: Author.

Atkins v. Virginia, 536 U.S. 304 (2002).

Baxstrom v. Herold, 383 U.S. 107 (1966).

Beers, C. W. (1908/2007). *A mind that found itself.* Las Vegas, NV: Filiquarian Publishing, LLC.

Campbell, D. T. (1975). Personal communication.

Columbia Law Review, Harvard Law Review, University of Pennsylvania Law Review, and Yale Law Journal (Compilers). (2020.) *The bluebook: A uniform system of citation. 21st edition.* Cambridge, MA: Harvard Law Review Association.

Daubert v. Merrell Dow Pharmaceuticals, Inc., 509 U.S. 579 (1993).

Drope v. Missouri, 420 U.S. 162 (1975).

Durham v. United States, 214 F.2d 862 (1954).

Ford v. Wainwright, 477 U.S. 399 (1986).

Hill v. Humphrey (Hill IV), 662 F.3d 1335 (11th Cir. 2011).

Jenkins v. United States, 307 F.2d 637 (113 U.S.App. D.C. 300, No. 16306) (1962).

Jones v. Mississippi, 593 U.S. ___, 141 S. Ct. 1307 (2021).

Kahler v. Kansas, 589 U.S. ___, 140 S. Ct. 1021 (2020).

Kent v. United States, 383 U.S. 541 (1966).

Lockett v. Ohio, 438 U.S. 586 (1978).

McCleskey v. Kemp, 481 U.S. 279 (1987).

Miller v. Alabama, 567 U.S. 460 (2012).

Montana v. Egelhoff, 518 U.S. 37 (1996).

Moore v. Texas, 581 U.S. 1039, 137 S. Ct. 1039 (2017).

Moore v. Texas, 586 U.S. 666 (2019).

State v. Wilson, 306 S.C. 498, 413 S.E.2d 19 (South Carolina, 1992).

United States v. Denny-Shaffer, 2 F3d 999 (10th Cir., 1993).

Acknowledgements

Jonathan Venn, Ph.D.
https://orcid.org/0000-0003-3327-2371

I wish to thank my lovely wife Mary Ann for her good will and constant reassurance.

I want to acknowledge the other 339 members of the American Academy of Forensic Psychology for educating me in this dynamic field. Without your input, this book would not have been possible. I want especially to say thank you to my mentor, Geoffrey R. McKee, Ph.D., ABPP, of the University of South Carolina, whose many contributions to my career went well beyond the call of duty, especially his assistance with the section on sexually violent predators in Chapter 16. I want to thank Daniel Neller, Ph.D., ABPP, for his assistance with Appendix O regarding the statistics of risk assessment instruments. I want it known that I accept full responsibility for this appendix because I know that Dan would have written it differently. I want to thank Professors Joel Dvoskin, J. Reid Meloy, Thomas Grisso, and Kirk Heilbrun, who read early versions of the manuscript and made helpful comments, especially Reid for his suggestion to include illustrations. I wish to thank Professor Stephen J. Morse of the University of Pennsylvania for his assistance in understanding the philosophical issues involved in *State v. Wilson* (1992; see Chapter 23).

I wish to thank Professor John H. Blume of Cornell University (attorney for Jamie Wilson) for his assistance with Chapter 23, and also my own attorney, Ryan Fox, who greatly improved upon this manuscript. I have drawn some criticism for writing about the law when I am not a lawyer myself, but I want it known that lawyers are available who will consult on manuscripts and will keep an author on the right track.

Thank you to the many mental health professionals who freely shared their ideas and research without thought of personal gain. This includes Dr. Bob Wildman, author of the Georgia Court Competency Test.

I thank Springer Nature for giving their permission to publish Table 10.1, regarding competency to stand trial.

Two of my cases presented here touch upon issues related to sexual minorities. I want to thank a number of people for their guidance in composing these sections: Gregory M. Herek, Professor Emeritus at the University of California at Davis; Noah Buchanan of the Trans Radical Activist Network; and Rose Dhaliwal and Amy Prescott – both doctoral candidates in Clinical Psychology at La Verne University who have published on issues related to sexual minorities.

Finally, I wish to offer my thanks to the hundreds of attorneys, government officials, and senior military officers whose faith and confidence allowed me four decades of access to the corridors of justice. Without your trust in me, the experiences documented in this book would not have been possible.

Part I

Foundational concepts of law and mental health

A forensic mental health practitioner does not need to be an attorney or to know everything about the law in order to function within their profession, but six concepts are encountered with such regularity that some familiarity with them is recommended for anyone who wishes to practice in this field. Therefore, in the interests of helping the reader understand and function within the justice system, Part I lays out a set of foundational principles that are essential to understanding the nature of forensic mental health practice:

- the due process of law (Chapter 1)
- the nature of expert testimony (Chapters 2 and 3)
- pleas and verdicts (Chapter 4)
- the standards of evidence (Chapter 5)
- the goals of sentencing (Chapter 6)
- the doctrine of mens rea (Chapters 7 and 8).

In the chapters that follow, each of these concepts will be discussed in detail and relevant case material will be presented. (Laws vary between jurisdictions. The material presented in these chapters is not intended to serve as legal advice or to be construed as an authoritative representation of the law in every jurisdiction.)

DOI: 10.4324/9781003385028-1

1 Due process of law

We have living among us persons who are so dangerous that it would be irresponsible for the rest of us to let them have their freedom. In the aftermath of an act of violence, a host of citizens are tasked with figuring out what happened and what to do about it. This host of citizens includes police officers, investigators, prosecutors, defense attorneys, judges, juries, grand juries, correctional employees, and mental health professionals.

These relationships are triangular in nature: The strong protect the weak from the dangerous. Ordinary citizens need protection from dangerous people. We expect our government to protect us, and government assumes that it has the right, the duty, and the power to do so. Because strength can make people dangerous, these relationships tend to "flip," so that the strong become dangerous and the formerly dangerous become the weak. The duty of a civilized society is to remain alert to this "flip" and prevent abuses by government employees. A tremendous amount of denial and rationalization accompanies the "flip." People like to believe they are doing the right thing, and a healthy level of awareness is not always achieved. But if we do not remain alert to the "flip," then our systems lose their credibility and our enforcers become like our offenders. A civilized society is obliged to remain vigilant and judge not only the defendant in the docket but also judge ourselves and overcome the massive denials and rationalizations that tell us we are always doing the right thing. It is our duty to treat all parties with dignity and respect, regardless of who that person is and what they may have done. To do anything less is to treat people like objects and not like people. The process of treating people fairly in legal proceedings is known as "due process."

Criminal justice stands at the intersection between the most brutal realities of human existence and a set of fine abstractions – honed over the millennia – about human nature and moral responsibility. All of this lies embedded in a framework of past legal decisions and an ever-changing set of administrative procedures that govern our criminal justice system. Due process includes such factors as:

DOI: 10.4324/9781003385028-2

- presumption of innocence (i.e., innocent until proven guilty)
- burden of proof (e.g., the state is required to prove its case against you)
- verbatim recording of proceedings
- sentencing that is proportional to the crime
- standards of evidence (see Chapter 5), of which three are commonly used in the U.S.:

  - beyond a reasonable doubt
  - clear and convincing evidence
  - preponderance of the evidence (sometimes called "more likely than not")

and the rights to:

- know the charges against you (Sixth Amendment)
- be informed of your rights (*Miranda v. Arizona*, 1966, see Chapter 9)
- request a hearing on your own behalf (habeas corpus)
- have an effective defense attorney (Eighth Amendment)
- have a jury trial (Sixth Amendment)
- confront your accusers (Sixth Amendment)
- cross-examine the witnesses against you (Sixth Amendment)
- submit evidence in your defense, which includes presenting your own witnesses (Sixth Amendment)
- testify on your own behalf
- have a unanimous verdict
- be competent to stand trial (*Dusky v. United States,* 1960)

and protection from:

- unreasonable searches and seizures (Fourth Amendment)
- self-incrimination (Fifth Amendment)
- double jeopardy (Fifth Amendment)
- unreasonable delays (Sixth Amendment)
- cruel and unusual punishments (Eighth Amendment)
- perjury
- invalid and abusive interrogations
- prosecutorial misconduct
- ex post facto laws (i.e., laws that are passed after your alleged crime, so that what you did was legal when you did it but now it is a crime; Article I, Section 9 of the U.S. Constitution).

Before we address the roles of mental health professionals in U.S. courts, let us review briefly the nature of due process and the history of how these laws evolved and how they have been applied. This material is covered in greater detail in Appendices D and J. A brief foray into this history will set the proper tone for the discussion of law that follows.

Seven documents are essential to understanding the history of due process in Anglo-American law: the Charter of Liberties of 1100, the Magna Carta Libertatum of 1215, the Six Statutes of King Edward III of 1354, the English Bill of Rights of 1689, the Virginia Declaration of Rights of 1776, the U.S. Bill of Rights of 1791, and the Fourteenth Amendment of 1868. A thorough study of these documents – which would include their historical, political, philo-sophical, theological, and military contexts – is beyond the scope of this book, but a brief review is included as Appendix D. Suffice it to say that due process rights in England and America were borne out of strife, revolution, and civil war.

THE INCORPORATION OF DUE PROCESS RIGHTS

The Bill of Rights of 1791 and the Fourteenth Amendment of 1868 are federal laws that guarantee due process rights, but it would be naïve to imagine that they were applied to the states without a struggle. The process by which the Bill of Rights and the Fourteenth Amendment were applied to the states is known as "incorporation." During the nineteenth and twentieth centuries, the U.S. Supreme Court ruled repeatedly that the Bill of Rights and the Fourteenth Amendment were federal laws that did not apply to the states. Cases where the U.S. Supreme Court ruled against incorporation include *Barron v. Baltimore* (1833), *The Slaughter-House Cases* (1873), *United States v. Cruikshank* (1876), *Presser v. Illinois* (1886), *Twining v. New Jersey* (1908), and *Adamson v. California* (1947). Cases in which the U.S. Supreme Court incorporated constitutional due process rights include *Gitlow v. New York* (1925), *Malloy v. Hogan* (1964), and *Timbs v. Indiana* (2019).

An understanding of the history of incorporation is one of the best ways to appreciate the nature of our judicial system and the racial and political divisions that exist within our country. For example, the political back-drop to *Barron* (1833) included issues of states' rights, slavery, and the rising tensions of an impending civil war. *Cruikshank* (1876) involved the 1873 massacre of at least 150 Black men (the exact number is unknown) by Confederate veterans of the Civil War at a courthouse in Louisiana over a disputed gubernatorial election (Keith, 2008; Lane, 2008). *Gitlow* involved the prosecution of a member of the Communist Party during the First Red Scare (which followed the Bolshevik Revolution of 1917).

As late as 2018, the State of Indiana still argued that the Bill of Rights did not apply to the states. Associate Justice Neil Gorsuch looked down from the bench at the Indiana State Solicitor and said, "Here we are in 2018 still litigating incorporation of the Bill of Rights. Really?" Gorsuch's question was 227 years in the making. The Court ruled 9–0 in favor of defendant Tyson Timbs. (For a discussion of *Timbs* and other cases in the history of incorporation, please see Appendix J.)

THE DUE PROCESS REVOLUTION OF THE 1960S

The 1960s was a decade of radical social change during which a series of landmark decisions by the U.S. Supreme Court revolutionized the practice of criminal and juvenile justice. This was the court of Chief Justice Earl Warren (1891–1974), a progressive Republican and former governor of California, who served as Chief Justice from 1953 to 1969. Four of the landmark adult cases in this series were:

- *Dusky v. United States* (1960; see Chapter 10), which defined competency to stand trial
- *Gideon v. Wainwright* (1963), which required the states to provide a defense attorney to every indigent defendant
- *Miranda v. Arizona* (1966; see Chapter 9), which required police to notify suspects of their Fifth and Sixth Amendment rights before they begin an interrogation
- *Baxstrom v. Herold* (1966; see Chapter 12), which released 967 inmates from the Dannemora State Hospital in New York – inmates whose psychiatrists believed were too dangerous to be released.

Two important juvenile cases in this series were:

- *Kent v. United States* (1966; see Chapter 11), regarding the conditions under which a juvenile can be tried as an adult
- *In re Gault* (1967), regarding the interrogation, arrest, detention, trial, and incarceration of juveniles.

The Warren court changed the lives of Americans. Those of us who were here during those years will remember the thousands of billboards, signs, and lapel buttons that urged Americans to "Impeach Earl Warren." The campaign to impeach Earl Warren never bore fruit. Harvard law professor William J. Stuntz saw Warren as the victim of "bad timing." His program of "protecting civil rights for black Americans and expanding civil liberties for all Americans – helped usher in the harsh politics of crime that characterized the twentieth century's last decades ... [Expanding] criminal defendant's rights in a period of steeply rising crime" did not sit well with voters. "The upshot was a nationalized and punitive politics of street crime that lasted a generation" (Stuntz, 2011, pp. 216–217). The Warren court changed our country and helped to convert the South from Democrat to Republican.

The landmark decisions in *Miranda, Dusky, Kent,* and *Baxstrom* greatly expanded the involvement of mental health professionals in guaranteeing the due process rights of criminal defendants and juvenile respondents. These four cases are reviewed in Chapters 9, 10, 11, and 12, respectively, as part of our larger discussion of the roles that mental health professionals have in the courts (discussed in Parts I, II, III, and IV). Today thousands of mental health professionals are employed daily in these enterprises.

TEN AREAS WHERE FORENSIC MENTAL HEALTH EVALUATIONS ASSIST WITH DUE PROCESS OF LAW

As the decades unfolded, courts continued to find new ways for mental health professionals to contribute meaningfully to decisions regarding the due process of law for individual defendants. In Chapters 9 through 24, we will review ten psycholegal questions.

Part II (Chapters 9 through 11) will address three types of mental health evaluation that can be relevant before a trial:

- waiver of Fifth and Sixth Amendment rights
- competency to stand trial
- transfer of juveniles to adult court.

Part III (Chapters 12 through 18) reviews six psycholegal questions that may be relevant after a conviction:

- risk of violence
- mitigation
- juvenile sentencing
- commitment of sexually violent predators
- capital punishment for persons with intellectual developmental disorder
- competency to be executed.

Part IV (Chapters 19 through 24) is devoted to a discussion of the insanity defense, which is argued at trial.

For each of these ten psycholegal questions, one or more landmark cases defines the issues and defines the roles that forensic mental health practitioners have in answering them. Chapters 9 through 24 review these ten questions and their essential landmark decisions from the United States and the United Kingdom. I also will present some cases from my own practice when they are relevant to the discussion. Where mental health professionals have developed psychometric tests to measure the relevant qualities of individual defendants, these tests are reviewed and evaluated.

An elementary understanding of statistics is needed to interpret and evaluate psychometric tests. Therefore I have included Appendix O, which provides a basic introduction to the statistics that are used to interpret and evaluate psychometric tests.

By limiting the discussion of psycholegal questions to these ten areas, I have intentionally left out several areas where mental health professionals contribute to the due process of law. Six of these areas are: (1) false confessions (Fulero, 2004; Kassin et al., 2010, 2015); (2) false memories (Loftus, 2005); (3) eyewitness identification (Loftus, 1996; Steblay, 2015); (4) battered woman syndrome (Follingstad, 2003; Walker, 2016); (5) child sexual abuse accommodation syndrome (CSAAS; Summit, 1983; Weiss & Alexander, 2013); and (6) testimonial capacity (e.g., the capacities of children to serve as witnesses in legal proceedings; Poole et al., 2015). I have omitted these six areas for several reasons. Landmark court decisions establishing their significance are not as readily identified. In fact, there have been occasions when expert testimony was rejected by the courts. In *State v. Kowalski* (2012), for example, a trial court in Michigan held that testimony regarding false confessions was not based on valid principles and proper methodologies and therefore did not meet the standards for admissibility set forth in *Daubert v. Merrell Dow Pharmaceuticals, Inc.,* 1993 (see Chapter 3 for a discussion of *Daubert*). This decision was upheld by the Michigan Supreme Court.

In *State v. J.L.G.* (2018), the Supreme Court of New Jersey held that the only feature of child sexual abuse accommodation syndrome (CSAAS) that is supported by the evidence is the fact that children may delay in reporting sexual abuse.

In *Ibn-Tamas v. United States* (1979), a court in the District of Columbia held that testimony on the battered woman syndrome did not meet the standard for admissibility of evidence set forth in *Frye v. United States,* 1923 (see Chapter 3 for a discussion of *Frye*). Blowers and Bjerregaard (1994) have documented the tortuous process by which testimony on battered woman syndrome gained acceptance in most courts.

Furthermore, testimony in these other areas sometimes relies on summaries of research findings and not on the intensive mental health evaluation of individual defendants. I have chosen to limit the discussions in this book to those ten areas where the courts depend regularly and reliably on mental health testimony, where testimony tends to be based on the intensive evaluation of individual defendants (and not on research summaries), and where landmark decisions by the U.S. Supreme Court are readily identified.

In order to build a foundation for our discussion of these ten psycholegal questions, we will first address five additional areas of the law that are fundamental and will help the reader understand the ideas that follow. These topics comprise the remainder of Part I, and they entail:

- expert testimony (Chapters 2 and 3)
- pleas and verdicts (Chapter 4)
- the standards of evidence (Chapter 5)
- the goals of sentencing (Chapter 6)
- the doctrine of mens rea (Chapters 7 and 8).

A forensic mental health practitioner does not need to be an attorney or know everything about the law in order to function within their profession, but these five areas are encountered with such regularity that some familiarity with them is recommended.

REFERENCES

Adamson v. California, 332 U.S. 46 (1947).

Barron v. Baltimore, 32 U.S. (7 Pet.) 243 (1833).

Baxstrom v. Herold, 383 U.S. 107 (1966).

Blowers, A. N., & Bjerregaard, B. (1994). The admissibility of expert testimony on the battered woman syndrome in homicide cases. *Journal of Psychiatry and Law*, 22(4), 527–560. doi:10.1177/009318539402200404.

Daubert v. Merrell Dow Pharmaceuticals, Inc., 509 U.S. 579 (1993).

Dusky v. United States, 362 U.S. 402 (1960).

Follingstad, D. R. (2003). Battered woman syndrome in the courts. In A. M. Goldstein & I. B. Weiner (Eds.) *Handbook of psychology. Volume 11: Forensic psychology* (pp. 485–507). New York: Wiley.

Frye v. United States, 293 F. 1013 (D.C. Cir. 1923).

Fulero, S. M. (2004). Expert psychological testimony on the psychology of interrogations and confessions. In G. Lassiter (Ed.) *Interrogations, confessions, and entrapment* (pp. 247–263). New York: Kluwer Academic/Plenum Press. doi:10.1007/978-0-387-38598-3_11.

Gideon v. Wainwright, 372 U.S. 335 (1963).

Gitlow v. New York, 268 U.S. 652 (1925).

Ibn-Tamas v. United States, 407 A.2d 626 (District of Columbia, 1979).

In re Gault, 387 U.S. 1 (1967).

Kassin, S. M., Drizin, S. A., Grisso, T., Gudjonsson, G. H., Leo, R. A., & Redlich, A. D. (2010). Police-induced confessions: Risk factors and recommendations. *Law & Human Behavior*, 34, 3–38. doi:10.1007/s10979-009-9188-6.

Kassin, S. M., Perillo, J. T., Appleby, S. C., & Kukucha, J. (2015). Confessions. In B. L. Cutler & P. A. Zapf (Eds.) *APA handbook of forensic psychology. Volume 2: Criminal investigation, adjudication, and sentencing outcomes* (pp. 245–270). Washington, D.C.: American Psychological Association.

Keith, L. (2008). *The Colfax massacre: The untold story of black power, white terror, and the death of Reconstruction*. Oxford: Oxford University Press.

Kent v. United States, 383 U.S. 541 (1966).

Lane, C. (2008). *The day freedom died: The Colfax massacre, the Supreme Court, and the betrayal of Reconstruction.* New York: Holt.

Loftus, E. (1996). *Eyewitness testimony. Second edition.* Cambridge, MA: Harvard University Press.

Loftus, E. (2005). Planting misinformation in the human mind: A 30-year investigation of the malleability of memory. *Learning and Memory, 12*(4), 361–366. doi: 10.1101/lm.94705.

Malloy v. Hogan, 378 U.S. 1 (1964).

Miranda v. Arizona, 384 U.S. 436 (1966).

Poole, D. A., Brubacher, S. P., & Dickinson, J. J. (2015). Children as witnesses. In B. L. Cutler & P. A. Zapf (Eds.) *APA handbook of forensic psychology. Volume 2: Criminal investigation, adjudication, and sentencing outcomes* (pp. 3–31). Washington, D.C.: American Psychological Association.

Presser v. Illinois, 116 U.S. 252 (1886).

Slaughter-House Cases, 83 U.S. 36, 21 L. Ed. 394, 872 U.S. 1139, 16 Wall. 36 (1873).

State v. J.L.G. (A-50-16) (078718) (New Jersey, 2018).

State v. Kowalski, 821 N.W.2d 14 (Michigan, 2012).

Steblay, N. K. (2015). Eyewitness memory. In B. L. Cutler & P. A. Zapf (Eds.) *APA handbook of forensic psychology. Volume 2: Criminal investigation, adjudication, and sentencing outcomes* (pp. 187–224). Washington, D.C.: American Psychological Association.

Stuntz, W. J. (2011). *The collapse of American criminal justice.* Cambridge, MA: Harvard University Press.

Summit, R. C. (1983). The child sexual abuse accommodation syndrome. *Child Abuse & Neglect, 7*(2), 177–193. doi: 10.1016/0145-2134(83)90070-4.

Timbs v. Indiana, 586 U.S. ____, 139 S. Ct. 682 (2019).

Twining v. New Jersey, 211 U.S. 78 (1908).

United States v. Cruikshank, 92 U.S. 542 (1876).

Walker, L. E. (2016). *The battered woman syndrome. Fourth edition.* New York: Springer.

Weiss, K. J., & Alexander, J. C. (2013). Sex, lies, and statistics: Inferences from the child sexual abuse accommodation syndrome. *Journal of the American Academy of Psychiatry & Law, 41*(3), 412–420. PMID: 24051595.

2 Mental health professionals in court

PSYCHOLOGISTS IN COURT

The earliest testimony by psychologists in American courts probably occurred in Cook County, Illinois, where the first juvenile court was established in 1899 through the efforts of social worker Jane Addams and her colleagues at Hull House (Brigham & Grisso, 2003; Tavil, 2017–2018). If we accept 1879 as the year that scientific psychology was born (i.e., the year that Wilhelm Wundt established the first psychological laboratory at the University of Leipzig), then the fledgling profession was a mere 20 years old when the first juvenile court was established. Juvenile court was intended to be more protective and less punitive than adult court (an intention that would erode over the next 100 years, as we will see), so the inclusion of mental health professionals was a good fit.

Only appellate decisions are published, so the earliest examples of psychological testimony are not available to us. The earliest recorded testimony by a psychologist in the United States did not concern juvenile delinquency but lie detection. In *State v. Driver* (1921) – regarding the attempted rape of a 12-year-old girl – the West Virginia Supreme Court excluded the testimony of a psychologist who would have testified for the defense. The court did not accept that the psychologist was an expert in lie detection. It would take another four decades and a world war before psychology gained acceptance in court. Other early cases in this series were *People v. Hawthorne* (1940; reviewed below) and *Hidden v. the Mutual Life Insurance Company of New York* (1954), both cases in which testimony by a psychologist was excluded – either at trial or at the appellate level – by judges who did not believe that psychologists were qualified to testify. During those early years – and consistent with decisions like *In re Petition of Crosswell* (1907) – mental illness was regarded as a medical problem and only medical doctors were allowed to testify.

In *People v. Hawthorne* (1940), the majority opinion by the Supreme Court of Michigan was that the trial court had erred in excluding the psychologist's testimony. Justice J. Butzel wrote in the majority opinion

DOI: 10.4324/9781003385028-3

that a court needs the best evidence it can get and, if that evidence comes from a psychologist, then the evidence should be heard. The true measure of an expert is not what academic degree they hold but their knowledge of a particular subject. Justice Butzel wrote, "There is no magic in particular titles or degrees" (*People v. Hawthorne*, 1940, at 25).

In the next few years following the *Hawthorne* decision, World War II created opportunities for psychologists, who proved their value in government functions like screening military inductees and treating veterans. The young profession grew in credibility and respect. Psychological testimony regarding children's development of racial identity was admitted in *Brown v. Board of Education* (1954). The issue of whether a psychologist could testify regarding mental illness was laid to rest in 1962 in *Jenkins v. United States,* a decision by the Court of Appeals for the District of Columbia.

Psychologists are allowed to testify in court: *Jenkins v. United States* (D.C. Cir. 1962)

Arguably no judge in U.S. history has had as much impact on mental health law as David Bazelon (1909–1993) of the Court of Appeals for the District of Columbia. Judge Bazelon wrote such pioneering opinions as *Durham v. United States* (1954), which confirmed the "product test" of insanity (see Chapter 19), and *Jenkins v. United States* (1962), which allowed psychologists to testify as experts on mental illness. Judge Bazelon's dedication to mental health law was memorialized when the Mental Health Law Project in Washington, D.C. (which had argued such landmark cases regarding the treatment of mental patients as *Wyatt v. Stickney*, 1972, and *O'Connor v. Donaldson*, 1975), was renamed the Bazelon Center in his honor.

Vincent Jenkins was accused of entering a woman's home with a weapon and trying to rape her. At his trial he pleaded not guilty by reason of insanity. Jenkins' attorneys presented the testimony of three psychologists: Dr. Margaret Ives, Chief Psychologist at St. Elizabeths Hospital in Washington, D.C., and a Diplomate of the American Board of Examiners in Professional Psychology (ABEPP); Dr. Bernard Levy, Chief Psychologist of the District of Columbia General Hospital; and Dr. Lawrence Tirnauer, a staff psychologist at St. Elizabeths. (There is no apostrophe in "St. Elizabeths" because, believe it or not, the name is older than the apostrophe. The hospital sits on land that was named in the seventeenth century, before the apostrophe was in common usage; see Wiener, 2013.)

All three psychologists testified that Jenkins had schizophrenia. Two of them testified that Jenkins' crimes were the product of his mental illness. The third psychologist testified that he had no opinion regarding the connection between Jenkins' crime and his mental illness. The trial judge instructed the jury to disregard the testimony of all three psychologists on the grounds that "A psychologist is not competent to give a medical opinion as to a mental disease or defect" (*Jenkins v. United States*, 1962, at 639).

Two psychiatrists also testified for the defense: Drs. Mary McIndoo and Richard Schaengold, Chief Psychiatrist and Assistant Chief Psychiatrist, respectively, of the District of Columbia General Hospital. The trial judge instructed the jury to ignore their testimony also because it lacked a "proper basis" (at 639).

One of the issues at Jenkins' trial was his intellectual functioning. His IQ had been tested three times in the course of one year. In October 1959, he obtained an IQ score of 63, which placed him in the range of "mild mental retardation" as it was known at that time. (The diagnostic terminology has changed and this condition is now known as "intellectual developmental disorder.") Then, in February–March 1960, Jenkins obtained an IQ score of 74, which placed him in the range of "borderline intellectual functioning." Then, in October 1960, he obtained an IQ score of 90, which is at the low end of the average range. This increase in IQ scores is open to interpretation. In my own practice I have seen it occur in two situations. One is where a defendant malingers at the earlier testing, but if that is your explanation then you have to explain why the defendant chose to stop malingering at the later testing. I also have seen this sort of improvement in IQ scores when a defendant with a mental illness is incarcerated and "off the streets" for the first time in a while. The defendant now has a roof over their head, gets regular sleep and meals, withdraws from street drugs and alcohol, stabilizes on psychotropic medication, and has the social stimulation of regular interaction with staff. The record of Jenkins' trial does not provide enough information for us to know which of these two interpretations might apply, but we do know that the change in IQ scores caused the defense psychiatrists to change their opinions. Dr. McIndoo changed her diagnosis to schizophrenia. Dr. Schaengold explained that, when he first interviewed Jenkins, he could not decide if Jenkins' cognitive blunting was due to "mental retardation" or to an undifferentiated psychosis. When Dr. Schaengold saw the first IQ score (63), he decided that Jenkins had "mental retardation." When he saw the later IQ scores, he changed his diagnosis to "undifferentiated psychosis." As stated above, the trial judge instructed the jury to disregard all of this testimony because it lacked a "proper basis" (at 639). Vincent Jenkins was found guilty of assault with intent to rape, assault with a dangerous weapon, and housebreaking with intent to commit assault, and he was sentenced to prison.

Jenkins' appeal pitted the two APAs against each other, that is, the American Psychiatric Association and the American Psychological Association. Both organizations submitted amici curiae briefs. (To my knowledge, this was the first amici curiae brief written by the American Psychiatric Association.) The psychiatrists urged the Court of Appeals to affirm the trial court's decision and exclude testimony by psychologists. The psychologists argued that they were well-trained, had good oversight of their training programs, and had a solid code of ethics. They urged the Court of Appeals to reverse the lower court's decision and let the psychologists' testimony stand. The psychologists pointed to *People v. Hawthorne* (1940; reviewed above) in which a trial court judge excluded the testimony of a psychologist, only to have the Supreme Court of Michigan rule that this was an error. As stated in *Hawthorne*, a court needs the best information available and should not rely solely on what degrees are held by the experts.

The D.C. Court of Appeals took the side of the psychologists and re-versed the trial court's decision. Judge Bazelon reviewed a series of cases in which non-medical personnel – including optometrists and a toxicologist – had testified as experts regarding medical illnesses. He wrote,

> The general rule is that "anyone who is shown to have special knowledge and skill in diagnosing and treating human ailments is qualified to testify as an expert, if his learning and training show that he is qualified to give an opinion on the particular question at issue." ... "It is not essential that the witness be a medical practitioner" [quoting 32 C.J.S. Evidence § 537 (1942)] ... The principle to be distilled from the cases is plain: if experience or training enables a proffered expert witness to form an opinion which would aid the jury, in the absence of some countervailing consideration, his testimony will be received. (*Jenkins v. United States*, at 644)
>
> The critical factor in respect to admissibility is the actual experience of the witness and the probable probative value of his opinion. (at 646)

That is, the test of admissibility is not the academic degree held by the witness but rather their "experience or training" and the "probative value" of their testimony. With the *Jenkins* decision, psychologists won their place in American courts.

Court-related mental health services are useful only if the courts actu-ally employ them. The next case reviewed, *Ake v. Oklahoma* (1986), guaranteed that defendants would have access to forensic mental health evaluations.

THE STATES MUST PROVIDE INDIGENT DEFENDANTS WITH FORENSIC MENTAL HEALTH SERVICES: *AKE V. OKLAHOMA* (U.S. 1986)

Glen Ake was arrested in 1979 for killing two people and wounding their two children. In jail and at arraignment, his behavior was so bizarre that the judge ordered a psychiatric examination. The psychiatrist who saw him concluded that he was delusional and probably had paranoid schizophrenia. Ake claimed to be God's "'sword of vengeance' ... and said that he will sit on the left hand of God in heaven" (*Ake v. Oklahoma*, 1986, at 71).

Ake was transferred to a psychiatric hospital, where he was found incompetent to stand trial. He was stabilized on a daily dose of 600 mg of Thorazine (a large dose). He was examined by psychiatrists, who at no time inquired into what his state of mind may have been at the time of the crime. Six weeks later his condition had improved, and he was found competent to stand trial. His attorney informed the court that he intended to plead not guilty by reason of insanity and, because Ake was indigent, he asked the state to pay for a psychiatric examination. He argued that the U.S. Constitution requires the state to provide the assistance of a psychiatrist when that assistance is necessary to the defense. The judge disagreed and denied the motion. Ake went to trial, where he pleaded insanity, but his defense had no supporting testimony. The jury rejected his plea and Ake was found guilty on two counts of murder in the first degree and two counts of shooting with intent to kill. At the penalty phase, the prosecution presented the testimony of psychiatrists, who said that Ake was a danger to society. Ake was sentenced to death and was given 500 years each for two counts of shooting with intent to kill.

The U.S. Supreme Court disagreed 8–1 with the trial court's opinion and remanded for a new trial. Justice Thurgood Marshall wrote the opinion for the majority:

> This Court has long recognized that, when a State brings its judicial power to bear on an indigent defendant in a criminal proceeding, it must take steps to assure that the defendant has a fair opportunity to present his defense. This elementary principle, grounded in significant part on the Fourteenth Amendment's due process guarantee of fundamental fairness, derives from the belief that justice cannot be equal where, simply as a result of his poverty, a defendant is denied the opportunity to participate meaningfully in a judicial proceeding in which his liberty is at stake. (*Ake v. Oklahoma*, 1986, at 76)

The Ake decision guarantees that every defendant who needs evaluation by a forensic mental health professional will get one. An indigent defendant is entitled to the services of a mental health professional, both in presenting an insanity defense and in rebutting prosecution testimony about future dangerousness. These services must be provided at the state's expense.

THE ROLES OF PROFESSIONAL ORGANIZATIONS

The functions of expert witnesses are shaped by sets of standards that include: (a) the Rules of Evidence that are passed into law by the legislatures of every jurisdiction; (b) case law like *Frye v. United States* (1923) and *Daubert v. Merrell Dow Pharmaceuticals, Inc.* (1993) that set the standards for the admissibility of scientific evidence in court (see Chapter 3); (c) codes such as the Department of Justice Code of Professional Responsibility for the Practice of Forensic Science (included here as Appendix B); and (d) professional organizations that promulgate standards and guidelines for forensic work and administer certification programs that recognize advanced levels of professional competency. Professional organizations that impact the functions of forensic mental health professionals include:

- the American Board of Forensic Psychology (ABFP)
- the American Academy of Forensic Psychology (AAFP)
- Division 41 of the American Psychological Association (also known as the American Psychology-Law Society or APLS)
- the National Organization of Forensic Social Work (NOFSW)
- the American Academy of Psychiatry and the Law (AAPL).

These organizations publish codes and guidelines for forensic work, and they provide certification programs that recognize advanced levels of practice. APLS and AAFP jointly published the "Specialty Guidelines for Forensic Psychologists" (American Psychological Association, 2013, included here as Appendix A). NOFSW has a certification program in forensic social work. ABFP and AAPL provide Board certification in forensic psychology and forensic psychiatry, respectively.

The American Board of Forensic Psychology (ABFP) is the certifying body for forensic psychology in the United States. It was created in 1977 under the leadership of its first president, Dr. Florence Kaslow. The ABFP later came under the sponsorship of the American Psychological Association (APA), which in 1947 created the American Board of Examiners in Professional Psychology (ABEPP; later known as the American Board of Professional Psychology, ABPP) for the purpose of creating boards that would administer examinations to individual providers and recognize advanced levels of competence. AAFP was created in 1978 to serve as a membership organization for psychologists who had earned board certification in Forensic Psychology from ABFP. (For a further discussion of the early history of ABFP, see Kaslow, 2021.)

Figure 2.1 Florence Kaslow, Ph.D., ABPP, founding President of the American Board of Forensic Psychology (ABFP) and President for its first three years, from 1977 to 1980.

REFERENCES

Ake v. Oklahoma, 470 U.S. 68 (1986).
American Psychological Association. (2013). Specialty guidelines for forensic psychologists. *American Psychologist*, 68(1), 7–19. doi.org/10.1037/a0029889.

Brigham, J. C., & Grisso, J. T. (2003). Forensic psychology. In D. K. Freedheim (Ed.) *History of psychology* (pp. 391–411). Hoboken, NJ: Wiley.

Brown v. Board of Education, 347 U.S. 483 (1954).

Daubert v. Merrell Dow Pharmaceuticals, Inc., 509 U.S. 579 (1993).

Durham v. United States, 214 F.2d 862 (1954).

Frye v. United States, 293 F. 1013 (D.C. Cir. 1923).

Hidden v. the Mutual Life Insurance Company of New York, 217 F.2d 818 (4th Cir. 1954).

In re Petition of Crosswell, 28 R.I. 137 (66 A. 55, 13 Ann. Cas. 874) (Rhode Island, 1907).

Jenkins v. United States, 307 F.2d 637 (113 U.S.App.D.C. 300, No. 16306) (1962).

Kaslow, F. W. (2021). The founding and early years of the American Board of Forensic Psychology. In T. Grisso & S. L. Brodsky (Eds.) *The roots of modern psychology and law: A narrative history* (pp. 195–206). Oxford: Oxford University Press.

O'Connor v. Donaldson, 422 U.S. 563 (1975).

People v. Hawthorne, 293 Mich. 15, 291 N.W. 205 (Michigan, 1940).

State v. Driver, 107 S.E. 189 (West Virginia, 1921).

Tavil, P. (2017–2018). Mandatory transfer of juveniles to adult court: A deviation from the purpose of the juvenile justice system and a violation of their Eight Amendment rights. *Revista Jurídica U.I.P.R.* 52(2), 377–409.

Wiener, A. (2013). The answer's column: What's with the lack of apostrophe in St. Elizabeths? Retrieved 10/06/2022 from https://washingtoncitypaper.com/article/453882/the-answers-column-whats-with-the-lack-of-apostrophe-in-st-elizabeths/.

Wyatt v. Stickney, 344 F. Supp. 387 (M.D. Ala. 1972).

3 Expert testimony

THE ADMISSIBILITY OF EXPERT TESTIMONY

Trials proceed by presenting evidence to triers of fact, and evidence is presented through the testimony of witnesses, sometimes including expert witnesses. The gatekeeper of expert testimony is the trial judge who decides whether a particular piece of scientific testimony will or will not be admitted into evidence. This is one of the judge's duties as the trier of law. To understand how judges make these decisions we will review the Rules of Evidence and two landmark cases: *Frye v. United States* (D.C Cir. 1923) and *Daubert v. Merrll Dow Pharmaceuticals, Inc.* (U.S. 1993). Please bear in mind that these standards apply only to the admissibility of expert testimony – i.e., whether or not the testimony will be entered into evidence. These standards do not address the weight of that testimony – i.e., how much credibility that testimony deserves. Weight of testimony is equally important in determining the outcome of a trial and it is the topic of a later section in this chapter.

Rules of Evidence

Every jurisdiction has its own Rules of Evidence, which are passed into law by the legislature of that jurisdiction. For convenience's sake we will address only the Federal Rules, which are similar to those of the other jurisdictions.

Rule 402 clarifies that all relevant evidence is admissible unless contravened by other authority:

> *Rule 402. General Admissibility of Relevant Evidence.* Relevant evidence is admissible unless any of the following provides otherwise: the United States Constitution; a federal statute; these rules; or other rules prescribed by the Supreme Court. Irrelevant evidence is not admissible.

DOI: 10.4324/9781003385028-4

The 700 series of the Federal Rules contains six important rules that define the nature of testimony. We will review the first three Rules here. Rule 701 concerns the "lay witness." In some jurisdictions this is known as a "fact witness" or "percipient witness," because this witness testifies about their own perceptions and facts they have observed. That is, the lay witness has direct sensory experience of the matter that has come to trial. They may have witnessed the alleged crime, or they may have seen or heard something related to the alleged crime. Generally speaking, a lay witness can testify only regarding their direct sensory experience and is not allowed to offer opinions (although Rule 701 does specify some conditions under which a lay witness can give opinions).

Rule 701. Opinion Testimony by Lay Witnesses. If a witness is not testifying as an expert, testimony in the form of an opinion is limited to one that is:

a rationally based on the witness's perception;
b helpful to clearly understanding the witness's testimony or to determining a fact in issue; and
c not based on scientific, technical, or other specialized knowledge within the scope of Rule 702.

Rule 702 defines the "expert witness." Generally speaking, the difference between a lay and an expert witness is that an expert witness is allowed to state both facts and opinions in court.

Rule 702. Testimony by Expert Witnesses. A witness who is qualified as an expert by knowledge, skill, experience, training, or education may testify in the form of an opinion or otherwise if:

a the expert's scientific, technical, or other specialized knowledge will help the trier of fact to understand the evidence or to determine a fact in issue;
b the testimony is based on sufficient facts or data;
c the testimony is the product of reliable principles and methods; and
d the expert has reliably applied the principles and methods to the facts of the case.

Please note that nothing in Rule 702 requires the expert to have a degree from a college or university. Experts can acquire their expertise through experience and employment. I consulted on a case where a truck driver with twenty years of experience testified as an expert. A truck had gone off the road and hit a parked car with a woman inside. Witnesses who approached the crashed truck found the windows rolled all the way down and the radio turned all the way up. The expert truck driver testified that – because the windows were rolled down and the radio was all the way up – the driver had been fighting to stay awake.

Rule 703 allows experts to use information that would be considered hearsay. This is an important distinction because hearsay evidence is not generally allowed in court. Rule 703 is essential to forensic mental health evaluation because so much of the information that the examiner relies upon is hearsay, e.g., information gathered from records and from interviews with defendants, victims, and witnesses. "Hearsay," defined in Rule 801, is "a statement that: (1) the declarant does not make while testifying at the current trial or hearing; and (2) a party offers in evidence to prove the truth of the matter asserted in the statement."

Rule 703. Bases of an Expert. An expert may base an opinion on facts or data in the case that the expert has been made aware of or personally observed. If experts in the particular field would reasonably rely on those kinds of facts or data in forming an opinion on the subject, they need not be admissible for the opinion to be admitted. But if the facts or data would otherwise be inadmissible, the proponent of the opinion may disclose them to the jury only if their probative value in helping the jury evaluate the opinion substantially outweighs their prejudicial effect.

That is, expert witnesses can testify regarding opinions they have developed from hearsay evidence, if it is the kind of evidence that experts in that field "would reasonably rely on." The hearsay evidence itself can be admitted if its prejudicial effect is outweighed by its probative value, i.e., its potential to help the trier of fact evaluate the facts of the case.

The general acceptance test: *Frye v. United States* (D.C. Cir. 1923)

For seven decades, the *Frye* decision by the Court of Appeals of the District of Columbia held sway as the leading standard for determining the admissibility of expert testimony. Today it has largely been replaced by the *Daubert* standard of 1993 (see below) but, by itself or in combination with other standards, it remains the rule in a number of jurisdictions (see Table 3.1).

James Frye was convicted of second degree murder. At his trial he tried to introduce evidence that he could not be guilty of the crime because he had passed a lie detector test. This lie detector test involved the measurement of systolic blood pressure. The judge did not allow this evidence into court. Frye appealed, arguing that he should have been allowed to introduce his evidence. In a unanimous decision the Court of Appeals approved the exclusion of this evidence and Frye's conviction was affirmed.

The *Frye* court adopted what is known as the "general acceptance" test. When a scientific method has reached a level of recognition where it is generally accepted by members of that profession, then it can be introduced as evidence under the *Frye* standard. Using systolic blood pressure to detect lies was not generally accepted by the scientific community and therefore was not admitted as evidence. By the *Frye* standard, any new method, no matter how valid, is excluded from testimony until it has reached a level of general acceptance. The weakness of the *Frye* standard is that perfectly valid methods may be excluded from evidence simply because the rest of the scientific community has not accepted them.

Forty-seven states adopted the *Frye* standard. The three states that never adopted *Frye* were North Carolina, North Dakota, and South Carolina. North Carolina adopted the *Daubert* standard in 1995. North Dakota adopted its own standard in *State v. Hernandez* (2005). South Carolina adopted its own standard in *State v. Council* (1999), which relied on its earlier decision in *State v. Jones* (1979) and on a California case, *People v. Marx* (1975). (See Venn, 2002, 2003a, 2003b, 2004).

The *Daubert* factors: *Daubert v. Merrell Dow Pharmaceuticals, Inc.* (U.S. 1993)

In the decades after *Frye*, its one-dimensional "general acceptance" test was increasingly called into question. For example, law review articles by McCord (1986, 1987) and by McCormick (1982) identified a large number of factors that could be used to determine the admissibility of scientific evidence. The *Frye* standard faced its most severe test in 1993 when two families sued Merrell Dow Pharmaceuticals.

Jason Daubert and Eric Schuller were both born with serious birth defects. Their mothers had taken the drug Bendectin, a prescription drug used to control nausea. The two families sued for damages.

Merrell Dow presented testimony by a physician and epidemiologist who had read the entire literature on Bendectin – more than 30 studies with more than 130,000 subjects – and concluded that Bendectin did not cause birth defects. The Daubert and Schuller families did not deny that this was the published record. The families presented eight witnesses of their own, all with good scientific credentials, who argued that Bendectin did cause birth defects. Some of these opinions were based on unpublished data. The District Court granted Merrell Dow's motion for summary judgment on the grounds that the opinions expressed by Daubert and Schuller's experts had not found general acceptance in the scientific community. Under the *Frye* standard of general acceptance, they could not have found otherwise. The Court of Appeals for the Ninth Circuit affirmed.

The U.S. Supreme Court agreed to hear the case (a process known as "certiorari") because of recent "sharp divisions" between courts regarding the admissibility of scientific evidence in cases such as *DeLuca v. Merrell Dow Pharmaceuticals, Inc.* (1990), which also involved the drug Bendectin, and *United States v. Williams* (1978), which involved spectrographic voice analysis. The *Williams* court had held that *Frye* was superseded by the Rules of Evidence. In *Daubert v. Merrell Dow,* the *Frye* standard itself was on trial.

The U.S. Supreme Court agreed with the *Williams* court that the Rules of Evidence, specifically Rules 402 and 702, superseded *Frye*. Rule 402 declares that "All relevant evidence is admissible," and Rule 702 defines "expert witness" (as explained above). Justice Harry Blackmun wrote in the majority opinion,

> The drafting history (of Rule 702) makes no mention of *Frye*, and a rigid "general acceptance" requirement would be at odds with the "liberal thrust" of the Federal Rules and their "general approach of relaxing the traditional barriers to 'opinion' testimony" … Given the Rules' permissive backdrop and their inclusion of a specific rule on expert testimony that does not mention "general acceptance," the assertion that the Rules somehow assimilated *Frye* is unconvincing. *Frye* made "general acceptance" the exclusive test for admitting expert scientific testimony. That austere standard, absent from, and incompatible with, the Federal Rules of Evidence, should not be applied in federal trials.
>
> That the *Frye* test was displaced by the Rules of Evidence does not mean, however, that the Rules themselves place no limits on the admissibility of purportedly scientific evidence. Nor is the trial judge disabled from screening such evidence. To the contrary, under the Rules the trial judge must ensure that any and all scientific testimony or evidence admitted is not only relevant, but reliable. The primary locus of this obligation is Rule 702, which clearly contemplates some degree of regulation of the subjects and theories about which an expert may testify. "If scientific, technical, or other specialized knowledge will assist the trier of fact to understand the evidence or to determine a fact in issue" an expert "may testify thereto." (*Daubert v. Merrell Dow Pharmaceuticals, Inc.,* 1993, at 588–589)

As can be seen in the above quote, the *Daubert* court affirmed the role of the trial judge as gatekeeper in determining whether expert testimony will be admitted.

This decision by the U.S. Supreme Court reversed the decision by the Court of Appeals and ruled that the unpublished evidence about Bendectin should have been admitted into evidence. The *Daubert* court identified five non-exclusive factors that trial judges can use when deciding whether to admit scientific testimony. These five factors are familiar territory to every scientist. (I have added numerals and line breaks to improve readability):

Many considerations will bear on the inquiry, including

1 whether the theory or technique in question can be (and has been) tested,
2 whether it has been subjected to peer review and publication,
3 its known or potential error rate,
4 and the existence and maintenance of standards controlling its operation,
5 and whether it has attracted widespread acceptance within a relevant scientific community. (*Daubert v. Merrell Dow Pharmaceuticals, Inc.*, 1993, at 580)

The "acceptance" standard that defined *Frye* was considered to be too "rigid" and "austere" by the *Daubert* court and, instead of being the sole criterion for admissibility, became the fifth of five factors that judges are encouraged to consider when deciding whether to admit expert testimony.

A serious problem remained in that most judges are not trained in science and did not feel confident about evaluating scientific evidence. A survey taken around the time of the *Daubert* decision found that only 4 percent of judges felt confident in their ability to evaluate scientific evidence. The Federal Judicial Center responded in 1994 by publishing the *Reference Manual on Scientific Evidence*, which is now in its third edition (Federal Judicial Center, 2011).

The third *Daubert* factor, "known or potential error rate," requires an elementary understanding of statistics and this topic is covered in Appendix O.

Each jurisdiction adopts its own set of standards for the admissibility of expert testimony, and these standards have been in flux since the years leading up to the *Daubert* decision. As can be seen in Table 3.1, many states, the District of Columbia, and the federal courts, have adopted the *Daubert* standard in one form or another, or in one context or another, sometimes in combination with other standards. Other states have either ignored or rejected *Daubert* and have either adhered to *Frye* or have developed their own unique standards.

Table 3.1 Judicial standards for the admissibility of expert testimony

Jurisdiction	Standard	Adopted
Alabama	*Daubert*	The Alabama Supreme Court adopted Alabama Code § 12-21-160 into Rule 702 of the Alabama Rules of Evidence on January 1, 2012.
Alaska	*Daubert*	*State v. Coon* (1999) and *State v. Sharpe* (2019).
Arizona	*Daubert*	The Arizona Supreme Court amended Arizona Rule of Evidence 702 on January 1, 2012.
Arkansas	*Daubert*	*Farm Bureau Mutual Insurance Company v. Foote*, 341 Ark. 105 (April 20, 2000).
California	*Daubert/Kelly*	The Supreme Court of California adopted *Daubert* for opinion testimony, except for testimony on new scientific techniques, which continues to be subject to the *Kelly* general acceptance test. See *People v. Robert Emmett Kelly* (1976); *Sargon Enterprises, Inc. v. University of Southern California* (2012, at 28).
Colorado	*Shreck/Daubert*	*People v. Shreck* (2001).
Connecticut	*Porter/Daubert*	*State v. Porter* (1997).
Delaware	*Daubert*	*Tolson v. State* (2006, at 645).
District of Columbia	*Daubert/* Rule 702	*Motorola, Inc., et al. v. Michael Patrick Murray, et al.* (2016).
Federal	*Daubert*	*Daubert v. Merrell Dow Pharmaceuticals, Inc.* (1993).
Florida	*Daubert*	By decision of the Florida Supreme Court: *In re: Amendments to the Florida Evidence Code*, No. SC19–107 (Florida, May 23, 2019).
Georgia	*Daubert*	*Daubert* was adopted by the Georgia General Assembly on March 20, 2022.
Hawaii	modified *Daubert*	*Daubert* is not required for admissibility but is used in the analysis of expert testimony. *In re Doe* (1999).
Idaho	partial *Daubert*	Idaho has applied *Daubert* only in criminal cases. See *State v. Parkinson* (1996, at 652) using *Daubert* for "guidance." The court then broadened its usage in *State v. Siegel* (2002).
Illinois	*Frye*	*Frye* was upheld in *Turner v. Williams* (2001).
Indiana	modified *Daubert*	Indiana courts routinely apply *Daubert*, although it is non-binding. See *Smith v. Yang* (2005, at 626–627).

(*Continued*)

Table 3.1 (Continued)

Jurisdiction	Standard	Adopted
Iowa	modified *Daubert*	Courts are strongly encouraged to apply *Daubert* but are not required to do so. See *In re Detention of Rafferty* (2002).
Kansas	*Daubert*	*Daubert* was adopted by statute on July 1, 2014. See Kansas Statutes Annotated §§ 60–456, 60–457, 60–458.
Kentucky	*Daubert/Frye*	The Supreme Court of Kentucky adopted *Daubert*, although it retained *Frye* for the admissibility of DNA evidence. See *Harris v. Commonwealth* (1992); *Mitchell v. Commonwealth* (1995).
Louisiana	*Daubert*	*In State v. Foret* (1993), the Louisiana Supreme Court adopted a variant of *Daubert* for criminal trials. *Daubert* has generally been applied in civil cases, although its applicability to non-jury trials has been disputed.
Maine	*Williams/ Daubert*	*State v. Williams* (1978). Then in *Searles v. Fleetwood Homes of Pennsylvania, Inc.* (2005) the Supreme Judicial Court of Maine cited *Daubert* favorably but did not adopt it.
Maryland	*Daubert*	See the decision by the Maryland Court of Appeals in *Rochkind v. Stevenson* (2020).
Massachusetts	*Daubert*	See the decision by the Supreme Judicial Court of Massachusetts in *Commonwealth v. Lanigan* (1994).
Michigan	*Daubert*	Michigan amended its rules and adopted *Daubert* on January 1, 2004. This was confirmed by the Supreme Court of Michigan in *Gilbert v. DaimlerChrysler Corp.* (2004, at 781).
Minnesota	*Frye/Mack*	Courts must apply the *Frye* standard and must ensure that evidence has a reliable scientific foundation. See *State v. Mack* (1980).
Mississippi	*Daubert*	Mississippi adopted the *Daubert* standard in May 2003. In *Hill v. Mills* (2010, at 336) the Supreme Court of Mississippi ruled that trial courts must consider the five *Daubert* factors.
Missouri	*Daubert*	Amendments were signed into law on March 15, 2017.
Montana	modified *Daubert*	In *State v. Clifford* (2005), a trial court limited *Daubert* to cases that involve novel scientific evidence, but the Montana Supreme Court held that this limitation was improper.

(*Continued*)

Table 3.1 (Continued)

Jurisdiction	Standard	Adopted
Nebraska	*Daubert*	Decision by the Supreme Court of Nebraska *in Schafersman v. Agland Coop* (2001).
Nevada	*Higgs*	Nevada's Rules of Evidence have their own three-prong test of admissibility, which bears similarities to *Daubert*. See *Higgs v. State* (2010).
New Hampshire	*Daubert*	The Supreme Court of New Hampshire adopted *Daubert* in *Baker Valley Lumber, Inc. v. Ingersoll-Rand Company* (2002).
New Jersey	*Daubert/Frye*	*Daubert* applies to civil cases; see *In re Accutane Litigation* (2018). *Frye* applies in criminal cases; see *State v. J.L.G.* (2018).
New Mexico	*Daubert/Alberico*	In *State v. Alberico* (1993, at 203), the Supreme Court of New Mexico replaced *Frye* with *Daubert* and added a unique factor: "whether the scientific technique is based upon well-recognized scientific principle and whether it is capable of supporting opinions based upon reasonable probability rather than conjecture."
New York	*Frye*	*People v. Wesley* (1994); *Parker v. Mobil Oil* (2006); *Cornell v. 360 W. 51st St. Realty* (2014); and *Sean R. v. BMW of North America* (2016).
North Carolina	*Daubert*	*State v. Goode* (1995, at 639).
North Dakota	*Hernandez*	North Dakota never adopted *Frye*. It rejected the *Daubert* standard in *State v. Hernandez* (2005).
Ohio	*Daubert*	*Daubert* has not been adopted explicitly but has been applied in civil and criminal cases. See *State v. Wilson* (2005).
Oklahoma	*Daubert*	The Court of Criminal Appeals of Oklahoma adopted *Daubert* in criminal trials in *Taylor v. State* (1995, at 328–329). The Supreme Court of Oklahoma adopted *Daubert* in civil cases in *Christian v. Gray* (2003). The Court of Civil Appeals of Oklahoma has limited *Daubert* to novel expert testimony or to situations in which the expert's method is not established; see *Cline v. DaimlerChrysler Co., Corp.* (2005).

(*Continued*)

Table 3.1 (Continued)

Jurisdiction	Standard	Adopted
Oregon	*Brown*	The Oregon Supreme Court was nine years ahead of *Daubert* when it adopted *Brown*, which listed seven factors for determining "the relevance or probative value of proffered scientific evidence" (*State v. Brown*, 1984, at 759). In a footnote, *Brown* referred to 11 factors identified by McCormick (1982).
Pennsylvania	*Frye*	The Supreme Court of Pennsylvania confirmed its adherence to *Frye* in *Grady v. Frito-Lay, Inc.* (2003).
Rhode Island	*Daubert*	*State v. Morel* (1996, at 1355).
South Carolina	*Council*	South Carolina adopted its own standard in *State v. Council* (1999), which relied on its earlier decision in *State v. Jones* (1979) and on a California case involving bite mark analysis (*People v. Marx*, 1975).
South Dakota	*Daubert*	*State v. Hofer* (1994, at 484).
Tennessee	*McDaniel/Kiser*	In *McDaniel v. CSX Transportation, Inc.* (1997, at 265), the Supreme Court of Tennessee chose not to adopt *Daubert* but did find some of its factors useful and added a factor of its own: "whether the expert's research in the field has been conducted independent of litigation." See also *State v. Kiser* (2009).
Texas	*Kelly/ Daubert/ Robinson*	The Court of Criminal Appeals of Texas presaged *Daubert* in 1992 by identifying seven factors that can be used to determine the admissibility of expert testimony. These included some unique factors, such as "(6) the clarity with which the underlying scientific theory and technique can be explained to the court" (*Kelly v. State*, 1992, at 573). In *E. I. du Pont de Nemours and Co. v. Robinson* (1995, at 556), the Supreme Court of Texas affirmed the *Kelly* and *Daubert* standards. In *Ablanedo v. Texas* (2005, at 10) the Texas Court of Appeals affirmed the "'*Daubert, Robinson,* and *Kelly*' trilogy."
Utah	*Rimmasch*	The Supreme Court of Utah presaged *Daubert* by four years in *State v. Rimmasch* (1989), a criminal trial that concerned the ability of mental health

(*Continued*)

Table 3.1 (Continued)

Jurisdiction	Standard	Adopted
		professionals to tell whether a child has been abused. The *Rimmasch* court recognized that the "general acceptance" standard of *Frye* does not apply to new scientific evidence. (In a concurring opinion, Justice Durham drew attention to two law review articles by Professor David McCord published in 1986 and 1987 concerning "novel" or "nontraditional psychological evidence." Those articles reviewed various judicial schemes for assessing the admissibility of scientific evidence and proposed a four-factor model based on necessity, reliability, understandability, and importance). In *State v. Crosby* (1996, at 642), the Utah Court of Appeals asked the Supreme Court of Utah to rule whether *Daubert* was the proper standard for the admissibility of scientific evidence, and that court chose the *Rimmasch* standard.
Vermont	*Daubert*	Vermont amended its Rules of Evidence on July 1, 2004, to adopt the *Daubert* standard in both civil and criminal matters.
Virginia	*Spencer*	*Spencer v. Virginia* (1990, at 621). In *Padula-Wilson v. Wilson* (2015), a circuit court used *Daubert* to evaluate proffered expert testimony. The Virginia Court of Appeals ruled that this was an error and reaffirmed the *Spencer* standard.
Washington	*Frye*	Affirmed in *Anderson v. Akzo Nobel Coatings Inc.* (2011).
West Virginia	*Wilt/Daubert*	*Wilt v. Buracker* (1993, at 203), a decision by the West Virginia Supreme Court of Appeals, is a modified version of *Daubert*. The West Virginia Supreme Court of Appeals revised its Rules of Evidence in 2014 and, in some cases, chose not to adopt the *Daubert* standard.
Wisconsin	*Daubert*	The Wisconsin Legislature amended Wisconsin Statutes § 907.02 to adopt the *Daubert* standards in both civil and criminal matters, effective February 1, 2011.

(*Continued*)

Table 3.1 (Continued)

Jurisdiction	Standard	Adopted
Wyoming	*Daubert*	*Bunting v. Jamieson* (1999). Interestingly, the Supreme Court of Wyoming held in *Wise v. Ludlow* (2015, at 15) that if an expert witness "did not correctly follow the methodology of differential diagnosis, that could affect the weight and persuasiveness of her opinions, but does not render that evidence inadmissible under *Daubert.*"

Source: Adapted from LexVisio (2020) and used with their permission.

THE WEIGHT OF EXPERT TESTIMONY

This discussion has addressed the admissibility of expert testimony. We will now discuss the weight of testimony, which is equally important when determining how much effect a bit of testimony will have on a trier of fact (i.e., the judge or jury). Once testimony has been admitted into evidence, the trier of fact then decides how much weight to give that evidence. The opposing attorney may try to diminish the weight or importance of the testimony in the eyes of the trier of fact: a process known as "impeachment." The opposing attorney may attack the value of the testimony itself or the credibility of the witness giving that testimony. For example, a cross-examining attorney may argue that the witness did not do an adequate job, did not use the proper methods, did not reach the proper conclusions, left stones unturned, or is biased in favor of their client. The very fact that an expert witness charges a fee for their services – and that the size of the fee must be enough for the expert to keep their practice running – exposes the expert witness to accusations of bias. The opposing attorney may try to impeach the witness with statements the witness has made at previous trials, seeking to expose inconsistencies and self-contradictions, and thereby discredit the witness in the eyes of the trier of fact. Opposing attorneys may resort to ad hominem arguments and try to convince the trier of fact that this witness does not have the education, training, experience, or sufficiently good character to offer an opinion on the matter at hand.

"A REASONABLE DEGREE OF SCIENTIFIC CERTAINTY"

A question that is sometimes heard in courtrooms regarding expert opinion and expert testimony is "Doctor, did you arrive at your opinion to a reasonable degree of scientific certainty." Sometimes the phrase is modified to identify an expert's profession, as in "a reasonable degree of medical certainty" or "a reasonable degree of psychological certainty." Superficially, the phrase sounds like it conveys something meaningful about expert opinion and expert testimony. Upon close inspection, however, the phrase loses meaning and may mislead a jury.

The phrase first appeared in 1935 in an Illinois case involving a boating accident. A witness was "asked whether he could determine with reasonable scientific certainty the cause of the capsizing of the boat" (*Herbst v. Levy*, 1935, at 358). Please note that the phrase was not invented by a legislature, judge, expert, or professional organization, but was invented by a trial attorney who must have thought it would communicate something meaningful and persuasive about expert opinion and expert testimony.

In reality the phrase is little more than a way for experts to say that (a) they believe what they are saying is true, and (b) they believe that other experts in their field would probably say the same thing. Therefore the phrase is redundant and unnecessary because (a) experts don't say what they don't believe, and (b) if the expert has followed the procedures of their profession – and if other experts in the same profession follow the same procedures – then they should arrive at the same or similar conclusions.

A "reasonable degree of scientific certainty" is a type of certainty that is not unreasonable, speculative, fanciful, whimsical, or imaginary. Again, the phrase is unnecessary and redundant, because no testifying expert is expected to say things that are unreasonable, speculative, fanciful, whimsical, or imaginary.

The problem with definitions of "reasonableness" is that they are tautological: A reasonable action is defined as something that a reasonable person would do. All definitions of "reasonableness" suffer from this circularity. For example, in the glossary attached to the "Specialty Guidelines for Forensic Psychologists" (SGFP; American Psychological Association, 2013; reproduced in this book as Appendix A), "reasonable" is defined as "the conduct of a prudent and competent forensic practitioner who is engaged in similar activities in similar circumstances" (p. 19). Elsewhere in the SGFP, "competent practice" is defined as "the conduct of a reasonably prudent forensic practitioner engaged in similar activities in similar circumstances" (p. 8). With all due respect to the authors of the SGFP, little or nothing is gained, in terms of definition, by shuffling and reshuffling the words "prudent," "competent," and "reasonable."

The words "reasonable" and "reasonably" are used quite often in the SGFP, and as the authors explain they are used:

in recognition of the need for professional judgment on the part of forensic practitioners; [they] ensure applicability across the broad range of activities conducted by forensic practitioners; and reduce the likelihood of enacting an inflexible set of guidelines that might be inapplicable as forensic practice evolves. (p. 8)

The words "reasonable" and "reasonably" thus indicate the fallible nature of human judgment and potentially mollify the perfectionism and rigidity that might otherwise creep into forensic practice. In this sense, they are useful words.

"Reasonableness" is subjective and is open to interpretation. Omissions that looked "reasonable" to an expert can be made to look unreasonable during cross-examination, and then a third party like a trier of fact must decide which side is being more reasonable.

The National Commission on Forensic Science (a division of the U.S. Department of Justice) found no scientific basis for the phrase and does not advocate its use. Accordingly, Attorney General Loretta Lynch on September 6, 2016, issued a memorandum instructing the scientists and attorneys employed by the U.S. Department of Justice not to use the phrase in their reports, testimony, or questions. (She attached to her memorandum the new Code of Professional Responsibility, which is included here as Appendix B.)

At its worst, the phrase might mislead a jury. A jury might confuse "reasonable degree of scientific certainty" with "beyond a reasonable doubt" (see Chapter 5). The resulting confusion could be disastrous in terms of public safety or the life and liberty interests of a defendant. Giannelli (2010, p. 41) has argued that, because the phrase could mislead a jury, it should be excluded under Federal Rule 403, which is included here for the reader's convenience:

Rule 403. The court may exclude relevant evidence if its probative value is substantially outweighed by a danger of one or more of the following: unfair prejudice, confusing the issues, misleading the jury, undue delay, wasting time, or needlessly presenting cumulative evidence.

Federal court (*United States v. Mornan*, 2005, at 381) and the Supreme Courts of Hawaii (*State v. DeLeon*, 2014, at 403) and Ohio (*State v. Lang*, 2011, at 617; *State v. Thompson*, 2014, at 1129) have found the phrase to be unnecessary. In *United States v. Glynn* (2008, at 574–575) a ballistics expert was instructed to say only that his opinion was "more likely than not" (see Chapter 5) and not to say "to a reasonable degree of ballistic certainty" or characterize his testimony in any other way.

BIAS IN EXPERT TESTIMONY

An abiding concern regarding the quality of expert testimony has been the potential for bias. Practitioners may or may not be aware of their own biases. It behooves an expert witness to grow in their awareness of their own biases and find ways to prevent them. Accordingly, Martinez (2014) identified eight potential sources of bias in forensic mental health examinations and twenty-four methods for overcoming them. This information is reproduced here in Table 3.2. These procedures identified by Martinez (2014) have potential for reducing bias in forensic work.

For further discussion of bias in forensic mental health assessment, see Neal and Grisso (2014).

BIAS IN THE ADVERSARIAL SYSTEM

A perennial challenge to the credibility of any expert witness is the inescapable fact that, in the adversarial system of justice, an expert is hired by either one side or the other. Experts are subject to the accusation that they are merely "hired guns" who receive payment for rendering opinions that are favorable to the party who retains them. These challenges will persist for as long as the justice system remains adversarial and each side hires their own experts. It is important for us to remember that the experts did not create this system: The legal profession did. If there were a suitable alternative, I believe that experts would be glad to go along with it.

A possible solution is to centralize the hiring and reimbursement of experts, so that experts are appointed and paid by the court or by a neutral government agency and not by the adversaries themselves. The mechanism for this already exists in Rule 706, which provides for the appointment and reimbursement of expert witnesses and applies to both civil and criminal proceedings. For the reader's convenience, Federal Rule 706 is reproduced here (Federal Rules of Evidence, 2021). Similar rules exist in the states.

Table 3.2 Eight potential sources of bias in forensic reports, and twenty-four methods for overcoming them

Anchoring or primacy bias	Information received at the outset of a case may lead to initial ideas and formulations that are difficult to abandon.	• Ask the retaining attorney or referral source to provide not only facts that support their position, but also the facts that the opposing side will likely argue. • Utilize systematic data gathering (e.g., structured interviews). • Avoid lengthy pre-evaluation interviews with attorneys. • Engage in rigorous consideration of alternative hypotheses.
Confirmatory bias	Focusing on evidence that supports rather than disconfirms a hypothesis.	• Generate a list of possible hypotheses near the outset of a case relevant to the legal question that are competing and seek out confirming and disconfirming evidence. • Modify initial impressions based on disconfirming information.
Underutilization of base rates	Failing to consider base rates when making judgments and predictions may result in overprediction or underprediction of the outcome of interest.	• Seek out reliable estimates of conditions or outcomes relevant in a particular case. • Absent specific base rate information, consider base rates of similar conditions or outcomes in other similar populations. • Appreciate that infrequently occurring conditions or outcomes are by their very nature difficult to predict but often the issues that forensic psychologists are called to address.
Inaccuracy from overreliance on memory	An overreliance on memory in forensic evaluations has the likelihood to result in a decrease in accurate information recall and increase in judgment bias.	• Record information immediately throughout the evaluation process or as soon as possible. • Consider utilizing video or audiotaping in addition to note taking. • Utilize an organization system for documenting available information (e.g., process for indexing large amounts of records for later referencing).

(Continued)

Table 3.2 (Continued)

Diagnosis momentum	Assigning a particular diagnosis without adequate evidence, which gathers momentum over time to the point that it may appear accurate.	• Avoid accepting a previous diagnosis as accurate without independently considering confirming and disconfirming evidence. • Withhold assigning a diagnosis in the event there is insufficient information. • Consider listing a previous diagnosis but indicate lack of information to support presently.
Allegiance effect	Formation of opinions in favor of the retaining party rather than on an objective assessment of available evidence.	• Form a list of potential hypotheses early in the evaluation process. • Diversifying a forensic practice may reduce pressure to satisfy the referral source due to interest in future referrals. • Strive to utilize objective and systematic methods for evaluation and forming conclusions. • Clearly state at the outset of a professional relationship that conclusions are based on the data available and may not support the retaining party's position.
Fundamental attribution error	Attributing more weight to dispositional qualities rather than situational circumstances when considering the reasons for someone's behavior.	• While considering hypotheses, confirming and disconfirming evidence should also include situational variables that may explain a particular condition or outcome.
Overconfidence	Overconfidence may lead to insufficient data collection and synthesizing of information prematurely.	• Identify competing hypotheses and consider evidence that supports and disconfirms each. • Consider the differences in validity of the information being considered and its relationship to a valid opinion or prediction. • If systematic feedback is available after forming conclusions, it may assist in forming knowledge of predictive validity. • Acknowledge areas of limitation.

Source: Martinez (2014).

Rule 706: Court-Appointed Expert Witnesses

a APPOINTMENT PROCESS. On a party's motion or on its own, the court may order the parties to show cause why expert witnesses should not be appointed and may ask the parties to submit nominations. The court may appoint any expert that the parties agree on and any of its own choosing. But the court may only appoint someone who consents to act.

b EXPERT'S ROLE. The court must inform the expert of the expert's duties. The court may do so in writing and have a copy filed with the clerk or may do so orally at a conference in which the parties have an opportunity to participate. The expert:

1 must advise the parties of any findings the expert makes;
2 may be deposed by any party;
3 may be called to testify by the court or any party; and
4 may be cross-examined by any party, including the party that called the expert.

c COMPENSATION. The expert is entitled to a reasonable compensation, as set by the court. The compensation is payable as follows:

1 in a criminal case or in a civil case involving just compensation under the Fifth Amendment, from any funds that are provided by law; and
2 in any other civil case, by the parties in the proportion and at the time that the court directs – and the compensation is then charged like other costs.

d DISCLOSING THE APPOINTMENT TO THE JURY. The court may authorize disclosure to the jury that the court appointed the expert.

e PARTIES' CHOICE OF THEIR OWN EXPERTS. This rule does not limit a party in calling its own experts.

Although Rule 706 and the centralized hiring of experts is available to the courts, experience shows that it is rarely used. Each side of an adversarial process typically hires its own experts both in civil and in criminal proceedings. (Exceptions exist at times, for example, in disability determinations, worker's compensation claims, and child custody contests, where experts are sometimes hired by a centralized government authority. In the United Kingdom, the hiring of forensic experts is centralized in both criminal and civil cases, which may help to reduce bias.)

Despite the potential for reducing bias, however, it does not seem likely that the hiring of experts will become centralized in most venues in the United States. It would not eliminate the suspicions that opposing attorneys have of each other and of the systems in which they function. Mistrust prevails. Attorney misconduct is real. Data from the American Bar Association indicates that 0.20 to 0.38% of attorneys are disciplined annually for misconduct (American Bar Association, 2022). Also, evidence from criminal trials indicates that experts who are appointed by the court tend to favor the prosecution (Blais & Forth, 2014; Grøndahl et al., 2013). It may not be possible in the United States to create a system that is not biased. It is likely that, in the United States, both sides of an adversarial proceeding will continue to insist upon their rights to present their own evidence and hire their own experts.

When the "hired gun" phenomenon is a conscious process, it means that an expert knowingly and purposely favors the side who hires them. Surely this happens at times, although it is forbidden by ethical guidelines like the "Specialty Guidelines for Forensic Psychologists" (SGFP; American Psychological Association, 2013; reproduced here as Appendix A). In addition to conscious bias, however, there is also the unconscious bias involved in the social-psychological process known as "adversarial allegiance" (Murrie et al., 2009; Murrie & Boccaccini, 2015; Zapf et al., 2018). This phenomenon is related to normal processes of cognitive dissonance and confirmation bias, and it is widespread. It has been observed in insanity evaluations (Otto, 1989), assessments of sexually violent predators (Murrie et al., 2009), civil lawsuits (Zusman & Simon, 1983), and child interviews in allegations of sexual abuse (McAuliff & Arter, 2016). In order to more fully prevent bias, practitioners are advised to bring these unconscious processes into their awareness and to find ways to address them.

REFERENCES

Ablanedo v. Texas, S.W.3d (Tex.App., Austin, 2005).

American Bar Association. (2022). Lawyer discipline. Retreved 11/11/2023 from https://www.abalegalprofile.com/discipline.php#anchor1.

American Psychological Association. (2013). Specialty guidelines for forensic psychologists. *American Psychologist*, 68(1), 7–19. doi.org/10.1037/a0029889.

Anderson v. Akzo Nobel Coatings Inc., No. 82264-6, Wash. Sup. (Washington, September 8, 2011).

Baker Valley Lumber, Inc. v. Ingersoll-Rand Company, 148 N.H. 609; 813 A.2d 409 (New Hampshire, 2002).

Blais, J., & Forth, A. E. (2014). Prosecution-retained versus court-appointed experts: Comparing and contrasting risk assessment reports in preventative detention hearings. *Law and Human Behavior*, 38(6), 531–543. doi:10.1037/lhb0000082.

Bunting v. Jamieson, 984 P.2d 467 (Wyoming, 1999).

Christian v. Gray, No. 96, 813 Ok. 10, 65 P.3d 591 (Oklahoma, 2003).

Cline v. DaimlerChrysler Co., Corp., 2005 Ok. Civ. App. 31, 114 P.3d 468 (Div. 3, 2005), cert. denied.

Commonwealth v. Lanigan, 641 N.E.2d 1342 (Massachusetts, 1994).

Cornell v. 360 W. 51st St. Realty, 22 N.Y.3d 762 (2014).

Daubert v. Merrell Dow Pharmaceuticals, Inc., 509 U.S. 579 (1993).

DeLuca v. Merrell Dow Pharmaceuticals, Inc., 911 F. 2d 941, 955 (CA3 1990).

E. I. du Pont de Nemours and Co. v. Robinson, 923 S.W.2d 549 (Texas, 1995).

Farm Bureau Mutual Insurance Company v. Foote, 341 Arkansas 105 (April 20, 2000).

Federal Judicial Center. (2011). *Reference Manual on Scientific Evidence. Third edition*. Washington, D.C.: National Academies Press.

Federal Rules of Evidence. (2021). Grand Rapids, MI: Michigan Legal Publishing, Ltd.

Frye v. United States, 293 F. 1013 (D.C. Cir. 1923).

Giannelli, P. C. (2010). Reasonable scientific certainty: A phrase in search of a meaning. Criminal Justice, 25(1), 40. Retrieved November 17, 2022, from https://scholarlycommons.law.case.edu/faculty_publications/963.

Gilbert v. DaimlerChrysler Corp., 470 Michigan 749 (2004).

Grady v. Frito-Lay, Inc., 576 Pa. 546, 839 A.2d 1038 (Pennsylvania, 2003).

Grøndahl, P., Stridbeck, U., & Grønnerød, C. (2013). The truth and nothing but the truth: Court-appointed forensic experts' experience with testifying and their perceptions of legal actors in the criminal courts. *Journal of Forensic Psychiatry & Psychology*, 24(2), 192–204. doi:10.1080/14789949.2013.771278.

Harris v. Commonwealth, 846 S.W.2d 678 (Kentucky, 1992).

Herbst v. Levy, 279 Ill. App. 353 (Ill. App. Ct. 1935).

Higgs v. State, 222 P.3d 648 (Nevada, 2010).

Hill v. Mills, 26 So.3d 322 (Mississippi, 2010).

In re Accutane Litigation, 191 A.3d 560 (New Jersey, 2018).

In re: Amendments to the Florida Evidence Code, No. SC19-107 (Florida, May 23, 2019).

In re Detention of Rafferty, 2002 WL 31113930 (Iowa App., 2002).

In re Doe, 981 P.2d 723 (Hawaii Court of Appeals, 1999).

Kelly v. State, 824 S.W.2d 568 (Texas Crim. App. 1992).

LexVisio. (J. L. Hill, Editor). (2020). The states of Daubert after Florida. Retrieved 11/13/2022 from www.lexvisio.com/article/2019/07/09/the-states-of-daubert-after-florida.

Martinez, M. A. (2014). Expert opinion: Good habits start early: Identifying and managing potential bias in forensic evaluations as an early career forensic psychologist. What can early career forensic psychologists do to avoid bias in their evaluations? *AP-LS News*. Retrieved 12/27/2022 from www.apadivisions.org/division-41/publications/newsletters/news/2014/10/expert-opinion.

McAuliff, B. D., & Arter, J. L. (2016). Adversarial allegiance: The devil is in the evidence details, not just on the witness stand. *Law and Human Behavior*, 40(5), 524–535. doi:10.1037/lhb0000198.

McCord, D. (1986). Expert psychological testimony about child complainants in sexual abuse prosecutions: A foray into the admissibility of novel psychological evidence. *Journal of Criminal Law and Criminology*, 77(1), 1–68. doi:10.2307/1143590.

McCord, D. (1987). Syndromes, profiles and other mental exotica: A new approach to the admissibility of nontraditional psychological evidence in criminal cases. *Oregon Law Review, 66*(1), 19–108.

McCormick, M. (1982). Scientific evidence: Defining a new approach to admissibility. *Iowa Law Review, 67*(5), 879–916.

McDaniel v. CSX Transportation, Inc., 955 S.W.2d 257 (Tennessee, 1997).

Mitchell v. Commonwealth, 908 S.W.2d 100 (Kentucky, 1995).

Motorola, Inc., et al. v. Michael Patrick Murray, et al., 2016 WL 6134870 (District of Columbia, October 20, 2016).

Murrie, D. C., & Boccaccini, M. T. (2015). Adversarial allegiance among expert witnesses. *Annual Review of Law and Social Science, 11*(1), 37–55. doi:10.1146/annurev-lawsocsci-120814-121714.

Murrie, D. C., Boccaccini, M. T., Turner, D. B., Meeks, M., Woods, C., & Tussey, C. (2009). Rater (dis)agreement on risk assessment measures in sexually violent predator proceedings: Evidence of adversarial allegiance in forensic evaluation? *Psychology, Public Policy, and Law, 15*(1), 19–53. doi:10.1037/a0014897.

Neal, T. M. S., & Grisso, T. (2014). The cognitive underpinnings of bias in forensic mental health evaluations. *Psychology, Public Policy, and Law, 20*(2), 200–211. doi:10.1037/a0035824.

Otto, R. K. (1989). Bias and expert testimony of mental health professionals in adversarial proceedings: A preliminary investigation. *Behavioral Sciences & the Law, 7*(2), 267–273. doi:10.1002/bsl.2370070210.

Padula-Wilson v. Wilson, 1203-14-2 (Virginia Court of Appeals, 2015).

Parker v. Mobil Oil, 7 N.Y.3d 434 (2006).

People v. Marx, Cr. 26579 (California, 1975).

People v. Robert Emmett Kelly, 17 Cal.3d 24, Crim. No. 19028, Supreme Court of California (1976).

People v. Shreck, 22 P.3d 68 (Colorado, 2001).

People v. Wesley, 83 N.Y.2d 417 (New York, 1994).

Rochkind v. Stevenson, 236 A.3d 630 (Maryland, 2020).

Sargon Enterprises, Inc. v. University of Southern California (November 26, 2012, S191550) 2012 Cal Lexis 10713.

Schafersman v. Agland Coop., 262 Nebraska 215 (2001).

Sean R. v. BMW of North America, 26 N.Y.3d 801 (2016).

Searles v. Fleetwood Homes of Pennsylvania, Inc., 878 A.2d 509 (Maine, 2005).

Smith v. Yang, 829 N.E.2d 624 (Court of Appeals of Indiana, 2005).

Spencer v. Virginia, 393 S.E.2d 609, 621 (1990).

State v. Alberico, 861 P.2d 192 (New Mexico, 1993).

State v. Brown, 687 P.2d 751 (Oregon, 1984).

State v. Clifford, 328 Montana 300, 121 P.3d 489 (2005).

State v. Coon, 974 P.2d 386 (Alaska, 1999).

State v. Council, No. 24932 (South Carolina, 1999).

State v. Crosby, 927 P.2d 638 (Utah, 1996).

State v. DeLeon, 319 P.3d 403 (Hawaii, 2014).

State v. Foret, 628 So. 2d 1116 (Louisiana, 1993).

State v. Goode, 461 S.E.2d 631 (North Carolina, 1995).

State v. Hernandez, 707 N.W.2d 449 (North Dakota, 2005).

State v. Hofer, 512 N.W.2d 482 (South Dakota, 1994).

State v. J.L.G. (A-50-16) (078718) (New Jersey, July 31, 2018).

State v. Jones, 273 S.C. 723, 259 S.E.2d 120 (South Carolina, 1979).

State v. Lang, 954 N.E.2d 596 (Ohio, 2011).

State v. Mack, 292 N.W.2d 764 (Minnesota, 1980).

State v. Marlon Duane Kiser, No. E2005-02406-SC-DDT-DD (Tennessee, 2009).

State v. Morel, 676 A.2d 1347 (Rhode Island, 1996).

State v. Parkinson, 909 P.2d 647 (Court of Appeals of Idaho, 1996).

State v. Porter, 241 Conn. 57 (Connecticut, 1997).

State v. Rimmasch, 775 P.2d 388 (Utah, 1989).

State v. Sharpe, 435 P.3d 997 (Alaska, 2019).

State v. Siegel, 137 Idaho 538, 50 P.3d 1033 (Court of Appeals of Idaho, 2002).

State v. Thompson, 23 N.E.3d 1096 (Ohio, 2014).

State v. Williams, 388 A.2d 500 (Maine, 1978).

State v. Wilson, Slip Opinion, 2005 WL 3112874 (Ohio App. 5 Dist., 2005).

Taylor v. State, 889 P.2d 319 (Court of Criminal Appeals of Oklahoma, 1995).

Tolson v. State, 900 A.2d 639 (Delaware, 2006).

Turner v. Williams, 762 N.E.2d 70, 326 Ill. App. 3d 541, 260 Ill. Dec. 804 (Illinois, 2001).

United States v. Glynn, 578 F. Supp. 2d 567, 574 (S.D.N.Y. 2008).

United States v. Mornan, 413 F.3d 372 (3d Cir. 2005).

United States v. Williams, 583 F. 2d 1194 (CA2 1978).

Venn, J. (2002). Forensic Focus: The *Council* standard. *Feedback*. South Carolina Psychological Association, p. 12.

Venn, J. (2003a.) Forensic Focus: The *Council* standard part 2. *Feedback*. South Carolina Psychological Association, p. 15.

Venn, J. (2003b). Forensic Focus: The *Council* standard part 3: "It can't happen here." *Feedback*. South Carolina Psychological Association, p. 13.

Venn, J. (2004). Forensic Focus: The *Council* standard part 4: The *Jones* factors. *Feedback*. South Carolina Psychological Association, p. 9.

Wilt v. Buracker, 443 S.E.2d 196 (West Virginia, 1993).

Wise v. Ludlow, 346 P.3d 1 (Wyoming, 2015).

Zapf, P. A., Kukucka, J., Kassin, S. M., & Dror, I. E. (2018). Cognitive bias in forensic mental health assessment: Evaluator beliefs about its nature and scope. *Psychology, Public Policy, and Law*, 24(1), 1–10. doi:10.1037/law0000153.

Zusman, J., & Simon, J. (1983). Differences in repeated psychiatric examinations of litigants to a lawsuit. *American Journal of Psychiatry*, 140(10), 1300–1304. doi:10.1176/ajp.140.1300.

4 Pleas and verdicts

Before trial, a defendant goes to an arraignment where they must choose one of the pleas that are available to them according to the laws of their jurisdiction. Each jurisdiction has its own set of pleas, and some pleas are defined differently in different jurisdictions. When the proceedings are complete and the ultimate decision has been reached, the phrase that once described a "plea" may now refer to a "verdict." Eight pleas (and verdicts) are discussed in this chapter:

- guilty
- not guilty
- nolo contendere (also known as "nun vult" or "no contest")
- not guilty by reason of insanity (NGRI)
- guilty but mentally ill (GBMI)
- guilty but insane
- guilty but with intellectual disability
- *Alford* plea.

We will review these eight pleas and discuss their histories, consequences, and positions within the judicial system.

GUILTY

Defendants who plead "guilty" admit that they committed the crime. They are required to state publicly in court that they did in fact commit the crime.

The large majority of defendants choose to plea bargain; that is, they enter a plea of guilty in exchange for a lesser offense (e.g., manslaughter instead of murder) and a reduced sentence. The number of cases that go to trial has grown smaller over the years. In a twelve-month period from October 2017 to September 2018, the federal courts processed 79,704 criminal defendants

DOI: 10.4324/9781003385028-5

(not including defendants who pleaded nolo contendere). Of those defendants, 8 percent were dismissed, 90 percent pleaded guilty, and only 2 percent went to trial. Of those who went to trial, 83 percent were convicted and 17 percent were acquitted. Juries tended to be harsh and acquitted only 14 percent of defendants. Defendants stood a better chance with bench trials (i.e., where the trier of fact is a judge and not a jury), where 38 percent were acquitted. These statistics summarized all federal crimes including immigration, drug, and property crimes. Among violent crimes, the trial rate was higher but still rather small, with only 7 percent of 2,879 violent crimes going to trial (Gramlich, 2019).

NOT GUILTY

The defendant who pleads "not guilty" challenges the prosecution to prove their case against them. The prosecution then has the option to dismiss the charges or to take them before a trier of fact. In most jurisdictions (North Carolina is an exception; see the discussion of *North Carolina v. Alford*, 1970, later in this chapter), a defendant can waive their right to a jury trial and opt for a bench trial.

Some defendants plead "not guilty" because they insist they did not commit the crime. Other defendants are reluctant to plead "not guilty," even if they are innocent, because they know that judges and juries are notoriously harsh with verdicts and sentences. Pleas of "not guilty" have grown increasingly rare and have been replaced by plea bargains (as described in the previous section). Trials are enormously expensive and labor-intensive endeavors, which creates incentives for prosecutors to resolve cases out of court through plea bargains. This creates incentives for prosecutors to inflate charges and sentences in order to persuade defendants to choose plea bargains instead of trials. That is, a hazard of the plea bargaining process is that innocent defendants will be coerced into pleading guilty in order to evade harsher punishments (Bar-Gill & Ben-Shahar, 2009).

NOLO CONTENDERE (ALSO KNOWN AS "NUN VULT" OR "NO CONTEST")

By pleading nolo contendere or "no contest," the defendant accepts the punishment but does not admit that they committed the crime. The judge then proceeds to give a sentence.

An advantage to the defendant who pleads nolo contendere is that they have not made an admission of guilt which might be used against them to establish their liability if there is a subsequent civil action for damages related to the crime.

NOT GUILTY BY REASON OF INSANITY (NGRI)

The special verdict of "not guilty by reason of insanity" was created in the United Kingdom in 1800, after James Hadfield fired a pistol over the head of King George III (see Chapter 20). The insanity defense is such a large topic that the entirety of Part IV (Chapters 19 through 24) is devoted to its discussion. When a defendant pleads not guilty by reason of insanity (NGRI), they are claiming that they are not responsible for their behavior because they had a mental illness at the time of the offense.

NGRI is an "affirmative defense"; that is, the defendant affirms that they committed the actus reus (see Chapter 7), but they assert that they are not guilty because of extenuating circumstances, namely, they have a mental illness. (Other examples of affirmative defenses include duress and self-defense. In duress, the defendant admits that, yes, they committed the actus reus, but they argue that they are guilt-free because they were forced to do it by another person. In self-defense the defendant affirms that, yes, they did commit the actus reus, but they argue that they are guilt-free because they needed to protect themselves.)

Insanity acquittees are not sent to prison, because these are acquittals and not convictions. They may be committed to hospitals, where they may be kept for indefinite periods of time until they no longer present a danger to the public or to themselves. The amount of time they spend in the hospital may exceed the time they would have spent in prison had they been found guilty of the crime (*Jones v. United States*, 1983).

The plea of NGRI is not available in the four states that have abolished the insanity defense: Idaho, Kansas, Montana, and Utah (see Chapter 24 and Appendix M).

GUILTY BUT MENTALLY ILL (GBMI)

The defendant who is found guilty but mentally ill (GBMI) goes to a prison and not a hospital, because these are convictions and not acquittals. This verdict was suggested by Queen Victoria in 1882, in response to the eight attempts against her life (see Chapter 20). Victoria's idea finally bore fruit in the state of Michigan, where the plea of GBMI first appeared in 1975. Around that time, sixty-four Michigan defendants were found not guilty by reason of insanity (NGRI) and were sent to state hospitals. Subsequently these defendants appeared at civil commitment hearings where they were released. Two of them committed violent crimes shortly after their release. Michigan citizens were outraged, and their legislature created the verdict of GBMI. Defendants who are found GBMI are found to be guilty of crimes and deserving of punishment. They are sentenced to prison, where they may begin their sentence at a prison hospital, but they are not sent to hospitals outside of prisons. They may be released when they complete their sentences, or they may be released by a parole board, but they are not released at commitment hearings.

Mickenberg (1987) was quite sanguine about this process. Other writers have questioned the ability of the GBMI verdict to dispense justice properly (Emanuel, 1989; McGraw et al., 1985; Slobogin, 1985).

The State of Indiana in 1981 – after the insanity plea was pursued in a particularly heinous crime – became the second state to pass a GBMI law. Also in 1981, John Hinckley, Jr., shot President Ronald Reagan and was acquitted by reason of insanity. Within two years, ten more states had GBMI laws.

As of the 2006 U.S. Supreme Court decision in *Clark v. Arizona* (see Chapter 22), eleven states had GBMI laws: Alaska, Delaware, Georgia, Illinois, Indiana, Kentucky, Michigan, New Mexico, Pennsylvania, South Carolina, and South Dakota. GBMI is defined differently in the various jurisdictions. In Delaware, Pennsylvania, and South Carolina, the definition of GBMI includes volitional incapacity (defined in Chapter 19; see 11 Delaware Code Section 401(b), 18 Pennsylvania Consolidated Statutes Section 314, and South Carolina Code of Laws Section 17-24-20). Pennsylvania and South Carolina both define GBMI as volitional incapacity. The Delaware statute is less restrictive and includes volitional incapacity as one possible instance of GBMI. The South Carolina law figured prominently in the trial of school shooter Jamie Wilson, who is the subject of Chapter 23.

Defendants who plead GBMI declare that they are guilty of the crime and that they had a mental illness at the time. They tacitly acknowledge that they do not qualify for a verdict of NGRI. Most defendants would prefer a verdict of NGRI – if they could qualify for it – because then they would go to a hospital and not a prison, and they would be eligible for release at a commitment hearing.

The benefit to a defendant of pleading GBMI instead of guilty involves acknowledgement by the court that the defendant had a mental illness, and this might entail certain advantages. For example, mental illness may be a mitigating factor in the death penalty. In the murder trial of Reginald Sanders (*Sanders v. State*, 1990; see Chapter 23), the fact that Sanders had been found GBMI instead of guilty prompted the Delaware Supreme Court to vacate the death penalty and spare his life.

GUILTY BUT INSANE

Three of the "abolitionist" states – Idaho, Montana, and Utah (see Chapter 24) – have a special verdict of "guilty but insane" that allows the defendant to go to a hospital instead of a prison. These states have bifurcated proceedings, in which a first hearing is held to decide whether the defendant committed the crime (i.e., the "guilt phase"), and then a second hearing (i.e., a "sentencing phase") is held to determine whether the defendant goes to a prison or to a mental hospital.

Arizona has a "guilty except insane" verdict, by which a defendant is committed to a state mental facility for treatment. (See Arizona Revised Statutes Section 13-502.)

Other states define "guilty" and "insane" differently so that they are two contradictory and mutually exclusive categories. When a defendant is found to be insane in those states, it means that no crime was committed.

GUILTY BUT WITH INTELLECTUAL DISABILITY

The State of Georgia has a special plea and verdict of guilty but with intellectual disability (Georgia Code Section 17-7-131(j)(2)). Under this section of the Georgia code, defendants in capital proceedings who are found guilty but with intellectual disability are not executed but are sent to the Georgia Department of Corrections for life. (See the discussion of Georgia law in Chapter 17.)

ALFORD PLEA: *NORTH CAROLINA V. ALFORD* (U.S. 1970)

Ordinarily, a defendant who pleads guilty to a crime must state publicly in court that they did in fact commit the crime. In *North Carolina v. Alford* (1970), however, the U.S. Supreme Court recognized that exceptions can be made when a defendant pleads guilty to a lesser offense in order to avoid a more serious penalty. In these cases, defendants are allowed to plead "guilty" and still assert that they did not commit the crime.

On November 22, 1963, a man in Winston-Salem, North Carolina, responded to a knock at his door. He opened the door slightly and was cut down by a shotgun blast. No one saw the killer.

Earlier that evening Henry Alford, a man with a long criminal record, had visited that house with a woman and they had rented a room for one dollar. They purchased liquor by the drink, which was illegal in North Carolina. Alford and the woman went to the room together, but they left after several minutes because Alford had run out of money. Alford insisted that the woman leave with him. The proprietor of the house (who was not the murder victim) said, "She could stay here if she wishes." An argument ensued, and Alford ran off with the woman's coat. He was chased by the murder victim and by another man. There was the knock at the door 15 to 20 minutes later, followed by the shotgun blast.

Alford was indicted for murder in the first degree. A conviction could have resulted in the death penalty, but a guilty plea would result in a life sentence. No one saw Alford pull the trigger, but numerous witnesses provided circumstantial evidence to a police investigator. A woman who had been living with Alford for three years told the investigator that Alford said he was going to kill the two men who had chased him, and he named the murder victim. She saw him get his shotgun and four shells and leave the house. He came back 30 to 35 minutes later and told her that he had killed the man and that she could have the furniture. Another woman who was in the house at the time saw Alford get his shotgun and say that he was going to kill somebody. A witness who was at a store half a block away said that she saw Alford walk past her with the shotgun. Later that evening Alford took another woman out for drinks and told her that he had shot a man and that he would be gone for a long time. Alford also told a neighbor that he had killed the victim. The arresting officer smelled the shotgun and testified that it had recently been fired.

Alford took the witness stand and denied shooting anyone. He pleaded guilty to murder in the second degree, which carried a sentence of 2 to 30 years in prison. He was sentenced to 30 years.

Several months later, Alford began to file a series of petitions, complaining that his guilty plea had not been given freely and voluntarily but had been coerced from him in order to save himself from the death penalty. The U.S. Court of Appeals for the Fourth Circuit agreed with Alford that his plea had been coerced. The State of North Carolina appealed to the U.S. Supreme Court.

The U.S. Supreme Court vacated this decision by the U.S. Court of Appeals and found that Alford had given his plea "intelligently" (*North Carolina v. Alford*, 1970, at 26). Alford had weighed his options – namely, the death penalty, life in prison, or 2 to 30 years – and the trial court had not erred in accepting his plea. The court ruled that:

a A guilty plea that represents a voluntary and intelligent choice among the alternatives available to a defendant, especially one represented by competent counsel, is not compelled within the meaning of the Fifth Amendment because it was entered to avoid the possibility of the death penalty. *Brady v. United States*, 397 U.S. 742.

b *Hudson v. United States*, 272 U.S. 451, which held that a federal court may impose a prison sentence after accepting a plea of nolo contendere, implicitly recognized that there is no constitutional bar to imposing a prison sentence upon an accused who is unwilling to admit guilt but who is willing to waive trial and accept the sentence.

c An accused may voluntarily, knowingly, and understandingly consent to the imposition of a prison sentence even though he is unwilling to admit participation in the crime, or even if his guilty plea contains a protestation of innocence, when, as here, he intelligently concludes that his interests require a guilty plea and the record strongly evidences guilt.

d The Fourteenth Amendment and the Bill of Rights do not prohibit the States from accepting pleas to lesser included offenses. (*North Carolina v. Alford*, 1970, at 25–26)

A dissenting opinion by Justice Brennan, in which he was joined by Justices Douglas and Marshall, argued that this decision, along with similar recent decisions (*Brady v. United States*, 1970; *Parker v. North Carolina*, 1970) transformed the death penalty into an "unconstitutional threat" by which "to induce a guilty plea from a defendant who was unwilling to admit his guilt" (*North Carolina v. Alford*, 1970, at 40). Apparently, those dissenting justices were aware of the process, mentioned above, by which prosecutors inflate charges and sentences in order to wrest guilty pleas from defendants and thereby avoid expensive and risky trials.

REFERENCES

Bar-Gill, O., & Ben-Shahar, O. (2009). The prisoners' (plea bargain) dilemma. *Journal of Legal Analysis* 1(2), 737–773. Retrieved 11/20/2022 from https://home.uchicago.edu/omri/pdf/articles/Plea_Bargain_JLA.pdf.

Brady v. United States, 397 U.S. 742 (1970).

Clark v. Arizona, 548 U.S. 735 (2006).

Emanuel, A. S. (1989). Guilty But Mentally Ill verdicts and the death penalty: An Eighth Amendment analysis. *North Carolina Law Review*, 68(1), 37–67. Retrieved 11/20/2022 from https://scholarship.law.unc.edu/nclr/vol68/iss1/9.

Gramlich, J. (June 11, 2019). Only 2% of federal criminal defendants go to trial, and most who do are found guilty. Pew Research Center. Retrieved 11/20/2022 from www.pewresearch.org/fact-tank/2019/06/11/only-2-of-federal-criminal-defendants-go-to-trial-and-most-who-do-are-found-guilty/.

Hudson v. United States, 272 U.S. 451 (1926).

Jones v. United States, 463 U.S. 354 (1983).

McGraw, B. D., Farthing-Capowich, D., & Keilitz, I. (1985). The "guilty but mentally ill" plea and verdict: Current state of the knowledge. *Villanova Law Review*, 30, 117–191.

Mickenberg, I. (1987). A pleasant surprise: The guilty but mentally ill verdict has both succeeded in its own right and successfully preserved the traditional role of the insanity defense. *University of Cincinnati Law Review*, 55, 943–973. NCJ Number 114711.

North Carolina v. Alford, 400 U.S. 25 (1970).

Parker v. North Carolina, 397 U.S. 790 (1970).

Sanders v. State, 585 A.2d 117 (Delaware, 1990).

Slobogin, C. (1985). The guilty but mentally ill verdict: An idea whose time should not have come. *George Washington Law Review*, 53, 494–526. Retrieved 11/20/2022 from https://scholarship.law.vanderbilt.edu/faculty-publications/1051.

5 Three standards of evidence

The standards of evidence that are applied in U.S. courts are fundamental to understanding the nature of legal proceedings. The three standards that are applied most commonly in U.S. courts are (in decreasing order of stringency; see generally McKenna & Fishman, 2004, §3.10):

- beyond a reasonable doubt (BRD)
- clear and convincing evidence (CCE)
- preponderance of the evidence (POE; sometimes called "more likely than not").

Every type of litigation is associated with one of these standards of evidence, and each jurisdiction decides its own set of standards. These are not mere philosophical abstractions: The differences between standards of evidence are used to make decisions that profoundly affect the lives of individual defendants. In *Addington v. Texas* (1979), for example, the difference between CCE and POE was essential in making the determination of civil commitment (see below). When Warren Lee Hill was executed in 2015, the distinction between BRD and the lower standards of evidence may have been essential in making the determination that ended his life (see Chapter 17). Let us now examine the three standards one at a time and consider some of the ways in which they are applied.

BEYOND A REASONABLE DOUBT (BRD)

Beyond a reasonable doubt, or BRD, is the highest of the three standards of evidence. It is the standard that is generally applied in criminal law, where issues of the utmost importance are at stake, namely, a defendant's life or liberty. It was created to protect individual liberties from governmental overreach. Before citizens can be deprived of their life or liberty, the prosecution must meet this very high standard of proof.

DOI: 10.4324/9781003385028-6

The term "reasonable doubt" eludes clear definition, despite the fact that numerous courts have attempted to define it, and despite the fact that it is used and defined by judges almost every day as they give their instructions to juries. "Reasonable doubt" has been defined as the doubt that a reasonable person might have. It is doubt that is based on reason and evidence. It is not a vague, speculative, or imaginary doubt. It is not a doubt that is conjured up in order to avoid an unpleasant duty or task. It is a doubt that would cause a prudent person to hesitate before they act on a matter that is important to themselves (*United States v. Johnson*, 2d Cir., 1965).

The problems with these definitions include (1) the tautological nature of defining "reasonable doubt" as something that a "reasonable person" would have, and (2) the implication that the lower standards of evidence might somehow be based on speculation or imagination or be characteristic of imprudent and unreasonable persons. There is nothing in the definitions of BRD that does not apply equally well to the lower standards of evidence. The attempts at definition do not support the special, high status that is given to BRD in our courts of law. There appears to be no good referent for BRD without resorting to tautology and universality. The *Johnson* court summarized when they wrote that these definitions are "safe but somewhat uninformative" (1965, at 7). The true meaning of "beyond a reasonable doubt" lies more in its pragmatics than in its content: When the law says "beyond a reasonable doubt," it is telling the triers of fact that the matter before them has the utmost importance and they must be careful to get it right.

Two elements of a felony – guilt and mens rea (see Chapters 7 and 8) – must be proved beyond a reasonable doubt (*In re Winship*, 1970). BRD is the standard that juvenile courts apply when a juvenile is accused of doing something that would be a crime if committed by an adult (*In re Winship*, 1970).

In 1952, Oregon was the only state in the union that required proof BRD in order to prove insanity. The U.S. Supreme Court upheld the Oregon standard in *Leland v. Oregon* (1952), thereby affirming the autonomy of the states in matters related to the insanity defense. Oregon changed its law in 1971, so that now insanity is established "by a preponderance of the evidence" (Oregon Revised Statutes 161.055).

Georgia is the only state in the Union that requires proof BRD to demonstrate intellectual developmental disorder (IDD, formerly known as "mental retardation") in criminal proceedings. Probably because of this standard of evidence, no defendant in the state of Georgia accused of malice murder has ever been found to have IDD (Lucas, 2017). This controversial law – Georgia Code Section 17-7-131 – is discussed below in Chapter 17 regarding the execution of persons who have IDD.

CLEAR AND CONVINCING EVIDENCE (CCE)

Clear and convincing evidence (CCE) is a less rigorous standard than BRD. It has been defined as evidence that is "highly probable" (*Weber v. Anderson*, 1978, at 895) and of a "reasonable certainty" (*Lepre v. Caputo*, 1974, at 656). In practical terms, it lies somewhere between BRD and preponderance of the evidence.

CCE is the standard for proving insanity in some jurisdictions, for example, in federal courts (18 U.S.C. § 17(b)) and in the State of Arizona (Arizona Revised Statutes Section 13–502(C)).

CCE has been the usual standard for civil commitment to mental institutions since *Addington v. Texas* (1979). Previously, the standard for commitment was the less stringent "preponderance of the evidence." In *Addington*, the court recognized the substantial liberty interest at stake in civil commitments and adopted the higher standard of evidence.

PREPONDERANCE OF THE EVIDENCE (POE; ALSO KNOWN AS "MORE LIKELY THAN NOT")

The least rigorous of the three standards is preponderance of the evidence or POE. It has been defined as evidence that is more convincing than the evidence that is offered in opposition (*Braud v. Kinchen*, 1975). POE is the usual standard in civil cases, where issues of life and liberty are not at stake.

In *Cooper v. Oklahoma* (1996), the U.S. Supreme Court ruled that POE is the appropriate standard for competency to stand trial in criminal proceedings. The elements of a criminal trial (e.g., guilt) require the highest standard of evidence (BRD), but it is consistent with due process and paramount to the interests of justice that a prosecutor never bring to trial a defendant who is not competent to stand trial. Therefore the U.S. Supreme Court adopted POE as the standard for competency in *Cooper* (competency to stand trial is the topic of Chapter 10).

Whereas "clear and convincing evidence" is the standard for the insanity defense in some jurisdictions, the U.S. Supreme Court – again respecting the autonomy of individual jurisdictions – upheld the lower standard "preponderance of the evidence" in the District of Columbia in *Jones v. United States* (1983). POE is also the standard of evidence for proving insanity in Oregon (since 1971; Oregon Revised Statutes 161.055(2)), in Delaware (Delaware Code Title 11 Section 304(a)), and in New Jersey (New Jersey Statutes Section 2C:4–1).

In *Patterson v. New York* (1977), the U.S. Supreme Court permitted New York State to use POE to establish the affirmative defense of "extreme emotional disturbance" in reducing second degree murder to manslaughter.

The important difference between standards of evidence was illustrated by the trials of O. J. Simpson in 1994. When Simpson was accused of killing his wife Nicole Brown Simpson and her companion Ronald Goldman, he was found not guilty in criminal court where the standard of evidence is BRD. Then, when the Brown and Goldman families sued him in civil court, where the standard of evidence was the less stringent POE, the jury awarded the families $33.5 million (which Simpson later challenged successfully in court).

When four New York police officers shot and killed 23-year-old Amadou Diallo in front of his home in the Bronx on February 4, 1999, all four officers were indicted for second degree murder and were acquitted under the BRD standard. When Diallo's family brought a wrongful death suit for $81 million against the City and the four officers, and the less stringent standard of POE applied, the City settled for $3 million.

Of the three standards of evidence, POE is the only standard that can be expressed in mathematical terms, as follows:

$$p(A) > p(-A)$$

where $p(A)$ is the probability that one theory (theory A) is correct and $p(-A)$ is the probability that theory A is wrong. Or, if we are considering two alternative theories – theory A and theory B – preponderance of the evidence can be expressed as follows:

$$p(A) > p(B)$$

where $p(A)$ is the probability that theory A is correct and $p(B)$ is the probability that theory B is correct. Preponderance of the evidence (POE) means that one side presents better evidence than the other side in an adversarial contest (*Braud v. Kinchen*, 1975).

In literal terms, the phrase "more likely than not" can also be expressed mathematically as:

$$p(A) > 0.5$$

where $p(A)$ is the probability that theory A is right. If that probability is greater than half (i.e., greater than 0.5), then it is more likely than not that theory A is correct. We can use the error matrix (described in Appendix O) to determine whether a prediction that is based on a psychometric test is "more likely than not." Table O.10, for example, presents data from Rice and Harris (1995) which indicate that their method for predicting acts of violence (VRAG) was accurate 68 percent of the time. Whether or not we should be impressed with a psychometric test that is accurate 68 percent of the time is a matter of judgment that will vary with the stakes at hand (e.g., the life and liberty interests of a defendant; see, for example, the debate reviewed in Chapter 12 regarding whether the PCL-R is a good-enough test to predict the occurrence of violence in prisons). What we cannot deny is that 68 percent is greater than 50 percent and therefore meets the mathematical definition of "more likely than not."

REFERENCES

Addington v. Texas, 441 U.S. 418, 99 S.Ct. 1804 (1979).
Braud v. Kinchen, 310 So. 2d 657 (Louisiana Court of Appeals, 1975).
Cooper v. Oklahoma, 517 U.S. 348 (1996).
In re Winship, 397 U.S. 358 (1970).
Jones v. United States, 463 U.S. 354 (1983).
Leland v. Oregon, 343 U.S. 790 (1952).
Lepre v. Caputo, 328 A.2d 650 (N.J. Super. Ct. App. Div. 1974).
Lucas, L. S. (2017). An empirical assessment of Georgia's beyond a reasonable doubt standard to determine intellectual disability in capital cases. *Georgia State University Law Review*, 33(3), 553–608. Retrieved 05/11/2022 from https:// readingroom.law.gsu.edu/gsulr/vol33/iss3/1.
McKenna, A. T., & Fishman, C. S. (2004). *Jones on evidence: Civil and criminal. Seventh edition.* (January 2023 update): Toronto, ON: Thomson Reuters.
Patterson v. New York, 432 U.S. 197 (1977).
Rice, M. D., & Harris, G. T. (1995). Violent recidivism: Assessing predictive validity. *Journal of Consulting and Clinical Psychology*, 6(5), 737–748. doi:10. 1037/0022-006X.63.5.737.
United States v. Johnson, 343 F.2d 5 (2d Cir. 1965).
Weber v. Anderson, 269 N.W.2d 892 (Minn. 1978).

6   Four goals of sentencing

A "sentence" is defined as a hardship or loss that is imposed by an authority upon a defendant because of a crime. Sentences are the ways in which judges enforce the laws. As Illinois Supreme Court Justice Walter Schaefer famously said in 1956 when he delivered the Oliver Wendell Holmes lecture at Harvard Law School, "The quality of a nation's civilization can be largely measured by the methods it uses in the enforcement of its criminal law" (Schaefer, 1956).

Sentences of the Tudor era included boiling in oil and beheading. In colonial times, sentences included flogging, banishment, dungeons, and public humiliation. In our own era, sentences include fines, jail, prison, parole, probation, suspended sentences, house arrest, ankle monitors, community service, deportation, and the various forms of capital punishment, namely, electrocution, lethal injection, firing squads, and asphyxiation in gas chambers.

When courts impose sentences, they seek to accomplish one or more of four goals: retribution, deterrence, incapacitation, and rehabilitation (Campbell, 1991, §2.1; LaFave & Scott, 1986). Other schemes for classifying the goals of sentencing have been suggested (e.g., Nadelhoffer, 2013, p. xvi). The system discussed in this chapter is the one adopted by the U.S. Supreme Court in cases like *Enmund v. Florida* (1982), *Atkins v. Virginia* (2002), and *Miller v. Alabama* (2012).

RETRIBUTION

"Retribution" occurs when a defendant gets what they deserve. In colloquial terms we might call it "payback." The phrase used by the U.S. Supreme Court in *Atkins v. Virginia* (2002) is "just deserts":

> With respect to retribution – the interest in seeing that the offender gets his "just deserts" – the severity of the appropriate punishment necessarily depends on the culpability of the offender. (*Atkins v. Virginia*, 2002, p. 319)

Of the four goals of sentencing, retribution is the goal that is least concerned with a defendant's well-being. It was probably the first of the

DOI: 10.4324/9781003385028-7

four goals to be articulated. Written records supporting the goal of retribution are at least 3,000 years old:

> But if there is serious injury, you are to take life for life, eye for eye, tooth for tooth, hand for hand, foot for foot, burn for burn, wound for wound, bruise for bruise. (Exodus 21:23–25)

As Barnet wrote in 1985, punishment by retribution tries to lower the defendant to the same level to which the defendant lowered the victim (in contrast to restitution, which tries to force the defendant to raise the victim to the level they were at before the crime). Retribution is consistent with the doctrine of mens rea (see Chapter 7) in that it punishes people not only for what they do but for what they were thinking at the time. It punishes people not only for what they do, but for having "bad" character. It is open to interpretation by corruptible people who happen to be in power at the time.

Some commentators have perceived an element of revenge in retribution, but revenge is not a necessary part of retribution. Retribution can be based on abstract concepts of justice and moral responsibility, without revenge. A court can administer justice by retribution when no one is present who wants revenge against the defendant (Moore, 1997).

Among legal scholars, criminologists, philosophers, and correctional officials, the philosophy of retribution has gone in and out of style. The 1966 edition of the *Manual of Correctional Standards* published by the American Correctional Association said, "Punishment as retribution belongs to a penal philosophy that is archaic and discredited by history." LaFave and Scott (1972), in their authoritative textbook on criminal law, called retribution "the oldest theory of punishment, *and the one which is least accepted today by theorists*" (italics added). Then, in the 1970s, the philosophy of retribution enjoyed a resurgence. When LaFave and Scott published the second edition of their book in 1986, they left out the phrase italicized above.

In 1976, Martin Gardner wrote,

> [Retribution] is suddenly being seen by thinkers of all political persuasions as perhaps the strongest ground, after all, upon which to base a system of punishment. (p. 784)

And Dolinko wrote in 1992 that

> retributivism, once treated as an irrational vestige of benighted times, has enjoyed in recent years so vigorous a revival that it can fairly be regarded today as the leading philosophical justification of the institution of criminal punishment. (p. 1623)

Retribution, however, did not maintain its favor. In 2016, Stohr and Walsh wrote that most criminologists did not support it as a valid theory of justice. Scholars have questioned its legitimacy (Braithwaite & Pettit, 1990) and have found it to be incomplete (Shafer-Landau, 1996). It has been criticized as flawed both in theory and in practice (Murphy, 1985), and for not supporting the values that it sets out for itself.

Barnet (1985) compared retribution with restitution and identified three practical problems, as follows:

1 The greater the punishment, the more procedural safeguards must be put into place to protect against errors. This results in fewer punishments being imposed. (It also increases the cost of punishment. For example, the average death penalty appeal takes more than 20 years. With accompanying court costs and other fees, administering the death penalty is more expensive than a life sentence. See Death Penalty Information Center, 2022.)
2 Prison is the most common and most acceptable form of retribution, but it is more expensive than restitution and it results in fewer sanctions being imposed.
3 When little or nothing is gained by the prosecution of criminals, victims are reluctant to report crimes and are reluctant to participate in their prosecution. (Note, for example, that 65 percent of rapes and sexual assaults go unreported. See Bureau of Justice Statistics, 2012. In the military, sexual assaults go unreported by 62 percent of female victims, and 83 percent of male victims. See Department of Defense, 2018. Also, when little or nothing is gained by prosecuting criminals, police are reluctant to make arrests. See Appendix L for an account of the California experience with the de-felonization of larceny.)

Of the four goals of sentencing, retribution is the one that is most related to theories of moral responsibility. Retribution assumes that the defendant had the capacity to understand and obey the law, and they chose not to do so. The other three goals – deterrence, incapacitation, and rehabilitation – are practical in nature and are valued for their effects on present and future defendants. Retribution, on the other hand, has no purpose beyond itself. The other three goals are not related to philosophical abstractions about a defendant's moral responsibility. Retribution alone is based on an abstract concept of justice. Seen from this perspective, retribution may not be the lowliest of the four goals but in fact may be the loftiest. Retribution is justified only by the moral blameworthiness of the defendant (Duff, 2001; Von Hirsch, 1993). When moral blameworthiness cannot be assigned to a defendant, then punishment for the purpose of retribution is not justified. Wojciech (1985) summarized,

Retributivism is the only theory of punishment which takes the notion of human responsibility seriously because it justifies punishment solely on the basis of acts and situations which were under the control of the perpetrator concerned. Only those facts which are believed to be free human acts are relevant in assessing guilt and deciding about punishment. (Wojciech, 1985, p. 241)

The problems in its application are weighty, however, as described above.

Retribution and proportionality

In the United States we do not embrace the strict "eye for an eye" proportionality of Exodus 21, but proportionality in sentencing is the law of the land. Punishments that are excessive in relation to the offense have been called the "exacting of mindless vengeance" (quoting *Ford v. Wainwright,* 1986, at 410). In *Coker v. Georgia* (1977), the U.S. Supreme Court ruled that it was disproportionate to sentence a defendant to death for the rape of an adult. The death penalty for rape of a child persisted in some jurisdictions until 2008, when the U.S. Supreme Court in *Kennedy v. Louisiana* added the rape of a child to the list of crimes that do not warrant capital punishment.

In a concurring opinion in *Furman v. Georgia* (1972) – the decision that created a national moratorium on the death penalty from 1972 to 1976 – Associate Justice Thurgood Marshall pointed out the history of racial disparity in executions for rape. Between 1930 and 1972, a total of 455 persons were executed for rape. This included 48 Whites and 405 Blacks. Racial disproportionality in the death penalty for rape was seen as a legalized form of lynching. (The series of cases around *Furman* are explored further in Chapter 13, and the question of racial disparities in the death penalty is discussed further in Chapter 8 and again in Appendix K.)

The severest penalties (i.e., capital punishment and life imprisonment) reflect a belief that crime is an expression of character. This is the belief that some crimes are so heinous that the perpetrators are irredeemable and fit only for the death penalty or for life in prison. These sentences assume that these crimes are expressions of immalleable character and that the defendants are not capable of change.

DETERRENCE

The U.S. Supreme Court in *Atkins* (2002) defined "deterrence" as "the interest in preventing (capital) crimes by prospective offenders" (p. 319).

Unlike retribution, which is based upon past deeds by the defendant, deterrence is pointed toward the future. The goals of deterrence are (1) to convince the defendant not to commit another crime (sometimes called "specific deterrence"), and (2) to convince the general public not to commit crimes (sometimes called "general deterrence"). Deterrence is not strictly a matter for the individual defendant but is directed to the public in a way that does not pertain to the other three goals of sentencing.

The Roman Empire appreciated the power of general deterrence 2,000 years ago. Golgotha, or the Place of the Skull, where Jesus Christ was crucified, was known to be on a hill along the main road to Jerusalem. The rhetorician Marcus Fabius Quintilianus (c. 35–c. 100 CE) explained,

> Whenever we crucify the guilty, the most crowded roads are chosen, where the most people can see and be moved by this fear. For penalties relate not so much to retribution as to their exemplary effect. (*Institutio Oratoria,* c. 95 CE, quoted in Yamauchi, 1982, p. 4)

Laws are verbal codes that people must comprehend and employ if those laws are going to guide and govern their behavior. For deterrence to be effective, a defendant (or a potential defendant) must be capable of rational thought, good decision-making skills, and healthy volitional controls. We cannot deter people who have intellectual disabilities or psychiatric impairments that render them incapable of understanding or conforming their conduct to the requirements of the law. Crimes committed in the heat of passion or during severe mental illness are not subject to deterrence. You cannot deter somebody who cannot control what they are doing.

Punishments are not likely to deter that subset of criminals who thrive on outsmarting, outmaneuvering, or outspending the legal system. This group of criminals is enticed and not deterred by law enforcement, and the more effective the law enforcement, the greater the enticement.

Effective sentencing also deters vigilantism. When the public perceives that sentences are disproportionately mild, citizens are likely to take the law into their own hands. They are likely to believe that this is necessary for their own protection and for the survival of their loved ones.

INCAPACITATION

It is not possible to imagine a civilized society that does not have some method for incapacitating dangerous persons. To borrow a phrase from Emile Durkheim (and to take it completely out of context), prisons are one of the "priceless instruments of civilization."

Incapacitation assumes that offenders lack the moral character or internal strength to do the right thing. Legal authority is needed to restrain them in the interests of public safety. Prisons protect the public by removing offenders from society and isolating them. House arrest with ankle bracelets and GPS tracking devices incapacitates offenders by limiting their mobility.

Incapacitation is directed toward the future. The sentence is given for a crime that was committed in the past, but the purpose of incapacitation is to prevent another crime from happening in the future.

The theory of incapacitation as a solution to the problems of crime prevailed in the early 1970s, replacing rehabilitation as the dominant theory in corrections. Brown (2003) called this "the death of rehabilitation." The 1970s saw unprecedented growth in prison systems, with increased rates of incarceration, longer prison sentences, and more consecutive life sentences. The 1970s also saw three States – Delaware, Maryland, and Alabama – enact habitual offender (or "three-strikes") laws that gave life sentences to repeat offenders. At the time of writing, the federal government and thirty states have habitual offender laws (see Table 6.1).

Table 6.1 Jurisdictions with habitual offender laws listed in chronological order

State	Enacted
New York	1797
Texas	1952
Delaware	1973
Maryland	1975
Alabama	1977
Washington	1993
federal	1994
California	1994
Colorado	1994
Connecticut	1994
Georgia	1994
Indiana	1994
Kansas	1994
Louisiana	1994
New Mexico	1994
North Carolina	1994
Tennessee	1994
Virginia	1994
Wisconsin	1994
Arkansas	1995
Florida	1995
Montana	1995
Nevada	1995
New Jersey	1995
North Dakota	1995
Pennsylvania	1995
South Carolina	1995
Utah	1995
Vermont	1995
Arizona	2005
Massachusetts	2012

A peak period for the enactment of these laws occurred in the years 1994 and 1995, when the federal government and twenty-two states enacted their habitual offender laws. These laws have been challenged in court and have been upheld as constitutional. In cases like *Ewing v. California* (2003), the U.S. Supreme Court ruled that habitual offender laws are not cruel and unusual punishment. (For a history of the "three-strikes" laws in California, see Appendix L.)

The rate of incarceration in the U.S. was stable from the 1920s to the early 1970s. Since then, that rate has more than quadrupled. From 1973 to 2009, the state and federal prison populations rose from about 200,000 to 1.5 million, with another 700,000 being held daily in local jails. The U.S. penal population of 2.2 million adults is the largest in the world. In 2012, close to 25 percent of the world's prisoners were held in American prisons, although the U.S. accounts for only about 5 percent of the world's population. Nearly 1 percent of U.S. adults were in jails or prisons, which was five to ten times higher than the rates in Western Europe and other democracies. The National Research Council concluded, "The growth in incarceration rates in the United States over the past 40 years is historically unprecedented and internationally unique" (2014, p. 2).

In 2018, the rate of incarceration in the U.S. was 655 per 100,000, giving the U.S. the highest rate of incarceration in the world at that time (Walmsley, 2018). Principal among the factors responsible for the increase in incarcerations were longer sentences, increased parole revocations, and increased incarceration for drug-related offenses (Levitt, 2004).

Economist Steven Levitt – winner of the John Bates Clark Medal for his work on the economics of crime, and co-author of the best-sellers *Freakonomics* and *SuperFreakonomics* – identified the growth in prison population as one of four factors that contributed to the dramatic and unexpected decrease in crime that occurred in the 1990s (2004). The other three factors were the increased number of police officers, the end of the crack cocaine epidemic, and the legalization of abortion (which meant fewer unwanted babies). Levitt attributed one-third of the reduction in crime to increased incarceration, but he noted that hiring more police officers was more cost-effective. He attributed the impact of longer sentences to the effects of incapacitation and deterrence, but he observed that increased incarcerations may reach a point of diminishing returns: "In other words, the two-millionth criminal imprisoned is likely to impose a much smaller crime burden on society than the first prisoner" (2004, p. 179).

Levitt also noted that increasing the prison population could have indirect costs related to the over-representation of young Black males in prisons and the alienation of this entire segment of our population. Hiring more police officers and giving longer sentences are social experiments that may be effective in the short run, but they may come at a cost and at some point might exceed their optimum benefit.

A related question is whether the resources that were used to hire more police officers and build more prisons in the 1990s could have been better spent on education, jobs, and mental health, and whether this would have had a similar effect on the crime rate. Research has demonstrated the effectiveness of child intervention programs in preventing juvenile delinquency (Foster et al., 2004; Loeber & Farrington, 2001). Educational programs for prisoners have been effective in reducing recidivism (these educational programs are discussed in the next section, on rehabilitation).

Incapacitation has a special significance in the juvenile justice system, where defendants mature rapidly and can be expected to have changed by the time of their release. Scientific knowledge about maturation during adolescence indicates that juveniles who are incarcerated during middle adolescence can be expected to have changed by the time they are released in late adolescence or early adulthood. We can expect them to have become more capable of rational thought, more risk-aversive, more future-oriented, and less susceptible to peer influence. The countervailing reality is that they will have spent these important developmental years in the company of serious offenders. They are likely to have been schooled in specialized knowledge of crime, to have acquired a variety of bad habits, and to have developed antisocial identities. The juvenile prisoner is likely to have changed by the time they are released, but society may not like the person it receives.

In the most sweeping change in the history of juvenile justice, Massachusetts closed its four juvenile prisons between 1970 and 1972 and tore those buildings down in response to the beatings and other abuses that were occurring inside those walls. Those prisons were replaced with community programs. The Massachusetts Department of Youth Services commissioner who oversaw these changes was Jerome G. Miller, whose 1991 book won the Edward Sagarin Prize of the American Society of Criminology. California followed suit, closed eight of its eleven juvenile prisons in 1996, and closed the last three in 2023 (Rainey & Queally, 2023; Rosales, 2021).

A theory of incapacitation is not complete unless it includes the many depredations that offenders are likely to face in prison. These may include beatings, rapes, robberies, thefts, drug use, impressment into gangs, abuse by authorities, lack of privacy, and schooling in the ways of crime. Furthermore, a prison sentence punishes an entire family. A family with a loved one in prison has a harder time staying intact. And, once released, it is harder for the offender to find a job, join the mainstream economy, and resist the lucrative underground economy (Leipold, 2006). Brown (2003) concluded, "In fact, offenders are more likely to commit a crime after release from prison than previous to incarceration." (p. 3)

REHABILITATION

Rehabilitation involves identifying the barriers to an offender's ability to succeed as a law-abiding citizen and then removing those barriers. Rehabilitation efforts include: (1) clinical treatment of physical and mental disorders; (2) social programs on issues like violence prevention, substance use, and parenting; (3) chaplaincy and pastoral counseling; and (4) vocational services that prepare offenders to enter the mainstream economy. Of the four goals of sentencing, rehabilitation is the goal that assumes the best about human nature and human potential.

Research has shown that the single best method for reducing recidivism is education. A meta-analysis of fifty-seven studies covering thirty-seven years of research from 1980 to 2017 indicates that inmates who received education in prison were 28 percent less likely to recidivate (Bozick et al., 2018). These findings are important, but convincing American voters to provide free education to prisoners – especially at the college level – is a hard sell. With 43 million Americans struggling and sacrificing for decades to pay off $1.6 trillion in federal student loans (Hahn & Tarver, 2022) – and with no one rewarding them for their years of law-abiding behavior – we cannot expect that they will want to pay for someone else's college education just because that other person broke the law. Education may be cheaper and healthier than recidivism, but at this point in our history we cannot expect American taxpayers to go for it.

Furthermore, many offenders have learning difficulties or are not motivated to learn. The disability that is most commonly reported by incarcerated offenders is cognitive disability, which is defined by the Bureau of Justice Statistics as difficulty with concentration, memory, or decision-making due to a physical, mental, or emotional problem. Examples given by the Bureau of Justice Statistics include learning disorder, attention deficit disorder, traumatic brain injury, intellectual disability, dementia, autism, and Down syndrome. Cognitive disabilities are reported by 20 percent of prisoners and 31 percent of jail inmates. Contrast these figures with the incidence of cognitive disabilities among the non-criminal U.S. population, estimated to be 5 percent (Bronson et al., 2015). Our jails and prisons are burdened with people who have cognitive difficulties and were unable to enter the mainstream economy. Many of them were incapable of learning. They acted out in school, disrupted their classrooms, got expelled, and entered a life of crime. The very people we are trying to rehabilitate in our crowded prison classrooms are the people who could not succeed in school the first time around.

Belief in rehabilitation was strongest during the period known as the Progressive Era (1890–1920). The primary goal of this era was to take down political bosses, but a secondary goal consisted of prison reform, which was related to the rights of prisoners. This was the period during which the first juvenile courts were established, as mentioned above, beginning in 1899 in

Cook County, Illinois, with the efforts of social worker Jane Addams (1860–1935) and her colleagues at Hull House in Chicago (Steinberg & Schwartz, 2000). Juvenile courts then were championed by Judge Benjamin Lindsey (1869–1943) of Colorado, who became a juvenile court judge in 1901 (Larsen, 1972). As mentioned above, the 1970s witnessed "the death of rehabilitation" (Brown, 2003) and the ascendancy of incapacitation as the dominant theory of incarceration, with unprecedented growth in rates of incarceration, length of sentences, and the construction of new prisons. Among juvenile courts as well, sentences have become less rehabilitative and more punitive.

Providing improved mental health services to juveniles has proved to be effective, decreasing initial involvement with the juvenile justice system by 31 percent and decreasing subsequent involvement by 28 percent (Foster et al., 2004).

A study of adult criminals who desisted from crime by Liverpool psychologist Shadd Maruna (2001) won the Hindelang Award from the American Society of Criminology. Important take-aways from this book include:

1 Desistance from crime is not generally complete. Even criminals who have "desisted" from crime are likely to "keep their hand in" a little bit, committing an occasional crime but not on the scale that they did before they "desisted." Criminal behavior is like other behavioral problems, including addictions, in that relapses can be expected.
2 Desistance is not a one-time event. It is not a conversion experience like that of St. Paul on the road to Damascus (Acts of the Apostles 9:3–4). Desistance from crime is a daily decision, much like desistance from an addiction. "One day at a time" is a familiar slogan from Alcoholics Anonymous, and it applies to criminal behavior as well.
3 Persons who have desisted from crime tell a similar story, which Maruna called "the redemption script" (p. 87). They see themselves – accurately – as people who grew up in disadvantaged environments in an indifferent world. Then somebody took an interest in them. This person could have been a teacher, pastor, counselor, or probation officer. That person opened a door for them to a new world of opportunity. Desistance from crime became a possibility and a reality.

In my own discussions with incarcerated felons, I have heard them describe their attitudes toward crime using expressions like "chump change" and "long green." I have heard them boast that they can make more money on the street in one hour ("long green") than their fathers make at their jobs in two weeks ("chump change"). Young prisoners say this with a sense of pride. But, by the time they have served a long prison sentence and reached the age of 40, the world starts to look different to them. It can occur to them that the people who are earning "chump change" and staying out of prison are the smart ones. A young felon's values are likely to revolve around money, sex, fast cars, violence, weapons, and drugs. As a prisoner ages, their body grows weaker, their values tend to change, and these excitements tend to lose their luster. It is not unusual for aging prisoners to examine their lives and experience a change of heart.

Within the philosophy of rehabilitation, offenders are disadvantaged, needy people who had limited opportunities and made bad decisions. The correctional system can help them to identify and remediate their needs, find new opportunities, and make better decisions.

The ideal of rehabilitation may be at its best today in the "problem-solving courts" (PSCs) that have evolved in certain jurisdictions, including drug courts, mental health courts, and domestic violence courts (Wolf, 2007).

Rehabilitation is directed toward the future and the prevention of crime, and toward developing a prisoner's resources, including good internal controls. The philosophy of rehabilitation regards offenders as being capable of developing good internal controls and desisting from a life of crime once their problems are solved. Rehabilitation assumes that the defendant has the capacity to benefit from remedial efforts and is capable of choosing to obey the law in the future. Of the four goals of sentencing, rehabilitation is the goal that is most optimistic about the potential of human beings.

Psychotherapy for antisocial traits

Traditional clinical wisdom has long held that nothing can be done to repair antisocial personality traits. Nevertheless, a number of cognitive behavioral strategies have been developed for this population. These include Reasoning and Rehabilitation therapy (R&R; Ross & Fabiano, 1985); Aggression Replacement Training (ART; Glick & Goldstein, 1987); Thinking for a Change (TFC; Bush et al., 1997); and Moral Reconation Therapy (MRT; Little & Robinson, 1988). These therapies were reviewed by Rosenfeld et al. (2015).

Other therapy models developed for offenders include the risk-need-responsivity (RNR) model by Andrews (2012), which was found to reduce recidivism by as much as 40 percent. A review of 42 studies by Salekin (2002) suggests that psychopathy may not be an untreatable disorder.

REFERENCES

American Correctional Association. (1966). *Manual of Correctional Standards*. Alexandria, VA: Author.

Andrews, D. A. (2012). The risk-need-responsivity (RNR) model of correctional assessment and treatment. In J. A. Dvoskin, J. L. Skeem, R. W. Novaco, & K. S. Douglas (Eds.) *Using social science to reduce violent offending* (pp. 127–156). New York: Oxford University Press.

Atkins v. Virginia, 536 U.S. 304 (2002).

Barnet, R. E. (1985). Pursuing Justice in a Free Society: Part One – Power vs. Liberty. 4 *Criminal Justice Ethics* 50. Retrieved 11/18/2022 from https://perma. cc/MY4S-K4K9.

Bozick, R., Steele, J. L., Davis, L. M., & Turner, S. (2018). Does providing inmates with education improve postrelease outcomes? A meta-analysis of correctional education programs in the United States. *Journal of Experimental Criminology*. Retrieved 08/06/2020 from www.rand.org/pubs/external_publications/EP67650.html.

Braithwaite, J., & Pettit, P. (1990). *Not just deserts: A republican theory of criminal justice*. Oxford: Clarendon Press.

Bronson, J., Maruschak, L. M., & Berzofsky, M. (2015). Disabilities among prison and jail inmates, 2011–2012. Retrieved 11/18/2022 from www.bjs.gov/content/ pub/pdf/dpji1112.pdf.

Brown, M. S. (2003). Penological crisis in America: Finding meaning in imprisonment post-rehabilitation. Unpublished Ph.D. dissertation. Indiana University.

Bureau of Justice Statistics. (2012). Nearly 3.4 million violent crimes per year went unreported to police from 2006 to 2010. Retrieved 11/18/2022 from www.ojp. gov/sites/g/files/xyckuh241/files/archives/pressreleases/2012/ojppr080912.pdf

Bush, J., Glick, B., & Taymans, J. (1997). *Thinking for a change: Integrated cognitive behavior change program*. Washington, D.C.: U.S. Department of Justice.

Campbell, A. W. (1991). *Law of sentencing* (September 2022 update). Deerfield, IL: Clark Boardman Callaghan.

Coker v. Georgia, 433 U.S. 584 (1977).

Death Penalty Information Center. (2022). *Time on death row*. Retrieved 11/18/2022 from https://deathpenaltyinfo.org/death-row/death-row-time-on-death-row.

Department of Defense. (2018). *Annual report on sexual assault in the military*. Retrieved 08/30/2020 from www.sapr.mil/sites/default/files/DoD_Annual_ Report_on_Sexual_Assault_in_the_Military.pdf.

Dolinko, D. (1992). Three mistakes of retributivism. *UCLA Law Review*, *39*, 1623–1657.

Duff, R. A. (2001). *Punishment, communication, and community*. Oxford: Oxford University Press.

Enmund v. Florida, 458 U.S. 782 (1982).

Ewing v. California, 538 U.S. 11 (2003).

Ford v. Wainwright, 477 U.S. 399 (1986).

Foster, E. M., Qaseem, A., & Connor, T. (2004). Can better mental health services reduce the risk of juvenile justice system involvement? *American Journal of Public Health*, *94*(5), 859–865. doi:10.2105/ajph.94.5.859.

Furman v. Georgia, 408 U.S. 238 (1972).

Gardner, M. R. (1976). The renaissance of retribution – An examination of doing justice. *Wisconsin Law Review*, 781–815.

Glick, B., & Goldstein, A. P. (1987). Aggression Replacement Training. *Journal of Counseling and Development*, *65*, 356–362. doi:10.1002/j.1556-6676. 1987.tb00730.x.

Hahn, A., & Tarver, J. (2022). 2022 student loan debt statistics: Average student loan debt. *Forbes Advisor*. Retrieved 06/10/2022 from www.forbes.com/advisor/student-loans/average-student-loan-statistics/.

Kennedy v Louisiana, 554 U.S. 407 (2008).

LaFave, W. R., & Scott, A. W. (1972). *Handbook on criminal law*. St. Paul, MN: West Publishing Co.

LaFave, W. R., & Scott, A. W. (1986). *Substantive criminal law*. St. Paul, MN: West Group Publishing.

Larsen, C. E. (1972). *The good fight: The life and times of Ben B. Lindsey*. New York: Quadrangle Books.

Leipold, A. D. (2006). Recidivism, incapacitation, and criminal sentencing policy. *University of St. Thomas Law Journal, 3*(3), 536–558. Available at SSRN: https://ssrn.com/abstract=988117.

Levitt, S. D. (2004). Understanding why crime fell in the 1990s: Four factors that explain the decline and six that do not. *Journal of Economic Perspectives, 18*(1), 163–190. Retrieved 11/18/2022, from www.ojp.gov/ncjrs/virtual-library/abstracts/understanding-why-crime-fell-1990s-four-factors-explain-decline-and.

Little, G. L., & Robinson, K. D. (1988). Moral Reconation Therapy: A systematic step-by-step treatment system for treatment resistant clients. *Psychological Reports, 62*(1), 135–151. doi:10.2466/pr0.1988.62.1.135.

Loeber, R., & Farrington, D. P. (Eds.) (2001). *Child delinquents: Development, intervention, and service needs*. Thousand Oaks, CA: Sage Publications, Inc.

Maruna, S. (2001). *Making good: How ex-convicts reform and rebuild their lives*. Washington, D.C.: American Psychological Association.

Miller, J. G. (1991). *Last one over the wall: The Massachusetts experiment in closing reform schools*. Columbus, OH: Ohio State University Press.

Miller v. Alabama, 567 U.S. 460 (2012).

Moore, M. S. (1997). *Placing blame: A theory of criminal law*. Oxford: Oxford University Press.

Murphy, J. G. (1985). Retributivism, moral education, and the liberal state. *Criminal Justice and Ethics, 4*(1), 3–11. doi:10.1080/0731129X.1985.9991766.

Nadelhofer, T. A. (2013). Introduction. In Thomas A. Nadelhoffer (ed.), *The future of punishment* (pp. xv–xxiv). Oxford: Oxford University Press.

National Research Council. (2014). *The growth of incarceration in the United States: Exploring causes and consequences*. Washington, D.C.: The National Academies Press. doi:10.17226/18613.

Rainey, J., & Quelly, J. (2023). Caifornia is closing its last youth prisons. Will what replaces them be worse? Retrieved 11/09/2023 from https://news.yahoo.com/california-closing-last-youth-prisons-120015540.html.

Rosales, B. M. (2021). New state law puts California's juvenile justice system at a crossroads. Retrieved 11/09/2023 from https://edsource.org/2021/quick-guide-new-state-law-puts-californias-juvenile-justice-system-at-a-crossroads/661962.

Rosenfeld, B., Howe, J., Pierson, A., & Foellmi, M. (2015). Mental health treatment of criminal offenders. In Cutler, B. L., & Zapf, P. A. (Eds.) *APA handbook of forensic psychology. Volume 1: Individual and situational influences in criminal and civil contexts* (pp. 159–190). Washington, D.C.: American Psychological Association.

Ross, R., & Fabiano, E. (1985). *Time to think: A cognitive model of crime and delinquency prevention and rehabilitation*. Johnson City, TN: Academy of Arts and Sciences.

Salekin, R. T. (2002). Psychopathy and therapeutic pessimism. Clinical lore or clinical reality? *Clinical Psychology Review*, 22(1), 79–112. doi:10.1016/s0272-7358(01)00083-6.

Schaefer, W. V. (1956). Federalism and state criminal procedure. *Harvard Law Review*, 70(1), 1–26. doi:10.2307/1337385.

Shafer-Landau, R. (1996). The failure of retributivism. *Philosophical Studies*, 82(3), 289–316. doi:10.1007/bf00355311.

Steinberg, L., & Schwartz, R. (2000). Developmental psychology goes to court. In T. Grisso and R. Schwartz (Eds.) *Youth on trial: A developmental perspective on juvenile justice* (pp. 9–31). Chicago, IL: University of Chicago Press.

Stohr, M., & Walsh, A. (2016). *Corrections: The essentials*. Thousand Oaks, CA: Sage.

Von Hirsch, A. (1993). *Censure and sanctions*. Oxford: Oxford University Press.

Walmsley, R. (2018). *World prison population List. Twelfth edition*. Institute for Criminal Policy Research. Retrieved 11/18/2022 from www.prisonstudies.org/sites/default/files/resources/downloads/wppl_12.pdf.

Wojciech, S. (1985). *Giving desert its due: Social justice and legal theory*. New York: Springer.

Wolf, R. V. (2007). *Principles of problem-solving justice*. U.S. Department of Justice. Office of Justice Programs. NCJ Number 234803. Retrieved 11/18/2022 from www.ojp.gov/library/publications/principles-problem-solving-justice.

Yamauchi, E. M. (1982). The crucifixion and docetic Christology. *Concordia Theological Quarterly*, 46(1), 1–20.

7 The doctrine of mens rea

The Anglo-American system of criminal justice is based not only on the actions of the defendant but on their state of mind at the time. As Justice Oliver Wendell Holmes, Jr., wrote, "Even a dog distinguishes between being stumbled over and being kicked" (Holmes, 1881/1991). For an act to be considered a crime, both elements must exist: the guilty act (actus reus) and the guilty mind (mens rea). Actus reus and mens rea are two of the "elements" of a crime, i.e., two of the factors that the prosecution must demonstrate in order to sustain a conviction. (Other elements of a crime described in the Model Penal Code are listed in the Glossary.)

This two-part system of justice (actus reus and mens rea) has an ancient history. Platt and Diamond (1966) traced the origins of mens rea to Hebrew or Talmudic law. The principle was understood in ancient Rome. Cicero (106–43 BCE) wrote, "Crimes are not to be measured by the issue of events but from the bad intentions of men." The essence of mens rea is expressed in the Latin phrase "*Actus reus non facit reum nisi mens sit rea*" ("The act is not culpable unless the mind is guilty"). Morse and Hoffman (2008) wrote,

> Virtually every civilization that has left a relevant record – including the Babylonians, Jews, Egyptians, Greeks, and Romans – recognized that the law must judge both the act and the intention. (p. 1072)

The distinction between intentional and unintentional homicide, for example, is a distinction based on mens rea and has been attributed to the Athenian lawmaker Draco (c. 650–600 BCE, whose name gave us the adjective "draconian"). In ancient Greece, intentional homicide (*hekousios phonos* or *phonos ek pronoias*) was punishable by death. Unintentional homicide (*akousios phonos*) was punishable by exile. Notice that mens rea determined not only the name of the crime but also the degree of punishment that was deserved. These remain important features of our justice system today.

DOI: 10.4324/9781003385028-8

In Saxon England, the principles of mens rea were recognized as early as the tenth century by King Æthelred (966–1016) and his successor King Canute (990–1035). In translating the tenth-century Laws of Æthelred, we read:

> And if it happens that a man commits a misdeed involuntarily, or unintentionally, the case is different from that of one who offends of his own free will, voluntarily and intentionally. And likewise he who is an involuntary agent of his misdeeds should always be entitled to clemency and better terms owing to the fact that he acted as an involuntary agent. (Quoted in Walker, 1968, p. 16)

In tenth-century England, the various levels of mens rea were accorded different punishments, just as they are today. From King Canute we read:

> Likewise, in many cases of evildoing, when a man is an involuntary agent, he is more entitled to clemency because he acted as he did from compulsion. And if anyone does anything unintentionally, the case is entirely different from that of one who acts deliberately. (Quoted in Walker, 1968, p. 17)

THE AMERICAN LAW INSTITUTE (ALI) AND THE MODEL PENAL CODE (MPC)

The best way I have found to understand the doctrine of mens rea as it is practiced today is to skip 3,000 years of ancient jurisprudence and go directly to the Model Penal Code (MPC) published in 1985 by the American Law Institute (ALI). In doing so, we skip over more than sixty legal terms that were used to describe varying shades of mental states during eight centuries of English common law. Some of those terms survive today, even though they sound old-fashioned. For example, the phrase "depraved mind," which was important in the 2021 murder trial of ex-Officer Derek Chauvin (*State v. Derek Michael Chauvin*, 2021; see Chapter 8), might be translated as "indifference to human life," a phrase that would communicate more meaningfully to readers in the twenty-first century. The old legal terms are poetic, but they lack precision. The list of outdated terms that describe mens rea includes Blackstone's "vitious will" (see Appendix G); "oblique intention" (a metaphor from geometry); and anatomical metaphors like "depraved heart" and "abandoned and malignant heart." What these terms possess in lyricism they lack in clarity. Since the nineteenth century, Anglo-American law has discovered more practical ways of saying things that better describe states of mind and communicate more effectively to all stakeholders, including judges, juries, defendants, attorneys, the press, the public, and mental health professionals.

Figure 7.1 Sir William Blackstone (1723–1780), Justice of the Common Pleas from 1770 to 1780. Along with Bracton, Coke, and Hale, he is recognized as one of the four great scholars of English common law.

The ALI is a non-profit organization that was founded in 1923 by a group of lawyers, judges, and law professors. Their self-appointed mission was to clarify American law by eliminating some of its uncertainties and unnecessary complexities. Among the founding members was William Howard Taft, twenty-seventh President of the United States (1909–1913) and tenth Chief Justice of the U.S. Supreme Court (1921–1930). The ALI wrote the Model Penal Code (MPC) and intended that it serve as a template by which the states and federal government might draft their own laws. The ALI reasoned, according to a concept known as "the principle of legality," that American society would function more effectively if the public knew and understood what was expected of them under the law.

Serious work on the Model Penal Code began in 1952 with a grant from the Rockefeller Foundation. After thirteen "Tentative Drafts," the "Proposed Official Draft" was published in 1962. A final version was published in 1985 (American Law Institute, 2008; the section numbers have been revised: for the latest version, please see Uniform Laws Annotated, 2023).

The MPC was influential, but it did not succeed in completely rewriting American law. More than two-thirds of the states adopted parts of the MPC. New Jersey, New York, and Oregon adopted almost all of it. Only one state adopted the ALI in its entirety – the state of Idaho, in 1971 – but this experiment lasted only two months and then was rejected, due chiefly to the MPC's provisions on gun control and its omission of laws regarding adultery, sodomy, and fornication.

The MPC identifies four levels of mens rea: purposely, knowingly, recklessly, and negligently. These are listed in order of decreasing blameworthiness. The most blameworthy states of mind deserve the most severe punishments. This chapter describes the four levels of mens rea by quoting the ALI definition and then rendering that definition into more familiar language. Examples are provided from actual cases. Also, each level is illustrated with the same hypothetical actus reus. The actus reus I have chosen is a scourge that is unique to our time. The study of history indicates that each era of human history has its own set of legal challenges that are unique to the technology of its time. For example, in the writings of King Alfred the Great (c. 847–899; see Appendix D), we find discussions of the liability involved when somebody borrows a horse and gets hurt, and when people leave their weapons stacked carelessly and they fall over and hurt somebody, and when somebody carries a spear over their shoulder and it accidentally pierces somebody. Alfred's world, apparently, was a place where people got hurt by borrowed horses and by long, sharp weapons. These examples reflect the technologies of Alfred's day. Our own time has its own plagues, not the least of which are the many pre-adolescent children who wander carelessly through parking lots while playing video games. Some of these children are accompanied by mindless parents who are equally oblivious on their cell phones. This has become such a problem in our society that I actually saw two near-misses in a single day. The hypothetical actus reus I have chosen for this chapter (and which I will reprise in Chapter 19 on insanity) involves a man who is driving through a parking lot when he hits a little boy who is playing a video game. This hypothetical will illustrate how moral responsibility and punishment vary not with the act itself but with the defendant's state of mind. By keeping the actus reus constant, we can illustrate the differences in the levels of mens rea.

For example, Driver W (for "Without mens rea") hits the little boy entirely by accident. (I later discovered that this illustration bears similarities to the hypothetical truck driver described by Williams, 1981, p. 28.) The little boy stepped out suddenly between two parked cars and Driver W did not have time to see him and did not have time to stop. Driver W did not have a "guilty mind." There was no mens rea. Therefore no crime was committed. (For purposes of clarity, we will revisit Driver W after we have discussed the four levels of mens rea.)

Purposely

According to the ALI definition: Model Penal Code, Section 2.02(2)(a):

A person acts purposely with respect to a material element of an offense when:

i if the element involves the nature of his conduct or a result thereof, it is his conscious object to engage in conduct of that nature or to cause such a result; and
ii if the element involves the attendant circumstances, he is aware of the existence of such circumstances or he believes or hopes that they exist

---

In other words, *purpose* exists when people (a) *know* what they are doing, (b) either *intend* to do what they are doing or (c) *intend* to cause the result that they cause, (d) are *aware* of their circumstances, and either (e) *know* that these are the circumstances or (f) *hope* that these are the circumstances.

An oft-used synonym for "purposely" is "intentionally."

In our parking lot example, the little boy was hit by the car *purposely* if Driver P (for "Purposely") *knew* he was going to hit the little boy, *intended* to hit the little boy, *intended* to hurt him, was *aware* of the circumstances, and either *knew* or *hoped* that the little boy would be hit and/or injured by their car. Because it is hard to imagine anyone so depraved as Driver P, let us develop a couple of scenarios, unlikely as they may seem.

> *First Scenario*: Driver P has a serious grudge against the little boy's family. He is motivated by revenge. He vows to himself that he is going to hurt the first person from that family that he sees, and that first person is the hapless little boy.
>
> *Second Scenario*: The parking lot happens to be at a medical center. Driver P has an urgent medical need and he has an emergency appointment, for which he is now late, because the parking lot is filled to capacity. Driver P has been waiting for 45 minutes. It is now 3:45 pm, and his doctor goes home at 4:00 pm. Just then an empty space opens up and Driver P speeds to it. He is almost there when the little boy's family comes from the opposite direction and slides into the parking space. Driver P is afraid for his own health, and he is furious. He is motivated by revenge. He lies in wait for people to come out of the car. (Lying in wait indicates purpose.) He runs down the first person who emerges from the car, who is the hapless little boy.

This second scenario not only illustrates purpose but it has the added benefit of introducing the difference between mens rea and insanity at this early stage of the discussion. Let us imagine that Driver P has a serious mental illness, that the doctor he is waiting to see is his psychiatrist, and that his medical emergency is an episode of uncontrollable rage. Mens rea is present: Driver P knew what he was doing, he developed a purpose, and he had a guilty mind. The question of insanity (specifically the form of insanity known as "volitional incapacity"; see Chapter 19) is whether Driver P was able to control his behavior at the time because of his mental illness.

The hypothetical crimes described in these two scenarios both indicate purpose, motive, intent, decision-making, planning, preparation, and premeditation. They include "malice aforethought," that is, planning, preparation, and the intent to do harm. If the little boy dies, Driver P may be guilty of first degree murder. If the boy dies and Driver P can demonstrate that he intended only to hurt him but not to kill him, then Driver P may be guilty of involuntary manslaughter. If the boy does not die, Driver P may be guilty of attempted murder, attempted manslaughter, assault with intent to kill, aggravated assault, or similar crimes as they are defined in his jurisdiction.

Knowingly

The Model Penal Code, Section 2.02(2)(b) defines "knowingly" as follows:

A person acts knowingly with respect to a material element of an offense when:

i if the element involves the nature of his conduct or the attendant circumstances, he is aware that his conduct is of that nature or that such circumstances exist; and

ii if the element involves a result of his conduct, he is aware that it is practically certain that his conduct will cause such a result.

Simply put, people commit crimes *knowingly* when they are (a) *aware* of their conduct, (b) *aware* of their circumstances, and (c) *aware* of the results that their behavior will cause. *Knowing* is the state of understanding that the action you are about to perform is morally and/or legally wrong. It involves awareness only, and does not imply motive or intent.

Knowing and *purpose* usually go hand-in-hand. In fact, if a crime is committed *purposely*, this implies that it was also committed *knowingly*. However some crimes do occur in which *knowing* can exist without *purpose*. In California several cases have been tried in which defendants were found guilty for *knowing* that they were giving their partner a sexually transmitted disease. The prosecution may not have been able to prove that the defendant acted with malice and *purposely* transmitted the disease, but if the prosecution can prove that the defendant *knew* they had the disease, then a crime was committed. In addition, sex crimes such as rape that are committed when a defendant *knows* they are HIV-positive are eligible for a three-year sentencing enhancement under California law (CA Penal Code § 12022.85).

Brink (2021) described the person who commits a crime *knowingly* although not *purposely* as someone who "tolerated the wrong without aiming at it" (p. 8).

Returning to our parking lot example, Driver "K" (for "Knowingly") sees the little boy in time but he does not brake or change course. Driver K knows that he is going to hit the boy and he knows that the boy will be hurt.

Because this is hard to imagine, let us develop a possible scenario. Perhaps Driver K was in the "freeze" mode of the "fight-flight-freeze" response, in which case he may *know* what he is doing even though he does not *intend* to do it. (Driver K may be able to argue that, while in the "freeze" mode, his mental state involved diminished capacity. See Chapter 21.)

Rather than search for those rare crimes where *knowing* exists without *purpose*, let us instead analyze the *knowing* aspect of mens rea by examining those behaviors where a *lack of knowing* may exclude the argument that a crime was committed. Riding in a stolen car, for example, may not be a crime if the defendant did not *know* that the car was stolen. (This example comes from the United Kingdom's Theft Act of 1968.) Marrying a person who is already married is a crime if you *know* that the person is already married. It may not be a crime if you *do not know* that the person is married. (This example comes from John Bouvier [1787–1851], who published the first American law dictionary in 1843.)

To do something *knowingly* is to do it without ignorance, accident, or mistake. The difference between doing something *knowingly* and doing something *purposely* is the difference between knowledge and intent. Driver P for "Purposely" intended and chose his action. Driver K for "Knowingly" chose his action only in the passive sense by which failure to act might be considered a choice.

If the child in our hypothetical dies, Driver K may go on trial for involuntary manslaughter. Three states (Florida, Minnesota, and Pennsylvania) also recognize the crime of third degree murder: these are homicides that involve *knowing* but do not involve planning or intent. (For an illustration of third degree murder, see the discussion in Chapter 8 of the murder of George Floyd by Officer Derek Chauvin; *State v. Derek Michael Chauvin*, 2021.)

Recklessly

In the words of the Model Penal Code, Section 2.02(2)(c):

> A person acts recklessly with respect to a material element of an offense when he consciously disregards a substantial and unjustifiable risk that the material element exists or will result from his conduct. The risk must be of such a nature and degree that, considering the nature and purpose of the actor's conduct and the circumstances known to him, its disregard involves a gross deviation from the standard of conduct that a law-abiding person would observe in the actor's situation.

Simply put, people act *recklessly* when they know that the action they are about to perform is grossly irresponsible and creates an unjustifiable risk.

In our parking lot example, imagine that Driver R (for "Recklessly") drives through the parking lot with his eyes shut. If this illustration sounds preposterous, then it serves our purpose, because *recklessness* involves preposterous behavior. Or perhaps Driver R was texting, taking a selfie, or playing a video game when he hits the little boy. Another common example is drunk driving. If the child dies, Driver R may be guilty of involuntary manslaughter.

Negligently

Model Penal Code, Section 2.02(2)(d) defines "negligently" as follows:

> A person acts negligently with respect to a material element of an offense when he should be aware of a substantial and unjustifiable risk that the material element exists or will result from his conduct. The risk must be of such a nature and degree that the actor's failure to perceive it, considering the nature and purpose of his conduct and the circumstances known to him, involves a gross deviation from the standard of care that a reasonable person would observe in the actor's situation.

Simply put, people behave *negligently* when they *do not know* that their actions are causing an unjustifiable risk, but they *should know.*

In our parking lot example, Driver N (for "Negligently") has not maintained his car. His brakes are shot. His tires are bald. He tries to stop, but he cannot stop in time. If the child dies, Driver N may be guilty of involuntary manslaughter.

AEROPERÚ FLIGHT 603

When Aeroperú Flight 603 from Lima, Peru, to Santiago, Chile, flew over the Pacific Ocean on the night of October 2, 1996, the pilots could not read their instruments and did not know their altitude, because the maintenance worker who had cleaned the outside of the airplane had put duct tape over the static ports and had neglected to remove it. The left wing hit the surface of the water and all 70 persons aboard were killed. The Peruvian maintenance worker was convicted of negligent homicide and served a two-year suspended sentence (Wrigley, 2021).

Summary: The four levels of mens rea in the MPC

The four levels of mens rea were presented above in the order of blameworthiness, and thereby in order of severity of punishment. The first three levels – purposely, knowingly, and recklessly – refer to states of mind. Negligence is a state of mind only in the sense in which it is the absence of the vigilant state of mind that we expect all citizens to have about themselves at all times.

One might summarize the four levels of mens rea by saying (1) acting *negligently* is failing to make the correct choice, (2) acting *recklessly* is making a choice that was unwise or preposterous, (3) acting *knowingly* is making a choice that you knew to be legally or morally wrong, and (4) acting *purposely* is putting that wrong choice into action.

ACTUS REUS WITHOUT MENS REA

Having examined the four levels of mens rea in the MPC, let us now consider actus reus in the absence of mens rea. Sometimes people get hurt and no crime was committed. Returning to our parking lot example, Driver W (for "Without mens rea"), the driver we considered at the top of this discussion, is a conscientious individual who kept his car in good working order. He kept the windshield clean. He watched where he was going. He was not fumbling with his car radio or looking in his glove compartment. He wore corrective lenses as required by the restriction on his driver's license. In short, there was no *negligence*.

Driver W was not driving while drinking or while taking a prescription medication with a warning label that reads, "Do not operate a motor vehicle while taking this medication." He did not engage in pranks like driving through parking lots with his eyes closed. He did not text or play video games while driving. That is, there was no *recklessness*.

Driver W did not see the child in time to stop or swerve. That is, the act was not done *knowingly*. The child stepped out suddenly from between two parked cars and Driver W had no time to react.

Driver W had no motive and he had nothing to gain by hurting the little boy. He held no grudge against the child or his family and no desire for revenge. He did not lie in wait and look for an opportunity. He had no plan or intent. That is, Driver W did not commit the act *purposely*.

If the child is killed or injured, this was not a crime (unless it happened during the commission of another crime, such as running a red light or fleeing the scene of a robbery, in which case Driver W may be guilty of involuntary manslaughter, aggravated assault, or another crime defined in his jurisdiction).

MOTIVE AND INTENT

The invisible internal life of defendants includes their motive and intent. "Motive" is the *reason why* somebody commits a criminal act. It is what the defendant hopes to gain from this victim or from this action. "Intent" involves the state of mind that the defendant had toward this victim at the time of this crime.

Many illustrations might be given of motive and intent. In the interests of making this discussion complex, let us select an example where behavior and circumstance demonstrate multiple levels of motivation, self-interest, and social pressure – the politically or religiously motivated suicide bomber. (I begin with a caveat: I have not known any suicide bombers. My knowledge of their motivation is based upon my reading and my surmise.)

The suicide bomber's intention is malicious, simple, and straightforward: They want to hurt their victims. Their motives may be complex and may include (1) making a public statement for their cause, (2) securing a place in paradise, (3) satisfying the expectations of their peers, (4) satisfying the expectations of their handlers, and (5) establishing their individual identity as a person who adheres to a certain moral code. Although they destroy themselves in the process, they demonstrate some of the self-interest that can be found inevitably in all human behavior. They elevate their status and self-worth, and, while they are alive, they obtain the approval of their peers and handlers. The religiously or politically motivated suicide bomber illustrates that the relationships between crime, personal interest, and personal loss can be complex. While it may be tempting to say that the suicide bomber made a free choice, their motives, their obedience to their code, and their desires to please their peers and handlers are such that the existence of free will cannot be proved. (I would argue that the existence of free will can never be proved, because an alternative reason can always be found for any human behavior, but that the existence of free will can be intuited. For an introduction to the philosophy of free will, see Kane, 2002.)

Intent cannot exist without motive. Motive, on the other hand, can exist without intent. Motive without intent is fantasy and remains in the realm of harmless imagination. Daydreaming about being a killer does not make one a killer. A person who entertains wishes, fantasies, or desires and does not act upon them does not commit a crime. (For the special case of criminal conspiracy, see the next section.)

But intent does not exist without motive. A person who intends to commit a crime always has a motive. Once an actus reus has occurred, it is the task of prosecutors, triers of fact, and forensic mental health professionals to analyze the defendant's behavior and draw inferences about their invisible motives and intentions. We infer motives and intentions from observable behaviors and from words spoken by the defendant. Planning an activity in advance indicates knowledge and purpose. Bringing a weapon to the scene of a crime indicates premeditation, knowledge, and purpose. Using bare hands or a random item like a clothes iron (see cases presented in Chapters 8 and 11) suggests lack of planning, whereas the use of a typical weapon like a gun or a knife suggests pre-meditation. Lying in wait (also known as "ambush") indicates pre-meditation and intent. Fleeing the scene, obscuring evidence, and other forms of evasion and deception indicate that the defendant knew they did something that could get them in trouble. Remorse indicates that the defendant knows they did something wrong. These common-sense ideas about intention and premeditation can be expressed in common-sense language that triers of fact will understand.

In the process of discerning a defendant's motive and intent, inter-viewing the defendant is not always helpful, because a canny defendant may choose to obscure what they were thinking at the time and what they had hoped to gain.

The model of human decision making and human action that emerges from these assumptions about motive and intent is one in which an agent who is faced with a predicament (such as how to pay the rent, how to resolve a dispute, or how to gratify their desires) (a) generates an array of alternative choices (unless they are so limited by intellectual, emotional, or cultural factors that they can generate only one choice); (b) reflects upon these alternatives (unless they are too impulsive to spend time reflecting on them); (c) eliminates undesirable alternatives; (d) prioritizes the remaining alternatives; (e) selects the most desirable alternative; and (f) puts it into action. In the case of an intentional crime, the agent has deliberately chosen an alternative that they knew to be illegal. The question is: Why would anybody do something so risky, so perverse, and so destructive of self and others as to knowingly commit a crime? To answer this question we posit a number of emotional and motivational states like rage, fear, greed, lust, envy, domination, selfishness, expediency, revenge, addiction, desperation, compulsion, and indifference. Also, the person who knowingly and pur-posely commits a crime may have imagined that they would not get caught, and indeed a large percentage of crimes go unreported and a large per-centage of reported crimes go unsolved (Thompson & Tapp, 2022). The U.S. Department of Justice conducts the National Crime Victimization Survey (NCVS) annually, in which it interviews about 240,000 individuals in 150,000 households. In 2021, only 30.8 percent of property crimes and only 45.6 percent of violent crimes (including only 21.5 percent of sexual assaults) were reported to the police. (Homicide is not included in these statistics because the NCVS is based on personal interviews with crime victims.) An annual report published by the FBI, Crime in the United States (CIUS), shows that in 2019 law enforcement agencies solved only 45.5 percent of violent crimes and only 17.2 percent of property crimes. This included 61.4 percent of murders, 52.3 percent of aggravated assaults, 32.9 percent of rapes, 30.5 percent of robberies, 23.8 percent of arsons, 18.4 per-cent of larcenies, 14.1 percent of burglaries, and 13.8 percent of auto thefts

(Federal Bureau of Investigation, 2019). If criminals believe that they have a good chance of getting away with a crime, they are right.

Because the emotional and motivational states of mind listed above may have neural substrates, certain neuroscientists have proposed that a science of "brain states" will someday replace our folk psychological system of "mental states." For example, Greene and Cohen (2006) predicted, "Neuroscience will challenge and ultimately reshape our intuitive sense of justice" (p. 208).

Denno (2016) wrote, "The entire modern criminal justice system is based on an outmoded psychology of mental states ... [It] is time for a scientific theory of mental states" (pp. 78, 80). Churchland (1981) envisioned a "completed neuroscience" that will replace "our commonsense conception of psychological phenomena" (p. 67). However, the brain is not a simple machine, and evidence suggests that the vision of a "completed neuroscience" may not materialize. For example, a meta-analysis of ninety studies by Elliott et al. (2020) suggests that fMRI experiments, rather than pulling us toward a completed neuroscience, are drowning in a sea of intra-subjective variability.

MENS REA IN CRIMINAL CONSPIRACY

The fact that conspiracy is a crime reflects how important intention and states of mind are to our system of justice. In criminal conspiracy, the actus reus is the mere sharing of an intention with another human being. If the defendants had kept their mouths shut and had kept their malicious intentions to themselves, their thoughts would have remained in the realm of harmless fantasy and no crime would have been committed.

In our parking lot example, two drivers we will name CC (for "Criminal Conspiracy") held a conversation in which they agreed that one of them would hurt the little boy. Even if they never act on their intention, Drivers CC may be guilty of conspiracy to commit murder.

STRICT LIABILITY CRIMES

This chapter, which has addressed the doctrine of mens rea, is not meant to imply that this noble doctrine has prevailed at all times and in all places. In what are known as "strict liability" crimes, a defendant's state of mind is not relevant and the actus reus alone determines culpability.

Early examples of strict liability crimes are found in the writings of King Alfred the Great (c. 847–899; see Appendix E). Another example of a strict liability crime was defined by King Henry VIII in 1530 after seventeen members of the household of the Bishop of Rochester were poisoned by their cook. Henry declared that homicide by poison was always high treason – without any consideration of the defendant's mens rea – and was punishable by boiling to death in oil. We might assume that Henry was worried about his own safety (Weinstock et al., 1996).

As Dubber wrote in 2011:

> Doctrinal rules about mens rea and actus reus, for instance, are but ancient broadsheets blowing in the wind of imminent threats to the authority of the sovereign or the welfare of the household under its/his control. Anachronistic slogans are no match for the rhetoric of emergency. (Dubber, 2011, p. 105)

In other words, acts of self-preservation by elites are likely to prevail despite all good intentions regarding due process.

Strict liability crimes in the United States today include failure to register as a sex offender and statutory rape (more specifically, statutory rape when the victim looks like an adult and when the victim consents – for an example, see the case of Eli discussed in Chapter 12). These are strict liability crimes because they are not defined by the defendant's state of mind but only by the defendant's action (or inaction) and the age of the victim.

REFERENCES

American Law Institute. (1953/1962/1985/2017). *Model Penal Code*. Philadelphia, PA: Author.

American Law Institute. (2008). *Model Penal Code Records*. University of Pennsylvania: Biddle Law Library. Retrieved 11/19/2022 from https://findingaids.library.upenn.edu/records/UPENN_BIDDLE_PU-L.ALI.04.005.

Bouvier, J. (1843). *A law dictionary: Adapted to the constitution and laws of the United States of America*. Philadelphia: T. and J. W. Johnson, Law Booksellers.

Brink, D. O. (2021). *Fair opportunity and responsibility*. Oxford: Oxford University Press.

Churchland, Paul M. (1981). Eliminative materialism and the propositional attitudes. *Journal of Philosophy*, 78(2), 67–90. Stable URL: http://links.jstor.org/sici?sici=0022-362X%28198102%2978%3A2%3C67%3AEMATPA%3E2.0.CO%3B2-8.

Denno, D. W. (2016). The place for neuroscience in criminal law. In D. Patterson & M. S. Pardo (Eds.) *Philosophical foundations of law and neuroscience* (pp. 69–83). Oxford: Oxford University Press.

Dubber, M. D. (2011). Foundations of state punishment in modern liberal democracies: Toward a genealogy of American criminal law. In R. A. Duff & S. P. Green (Eds.) *Philosophical foundations of criminal law* (pp. 83–106). Oxford: Oxford University Press.

Elliott, M. L., Knodt, A. R., Ireland, D., Morris, M. L., Poulton, R., Ramrakha, S., Sison, M. L., Moffitt, T. E., Caspi, A., & Hariri, A. R. (2020). What is the test-retest reliability of common task-functional MRI measures? New empirical evidence and a meta-analysis. *Psychological Science, 31*(7), 792–806. doi:10.11 77/0956797620916786.

Federal Bureau of Investigation. (2019). Crime in the United States. U.S. Department of Justice. https://ucr.fbi.gov/crime-in-the-u.s/2019/crime-in-the-u.s.-2019/topic-pages/clearances.

Greene, J., & Cohen, J. (2006). For the law, neuroscience changes nothing and everything. In S. Zeki & O. Goodenough (Eds.) *Law and the brain.* Oxford: Oxford University Press.

Holmes, O. W. (1881/1991). *The common law.* Garden City, NY: Dover Books.

Kane, R. (2002). Introduction. In R. Kane (Ed.) *Free will* (pp. 1–26). Malden, MA: Blackwell Publishing.

Morse, S. J., & Hoffman, M. B. (2008). The uneasy entente between legal insanity and mens rea: Beyond *Clark v. Arizona. Journal of Criminal Law and Criminology, 97*(4), 1071–1149. www.jstor.org/stable/40042860.

Platt, A., & Diamond, B. L. (1966). The origins of the "Right and Wrong" test of criminal responsibility and its subsequent development in the United States: An historical survey. *California Law Review, 54*(3), 1227–1260. doi:10.2307/34 79281.

State v. Derek Michael Chauvin, 27-CR-20-12646 (Minnesota, 2021).

Thompson, A., & Tapp, S. N. (2022). Crime victimization, 2021. U.S. Department of Justice. https://bjs.ojp.gov/content/pub/pdf/cv21.pdf.

Uniform Laws Annotated. *Model Penal Code.* Retrieved 3/31/2023 from https://1.next.westlaw.com/Document/NF747F2F0025B11DD8320AE42787FBF1D/View/FullText.html?originationContext=documenttoc&transitionType=CategoryPageItem&contextData=(sc.Default). (Subscription required.)

Walker, N. (1968). *Crime and insanity in England. Volume 1: The historical perspective.* Edinburgh: University of Edinburgh Press.

Weinstock, R., Leong, G. B., & Silva, J. A. (1996). California's diminished capacity defense: Evolution and transformation. *Bulletin of the American Academy of Psychiatry and Law, 24*(3), 347–366.

Williams, B. (1981). *Moral luck.* Cambridge: Cambridge University Press.

Wrigley, S. (2021). Aeroperú Flight 603. Retrieved 11/19/2022 from https://fearoflanding.com/accidents/accident-reports/aeroperu-flight-603/.

8   Applications of mens rea

The doctrine of mens rea, explained in Chapter 7, is applied in many contexts, including the distinction between murder and manslaughter.

MURDER VS. MANSLAUGHTER

First degree murder typically is defined by "malice aforethought." That is, the defendant intended to do harm without sufficient justification, and they planned the crime in advance (premeditation).

"Second degree murder" typically is defined as malicious intent without premeditation. When four police officers on patrol in New York City shot and killed Amadou Diallo on February 4, 1999, the officers were correctly charged with second degree murder, because the homicide was committed on the spur of the moment, without premeditation, even though the homicide was intentional. (The four officers were acquitted, but the City settled for $3 million. See the discussion in Chapter 5 regarding the difference in standards of evidence between criminal and civil trials.)

"Third degree murder" exists in only three states – Florida, Minnesota, and Pennsylvania – and it is defined differently in each of those states. The definition of third degree murder became crucial in *State v. Derek Michael Chauvin* (2021), i.e., the trial of Officer Derek Michael Chauvin for the murder of George Floyd (see below).

Voluntary manslaughter

Not all homicides are murders. A homicide is "voluntary manslaughter" when the defendant was in a compromised state of mind and lacked full capacity for criminal responsibility. Crimes of passion fall into this category. These are crimes where the victim has done something to provoke the defendant beyond their available self-control. Passion can be so overwhelming that a person may lose control of themselves and do something against their own best interest. The defendant may have

DOI: 10.4324/9781003385028-9

intended to harm or kill the victim, but the elements of planning, preparation, and premeditation that define first degree murder are absent.

Case study #1: Anthony – a crime of passion

I conducted Anthony's psychological evaluation after he found his wife having sex with another man and he killed them both. He was 27 years old and had a good employment history. There was no past or present indication of mental illness, including substance use disorder. He had no prior history of violence. He was found guilty of voluntary manslaughter and was sentenced to prison for a determinate period of time. Upon his release from prison, he returned to his former employment and went on with his life.

Involuntary manslaughter

"Involuntary manslaughter" is homicide without intent. In some jurisdictions, it is known as "negligent homicide." It may occur "accidentally" during the commission of another crime. For example, if I am fleeing the scene of a robbery and I inadvertently strike a pedestrian with my car, I may be guilty of involuntary manslaughter. Or if I intentionally run a red light and inadvertently kill a pedestrian in the process, I may be guilty of involuntary manslaughter. In both of these examples my intention was to commit a crime. Even though the crime I intended was not homicide, I may be guilty of involuntary manslaughter because my intention was to commit a crime. These examples help to underscore the centrality of intention or state of mind (mens rea) in the definition of crime.

The murder of Heather Heyer: a case of first degree murder: *United States v. James Alex Fields, Jr.* (W.D. Va. 2018)

On February 6, 2017, the City Council of Charlottesville, Virginia, met to decide the future of the Robert E. Lee statue that had stood in its location since 1924. Their meeting was part of a general movement throughout the Southern states to remove memorials dedicated to the Confederate States of America. The City Council of Charlottesville voted 3–2 to remove the statute.

A group called "Unite the Right" rallied in Charlottesville to protest this decision. The rally drew counter-protestors, and a number of violent skirmishes broke out.

James Alex Fields, Jr., age 20, a white supremacist, drove from Ohio to attend this rally. He accelerated his 2010 Dodge Challenger into a stopped car, which rolled forward, killing counter-protestor Heather Heyer (age 32) and wounding twenty-eight others. He fled the scene, injuring more people on his way out. Fields was found guilty of first degree murder, hit and run, and eight counts of malicious wounding. In order to avoid the death penalty, he pleaded guilty to twenty-nine counts of federal hate crimes. He was sentenced to two life sentences plus 419 years.

Fields' crime showed purpose, motive, planning, and intent to harm. He drove from Ohio to Virginia for the purpose of attending this demonstration. Although he may not have been contemplating murder when he left Ohio, at some point he did contemplate hurting other people, he chose to do so, and he acted upon his decision. Although he may not have intended specifically to kill Ms. Heyer, he did intend and plan – for however brief a duration – to knock a stopped car into a crowd of demonstrators. His motive was related to his political ideology. He showed malice aforethought, and his crime was first degree murder (*United States v. James Alex Fields, Jr.*, 2018).

The murder of George Floyd: a case of second degree murder, third degree murder, and second degree manslaughter: *State v. Derek Michael Chauvin* (Minn. App. 2021)

On May 25, 2020, Minneapolis police officer Derek Michael Chauvin (age 44) murdered George Floyd (age 46) in the process of arresting him for buying cigarettes with a counterfeit $20 bill. Chauvin and three junior officers at the scene were fired the next day. Protests erupted in 140 cities. The National Guard was called out in twenty-one states. Six people were killed in riots, many more people were injured, and thousands were arrested (Taylor, 2020). In Minneapolis alone protestors set fire to 220 buildings, including a police station, and caused an estimated $55 million in damage.

Ex-officer Chauvin was charged with several crimes reflecting various levels of mens rea. At first he was charged with third degree murder. This crime exists in only three states: Minnesota, Pennsylvania, and Florida. Each of these states defines the crime differently. Section 609.195 of the Minnesota Statutes defines third degree murder as occurring when a defendant "causes the death of another by perpetrating an act eminently dangerous to others and evincing a depraved mind, without regard for human life." The phrase "depraved mind" is an example of the poetic language that we inherited from eight centuries of English common law. It is evocative and polemical, but it needs clarification. The rest of the phrase, "without regard for human life," is easier for a modern reader to understand. Instead of saying "depraved mind," we might say that the crime of third degree murder in Minnesota is a homicide that is caused by indifference to human life.

Civil rights activist Reverend Al Sharpton appeared before the media and protested that Hennepin County, Minnesota, should have charged Officer Chauvin with first degree murder. First degree murder is defined in Section 609.185 of the Minnesota Statutes as occurring (inter alia) when a defendant

> causes the death of a human being with premeditation and with intent to effect the death of the person or of another.

By insisting that Chauvin be charged with first degree murder, Reverend Sharpton was asserting that Officer Chauvin had intended to kill George Floyd and had planned to do it.

Minnesota Governor Tim Walz gave control of the case to Minnesota Attorney General Keith Ellison, who on June 3, 2020, charged Chauvin with second degree murder. Second degree murder is defined in Section 609.19 of the Minnesota Statutes as occurring (inter alia) when a defendant "causes the death of a human being with intent to effect the death of that person or another, but without premeditation." This phrase "intent to effect the death" has a unique meaning in Minnesota law. In order to be convicted of second degree murder in Minnesota, it is not necessary that the defendant intend to kill the victim. A conviction for second degree murder is supported if the prosecution can demonstrate that the defendant intended to use any type of force against the victim. When the charge of second degree murder was entered – in addition to the charge of third degree murder – the attorney for the Floyd family issued a statement saying, "This is a source of peace for George's family in this painful time." He also encouraged the Attorney General to charge Chauvin with first degree murder (Johnson, 2020). The family was appeased and the tense situation was mollified.

In October 2020, Hennepin County District Judge Peter Cahill dismissed the charge of third degree murder against Derek Chauvin, on the grounds that there was no evidence that Chauvin's actions were "specifically directed at persons besides George Floyd." This was an unusual interpretation of the law, and the prosecution continued to urge that Chauvin be charged with third degree murder. On February 5, 2021, prosecutor Matthew Frank filed a motion asking that the charge of third degree murder be reinstated, based upon a recent decision by the Minnesota Court of Appeals that upheld a conviction for third degree murder against another Minneapolis police officer, Mohamed Noor. Noor is currently serving a 12-year prison sentence for shooting and killing Justine Ruszczyk Damond in 2017. Damond was an unarmed woman who had called 911 to report a possible sexual assault. The Court of Appeals said in its ruling that "a conviction for third-degree murder … may be sustained even if the death-causing act was directed at a single person" (Pross, 2021).

The trial of Derek Chauvin began on March 29, 2021. He was charged with second degree murder, third degree murder, and second degree manslaughter. Second degree manslaughter is defined in the Minnesota Statutes as occurring (inter alia) as death "by the person's culpable negligence whereby the person creates an unreasonable risk, and consciously takes chances of causing death or great bodily harm to another" (Section 609.205).

The jury in Derek Chauvin's trial faced important questions about mens rea, namely, questions about his knowledge, negligence, and intent. On April 20, 2021, they found Derek Chauvin guilty of all three charges. He was sentenced to twenty-two and a half years in prison.

In federal court on July 7, 2022, ex-officer Chauvin was sentenced to twenty one years in prison for violating George Floyd's civil rights (Hammond et al., 2022).

Chauvin's three co-defendants – ex-officers Thomas Lane, J. Alexander Kueng, and Tou Thao – were present at the murder of George Floyd. Lane held down Floyd's legs and Kueng restrained his torso. Thao held back a crowd of witnesses. Their trial in federal court in Minneapolis lasted one month and ended on February 24, 2022. They argued that they had not received proper training and that they had relied upon Officer Chauvin because he was the lead officer at the scene. Lane, in fact, was a rookie officer in his fourth day on the job. They were convicted by a jury for failure to render medical aid (all three co-defendants) and for failure to intervene (Kueng and Thao only; Lane twice asked if Floyd should be turned on his side – which Chauvin ignored – and was not convicted of failure to intervene). Kueng and Thao were sentenced to three years and three and a half years, respectively, in federal prison. Lane was sentenced to two and a half years in federal prison for his "minimal role" in the incident (quoting Judge Magnuson). In state court, Lane pleaded guilty to aiding and abetting second degree manslaughter and he was sentenced to three years in prison, to run concurrently with his sentence in federal prison (Levenson et al., 2022; Silva, 2022; Vercammen & Parks, 2022).

Kueng and Thao's trial in state court began on October 24, 2022. Kueng pleaded guilty to aiding and abetting second degree manslaughter. He was sentenced to three and a half years in prison, to run concurrently with his federal sentence (Associated Press, 2022; Sanchez & Parks, 2022). Tou Thao agreed to a trial by stipulated evidence (i.e., he accepted certain evidence against him, and he waived his right to testify and his right to a jury trial, which meant that the judge would decide his verdict). On May 1, 2023, Thao was found guilty of aiding and abetting manslaughter. On August 7, 2023, he was sentenced to four years and nine months in prison, to run concurrently with his federal sentence. This sentence exceeded the four years recommended under Minnesota state guidelines. On August 4, 2023,

Thao's federal sentence of three and a half years for violating George Floyd's civil rights was upheld in a court of appeals (Karnowski, 2023).

George Floyd's family filed a civil lawsuit in federal court in July 2020. The city of Minneapolis settled for $27 million (Brewster et al., 2021).

RACIAL DISCRIMINATION AND THE DEATH PENALTY: "RACIALLY DISCRIMINATORY PURPOSE" APPLIED TO DECISIONS BY THE JUDICIARY: *MCCLESKEY V. KEMP* (U.S. 1987)

The concept of "purpose" has been applied not only to crimes committed by individuals but also to actions by the judiciary. In *McCleskey v. Kemp*, it was argued that imposing the death penalty on defendant Warren McCleskey – a Black man convicted of murder in Georgia – was an act of racial discrimination. McCleskey's conviction and his sentence were upheld by the U.S. Supreme Court because McCleskey could not demonstrate that the alleged discrimination by the court had been done purposefully. (For a discussion of *McCleskey* and further questions about race and the death penalty, see Appendix K.)

ALTERED STATES OF CONSCIOUSNESS

Because our system of justice is based on states of mind (mens rea), serious questions arise when a defendant is in an altered state of consciousness, such as occurs during intoxication, illness, and sleep. It is hard enough for people to make sound moral decisions when they are awake and sober. When a defendant carries the extra burden of intoxication, illness, or sleep, their capacities for forming intentions and making decisions may be impaired. These may be situations where actus reus has occurred without mens rea, i.e., situations where the actus reus was performed without the defendant's awareness or control. It can occur in disorders like epilepsy, delirium, dissociation, febrile states, head injuries, settled insanity (see below), and sleepwalking (somnambulism). It can occur in toxic states, including involuntary intoxication, and in non-pathological states like hypnosis.

Intoxication

Most intoxications are voluntary. Involuntary intoxication, in which a person ingests an intoxicating substance without their knowledge or choice, may excuse that person's antisocial behavior. The traditional, common-law view of voluntary intoxication is that the trier of fact may regard the intoxicated defendant as if they had committed the crime while sober. The voluntarily intoxicated defendant may have been impaired at the moment of the crime, but they were not impaired earlier in the day when they chose to ingest the intoxicating substance.

Voluntary intoxication tends to be mitigating only at the highest level of punishment (i.e., capital punishment). Substance use clouds a person's judgment. Judges and juries may be unwilling to impose the death penalty on a defendant who was intoxicated at the time of the crime. (Only a jury and not a judge can impose the death penalty. The U.S. Supreme Court ruled in *Ring v. Arizona*, 2002, that – under the Sixth Amendment right to a jury trial – only a jury and not a judge can find the aggravating factors necessary for imposing the death penalty. In certain circumstances judges have vacated a death penalty and downgraded it to a lesser sentence.) Arguments about voluntary intoxication are not likely to keep a defendant out of prison, but they can make the difference between the death penalty and life in prison. If capital punishment is to be reserved only for those killers who commit the most serious offenses at the highest levels of mens rea (i.e., with knowledge, purpose, and premeditation), then intoxicated killers who are not thinking clearly do not fit the definition.

The U.S. Supreme Court addressed the issue of murder and voluntary intoxication in *Montana v. Egelhoff* (1996) and upheld the Montana state law that courts may not consider voluntary intoxication as a factor that might negate mens rea in murder.

MONTANA LAW DOES NOT VIOLATE DUE PROCESS RIGHTS: *MONTANA V. EGELHOFF* (U.S. 1996)

James Allen Egelhoff was camping in northwestern Montana where he met and befriended John Christenson and Roberta Pavola. They spent the night of Sunday, July 12, 1992, drinking in bars and at a private party. They left the party in Christenson's 1974 Ford Galaxy station wagon. Egelhoff remembered that he and Christenson were "sitting on a hill or a bank passing a bottle of Black Velvet back and forth" (*State v. Egelhoff*, 1995, at 118).

Around midnight that night, officers of the sheriff's department in Lincoln County, Montana, responded to reports of a possible drunk driver and found Christenson's station wagon stuck in a ditch. Egelhoff was lying in the rear of the car, drunk and yelling obscenities. His blood-alcohol content was .36 percent over one hour later. Christenson and Pavola were in the front seat, both dead from a single gunshot wound to the head. On the floor of the car near the brake pedal lay Egelhoff's .38-caliber handgun with four loaded rounds and two empty casings. Egelhoff had gunshot residue on his hands. He was charged with two counts of deliberate homicide, which in Montana is defined as "purposely" or "knowingly" causing the death of another human being (Montana Code Annotated Section 45-5-102, 1995). Egelhoff protested that he did not remember what had happened, that he was innocent because he was too drunk to kill anybody, and that an unidentified fourth person must have committed these murders.

Montana adheres to the common-law principle by which a voluntarily intoxicated defendant is regarded as if they had committed the offense while sober. Under Montana law, Section 45-2-203, voluntary intoxication "may not be taken into consideration in determining the existence of a mental state which is an element of [a criminal] offense." The jury found Egelhoff guilty on both counts and he was sentenced to 84 years in prison.

The Supreme Court of Montana reversed the court's decision, holding that Egelhoff's voluntary intoxication was relevant to the question of mens rea and that the jury should have considered it. The issue before the U.S. Supreme Court was the constitutionality of the Montana law: Does due process require that a defendant be allowed to present evidence of intoxication that could negate mens rea? The U.S. Supreme Court held that it does not. In a 5–4 decision, the court held that evidence of voluntary intoxication does not need to be considered at trial. Due process gives defendants the right to present evidence in their defense, but it does not give them the right to present all possible evidence. States can write laws regarding justifiable exclusions. A defendant who was voluntarily intoxicated at the time of an offense can be regarded as if they had committed the offense while sober.

Addiction and withdrawal

Similarly, the defendant who experiences an altered state of mind because of addiction to a drug and the accompanying withdrawal symptoms may not merit any special consideration from the court.

BRAND V. STATE (GA. APP. 1971): "AN OVERWHELMING PASSION FOR NARCOTICS"

D. W. Brand pleaded guilty to auto theft in 1965 and he was sent to prison for four years. He was released on December 14, 1969. Thirty-seven days later – on January 20, 1970 – he was arrested for the burglary of a pharmacy. He explained that he had become addicted to drugs while in prison, "and that the burglary of a medical pharmacy was the result of an overwhelming passion for narcotics brought on by withdrawal symptoms" (at 273). He was found guilty and was sentenced to fifteen years in prison.

On appeal, the Court of Appeals of Georgia adhered to the laws regarding insanity. Brand neither "lacked the mental capacity to distinguish between right and wrong" (i.e., moral incapacity; Georgia Code § 26–702), nor did he suffer "a delusional compulsion which overmastered his will" (i.e., a delusion causing volitional incapacity; Georgia Code § 26–703; see Chapter 19 for a discussion of moral and volitional incapacities). The Court affirmed Brand's prison sentence.

Settled insanity

Voluntary intoxications can lead to involuntary states of mind when those substances are ingested repeatedly for decades and cause irreversible brain damage. This condition is known in the law as "settled insanity." The defendant with settled insanity has suffered so much brain damage that they are no longer considered responsible for their behavior.

Case study #2: Arthur – a case of settled insanity

Arthur was an elderly homeless man who became my patient at a forensic hospital where I evaluated him for competency to stand trial and criminal responsibility. He had been arrested late at night in the home of a middle-aged woman who lived alone. She had been awakened by noises on the first floor of her home and came downstairs to find Arthur wearing her red dress.

Arthur was 68 years old and he had no prior history of burglary or cross-dressing. He and the victim of his crime were strangers to each other. Fifty years of heavy drinking had damaged his brain. The damage was permanent and irreversible.

Arthur could not remember what he had done on the night in question. He could not explain why he had entered the woman's home, entered her closet, and donned her red dress. My testimony was that he was not competent to stand trial due to profound cognitive deficits, and that he was not likely to regain competence because of irreversible brain damage. I testified further that he was not responsible for his behavior due to settled insanity. Arthur's cognitive impairment was so severe that his behavior had become aimless and purposeless, which was underscored by the lack of any possible use he could have had for the woman's red dress. He had performed these behaviors without developing a conscious intention to do so. In my opinion he lacked mens rea. I recommended that his behavior not be considered a crime and that he be committed to a state institution due to grave disability (i.e., inability to provide for his own needs).

Automatism

In certain conditions a person might move their extremities while they have no awareness or conscious control over their movements. These movements are called "automatisms." They can occur during sleep, hypnosis, or certain medical conditions. A summary in Melton et al. (2018, p. 213) includes cases of anoxia, hypoglycemia, and shock after a gunshot wound. The defendant with an automatism lacks mens rea because their behavior occurs outside their conscious control. These defendants are not considered blameworthy, and their behavior is not a crime.

The earliest description of such a case is that of Esther Griggs of London (Bucknill, 1862/2017). In January 1859, Griggs threw her baby out the window while she was having a nightmare that her house was on fire. She was trying to save her baby from the "fire" when she threw it out the window. The baby survived, and the grand jury did not indict her.

The first case of automatism that went to trial may have been that of Simon Fraser in Scotland (*H.M. Advocate v. Fraser*, 1878). On the night of April 9, 1878, Fraser killed his baby son by battering his skull against the wall of his room. Fraser had dreamed that a wild animal had jumped onto the bed. Fraser's father and sister testified that he had been a sleepwalker from an early age. His behavior while sleepwalking had involved previous acts of violence and imaginary rescues. He had, while asleep, struck his father, tried to strangle his sister, tried to pull his wife out of what he believed to be a burning house, and walked into a body of water to save his sister from an imaginary drowning. The jury was persuaded by the testimony of Fraser's father and sister and found that he was not responsible for the death of his son. The judge also wanted to hear the medical testimony that had been prepared. Three physicians – each one the superintendent of an asylum – testified that Fraser had been unaware of what he was doing and was not responsible for his behavior. Fraser promised that in the future he would sleep alone, and the judge dismissed the case.

In some jurisdictions these states of mind are called "unconsciousness," which is not meant to imply coma or immobility but means that the defendant was not aware of what they were doing. For example, the 2022 edition of the California Criminal Jury Instructions (CALCRIM) states, "Someone is unconscious when he or she is not conscious of his or her actions" (CALCRIM, No. 3425). Examples given in CALCRIM include epilepsy, delirium, involuntary intoxication, and somnambulism (sleepwalking).

Case study #3: Charles – a case of somnambulism

Charles was a 42-year-old gang member serving a life sentence for first degree murder. When I met him, he had been in prison for thirteen years and seven months. Before coming to prison, he had spent several years in jail awaiting trial.

I saw Charles for mental health evaluation after he assaulted his cellmate. At the time of our interview, Charles was housed in the

Administrative Segregation Unit (ASU) of a maximum-security prison. (For readers who are not familiar with the prison environment, an ASU is a prison inside a prison. It is the building where inmates are held after a serious violation of the rules.) Charles had assaulted his cellmate around midnight and had been transferred out of the general prison population and into the ASU. He was referred for mental health evaluation to assist the warden in understanding whether any factors related to his mental health should be considered when adjudicating this violation.

Charles had spent the first thirteen years of his prison term in protective custody. He had been moved into the general prison population only seven months before this assault took place. He already had diagnoses of post-traumatic stress disorder and sleepwalking. Information I obtained in my interview also suggested a mood disorder and a disorder on the schizophrenia spectrum. As it turned out, the only factor that was relevant to the adjudication of this assault was sleepwalking and not any of these other diagnoses.

Correctional officers had arrived at Charles' cell at 12:20 a.m. Charles had a split lip, and his cellmate looked as if he had been beaten. I was safe sitting in an interview room with Charles because he sat inside a plexiglass module the size and shape of a telephone booth. Charles cooperated with the interview. He looked miserable and his eyes were full of tears. He said,

> I grew up in a violent world of gangs. My father was the shotcaller of a really bad gang. All I know is what I was taught. My mind goes in circles. I can get madder than hell. Then I'm happy for a while. In the course of two weeks my mood goes from 1 to 10.

As a boy, Charles had seen his brother shot with a firearm (and survive). He had seen members of his father's gang commit murders. As a little boy, he had danced in circles around dying men, singing, "You are dying. You are dying." Charles told me,

> My whole childhood was tore up. I became the enforcer for the gang. That's how I was brought up. That's what I was brought up to be. I am so tired of it. I want to be done with it. I'm at this point in my life where I need to change. I would like to die in peace. This drives me crazy. I can't control it. I get so mad that I have to be careful. I get these violent thoughts and I try to suppress them but I can't do it.

Charles had been a mental health patient from the ages of 11 to 17, during which time he was treated with medication for anger and depression. "I was violent. Very violent," he explained. As an adult he had received mental health treatment in prison on only one occasion, twelve years earlier, after the death of his son.

Before prison, his drugs of choice were alcohol, LSD, and methamphetamine. He had been hospitalized for detoxification from barbiturates. When I met Charles, he had been sober for only three months. He had not had a visitor in fourteen years.

Charles had out-of-body experiences in his cell and felt that demons were taking control of him. "I used to call upon pre-Adamic demonic spirits," he said. He had a history of sleepwalking and sleeptalking. He had assaulted people in his sleep. These assaults had not involved weapons, but only his bare hands (which helped to indicate that they occurred spontaneously and were not premeditated).

Charles explained to me that his experience of anger was sudden and unplanned and that it could occur when he had not felt angry one second before. He said, "I go from 0 to 100 in a flash. I go straight into rage." Sometimes, after committing an assault, he could not remember what he had done. (Memory "blackouts" after an explosion of rage and aggression are known as "redouts." These are sudden moments of violence for which the assailant has no memory.) Charles had injured people in "redouts" while sober.

At the age of 28, while living with his wife, Charles had a hypnopompic hallucination (i.e., a hallucination while waking from sleep) of a demon sitting on his chest, stealing his breath away, and telling him to kill his wife. Charles told me that he had started crying, and when his wife turned on the light the demon disappeared. On another occasion he had awakened from sleep and found himself choking his wife.

At the time of his arrest for first degree murder, Charles had been planning to commit suicide in response to a command auditory hallucination. He had heard a girl's voice in the back seat of his car saying, "Do it [kill yourself]." He had 100 tablets of Valium that he was planning to swallow, and then he was going to shoot himself. Then he heard a different voice say, "Just do what I tell you to do and you're going to be alright." He did not hurt himself, and this second voice did not say anything further.

As mentioned above, Charles was moved out of protective custody and into the general prison population after thirteen years in protective custody and seven months before I met him. This means that he was still adjusting to the general population when this assault took place. His adjustment to the general population was poor. He was not sleeping well. In protective custody he had slept five to six hours a night, but in the general population he was sleeping only two to three hours a night. He complained of low energy and inability to concentrate. He had frequent, violent nightmares about real events, including the time he saw his brother get shot. He had little appetite for food, which he attributed to "anxiety." In seven months in the general population, he had lost twenty lbs., going from 215 to 195 lb.

Charles had been assigned to a vocational program in auto body repair. There he had argued with three other inmates, and he had learned they were planning to hit him with a hammer. He made plans to kill one of them, but he had not yet chosen a time to do this. "I was waiting to see if he would get relaxed," he said.

Charles assaulted his cellmate at midnight while both of them were asleep. The cellmate had been in the cell only two days. They had no prior relationship with each other. They had not argued. Before that, Charles had been celled alone. He said,

> I fell asleep. The next thing I knew we were fighting. I woke up swinging. At first I didn't know what I was doing or what I was swinging at. Then I came to and I saw that my cellmate was swinging at me, too. I realized what was happening, and I backed away, and he backed away, and that was that. He got hurt worse than I did. I guess you could say that I won that fight. My lip got busted pretty good, though.

Charles's description of the fight indicates lack of awareness. As soon as he became aware of what he was doing, he stopped and backed away, which indicates lack of intention. There was no evidence of a conscious intention to assault his cellmate.

Charles was planning to plead guilty to assault and battery. He asked me that, if he were going to be kept in ASU, he be given something to read, "Or else I'll lose it."

ASU is intended to be a punishment and an incapacitation. Inmates usually experience it as a high-stress environment. (A disproportionate number of suicides occur inside ASUs.) Charles, however, actually felt better in the ASU than he did in the general prison population because "I feel safer here," he said. "I don't have to worry about hurting people."

Sleepwalking is not uncommon. The American Psychiatric Association (2022, p. 454) reported a worldwide lifetime prevalence ranging from approximately 6.9 to 29.2 percent. Criminal behavior during sleepwalking, however, is rare.

Charles is a most unhappy and unfortunate individual who never had a chance to lead a normal life. From early childhood, he was traumatized by repeated exposure to violence. He had seen men killed by members of his father's gang. He had seen his own brother shot. As a child, he was schooled in the use of violence, and violence had been expected of him. His childhood circumstances had not allowed him to develop good internal controls. He was prone to rage and homicidal fantasy. His experience of anger involved sudden, unpredictable outbursts; assaults while asleep; and dissociative experiences like redouts even while he was awake and sober. At the age of 42, Charles was approaching middle age and violent actions and fantasies had become ego-dystonic. He wanted to desist from violence, but he found himself unable to do so.

After thirteen years in protective custody, Charles had been transferred into the general prison population, where his adjustment was poor. He was not sleeping well. He had lost his appetite and he was losing weight. His safety had been threatened. At the time of our interview, he was planning to kill another inmate. Also, he was withdrawing from polysubstance abuse. He had been sober only three months at the time of this assault.

I reported to the warden that the assault had been an automatism, that the assault had lacked mens rea, and that Charles should not be held accountable. I reported to the medical authorities of the prison that Charles had significant mental health issues that had not been recognized during the first sixteen years of his incarceration.

As mentioned above, the only feature of Charles' multiple mental illnesses that contributed to my opinion regarding mens rea was sleepwalking. His other mental health conditions – post-traumatic stress disorder, mood difficulties, interpersonal problems, substance use, and dissociative episodes including out-of-body experiences – helped to illuminate the totality of his condition and his need for mental health services, but they were not relevant to the question of mens rea and did not contribute to my opinion regarding his lack of responsibility for the assault. Charles had been unconscious during the assault, and this was the reason why he lacked mens rea.

TESTIFYING TO THE ULTIMATE ISSUE

In California and at the federal level, displeasure with mental health verdicts in high-profile cases like *People v. White* (1981; see Chapter 21) and *United States v. Hinckley* (1981; see Chapter 22) provoked legislation that curtailed the range of expert testimony in criminal trials (California Penal Code Section 29; Federal Rule of Evidence 704(b)). In California and in federal courts, expert witnesses are prohibited from addressing the "ultimate issue" regarding mens rea. The California law reads as follows:

> In the guilt phase of a criminal action, any expert testifying about a defendant's mental illness, mental disorder, or mental defect shall not testify as to whether the defendant had or did not have the required mental states, which include, but are not limited to, purpose, intent, knowledge, or malice aforethought, for the crimes charged. The question as to whether the defendant had or did not have the required mental states shall be decided by the trier of fact. (California Penal Code Section 29)

Rule 704 of the Federal Rules of Evidence reads:

Rule 704. Opinion on an Ultimate Issue

a In General – Not Automatically Objectionable. An opinion is not objectionable just because it embraces an ultimate issue.
b Exception. In a criminal case, an expert witness must not state an opinion about whether the defendant did or did not have a mental state or condition that constitutes an element of the crime charged or of a defense. Those matters are for the trier of fact alone.

Experts testifying in these courts may testify regarding the facts in their possession, and they may testify to limited opinions (e.g., diagnosis) that may lead up to the ultimate issue, but the ultimate issue of whether a defendant had the requisite state of mind (i.e., mens rea) is the province of the triers of fact, and expert witnesses, with their powers of persuasion, are not allowed to usurp that authority. In this way, these legislatures, in response to the public pressure following the verdicts in *Hinckley* and *White*, sought to curtail the influence that expert testimony can have upon a jury.

REFERENCES

Associated Press. (October 24, 2022). J. Alexander Kueng, officer who knelt on George Floyd's back, agrees to plea deal. Retrieved 11/19/2022 from www.cbc. ca/news/world/minn-george-floyd-officer-plea-1.6627275.

Brand v. State, 123 Ga. App. 273, 180 S.E. 2d 579 (Georgia, 1971).

Brewster, S., Griffith, J., & Gutierrez, G. (2021). City of Minneapolis reaches $27M settlement with George Floyd's family. *NBC News*. Retrieved 11/19/2022 from www.nbcnews.com/news/us-news/city-minneapolis-considering-settlement-george-floyd-s-family-n1260868.

Bucknill, J. C. (1862/2017). *A manual of psychological medicine*. (2017 edition): Miami, FL: HardPress.

California Criminal Jury Instructions (CALCRIM). (2022). Retrieved 11/19/2022 from www.justia.com/criminal/docs/calcrim/3400/3425/.

CBS Minnesota. (January 31, 2023). Fate of Tou Thao, last ex-cop charged in George Floyd's murder, lies with judge. Retrieved 03/02/2023 from www.msn.com/en-us/news/crime/fate-of-tou-thao-last-ex-cop-charged-in-george-floyds-murder-lies-with-judge/ar-AA16YbZQ.

Hammond, E., Sangal, A., Chowdhury, M., & Vogt, A. (July 7, 2022). Derek Chauvin sentenced for violating George Floyd's civil rights. Retrieved 11/19/2022 www.cnn.com/us/live-news/derek-chauvin-federal-sentencing-07-07-22/index.html.

H.M. Advocate v. Fraser, 4 Coup. 78 (1878).

Johnson, M. (June 3, 2020). Derek Chauvin charge upgraded to second-degree murder; other officers charged. Retrieved 11/19/2022 from https://thehill.com/homenews/state-watch/500949-chauvins-charges-upped-to-second-degree-murder-three-other-officers.

Karnowski, S. (August 7, 2023). Tuo Thao sentenced to nearly 5 years on state charge for role in George Floyd's death. *Associated Press*. Retrieved 08/07/2023 from www.abc12.com/news/national/tou-thao-sentenced-to-nearly-5-years-on-state-charge-for-role-in-george-floyd/article_eb0792e3-4346-54e7-9270-24772873d7e6.html.

Levenson, E., Parks, B., & Jimenez, O. (September 21, 2022). Former officer who held down George Floyd's legs gets 3 years in Prison for aiding and abetting manslaughter. Retrieved 11/19/2022 from www.cnn.com/2022/09/21/us/thomas-lane-sentencing/index.html.

McCleskey v. Kemp, 481 U.S. 279 (1987).

Melton, G. B., Petrila, J., Poythress, N. G., Slobogin, C., Otto, R. K., Mossman, D., & Condie, L. O. (2018). *Psychological evaluations for the courts: A handbook for mental health professionals and lawyers. Fourth edition*. New York: Guilford Press.

Montana v. Egelhoff, 518 U.S. 37 (1996).

People v. White, 117 Cal. App. 3d 270, 172 Cal. Rptr. 612 (Callifornia, 1981).

Pross, K. (February 5, 2021). Prosecution in George Floyd case asks to reinstate third-degree murder charge against Chauvin. Retrieved 11/19/2022 from www.inforum.com/news/prosecution-in-george-floyd-case-asks-to-reinstate-third-degree-murder-charge-against-chauvin.

Ring v. Arizona, 536 U.S. 584 (2002).

Sanchez, R., & Parks, B. (December 9, 2022). Former Minneapolis police officer who helped restrain George Floyd sentenced to 3-1/2 years in prison. *CNN*. www.cnn.com/2022/12/09/us/george-floyd-alexander-kueng-sentencing/index.html.

Silva, D. (July 7, 2022). Derek Chauvin sentenced to just over 20 years for violating George Floyd's civil rights. Retrieved 07/15/2023 from www.nbcnews.com/news/

us-news/derek-chauvin-sentenced-just-20-years-violating-george-floyds-federal-rcna36958.

State v. Derek Michael Chauvin, 27-CR-20-12646 (Minnesota, 2021).

State v. Egelhoff, 272 Montana 114, 900 P. 2d 260 (Montana, 1995).

Taylor, D. B. (June 22, 2020). George Floyd protests: A timeline. *New York Times*. Retrieved 11/19/2022 from www.nytimes.com/article/george-floyd-protests-timeline.html.

United States v. James Alex Fields, Criminal No. 3:18-CR-00011 (2018).

United States v. Hinckley, 525 F. Supp. 1342 (D.D.C. 1981).

Vercammen, P., & Parks, B. (July 21, 2022). Ex-Minneapolis police officer Thomas Lane sentenced to 2.5 years in prison for violating George Floyd's civil rights. Retrieved 11/19/2022 from www.cnn.com/2022/07/21/us/thomas-lane-george-floyd-sentence/index.html.

Yousif, N. (May 3, 2023). Final officer convicted on state charges over George Floyd death. *BBC News*. Retrieved 05/04/2023 from www.bbc.com/news/world-us-canada-65463223.

Part II

Due process before trial

Courts have found numerous ways for mental health professionals to contribute to the due process of law. These can be called "psycholegal questions." Ten of these are reviewed in Parts II, III, and IV of this volume. Part II addresses three psycholegal questions that may exist before a defendant goes to trial. These are:

- the defendant's capacity to waive their Fifth and Sixth Amendment rights before a police interrogation (relevant cases include *Miranda v. Arizona*, 1966)
- competency to stand trial (cases include *Dusky v. United States*, 1960)
- the transfer of juvenile defendants to adult court (cases include *Kent v. United States*, 1966).

Where mental health professionals have developed psychometric tests to help answer these questions, these tests will be described and evaluated in these chapters.

DOI: 10.4324/9781003385028-10

9 Waiver of Fifth and Sixth Amendment rights during police interrogations

Miranda v. Arizona (U.S. 1966)

The *Miranda* warnings are familiar to anybody who has ever watched a cop show on television. This fourfold waiver of rights was defined by the U.S. Supreme Court in *Miranda v. Arizona* (1966). They were intended to be read aloud to the defendant by the arresting officer, and the defendant's responses are recorded. Reading the warnings to a defendant is a police function. Assessing whether or not the defendant actually understands these rights is the province of a mental health evaluation. For a waiver of rights to be valid, it must be made knowingly, intelligently, and voluntarily, and these factors can be assessed by a mental health professional.

Ernesto Miranda was arrested in Phoenix, Arizona, on March 13, 1963. He was identified by a witness and was accused of kidnaping and rape. Two police officers questioned him for two hours, and he signed a written confession. The confession contained the typed statement:

> that the confession was made voluntarily, without threats or promises of immunity and "with full knowledge of my legal rights, understanding any statement I make may be used against me." (*Miranda v. Arizona*, 1970, at 492)

One of the officers who questioned Miranda testified that he read this statement to him only *after* Miranda had confessed. Miranda was found guilty and was sentenced to 20 to 30 years in prison.

The U.S. Supreme Court ruled that Miranda's confession was inadmissible because his right against self-incrimination had not been protected and he had not been advised of his right to an attorney. The Court wrote,

> The mere fact that he signed a statement which contained a typed-in clause stating that he had "full knowledge" of his "legal rights" does not approach the knowing and intelligent waiver required to relinquish constitutional rights. (at 492)

DOI: 10.4324/9781003385028-11

The Court ruled as follows (I have added numbers and line breaks for clarity):

that a four-fold warning be given to a person in custody before he is questioned, namely,

1 that he has a right to remain silent,
2 that anything he says may be used against him,
3 that he has a right to have present an attorney during the questioning, and
4 that, if indigent, he has a right to a lawyer without charge. (at 504)

(The right of an indigent defendant to be represented by a court-appointed attorney was decided by the U.S. Supreme Court in *Gideon v. Wainwright* (1963). To do otherwise would deprive a defendant of their due process rights guaranteed by the Fourteenth Amendment.)

Due process exists to protect citizens from intrusive actions by the government and by government employees. The *Miranda* safeguards were written to preserve elements of due process during police interrogations. They reflect the court's awareness of their duty to set limits on police activity. Police brutality is not limited to the physical dimension, but can be psychological as well. As the U.S. Supreme Court wrote in *Blackburn v. Alabama* (1960),

... [The] blood of the accused is not the only hallmark of an unconstitutional inquisition. (*Blackburn v. Alabama*, 1960, at 206)

At the time of the *Miranda* decision, several manuals had been written for police departments instructing them in methods of psychological manipulation for use during interrogations. These manuals are named and described in the *Miranda* decision. They include such methods as "Mutt and Jeff," which goes like this: "You had better talk to me now, because Mutt is a mean SOB, and when he gets here I don't know if I can control him."

The *Miranda* decision was condemned by "law and order" politicians like Richard Nixon (who at that time was a former vice president), who predicted that it would constrain the police from being able to do their jobs. Nixon promised that, as president, he would nominate only "strict constructionists" for the bench. He went on to nominate six candidates for the U.S Supreme Court during his term in office, two of whom (Clement Haynsworth and G. Harrold Carswell) were rejected by the Senate and were the first rejections of Supreme Court nominees since 1930.

Ernesto Miranda got a new trial. His confession had been ruled inadmissible and it was not presented at his second trial. He was again found guilty and again was sentenced to 20 to 30 years in prison.

Miranda was paroled in 1972. He returned to prison for one year when he violated his parole by being found in possession of a firearm. He was killed by a knife in a bar fight on January 31, 1976. A suspect was arrested, but there was no evidence against him, he maintained his right to remain silent, and he was released.

PSYCHOMETRIC TOOLS FOR EVALUATING COMPREHENSION OF THE *MIRANDA* WARNINGS

The first standardized methods for assessing a defendant's comprehension of the *Miranda* warnings were developed under the coordination of psychologist Saleem Shah in his role as director of the National Institute of Mental Health Center for Studies of Crime and Delinquency (Rogers & Fiduccia, 2015). Grisso (1998) developed a set of tests – the Instruments for Assessing Understanding and Appreciation of *Miranda* Rights (IAU) – that measured a subject's comprehension of the warnings. These were replaced in 2014 by the Miranda Rights Comprehension Instruments (MRCI; Goldstein et al., 2014).

Figure 9.1 Saleem A. Shah, Ph.D., ABPP (1931–1992), born in Allahabad, India, and educated at Pennsylvania State University. Dr. Shah did more than any other individual to create the field of forensic psychology in the United States. His leadership at the National Institute of Mental Health, as Director of the Center for Studies of Crime and Delinquency from 1968 to 1987, helped produce the first psychometric tools assessing competency to stand trial and comprehension of Miranda warnings.

The MRCI is a multi-method instrument consisting of four separate tests that measure a subject's comprehension in different ways. Written and visual materials are presented to the subject by means of an easel that sits atop a desk or table, and the subject's responses are recorded and scored. Norms were obtained for juvenile delinquents, adult offenders, and a community sample of middle- to upper-middle socioeconomic status juveniles. Norms are stratified by age, level of intelligence, and reading level.

As Goldstein et al. (2014) and Grisso (2003) pointed out, the results of testing may reflect a subject's comprehension of rights at the time of testing, but the relevant psycholegal questions are whether the subject understood and was able to exercise their rights at the time of the interrogation. This may require the forensic examiner to inquire into situational variables like the time of day, the defendant's fatigue at the time of the interrogation, and the pressures and anxieties related to questioning at a police station. Relevant to the evaluation is not only whether a defendant has an abstract understanding of their rights but also whether they understood their rights and were able to apply them in the interrogation situation. For example, did the subject understand the adversarial nature of the police-suspect relationship? Did the subject understand the advocacy and cooperative nature of the attorney-client relationship? Did the subject understand that the right to silence cannot be violated? A judge's decision regarding the validity of a defendant's waiver of rights takes into account the totality of the circumstances and is not determined solely by a score on a test (Goldstein et al., 2014, p. 7). The numerical scores on tests like the MRCI are useful in assessing individual defendants and in calculating the internal consistency, test-retest reliability, and interrater reliability of these measures (see Appendix O for a brief discussion of test-retest reliability and interrater reliability), but the numerical scores are not dispositive in the adjudication of an individual case. The ultimate decision regarding a defendant's comprehension of *Miranda* warnings is a qualitative decision made by a trier of fact.

As the authors of the MRCI explain, internal consistency measures are likely to be low, because the subtests of the MRCI contain a small number of items and because they measure a disparate array of competencies (e.g., just because you appreciate the adversarial nature of the police-suspect relationship does not necessarily mean that you also appreciate the collaborative nature of the attorney-client relationship; Goldstein et al. 2014, p. 41).

Comprehension of *Miranda* Rights-II (CMR-II)

The subject is shown a written version of the *Miranda* warnings, one by one (now expanded to five warnings, because of the common practice in many jurisdictions of informing the defendant that they have the right to stop the questioning at any time). The examiner reads the warning out loud to the subject and asks them to explain it in their own words. The subject's answers are scored on a three-point scale: 2 = adequate, 1 = questionable, 0 = inadequate. There are five *Miranda* warnings, so scores range from 0 to 10.

Internal consistency (Cronbach's α) ranged from 0.58 to 0.70 for the three samples (juvenile delinquents, adult offenders, and community juveniles). Average item-total correlations ranged from 0.61 to 0.68. Test-retest reliabilities ranged from 0.68 to 0.82. Interrater reliability as measured by intraclass correlation coefficients (ICCs) was excellent, ranging from 0.94 to 0.95.

Because this test requires the subject to paraphrase, it places a rather high demand on their capacity for verbal expression and may lose utility with subjects who have limited skills in this area.

Comprehension of *Miranda* Rights-Recognition-II (CMR-R-II)

In this test, the examiner presents various interpretations of the warnings and the subject reports whether they are the same as the warning or are different. Because this is a recognition task and does not require paraphrasing, it places less demand on a subjects' capacity for verbal expression than the CMR-II. The examiner replies simply "same" or "different" after each alternative interpretation is presented. Three alternatives are presented for each of the five *Miranda* warnings, so subjects' scores range from 0 to 15. Eight of the interpretations are the same as the warning, and seven are different. For each of the five warnings, there is at least one interpretation that is the same and one that is different. Internal consistency (Cronbach's α) ranged from 0.54 to 0.69. Average subtotal-total correlations ranged from 0.56 to 0.67. Test-retest reliabilities ranged from 0.67 to 0.75.

Comprehension of *Miranda* Vocabulary-II (CMV-II)

This test measures a subject's comprehension of sixteen words that are commonly used in *Miranda* warnings. The examiner reads the word out loud, uses it in a sentence, says the word again, and asks the subject to define it. A subject's answers are scored on a three-point scale: 2 = adequate, 1 = questionable, 0 = inadequate. There are sixteen words, so scores range from 0 to 32. Internal consistency (Cronbach's α) ranged from 0.75 to 0.82. Average item-total correlations ranged from 0.45 to 0.51. Test-retest reliabilities ranged from 0.84 to 0.88. Interrater reliability (ICC) was excellent, ranging from 0.96 to 0.97.

Function of Rights in Interrogation (FRI)

The CRM-II, CMR-R-II, and CMV-II all focus on a subject's comprehension of the language used in the *Miranda* warnings. In contrast, the FRI assesses the subject's understanding of how these rights function in the real world and their appreciation of how important these rights can be. For example, does the subject understand that maintaining their silence limits the discretionary power of judges and police? As Grisso (2003) wrote, "[Individuals] who understand *Miranda* warnings may or may not be aware of the function and significance of *Miranda* rights" (p. 185). The FRI is comprised of three subscales that assess the subject's comprehension in three areas:

- NI subscale: the nature of police interrogations and the jeopardy association with interrogation (i.e., does the subject understand the adversarial nature of the police-suspect relationship?)
- RC subscale: the right to counsel and the function of legal counsel (i.e., does the subject understand the advocacy and cooperative nature of the attorney-client relationship?)
- RS subscale: the right to silence, protections related to the right to silence, and the role of confessions (e.g., does the subject understand that the right to silence cannot be violated?)

Four pictures are shown to the subject, accompanied by brief vignettes, depicting two police interrogations, a consultation with a defense attorney, and a court hearing. The pictures and vignettes are generic in nature and do not suggest any particular sort of crime. Each picture and vignette are associated with a set of questions – fifteen in all – that assess a subject's understanding of the three subscales described above. Answers are scored on a three-point scale: 2 = adequate, 1 = questionable, 0 = inadequate. There are fifteen questions, so scores range from 0 to 30. Internal consistency (Cronbach's α) ranged from 0.54 to 0.59. Cronbach's α for the three subscales was relatively low, ranging from 0.20 to 0.31 for subscale NI, from 0.22 to 0.41 for subscale RC, and from 0.35 to 0.53 for subscale RS. Average subscale-total correlations ranged from 0.64 to 0.71. Test-retest reliabilities ranged from 0.53 to 0.55. Interrater reliability (ICC) was excellent, ranging from 0.87 to 0.91.

FAILURE TO READ *MIRANDA* WARNINGS TO A DEFENDANT DOES NOT ALONE PERMIT A POLICE OFFICER TO BE SUED: *VEGA V. TEKOH* (U.S. 2022)

The rights that the *Miranda* warnings refer to are the Fifth Amendment right against self-incrimination and the Sixth Amendment right to counsel. In *Vega v. Tekoh*, the U.S. Supreme Court stated, accurately, that the so-called "*Miranda* rights" are not actually rights in themselves but are warnings about these rights that are guaranteed by these amendments to the Constitution. The court pointed out that these constitutional rights can be enforced in court through other means, and they ruled that there is no constitutional duty to read these warnings to a defendant. That is, when a police officer does not read the *Miranda* warnings to a defendant, it does not violate that defendant's constitutional rights.

Terence Tekoh is an immigrant from Cameroon. At the age of 25, he was working as a certified nursing assistant at a medical center in Los Angeles, California, where his job was to transport patients from their rooms to the magnetic resonance imaging (MRI) department. A female patient accused him of touching her genitals while he was transporting her. Deputy Carlos Vega responded to the call.

Tekoh and Vega later gave contradictory versions of what transpired at this interrogation. It was undisputed that the interrogation took place in a small, soundproof room in the hospital that is used by doctors to read MRIs. It was undisputed that Vega did not give the *Miranda* warnings. By the end of this interrogation, Tekoh had written the following confession:

To who [*sic*] it may concern,

This is an honest and regrettable apology from me about what happened a few hours ago. It was I don't know what suddenly came over me, but it was certainly the most weakest moment I've ever been caught up with in my life. I've never ever found myself doing such a despicable act. and I am I don't think this is an excuse but I'm single and currently don't have a girlfriend and became very excited after I first saw her vagina accidently. So after dropping her off, I decided to go further by woking [*sic*] and spreading her vagina lip for a quick view and then went back to my duty post with the intention of masturbating, which I never did. (*Tekoh v. County of Los Angeles*, 2021, at 715)

In Vega's version of the interrogation, Tekoh began by saying, outside the interrogation room, "I made a mistake," and he asked if he could talk to Vega in private, away from his co-workers. Once inside the MRI reading room, Vega handed Tekoh a sheet of paper and asked Tekoh to write down what had happened. According to Vega, Tekoh wrote out his confession without any further prompting.

Tekoh gave a very different account. According to Tekoh, Deputy Vega asked if there was a place where they could talk in private, and Tekoh's co-workers suggested the MRI reading room:

a small, windowless, and soundproof room used by doctors to read MRIs. When one of Tekoh's co-workers tried to accompany Tekoh into the reading room, Deputy Vega stopped her and told her the interview was private.

Deputy Vega shut the door and stood in front of it, blocking Tekoh's path to the exit. He then accused Tekoh of touching the patient's vagina. Tekoh adamantly denied the allegation. After about 35 to 40 minutes of questioning during which Tekoh refused to confess, Deputy Vega told him (falsely) that the assault had been captured on video so he might as well admit to it. Still, Tekoh did not confess.

Tekoh then asked to speak to a lawyer, but Deputy Vega ignored the request. At that point, Tekoh grew frustrated and tried to get up and leave the room. Tekoh testified:

"I made one or two steps, and [Deputy Vega] rushed at me and stepped on my toes, put his hand on his gun and said, 'Mr. Jungle Nigger trying to be smart with me. You make any funny move, you're going to regret it. I'm about to put your black ass where it belongs, about to hand you over to deportation services, and you and your entire family will be rounded up and sent back to the jungle ... Trust me, I have the power to do it.'"

According to Tekoh, this outburst left him "shaking" and triggered flashbacks to his experiences with police brutality in Cameroon, where he was from.

Deputy Vega then grabbed a pen and paper, put them in front of Tekoh, and told him to "write what the patient said [he] did." When Tekoh hesitated, Vega put his hand on his gun and said he was not joking. According to Tekoh, Vega then dictated the content of the written confession and Tekoh, who was scared and "ready to write whatever [Vega] wanted," acquiesced and wrote the statement down. (*Tekoh v. County of Los Angeles*, 2021, at 715–716)

Tekoh was fired from his job. He went to trial twice. His first trial was declared a mistrial after the prosecution revealed evidence that had not been shared with the defense. Tekoh's confession was introduced into evidence at his second trial. Testimony was obtained from a professor of psychology, an expert on false confessions. The jury found Tekoh not guilty. Tekoh sued the County of Los Angeles, the Sheriff's Department, Deputy Vega, and 11 other defendants (Moran, 2014; Nanos, 2022; *Tekoh v. County of Los Angeles*, 2021).

The U.S. Court of Appeals for the Ninth Circuit held that using the un-*Mirandized* statement against him in a criminal proceeding violated his Fifth Amendment right against self-incrimination, and that he could sue the officer who obtained such a statement. The U.S. Supreme Court disagreed. In a 6–3 decision, the U.S. Supreme Court ruled that *Miranda* warnings are not required by the U.S. Constitution. Violating the *Miranda* decision does not violate the Fifth Amendment, and the arresting officer cannot be sued. Evidence that a confession was un-Mirandized still can be presented in a criminal trial, for consideration by the trier of fact, but such evidence cannot be used to sue the interrogating officer.

"Law and order" politicians have seen the *Miranda* warnings as an obstacle ever since their inception in 1966. With the U.S. Supreme Court decision in *Vega v. Tekoh*, there is now less personal incentive for officers to keep giving the warnings. We may anticipate that the administration of *Miranda* warnings will become less frequent, defendants will exercise their Fifth and Sixth Amendment rights less frequently, and police interrogations will yield more false confessions. If the need for mental health professionals to evaluate comprehension of *Miranda* warnings declines, the need for mental health professionals to evaluate false confessions may be expected to increase.

REFERENCES

Blackburn v. Alabama, 361 U.S. 199 (1960).

Gideon v. Wainwright, 372 U.S. 335 (1963).

Goldstein, N. E. S., Zelle, H., & Grisso, T. (2014). *Miranda Rights Comprehension Instruments (MRCI): Manual for juvenile and adult evaluations*. Sarasota, FL: Professional Resource Press.

Grisso, T. (1998). *Instruments for assessing understanding and appreciation of* Miranda *rights*. Sarasota, FL: Professional Resource Press.

Grisso, T. (2003). *Evaluating competencies: Forensic assessments and instruments. Second edition*. New York: Kluwer Academic/Plenum Publishers.

Miranda v. Arizona, 384 U.S. 436 (1966).

Moran, L. (March 21, 2014). Male nurse accused of sexually assaulting patient in Los Angeles County examination room. *New York Daily News*. Retrieved 11/21/2022 from www.nydailynews.com/news/national/male-nurse-accused-sexually-assaulting-patient-la-county-cops-article-1.1729193.

Nanos, E. (June 23, 2022). Justice Alito opinion deals major blow to rights. Retrieved 11/21/2022 from https://lawandcrime.com/supreme-court/justice-alito-opinion-deals-major-blow-to-miranda-rights/.

Rogers, R., & Fiduccia, C. E. (2015). Forensic assessment instruments. In B. L. Cutler & P. A. Zapf (Eds.) *APA handbook of forensic psychology. Volume 1: Individual and situational influences in criminal and civils contexts* (pp. 19–34). Washington, D.C.: American Psychological Association.

Tekoh v. County of Los Angeles, 985 F.3d 713 (9th Cir. 2021).

Vega v. Tekoh, 597 U.S. ____, 142 S. Ct. 2095 (2022).

10 Competency to stand trial (CST)

Dusky v. United States (U.S. 1960)

The Anglo-American system of due process exists to protect the individual defendant from intrusions by government employees. Accordingly, the government is not allowed to bring a defendant to trial unless that defendant is capable of defending themselves. This tradition began during the period of English common law with defendants who could not hear or speak. It has been traced back to the Dooms of King Alfred which were written in or around the year 893. People who cannot hear or speak cannot be examined and cannot defend themselves, and therefore they were not taken to court. Two cases from the nineteenth century that involved defendants who could not hear or speak were *Rex v. Esther Dyson* (1831), regarding a woman who beheaded her own child, and *Rex v. Pritchard* (1836), regarding a man accused of bestiality. The concepts that were employed in those cases continue to define our notions of competency today. In *Dyson*, Mr. Justice Parke told the jury that the question was whether the defendant had

> sufficient reason to understand the nature of this proceeding, so as to be able to conduct her defence with discretion.

The jury found Esther Dyson to be "insane," which at that time and in that context meant that she was not competent to stand trial.

In *Pritchard*, Baron Alderson told the jury to consider whether the accused was

> of sufficient intellect to comprehend the course of proceedings in the trial so as to make a proper defence – to know that he might challenge any of you to whom he may object, and to comprehend the details of the evidence.

The jury found Pritchard to be "insane," which, again, in the parlance of the day meant that he was not competent to stand trial (Walker, 1968, pp. 224–225).

DOI: 10.4324/9781003385028-12

Eventually, the same protections were extended to persons who had severe mental illness. It was not until the thirteenth century that persons with severe mental illness were even brought to trial. Evidence from the Old Bailey Sessions Papers indicates that the earliest case of a hearing regarding competency to stand trial for a defendant with severe mental illness may have been that of Robert Dyle, who was accused of murder in 1756. Dyle's lawyer found it impossible to work with his client and testified at the hearing, "I don't think he is capable of attending to or minding the evidence, or remembering it when he has heard it." The jury found Dyle to be "insane," which meant that he was incompetent to stand trial. There is no record of any further proceeding concerning Robert Dyle (Walker, 1968, pp. 222–223).

On January 21, 1790, King George III was driving in state to the House of Lords when a tall man named John Frith threw a stone at his coach. Frith was dressed eccentrically: a scarlet coat, striped waistcoat, black breeches, and a cocked hat with an orange cockade. When Frith testified in front of a jury, his mental illness was apparent. He said,

> When I first arrived at Liverpool I perceived I had some powers like those which St. Paul had; and the sun that St. Paul gives a description of in the Testament: an extraordinary power that came down upon me – the power of Christ; in consequence of my being persecuted and ill-used the public wanted to receive me as a most extraordinary kind of man ... When I went to St. Thomas's church I was there surprised to hear the clergyman preach a most extraordinary sermon upon me as if I was a god. (cited in Walker, 1968, pp. 223–224)

In today's clinical language, we would say that Frith had a delusion of grandiosity (that he had "extraordinary power") and a delusion of reference (that he was the subject of a preacher's sermon). Lord Kenyon instructed the jury, saying,

> The humanity of the law of England, falling into that which common humanity, without any written law, would suggest, has prescribed that no man shall be called upon to make his defence at a time when his mind is in that situation as not to appear capable of so doing. For however guilty he may be, the enquiring into his guilt must be postponed to that season when, by collecting together his intellects, and having them entire, he shall be able so to model his defence as to ward off the punishment of the law. (cited in Walker, 1968, p. 224)

The jury found Frith to be "insane," which meant incompetent to stand trial. There is no record of any further proceeding against John Frith (Walker, 1968, pp. 223–224).

COMPETENCY TO STAND TRIAL DEFINED: *DUSKY V. UNITED STATES* (U.S. 1960)

The qualities that render a defendant competent or incompetent to stand trial (CST or IST) are variables that can be assessed by mental health professionals. In the United States today, in every jurisdiction of the country, mental health professionals are employed daily in the evaluation of competency to stand trial. The case that defined these psycholegal issues is *Dusky v. United States* (1960).

Milton Dusky assisted in the kidnaping and rape of a young girl. At trial he was oriented to time and place, and he had some recollection of events. He was found guilty and was sentenced to 45 years in prison.

Dusky's attorneys argued that he had schizophrenia and had not been competent to stand trial. The U.S. Supreme Court held that it was not enough that a defendant be oriented to time and place and have some recollection of events. The defendant must also understand the proceedings against them and must be able to work together with an attorney in their own defense. The court issued a two-pronged standard for competency to stand trial (I have added numbers and line breaks for clarity):

1 whether he has sufficient present ability to consult with his lawyer with a reasonable degree of rational understanding and
2 whether he has a rational as well as factual understanding of the proceedings against him. (*Dusky v. United States*, at 402)

This definition of competency to stand trial is psychological in nature, as it concerns a defendant's cognition, motivation, and ability to work together with another person. The definition has endured and has generated a large amount of forensic and research activity among mental health professionals.

PSYCHOMETRIC TOOLS FOR EVALUATING COMPETENCY TO STAND TRIAL (CST)

By 1965 – only five years after the *Dusky* decision – mental health professionals were constructing lists of behaviors that reflect a defendant's competency to stand trial. The first such list was constructed by a psychiatrist: Ames Robey of Boston (Robey, 1965). Subsequent lists were developed by Bukatman et al. (1971); A. Louis McGarry and his associates at Harvard Medical School (Laboratory of Community Psychiatry, 1973); the Group for the Advancement of Psychiatry (1974); and Claudine Ausness of the University of Kentucky (1978). Some of the first standardized methods for assessing a defendant's competency to stand trial were developed with the consultation of psychologist Saleem Shah in

Table 10.1 Functional ability concepts associated with competence to stand trial

---

Consulting and assisting counsel
- understanding that counsel works for defendant
- understanding counsel's inquiries
- capable of responding to counsel's inquiries in a manner that provides relevant information for defense
- can provide consistent account of event relevant to charges and a defense
- can manage the demands of trial process (stress, maintaining demeanor)
- capable of testifying if necessary

Factual understanding
- that the defendant is accused of a crime
- that the court will decide on guilt or innocence
- that the trial could result in punishment
- of the various ways that defendants may plead
- that certain sentences are possible (their nature and seriousness)
- of the roles of various participants in the trial process
- of the general purpose of trials

Rational understanding (decisional abilities)
- beliefs about one's own trial process are not distorted by delusional beliefs
- appropriately motivated to further one's defense
- reasoning ability sufficient to process relevant information during decision making

---

Source: from Grisso (2003, p. 84), reprinted with permission of Springer Nature.

his role as director of the Center for Studies of Crime and Delinquency at the National Institute of Mental Health (Rogers & Fiduccia, 2015). Grisso (2003) summarized these lists as comprising three prongs (dividing *Dusky's* second prong into "factual understanding" and "rational understanding"), as presented in Table 10.1.

A number of mental health professionals in the U.S. and Canada have published standardized tests that evaluate competency to stand trial. These include measures designed specifically for the unique needs of juveniles (JACI; see below) and of defendants who have intellectual developmental disorder (CAST-MR; see below). However, most competency examinations conducted in the U.S. do not rely on any of the published tests, but rather are based upon freestyle interviews that are loosely structured around some version of the factors listed in Table 10.1. Neal and Grisso's (2014) survey of 434 forensic mental health practitioners indicated that CST instruments are not used frequently. Likewise, Rubenzer's (2018) nationwide survey of 55 CST examiners confirmed that standardized tests are not used frequently (p. 173).

Rogers et al. (2002) identified two generations of CST measures. They described a "first generation" that evaluated the *Dusky* factors but lacked test validation and norms. The "second generation" of CST measures began around 1998 and includes test validation and norms. This second generation includes the MacCAT-CA and the ECST-R (both of which are reviewed below). (For a basic explanation of the statistics used to evaluate psychometric tests, see Appendix O.)

"First generation" tests include (in chronological order):

- *Competence to Stand Trial Assessment Instrument (CAI) and Competence Screening Test (CST) (Laboratory of Community Psychiatry, 1973; lead author A. Louis McGarry)*

    The CAI was very influential and virtually all instruments for assessing competence to stand trial are indebted to it. The CAI – and its 1986 revision, the CAI-R – were critiqued by Grisso (2003) and by Rogers and Shuman (2005) and probably have been surpassed by newer methods.

    The CAI was used in practice primarily as a way of structuring forensic interviews and opinions around thirteen legally relevant functions similar to the variables identified in Table 10.1. Two or three interview questions are recommended for each function. Numerical ratings of 1 to 5 are given for each item. Clinicians were urged to be flexible in their approach to these questions and interviews.

    The CST is a sentence completion test that was designed to accompany the CAI. For example, one of the items on the CST reads, "When I go to court the lawyer will _____."

    Interrater reliabilities for the CAI averaged .92 for experienced raters and .87 for inexperienced raters (Laboratory of Community Psychiatry, 1973). CAI results corresponded to the consensus of expert panels in 78 percent of cases (Golding et al., 1984; Schreiber et al., 1987).

- *Georgia Court Competency Test (GCCT; Wildman et al., 1980)*

    The version of the GCCT that is used most often in forensic practice is the revision that was developed at Mississippi State Hospital in 1988 and is known as the GCCT-MSH (Nicholson, Briggs, & Robertson, 1988). It is based on four components of competency to stand trial: (1) knowledge of the charge, (2) knowledge of possible penalties, (3) understanding of courtroom procedures, and (4) ability to communicate rationally with an attorney in preparation of a defense. The GCCT-MSH consists of twenty-one questions and can be administered in a short amount of time. Seven of the questions utilize a drawing of an empty courtroom, upon which the subject indicates the locations of courtroom personnel. Answers are scored and totaled, with scores ranging from 0 to 100. A cut score of 69 or below has been applied. Internal consistencies (alpha coefficients) have ranged from .70 to .89 (Nicholson, Briggs, & Robertson, 1988; Rogers et al.,

2001; Ustad et al., 1996). Interrater reliabilities have ranged from .82 (Rogers et al., 2001) to .95 (Nicholson & Kugler, 1991). Sensitivity was found to be 71 percent (Nicholson, Briggs, & Robertson, 1988).

Among a sample of 140 defendants referred for CST evaluations, defendants found to be CST scored an average of 81.2, and defendants found to be IST scored an average of 51.3 (Nicholson, Robertson, Johnson, & Jensen, 1988).

Defendants in a competency restoration program whose competency was restored averaged a score of 81.8, and defendants who remained IST averaged 43.2 (Ustad et al., 1996).

A meta-analysis of four studies found that the GCCT correlated modestly (.42) with independent clinical judgments of CST (Nicholson & Kugler, 1991).

In recognition of the fact that many pre-trial defendants malinger and pretend to be IST, Gothard et al. (1995) added eight items to detect malingered psychosis. (Estimates of the base rate of malingering in CST examinations have ranged from 1 percent to 43 percent. See Rubenzer, 2018. Rubenzer's own research suggested that the median base rate of malingering in CST examinations is around 20 percent.) The eight items developed by Gothard et al. (1995) are scored on a three-point scale: 0 (for "no" or "does not apply"), 1 (for "sometimes" or a "qualified yes"), and 2 (for a "definite yes.") A cut score of ≥6 correctly classified 90 percent of the sample. Those authors judged that 12.7 percent of their sample were malingering.

A later study of the malingering items by Rogers et al. (2002) found that the cut score of ≥6 correctly classified 89.2 of their sample but had a sensitivity of only 31.8 percent. The optimal cut score was ≥3, which yielded a sensitivity of 72.7 percent and a specificity of 78.4 percent.

- *Fitness Interview Test (FIT; Roesch et al., 1984); Fitness Interview Test – Revised Edition (FIT-R; Roesch et al., 1998); and Fitness Interview Test – Revised (FIT-R; Roesch et al., 2006)*

  The original FIT was based on the CAI, with items added to reflect Canadian trial procedures. The FIT was revised extensively after Canada's 1992 revision of its Criminal Code, and the FIT-R was released in 1998. A second FIT-R, with minor changes in wording, was published in 2006, designed not only for Canadian courts but also for application in the United States and United Kingdom.

  Scoring criteria are relatively unstructured. Examiners use their own judgment to rate a defendant's capacities. Interrater reliability of overall competence to stand trial was excellent at .98 (Viljoen et al., 2002).

- *Competence Assessment for Standing Trial for Defendants with Mental Retardation (CAST-MR; Everington & Luckasson, 1992)*

  The CAST-MR consists of fifty questions that were written to be understood by people who have intellectual developmental disorder (IDD; formerly known as "mental retardation"). These questions are organized into three sections that cover (1) basic legal concepts, (2) skills to assist defense, and (3) understanding case events. The first two sections contain forty multiple-choice questions. Multiple-choice questions reduce the burden on the subject's expressive language skills and are easily scored without relying on the examiner's judgment. The third section consists of ten short, open-ended questions. Test-retest reliability is .90 (Everington, 1990).

  "Second generation" measures of competency to stand trial include:

- *MacArthur Competence Assessment Tool – Criminal Adjudication (MacCAT-CA; Poythress et al., 1999)*

  The MacCAT-CA is a structured interview of twenty-two items. It does not yield a total score but generates independent scores in three domains: Understanding, Reasoning, and Appreciation. Six Appreciation items are based on the defendant's appraisal of their own legal situation. Eight Understanding items and eight Reasoning items are based not on the defendant's own legal circumstances but on a hypothetical of two men who get into a bar fight while playing pool. Scoring criteria are highly structured (relative to other methods for determining CST).

  Interrater reliabilities for the three domains are .90 for Understanding, .85 for Reasoning, and .75 for Appreciation (Otto et al., 1998; Poythress et al., 1999).

  Internal consistencies (i.e., values which indicate that the items within each scale measure the same construct) are good, with Cronbach's α of .85 for Understanding, .81 for Reasoning, and .88 for Appreciation (Otto et al., 1998).

  Results from a hospital sample indicated that scores correlated modestly with staff determinations of competency: .36 for Understanding, .42 for Reasoning, and .49 for Appreciation (Otto et al., 1998; Poythress et al., 1999).

- *Evaluation of Competency to Stand Trial – Revised (ECST-R) (Rogers et al., 2004)*

  The ECST-R is a semi-structured interview that yields eighteen items and three scales that assess the three prongs of CST. Because CST evaluees very often attempt to malinger mental disorders, the ECST-R contains an additional twenty-eight items and five scales that assess atypical presentation.

  Interrater concordance rates have been good, with phi coefficients of .75 and .82 (Tillbrook, 1997, 2000). The ECST-R was effective in predicting whether the court would find defendants CST or IST (phi coefficient = .66; Tillbrook, 1997).

The twenty-eight items that assess atypical presentation (AP) were evaluated by Rogers et al. (2002) with a group of eighty-seven consecutive referrals from a jail program, of whom twenty-two (25 percent) were probably faking and sixty-five (75 percent) were probably not faking (as determined by the Structured Interview of Reported Symptoms [SIRS]; Rogers et al., 1992). Rather than seek an optimal cut score, the authors chose a cut score that would yield a sensitivity of 90 percent or more. This cut score (>4) yielded a sensitivity of .91, a specificity of .58, a positive predictive value of .43, a negative predictive value of .95, and a total predictive value of .67. These results are shown in an error matrix in Table 10.2. In a sample with a 25 percent base rate of malingering, the cut score of >4 was very useful in predicting when a defendant was not malingering (negative predictive value = .95). However, when this cut score was used to predict that a defendant was malingering, it was more likely to be wrong than right (false positives = 57 percent of positive predictions; positive predictive value = 43 percent). The atypical presentation (AP) items of the ECST-R probably would have performed better with a lower cut score and with a sample that had a higher base rate of malingering. However, a base rate of 25 percent malingering is probably close to what we would find in the real world (see Rubenzer, 2018).

- *Juvenile Adjudicative Competence Interview (JACI) (Grisso, 2005)*

The JACI is a structured interview of CST that was developed to meet the unique needs of juvenile defendants. Due to their immaturity and inexperience, juveniles are less likely than adults to understand the justice system. The need for such an instrument arose as the mission of juvenile courts became less rehabilitative and more punitive.

The twelve content areas of the JACI correspond to those that are found in all tests of CST. Tomei and Panza (2014) found that only two of these twelve content areas were good predictors of clinicians' assessments of CST, namely, understanding the role of the prosecutor (p = .003) and understanding the nature of plea bargaining (p = .007). That is, juveniles who did not understand (1) the adversarial nature of prosecution or (2) the nature of plea bargaining and how it would affect their future were not likely to be found CST by clinicians.

With all due respect to Rogers et al. (2002) and their distinction between first and second generation tests of CST, and with all due respect to the researchers who have published normative data on tests of CST, it can be argued that judgments about CST are qualitative and not quantitative in nature, which means that normative data are not particularly relevant. When tests of CST are used by practitioners in the field (and they are used infrequently; see above), they are likely to be used not as quantitative tests but as structured professional judgments (SPJs; see Chapter 12). This is because CST variables are qualitative and are not additive. A single variable

Table 10.2 Utility estimates for feigning on the ECST-R atypical presentation (AP) scale

		SIRS			
		Feigning	*Not feigning*	*Totals*	
ECST-R AP Scale	*Feigning*	20	27	47	Positive predictive value = .43
	Not feigning	2	38	40	Negative predictive value = .95
	Totals	22	65	87	
		Sensitivity = .91	Specificity = .58		Total predictive value = .67

Source: From Rogers et al. (2002).

can be powerful enough to render a defendant IST. For an example, see the case of Richard (Case study #4).

DEFENDANTS HAVE THE RIGHT TO A COMPETENCY EVALUATION: *DROPE V. MISSOURI* (U.S. 1975)

Dusky v. United States (1960) established the legal standards for competency to stand trial. *Drope v. Missouri* (1975) established the right of every defendant to have a competency evaluation.

When James Drope was indicted for raping his wife, he requested a continuance so that he could receive psychiatric treatment and a psychiatric evaluation. He attached to his motion a psychiatric report recommending treatment. His request was denied and his case went to trial. On day two of the trial he shot himself, but he survived. He spent the remainder of his trial in the hospital for treatment of his wound. In one of the truly bizarre decisions in judicial history, his request for a mistrial was denied, because his absence from the courtroom was deemed to be voluntary. Drope was found guilty and was sentenced to life in prison. (At that time he might have faced the death penalty for rape in Missouri. This was before the "proportionality" rule in *Coker v. Georgia*, 1977, established that a defendant cannot be given the death penalty for the rape of an adult. See Chapter 6.)

Drope's appeal reached the U.S. Supreme Court where his conviction was reversed and remanded in a unanimous decision. By denying him a competency evaluation, the trial court had violated his right to due process. A defendant who is too depressed or too suicidal to participate in their own defense is not competent and should not go to trial.

It is essential to due process that a defendant who is not competent is not taken to trial. Therefore, the threshold for granting a competency evaluation is low. Drope should have been granted a competency examination upon his initial request and again after he attempted suicide.

Case study #4: Richard – incompetency to stand trial (IST) in a severely depressed man

Richard was in prison for the murder of his wife and he was in the process of appealing his conviction. His crime was literally "close to home" for me, because he had dropped his wife's body on a paved road about one mile from my house.

Richard was transferred from the prison to the forensic hospital because he was incompetent to proceed with his appeal and he was not safe within the general prison population.

Richard was a 45-year-old, middle-class, professional man with a good work history. He was soft-spoken, mild-mannered, and well-educated. He had done well in school and he did well in his career. He had no prior history of mental illness or crime. Nothing in his life had prepared him for prison, and he was finding it to be an impossible adjustment.

The maximum security prison where Richard had been housed is the kind of soul-crushing environment where an inmate can be hired to kill another inmate. Several months after his arrival, Richard reportedly began looking for one of these contract killers. When it became known that the prisoner he wanted murdered was himself, he was transferred out of the general prison population and into the forensic hospital where I was employed. There he was found incompetent to stand trial (IST). A defendant who is so depressed that they want to die is not motivated to defend themselves and they cannot go to trial.

Richard is a good example of the reason why tests for competency to stand trial are qualitative in nature and not quantitative and why they should be used as structured professional judgments (see Chapter 12) and not as actuarial instruments that produce numerical scores. Richard was an intelligent and verbal individual who had no difficulty understanding the proceedings involved in his appeal and no difficulty communicating with his attorney. He was fully aware of the factual and rational aspects of those proceedings. He met every variable within the *Dusky* criteria, but he was not motivated to defend himself. He could not make the adjustment to prison life, was profoundly depressed, wanted to die, and did not care about the appeal that his attorney was sending forward to the court. He was self-destructive and the risk was too great that he might find ways to sabotage the proceedings and act against his own best interests. In my opinion, he was not competent to stand trial.

Richard was treated for depression in the hospital environment and his condition stabilized. After a number of months he was able to proceed with his appeal.

Case study #5: Clive – incompetency to stand trial (IST) in a man with severe brain injury after a failed suicide attempt

Clive was a resident of a skilled nursing facility that was operated by the state. He was escorted to the examination room in handcuffs and in a wheelchair. He could walk only a few steps on his own. Twenty years earlier he had killed his son with a shotgun and then had put the gun to his left temple and pulled the trigger. He lost about 25 percent of his brain tissue and survived. I had never seen a person lose so much of their brain tissue and live.

As would be expected in someone with severe damage to the left frontal lobe, Clive spoke only with great effort, and when he did speak most of his words were incomprehensible. He could not demonstrate an understanding of the facts of his case or the proceedings against him. He was not able to communicate meaningfully with an attorney. He was not competent and he never stood trial for his son's death. Every few years, the district attorney tried to take him to court, but Clive was not competent and I returned him to the skilled nursing facility.

When a forensic examiner reaches the opinion that a defendant is IST, we attach to our report an opinion regarding whether or not competency is likely to be restored. It had been twenty years since Clive had killed his son. His injury was permanent and his cognitive skills had not improved. My opinion was that competency was not likely to be restored. To my knowledge, Clive never stood trial for the death of his son and probably spent the remainder of his life in the skilled nursing facility operated by the state.

REFERENCES

Ausness, C. W. (1978). The identification of incompetent defendants: Separating those unfit for adversary combat from those who are fit. *Kentucky Law Journal*, 66(3), 666–706. Retrieved 11/21/2022 from https://uknowledge.uky.edu/klj/vol66/iss3/11.

Bukatman, B., Foy, J., & DeGrazia, E. (1971). What is competency to stand trial? *American Journal of Psychiatry*, 127, 1225–1229. doi:10.1176/ajp.127.9.1225.

Coker v. Georgia, 433 U.S. 584 (1977).

Drope v. Missouri, 420 U.S. 162 (1975).

Dusky v. United States, 362 U.S. 402 (1960).

Everington, C. (1990). The Competence Assessment for Standing Trial for Defendants with Mental Retardation (CAST-MR): A validation study. *Criminal Justice and Behavior*, 17(2), 147–168. doi:10.1177/0093854890017002001.

Everington, C., & Luckasson, R. (1992). *Competence Assessment for Standing Trial for Defendants with Mental Retardation: Test manual*. Worthington, OH: IDS Publishing Corp.

Golding, S., Roesch, R., & Schreiber, J. (1984). Assessment and conceptualization of competence to stand trial: Preliminary data on the Interdisciplinary Fitness Interview. *Law and Human Behavior*, 8(3–4), 321–334. doi:10.1007/BF01044699.

Gothard, S., Rogers, R., & Sewell, K. W. (1995). Feigning incompetency to stand trial: An investigation of the GCCT. *Law and Human Behavior*, 19, 363–373. doi:10.1007/BF01499137.

Grisso, T. (2003). *Evaluating competencies: Forensic assessments and instruments. Second edition.* New York: Kluwer Academic/Plenum Publishers.

Grisso, T. (2005). *Evaluating juveniles' adjudicative competence: A guide for clinical practice.* Sarasota, FL: Professional Resource Press.

Group for the Advancement of Psychiatry. (1974). *Misuse of psychiatry in the criminal courts: Competency to stand trial.* New York: Committee on Psychiatry and Law.

Laboratory of Community Psychiatry, Harvard Medical School. (1973). *Competency to stand trial and mental illness* (DHEW Publication No. ADM77-103). Rockville, MD: NIMH, Department of Health, Education and Welfare.

Neal, T. M. S., & Grisso, T. (2014). Assessment practices and expert judgment methods in forensic psychology and psychiatry: An international snapshot. *Criminal Justice and Behavior, 41*(12), 1406–1421. doi:10.1177/0093854814548449.

Nicholson, R., Briggs, S., & Robertson, H. (1988). Instruments for assessing competence to stand trial: How do they work? *Professional Psychology: Research and Practice, 19,* 383–394. doi:10.1037/0735-7028.19.4.383.

Nicholson, R., & Kugler, K. (1991). Competent and incompetent criminal defendants: A quantitative review of comparative research. *Psychological Bulletin, 109,* 355–370. doi:10.1037/0033-2909.109.3.355.

Nicholson, R., Robertson, H., Johnson, W., & Jensen, G. (1988). A comparison of instruments for assessing competence to stand trial. *Law and Human Behavior, 12,* 313–321. doi:10/1007/BF01044387.

Otto, R., Poythress, N., Edens, N., Nicholson, R., Monahan, J., Bonnie, R., Hoge, S., & Eisenberg, M. (1998). Psychometric properties of the MacArthur Competence Assessment Tool-Criminal Adjudication. *Psychological Assessment, 10*(4), 435–443. doi:10.1037/1040-3590.10.4.435.

Poythress, N., Nicholson, R., Otto, R., Edens, J., Bonnie, R., Monahan, J., & Hoge, S. (1999). *The MacArthur Competence Assessment Tool – Criminal Adjudication: Professional manual.* Odessa, FL: Psychological Assessment Resources.

Rex v. Esther Dyson 7 C. & P. 305 (1831).

Rex v. Pritchard, 7 C. & P. 303 (1836).

Robey, A. (1965). Criteria for competency to stand trial: A checklist for psychiatrists. *American Journal of Psychiatry, 122,* 616–623. doi:10.1176/AJP.122.6.616.

Roesch, R., Webster, C. D., & Eaves, D. (1984). *The Fitness Interview Test – A method for examining fitness to stand trial* (Research Report of the Centre of Criminology). Toronto, Ontario: University of Toronto.

Roesch, R., Zapf, P. A., & Eaves, D. (2006). *Fitness Interview Test – Revised: A structured interview for assessing competency to stand trial.* Sarasota, FL: Professional Resource Press.

Roesch, R., Zapf, P., Eaves, D., & Webster, C. (1998). *Fitness Interview Test. Revised edition.* Burnaby, British Columbia, Canada: Mental Health, Law and Policy Institute, Simon Fraser University.

Rogers, R., Bagby, R. M., & Dickens, S. E. (1992). *Structured Interview of Reported Symptoms (SIRS).* Odessa, FL: Psychological Assessment Resources.

Rogers, R., & Fiduccia, C. E. (2015). Forensic assessment instruments. In B. L. Cutler & P. A. Zapf (Eds.) *APA handbook of forensic psychology. Volume 1:*

Individual and situational influences in criminal and civil contexts (pp. 19–34). Washington, D.C.: American Psychological Association.

Rogers, R., Grandjean, N., Tillbrook, C., Vitacco, M., & Sewell, K. (2001). Recent interview-based measures of competence to stand trial: A critical review augmented with research data. *Behavioral Sciences and the Law, 19*(4), 503–518. doi:10.1002/bsl.458.

Rogers, R., Sewell, K. W., Grandjean, N. R., & Vitacco, M. J. (2002). The detection of feigned mental disorders on specific competency measures. *Psychological Assessment, 14*(2), 177–183. doi:10.1037/1040-3590.14.2.177.

Rogers, R., & Shuman, D. W. (2005). *Fundamentals of forensic practice.* New York: Springer.

Rogers, R., Tillbrook, C. E., & Sewell, K. W. (2004). *Evaluation of Competency to Stand Trial – Revised (ECST-R) and professional manual.* Odessa, FL: Psychological Assessment Resources, Inc.

Rubenzer, S. (2018). *Assessing negative response bias in competency to stand trial evaluations.* Oxford: Oxford University Press.

Schreiber, J., Roesch, R., & Golding, S. (1987). An evaluation of procedures for assessing competence to stand trial. *Bulletin of the American Academy of Psychiatry and the Law, 15*, 143–150. https://pubmed.ncbi.nlm.nih.gov/3435784.

Tillbrook, C. E. (1997). Validation of the Evaluation of Competency to Stand Trial (ECST) instrument: A preliminary assessment. Unpublished master's thesis, University of Alabama, Tuscaloosa.

Tillbrook, C. E. (2000). *Competency to proceed: A comparative appraisal of approaches to assessment.* Unpublished doctoral dissertation, University of Alabama, Tuscaloosa.

Tomei, J., & Panza, N. R. (2014). The Juvenile Adjudicative Competence Interview (JACI): Current usage in juvenile competence to stand trial evaluations. *Contemporary Issues in Juvenile Justice, 8*(1), Article 1. https://digitalcommons.pvamu.edu/cojjp-contemporaryissues/vol8/iss1/1.

Ustad, I., Rogers, R., Sewell, K., & Guarnaccia, C. (1996). Restoration of competency to stand trial: Assessment with the Georgia Court Competency Test and the Competency Screening Test. *Law and Human Behavior, 20*, 131–146. doi:10.1007/BF01499351.

Viljoen, J., Roesch, R., & Zapf, P. A. (2002). Interrater reliability of the Fitness Interview Test across four professional groups. *Canadian Journal of Psychiatry, 47*, 945–952. doi:10.1177/070674370204701006.

Walker, N. (1968). *Crime and insanity in England. Volume 1: The historical perspective.* Edinburgh: University of Edinburgh Press.

Wildman, R., Batchelor, E., Thompson, L., Nelson, F., Moore, J., Patterson, M., & deLaosa, M. (1980). *The Georgia Court Competency Test: An attempt to develop a rapid, quantitative measure for fitness for trial.* Unpublished manuscript, Forensic Services Division, Central State Hospital, Milledgeville, GA.

11   Transfer of juveniles to adult court

Kent v. United States (U.S. 1966)

Each state decides its own age of majority. In most states that age is 18. In Alabama, Delaware, and Nebraska the age of majority is 19. In Mississippi it is 21. In Arkansas, Nevada, Ohio, Tennessee, Utah, and Wisconsin the age of majority depends on whether you are still in high school.

The juvenile courts of every state can incarcerate a juvenile only up to a certain age, such as age 21. This presents a critical problem for the courts when a juvenile commits a serious offense like homicide, armed robbery, or rape. If that defendant is tried and sentenced under juvenile law, then they must be released on or before their 21st birthday, and this can pose a serious threat to public safety.

All states have laws that allow for the transfer (some states call it "waiver") of serious juvenile offenders to adult court. Adult courts can give longer sentences and, until *Roper v. Simmons* (2005), could give a juvenile the death penalty. In *Roper*, the U.S. Supreme Court ruled that persons who commit murder before the age of 18 cannot be given the death penalty. When the U.S. Supreme Court issued the *Roper* decision, four of my juvenile evaluees came off death row, including one of the cases presented below. At present, the maximum penalty that a juvenile can receive is life without parole, which also has been the subject of much judicial attention (and is the topic of Chapter 15).

The challenge to our legal system is to develop equitable procedures that are consistent with due process by which our judicial system can decide which juveniles will be transferred to adult court.

Morris Kent was arrested at age 16 in Washington, D.C. He was accused of burglary, robbery, and rape. Given the seriousness of the charges, the prosecutor sought transfer to adult court. Kent's attorney asked for a hearing on the transfer issue, so that witnesses could be cross-examined and evidence presented on Kent's behalf. The judge ignored the defense motion for a hearing and transferred Kent to adult court in camera – that is, without a hearing. Kent was found guilty in adult court and was sentenced to 30 to 90 years in prison.

DOI: 10.4324/9781003385028-13

The in camera procedure that this judge had followed was the standard practice in juvenile courts at that time. The process has been likened to the infamous Star Chamber of kings Henry VIII, James I, and others. The Star Chamber was a room in the royal Palace of Westminster which got its name from its ceiling that was decorated with gold stars. In this room judges met, rendered verdicts, and assigned punishments without safeguards of due process.

Kent's attorneys argued that transfer to adult court was such a serious matter that he was entitled to a hearing and that to do otherwise violated his right to due process. The U.S. Supreme Court agreed.

Kent was a landmark decision and part of the civil rights revolution that took place in the U.S. Supreme Court during the 1960s. Because of the decisions in *Kent* and *In re Gault* (1967), juvenile justice procedures were revised throughout the country.

In an appendix to *Kent*, the court listed eight criteria that can be used to decide whether a juvenile is transferred to adult court. These eight criteria are:

1 The seriousness of the alleged offense to the community and whether the protection of the community requires waiver.
2 Whether the alleged offense was committed in an aggressive, violent, premeditated or willful manner.
3 Whether the alleged offense was against persons or against property, greater weight being given to offenses against persons especially if personal injury resulted.
4 The prosecutive merit of the complaint, *i.e.*, whether there is evidence upon which a Grand Jury may be expected to return an indictment (to be determined by consultation with the United States Attorney).
5 The desirability of trial and disposition of the entire offense in one court when the juvenile's associates in the alleged offense are adults who will be charged with a crime in the U.S. District Court for the District of Columbia.
6 The sophistication and maturity of the juvenile as determined by consideration of his home, environmental situation, emotional attitude and pattern of living.
7 The record and previous history of the juvenile, including previous contacts with the Youth Aid Division, other law enforcement agencies, juvenile courts and other jurisdictions, prior periods of probation to this Court, or prior commitments to juvenile institutions.
8 The prospects for adequate protection of the public and the likelihood of reasonable rehabilitation of the juvenile (if he is found to have committed the alleged offense) by the use of procedures, services and facilities currently available to the Juvenile Court. (*Kent v. United States*, 1966, at 566–567)

Kent criteria 1, 3, 4, 5, and 7 are decisions that are made during judicial proceedings or are information that can be found in court records. Criteria 2, 6, and 8 are (or can be) the province of forensic mental health assessment.

Criterion 2, "Whether the alleged offense was committed in an aggressive, violent, premeditated or willful manner," can be evaluated by interviewing the defendant and by reviewing evidence relevant to the defendant's behavior and state of mind during the alleged offense. As explained in Chapter 7, variables like premeditation and will are inferred from a defendant's behavior. (It is important to note that in some jurisdictions – Colorado and South Carolina, in my experience – the contents of a pre-transfer psychological evaluation are not privileged, which means that the defendant's description of the crime can be used against them in court to prove that they committed the crime. In these jurisdictions, I advise forensic mental health examiners not to question defendants about the details of their crimes. Our role is to serve as mental health experts and not as police investigators.)

Criterion 6, "sophistication and maturity," refers to the defendant's status within the transition from child to adult. Is this defendant more like a child, whose behavior is experimental and malleable, or more like an adult, whose behavior and character are relatively fixed? Perhaps the biggest challenge in the forensic evaluation of juveniles is the fact that they are developing rapidly, which means that assessments of their character and predictions about their behavior are like trying to hit a moving target. (See the discussion of adolescent development in Chapter 15.) Presumably, there is greater potential for desistance from crime among juvenile defendants who are child-like and greater potential for recidivism among defendants who already are hardened criminals. Sophistication and maturity can be assessed through a combination of methods that include interviewing the juvenile, interviewing collateral persons (i.e., those who have information about the juvenile), reviewing relevant records including school and mental health records, and administering a battery of tests that might include tests of intelligence, adaptive behavior, personality, and suggestibility.

Criterion 8, "likelihood of reasonable rehabilitation," includes such factors as risk of violence, likelihood of recidivism, and amenability to treatment. Psychometric tools that are commonly used to predict juvenile violence include the Psychopathy Checklist: Youth Version (PCL:YV; Forth et al., 2003); the Structured Assessment of Violence Risk in Youth (SAVRY; Borum et al., 2002, 2006); and the Youth Level of Service/Case Management Inventory (YLS/CMI; Hoge & Andrews, 2002). These instruments for the prediction juvenile violence are reviewed in Chapter 15 in the discussion of juvenile sentencing.

Salekin (2004) published a semi-structured interview – the Risk-Sophistication-Treatment Inventory (RST-I) – which assesses three factors relevant to transfer decisions: (1) level of dangerousness, (2) sophistication or maturity, and (3) amenability to treatment. Each of these three scales contains both static and dynamic factors. ("Static" refers to variables that do not change over time, like age at first offense. "Dynamic" factors change over time, for example, ability to cope.) Each scale comprises three item clusters and fifteen items that are rated from 0 to 2 as follows: 0 = absence of the characteristic/ability, 1 = subclinical/moderate, and 2 = presence of the characteristic/ability. The three scales and their item clusters are:

Risk for dangerousness

- Violent and aggressive tendencies
- Planned and extensive criminality
- Psychopathic features

Maturity

- Autonomy
- Cognitive capacities
- Emotional maturity

Treatment amenability

- Psychopathology: degree and type
- Responsibility and motivation to change
- Consideration and tolerance of others.

Alpha coefficients for the three factors ranged from .78 to .83. Intraclass correlations ranged from .74 to .94, which indicates good interrater reliabilities. Leistico and Salekin (2003) found that RST-I scores predicted judicial decisions regarding transfer to adult court.

An unpublished self-report version (RSTI-SR; Iselin & Salekin, 2008) and an abbreviated version (RSTI-A; Gillen et al., 2015; Salekin, 2012) were created for research purposes. Early research results have been promising, but these instruments have not been published for forensic use.

Case study #6: Ronald – Transfer to adult court for serial rape and murder

Ronald lived with his family in a rural area. The facts against him indicated that his victims were adult women. He raped and killed his first victim when he was 14 years old. She was a neighbor who lived alone. He picked up a sharp stick that was lying in her front yard, thrust it under her ribcage, and raped her while she was dying. He raped and killed two more women before his 18th birthday.

Ronald never carried a weapon. He killed his victims quickly and brutally with a stick or a pipe that lay nearby. He raped one woman while she lay dying in bed next to her baby. He had killed three women when he was apprehended by the police shortly after his 18th birthday.

During psychological interviews Ronald was polite, respectful, and soft-spoken. His level of intelligence was just a little below average. He did not have any reading or learning difficulties. There was no indication of psychosis, dissociation, mood disorder, or other form of mental disorder. He could not explain why he had committed these crimes, and he was genuinely perplexed by his own behavior.

My testimony was that Ronald was not likely to be rehabilitated by the age of 21. He was transferred to adult court, where he was found guilty of murder and was sentenced to death. Then, in 2005, the U.S. Supreme Court ruled in *Roper v. Simmons* that a defendant cannot be executed for a murder committed before the age of 18. Ronald came off death row at that time. As Ronald matured in prison, he continued to struggle with the question of why he had committed these horrible crimes. He remained a mystery to himself.

Because a subtext of this book is to reflect what it is like to work as a forensic mental health professional, I will share that, after my first interview with Ronald (which lasted several hours and was held face-to-face in a small interview room deep inside a county jail), I was in a state of shock for three days.

Case study #7: Callie – transfer to adult court for a group homicide

Callie was 16 years old. She did not discuss her crime with me, and my knowledge of these events is based only on information that was gathered by investigators for her trial. She and two female friends were accused of killing and robbing a 36-year-old man in a hotel room. According to police records, the victim knew all three of the girls. They had approached him and offered him group sex if he would take them to a hotel. Each girl had concealed on her person a knife with a three-inch blade. While they were engaged in group sex – with the victim lying on his back and Callie on top of him – she buried her knife in his throat. "Callie, why are you killing me?" were his last words.

Callie was an attractive girl, despite scars on her face and chest that showed her life had not been an easy one. Her IQ was below average. She had not done well in school. She had no prior record with the juvenile court and no record with child protective services.

When I interviewed Callie, she was taciturn and emotionless. She gave short, uncomplicated, and non-committal answers to questions that told me very little about herself. She did not elaborate on her answers and did not volunteer any information. She denied having any history of involvement with crime or substance use. She denied having any history of child abuse. She attributed the scars on her face and chest to an innocent childhood accident: "I fell out of my high chair as a baby," she said.

Callie made eye contact with me, but her eyes were empty and devoid of feeling. She gave no indication of distress or remorse. She was indifferent to her victim, her crime, her circumstances, and her future. She gave no indication that it bothered her to have taken a life, to be in jail, or to be facing a long prison sentence.

Lack of emotion is typical of juveniles with conduct disorder, and given the nature of the charges against her I had no difficulty arriving at that diagnosis. For instructional purposes here, I wish to repeat and to emphasize that the biggest problem in evaluating juveniles is that they are changing rapidly. If, for example, Callie's emotional indifference was not a feature of conduct disorder but was a negative symptom of schizophrenia (i.e., "flat affect"), we may not have been able to confirm that diagnosis for years. (The typical age of onset of schizophrenia among women is in their late 20s; American Psychiatric Association, 2022, p. 117.) Callie gave no other indication of psychosis, and her alleged crime suggested severe antisocial tendencies, which confirmed the diagnosis of conduct disorder.

Callie's alleged offense "was committed in an aggressive, violent, premeditated or willful manner" (*Kent* criterion 2). Premeditation was indicated by the facts that she had conspired with co-defendants and had intentionally brought the murder weapon to the scene. She had concealed the weapon and had maneuvered the victim into a vulnerable position.

Regarding *Kent* criterion 6, Callie at the age of 16 had reached a level of criminal "sophistication and maturity" that was more typical of a hardened adult criminal than a malleable child. She had used her body and her sexuality in a calculated and savage manner, of which most women are not capable.

Callie's crime and the dim prospects for her future offered little hope for rehabilitation. The opinion I sent forward to the court was that Callie was not likely to be rehabilitated by the age of 21. She was transferred to adult court. She was convicted of armed robbery and sentenced to a long term in prison. For reasons unknown to me, she was not convicted of murder. She is currently serving her sentence in a state penitentiary.

Case study #8: Janice – transfer to adult court for a group homicide

A disproportionate number of juvenile crimes are committed in groups (Scott & Steinberg, 2008). Juveniles will do things in groups that they would not do alone, and this includes homicide. They have not yet developed the cognitive maturity that is required for independent thought and action.

Janice had lived with her aunt in a housing project. She was only 14 years old, but she was large and physically powerful. The facts in her case indicated that she was one of a group of teenage girls who attacked and killed a young adult woman who was visiting their housing project. The victim, I was told, was a regular visitor at the project. Why she visited the project, why she visited so frequently, and how she angered the wrong group of people were not known to me, but she must have been conspicuous at the housing project, being a well-dressed woman of another race, carrying a purse, and obviously having money and a middle-class lifestyle, in contrast to the people who lived there. Five teenage girls knocked her to the ground and kicked her. Janice delivered the fatal blows by kicking her in the throat with hard shoes, crushing her windpipe. The district attorney filed a motion to transfer Janice to adult court. Her co-defendants had not delivered the fatal kicks and they stayed in juvenile court.

Janice had no prior history in the juvenile justice system. Her IQ was below average, and she had not done well in school. Her parents were not involved with her and she had been a client of child protective services most of her life. She had been placed in one home after another, including group homes and foster homes operated by the state, and finally she had come to live with her aunt in the housing project.

Janice gave no indication of mental illness or other maladaptive traits. By all indications, this homicide was the result of a spontaneous outburst of rage by this group of girls. I had no indication that the homicide was premeditated or that Janice had intended to kill. No one had brought a weapon to the scene. Like many juvenile offenses, this was a group action and not an individual crime. It was not likely that Janice would have done this if she had acted alone. Middle adolescence is, in fact, the period of time during which juveniles are most responsive to peer pressure and most likely to go along with a group.

I interviewed Janice several times. She wept bitterly and inconsolably every time I saw her. She knew that she had destroyed her future in one regrettable moment. She had lost her freedom and her life would never be the same.

Jails and prisons are a harsh reality, and many incarcerated defendants are depressed and miserable. (Observe the high rate of suicide among prisoners, including juveniles. Suicide is the leading cause of death among juveniles in custody, and their rate of suicide is twice what it is for juveniles outside of custody; see Gallagher & Dobrin, 2006.) The challenge for the forensic examiner who is assessing an incarcerated defendant is to distinguish whether a defendant's misery is (1) regret for how they have ruined their life, (2) remorse for how they have damaged the cohesion and reputation of their family, (3) fear of retribution, (4) sorrow for damage they have done to the victim, (5) sorrow for the damage they have done to the victim's family, (6) remorse over violating a fundamental principle of moral conduct (and what this says about themselves and their character), (7) a reaction to the deprivations of incarceration, or (8) the pain of scrutiny itself. The juvenile mind is focused on itself, their family, and their immediate circle of friends. My own untested hypothesis, based on the evaluations of 1,000 juvenile defendants, is that it is not developmentally appropriate to expect a child of 14 to show remorse for how they have affected the life of someone who is outside their family or their immediate circle of friends. Conscience develops slowly, if it develops at all. (My experience in evaluating 1,000 incarcerated felons of all ages is that conscience, if it develops at all, is a phenomenon of midlife, roughly ages 45 to 60). My impression of Janice was consistent with my general impression of defendants at her age – that her misery was related mostly to how she had destroyed her future.

Whatever the reason for Janice's misery, it showed that she was capable of profound and appropriate emotion (unlike the cold indifference of Callie described in the previous case study). In terms of "sophistication and maturity" (*Kent* criterion #6), Janice at the age of 14, crying her eyes out for what she had done, was more girl than woman.

At her transfer hearing, Janice sat a few feet away from me at the defense table. She sobbed heavily throughout the proceeding. Most juvenile hearings have few observers – consistent with the protective mission of juvenile court – but at Janice's hearing the courtroom was packed with members of the victim's family. They stared at me intensely as I testified about Janice, her low level of intelligence, her learning difficulties, her life of poverty, the abandonment by her parents, the abuse and neglect she had suffered at the hands of her extended family, and the fact that she had been shuffled from one group home to another, one foster home to another, and one impoverished family member to another. Janice hid her face in her hands and wept bitterly as I told her life story. Toward the end of my testimony, the prosecutor blurted out caustically, "It sounds like you feel sorry for this girl!" I responded in a calm and straightforward manner. "I *do* feel sorry for this girl," I said. "She never had a chance to lead a normal life."

Due to the seriousness of her crime (*Kent* criterion #1) Janice was transferred to adult court, where she stood trial for murder. (Unfortunately I have no follow-up on Janice and do not know the outcome of her trial.)

Case study #9: Sarah – retention in juvenile court of a child abuse victim

Sarah had lived alone with her alcoholic mother, who was physically and psychologically abusive. One evening, when she was 16 years old, she called the police to their home. Her mother's body was inside the house, dead from a blow to the back of the head with a clothes iron.

Sarah was taken into custody and was held at a state hospital for juveniles, where I interviewed her. She recounted to me the details of the physical and psychological abuse she had suffered at the hands of her mother. She had no prior history of involvement with the juvenile justice system. She had no prior history of violence or other antisocial behavior. Her behavior at school and in her community had been exemplary. Her grades were good and she planned to attend college. She gave no sign of mental illness. By all indications she would have a good life if she could get beyond her current difficulties.

There was no indication that this homicide had been planned. Sarah had not brought a weapon to the scene. The murder weapon was not a typical weapon, like a gun or a knife, but a common household object that lay close at hand, suggesting that the homicide was related to a spontaneous outburst of emotion without planning.

Kent criterion 8, "likelihood of rehabilitation," includes risk of recidivism. Intra-familial violence such as matricide is different from predatory violence such as armed robbery or rape. Predatory violence is motivated by calculated self-interest, and the violence is instrumental – the predator wants something from the victim, and victims are little more than interchangeable means to an end. The homicide of a family member, on the other hand, involves a complex and unique relationship. Familial victims are not interchangeable, and they are less likely to be a means to an end. Matricide cannot be recidivated. You cannot kill your mother more than once. Some defendants who kill family members have patterns of unstable attachments and histories of repeated acts of violence, but this was not the case with Sarah. Her history of violence was limited to one eruption of uncontrollable rage; what mental health professionals used to call "catathymia."

I tendered my opinion that Sarah was likely to be rehabilitated in the juvenile justice system. She was retained in juvenile court, where she was adjudicated delinquent for homicide and given a suspended sentence. When she was able to leave the hospital, she was taken in by a sympathetic aunt. She continued to do well in school. Two years later she was accepted at a university 1,000 miles away. She left home and went on with her life.

MANDATORY TRANSFER OF JUVENILES TO ADULT COURT

Juvenile violence in America peaked in 1994 (Snyder, 1997). Transfer hearings are labor-intensive, and juvenile courts were severely bogged down with large numbers of serious offenders. Legislatures sought ways to reduce this burden and hit upon the idea of returning to the old days before *Kent*, when juveniles were transferred to adult court without a hearing. A number of states enacted mandatory transfer laws by which juveniles of a certain age accused of certain violent crimes were transferred automatically without a hearing and without a mental health evaluation. These mandatory transfer laws simplified the administrative processes and made them faster and much less expensive, but they were contrary to the U.S. Supreme Court decision in *Kent* (by which juveniles are entitled to a hearing before deciding their transfer to adult court) and contrary to the mission of juvenile court (which is intended to be more rehabilitative and less punitive than adult court; Tavil, 2017–2018). Furthermore, as documented by the Juvenile Sentencing Project in 2020, a racial disparity appeared in mandatory transfers – more Black juveniles than White juveniles were sent automatically to adult courts.

While these issues were being pursued in the courts and state legislatures, a number of states backed off and either rescinded their mandatory transfer laws (replacing them with *Kent*-like procedures) or modified them by narrowing the age range and types of crimes by which a juvenile can be transferred to adult court without a hearing (Juvenile Sentencing Project, 2020).

In the state of Ohio, which has a mandatory transfer law, these questions were pursued with mixed results. Juvenile defendant Alexander Quarterman was transferred automatically to adult court, where he pleaded guilty to aggravated robbery. His conviction was affirmed by the Court of Appeals of the Ninth Judicial District. That is, the Court of Appeals declared that his mandatory transfer to adult court was justified (*State v. Quarterman*, 2014).

The next case in this series, *State v. Aalim*, was heard twice by the Supreme Court of Ohio. In *State v. Aalim* (2016; known as *Aalim I*), the court ruled that mandatory transfer is not consistent with *Kent* and violates the due process and equal protection clauses of the Fourteenth Amendment. One year later, in *State v. Aalim* (2017; known as *Aalim II*), the composition of the court had changed, and the court declared that questions can be revisited when there is a change of personnel on the bench. The court reversed its decision in *Aalim I*, and mandatory transfers resumed in Ohio.

Juvenile transfer laws exist in every jurisdiction. Legislatures have created a variety of alternatives by which courts can address the serious questions of whether and when to return a dangerous juvenile to society (Office of Juvenile Justice and Delinquency Prevention, 2022). These alternatives include:

1 mandatory transfer, by which a juvenile is automatically transferred to adult court without a hearing, based on the juvenile's age and the type of offense (twelve states)
2 presumptive transfer, by which the burden is on the defense to argue why a defendant should be retained in juvenile court (eleven states and the District of Columbia)
3 direct file, by which a prosecutor has discretion to file in adult court (thirteen states and the District of Columbia)
4 reverse transfer, by which an adult court can return a defendant to juvenile court (twenty-eight states)
5 juvenile blended sentencing, by which a juvenile court has the authority to impose adult penalties (fifteen states)
6 adult blended sentencing, by which an adult court has the authority to impose juvenile dispositions (twenty-three states).

These variations are presented in Table 11.1. Three states – Alabama, Hawaii, and Washington – have juvenile transfer laws but do not have any of these six variations.

Table 11.1 Transfer laws at the end of the 2019 legislative session

Jurisdiction	Mandatory transfer	Presumptive transfer	Direct file	Reverse transfer	Juvenile blended sentence	Adult blended sentence
Alabama						
Alaska		X			X	X
Arizona			X	X		X
Arkansas			X	X	X	X
California				X		X
Colorado		X	X	X	X	X
Connecticut	X		X	X	X	
Delaware	X		X	X	X	
District of Columbia		X	X			
Florida			X			X
Georgia			X	X		X
Hawaii						
Idaho						X
Illinois		X		X	X	X
Indiana	X			X	X	X
Iowa						X
Kansas					X	
Kentucky	X			X		X
Louisiana	X		X			
Maine		X				
Maryland				X		
Massachusetts					X	X
Michigan		X	X		X	X
Minnesota		X			X	
Mississippi				X		
Missouri						X

(Continued)

Table 11.1 (Continued)

Jurisdiction	Mandatory transfer	Presumptive transfer	Direct file	Reverse transfer	Juvenile blended sentence	Adult blended sentence
Montana			X	X	X	X
Nebraska			X	X		X
Nevada		X		X		
New Hampshire		X				
New Jersey	X			X		
New Mexico					X	X
New York				X		
North Carolina	X			X		
North Dakota	X	X		X		
Ohio	X			X	X	
Oklahoma			X	X		X
Oregon				X		
Pennsylvania		X				
Rhode Island		X			X	
South Carolina	X			X		
South Dakota				X		
Tennessee						
Texas					X	
Utah		X				
Vermont				X		X
Virginia	X		X	X		X
Washington						
West Virginia	X			X		X
Wisconsin				X		X
Wyoming			X	X		

Source: Office of Juvenile Justice and Delinquency Prevention (2022).

TRANSFER TO ADULT COURT DOES NOT DETER JUVENILE DELINQUENCY

The transfer of juveniles to adult court serves the goal of incapacitation (see Chapter 6). It enables a state to incarcerate juveniles for long periods of time. However, transfers do not deter offenders. Research in New York state by Singer and McDowall (1988) and in Idaho by Jensen and Metsger (1994) found no deterrent effect on juvenile arrest statistics after transfer laws were enacted in those states.

New York passed a transfer law in 1978 that lowered the age of transfer to 13 for murder and 14 for assault, arson, burglary, kidnaping, and rape. Juvenile crime did not decline in the state of New York. Idaho passed its juvenile transfer law in 1981. Juvenile arrests in Idaho increased by 13 percent after that law went into effect. In contrast, juvenile arrests declined in the neighboring states of Montana and Wyoming, which did not yet have transfer laws.

Juvenile defendants who are transferred to adult court are more likely to reoffend after their release. Redding (2010) summarized this literature as follows: Six large studies, with sample sizes ranging from 494 to 5,476, all found that juveniles convicted in adult courts had higher recidivism rates than similar juveniles adjudicated delinquent in juvenile courts. That is, transfer to adult court did not deter crime, but may in fact have encouraged crime. Redding suggested four possible explanations:

- the stigmatization and other negative effects that come from being labeled a felon
- the sense of resentment and injustice that juveniles feel after being tried and punished as adults
- the schooling in criminal mores and behaviors that comes from being incarcerated with adult offenders
- the decreased emphasis on rehabilitation and family support that juveniles face in the adult system.

In the complex relationship between punishment and behavior, it seems likely that severe punishment can be counterproductive.

REFERENCES

American Psychiatric Association. (2022). *Diagnostic and Statistical Manual of Mental Disorders. Fifth edition. Text revision. DSM-5-TR.* Washington, D.C.: American Psychiatric Association.

Borum, R., Bartel, P., & Forth, A. (2002). *Manual for the structured assessment of violence risk in youth: Consultation version.* Tampa: University of South Florida, Florida Mental Health Institute.

Borum, R., Bartel, P., & Forth, A. (2006). *SAVRY: Structured assessment of violence risk in youth: Professional manual.* Lutz, Florida: Psychological Assessment Resources.

Forth, A. E., Kosson, D. S., & Hare, R. D. (2003). *The Hare Psychopathy Checklist: Youth Version.* Toronto: Multi-Health Systems.

Gallagher, C. A., & Dobrin, A. (2006). Deaths in juvenile justice residential facilities. *Journal of Adolescent Health, 38*(6), 662–668. doi:10.1016/J.JADOHEALTH.2005.01.002.

Gillen, T. A., MacDougall, E. A. M., Salekin, R. T., & Forth, A. (2015). The validity of the Risk-Sophistication-Treatment Inventory – Abbreviated (RSTI-A): Initial evidence in support of a measure designed for juvenile evaluations. *Psychology, Public Policy, and Law, 21*(2), 205–212. doi:10.1037/law0000044.

Hoge, R., & Andrews, D. (2002). *The Youth Level of Service/Case Management Inventory manual and scoring key.* Toronto: Multi-Health Systems.

In re Gault, 387 U.S. 1 (1967).

Iselin, A. M. R., & Salekin, R. T. (2008). *Risk-Sophistication-Treatment Inventory–Self Report.* Unpublished test. Tuscaloosa, AL: Department of Psychology, University of Alabama.

Jensen, E., & Metsger, L. (1994). A test of the deterrent effect of legislative waiver on violent juvenile crime. *Crime and Delinquency, 40*(1), 96–104. doi:10.1177/0011128794040001007.

Kent v. United States, 383 U.S. 541 (1966).

Juvenile Sentencing Project. (January 2020). Limiting transfer to adult court: Enhancing judicial oversight. Quinnipiac University School of Law. Retrieved 11/22/2022 from https://juvenilesentencingproject.org/wp-content/uploads/model_reforms_limiting_ransfers_to_adult_court.pdf.

Leistico, A. M., & Salekin, R. T. (2003). Testing the reliability and validity of the Risk, Sophistication-Maturity, and Treatment Amenability Instrument (RST-i): An assessment tool for juvenile offenders. *International Journal of Forensic Mental Health, 2*(2), 101–117. doi:10.1080/14999013.2003.10471182.

Office of Juvenile Justice and Delinquency Prevention. (2022). Provisions for imposing adult sanctions on minors, 2019. U.S. Department of Justice. Retrieved 11/22/2022 from www.ojjdp.gov/ojstatbb/structure_process/qa04115.asp.

Redding, R. E. (2010). Juvenile transfer laws: An effective deterrent to delinquency? *Juvenile Justice Bulletin.* U.S. Department of Justice, Office of Justice Programs, Office of Juvenile Justice and Delinquency Prevention. Retrieved 11/22/2022 from https://ojjdp.ojp.gov/library/publications/juvenile-transfer-laws-effective-deterrent-delinquency.

Roper v. Simmons, 543 U.S. 551 (2005).

Salekin, R. T. (2004). *Risk-Sophistication-Treatment Inventory (RSTI): Professional manual.* Lutz, FL: Psychological Assessment Resources.

Salekin, R. T. (2012). *Risk-Sophistication-Treatment Inventory – Abbreviated.* Unpublished clinical rating measure. Tuscaloosa, AL: Department of Psychology, University of Alabama.

Scott, E., & Steinberg, L. (2008). *Rethinking juvenile justice.* Cambridge, MA: Harvard University Press.

Singer, S., & McDowall, D. (1988). Criminalizing delinquency: The deterrent effects of the New York Juvenile Offender Law. *Law and Society Review*, 22(3), 521–536. doi:10.2307/3053628.

Snyder, H. N. (1997). *Juvenile arrests 1995*. Washington, D.C.: U.S. Department of Justice, Office of Justice Programs, Office of Juvenile Justice and Delinquency Prevention.

State v. Aalim (Aalim I), 150 Ohio St.3d 463, 2016-Ohio-8278, 83 N.E.3d 862 (2016).

State v. Aalim (Aalim II), 150 Ohio St. 3d 489 (2017).

State v. Quarterman, 140 Ohio St.3d 464, 2014-Ohio-4034 (2014).

Tavil, P. (2017–2018). Mandatory transfer of juveniles to adult court: A deviation from the purpose of the juvenile justice system and a violation of their eight amendment rights. *Revista Jurídica UIPR*, 52(2), 377–409.

Part III

Due process after conviction

A number of psycholegal questions and due process rights may pertain after a defendant has been convicted of a crime. Six of these areas are reviewed in Part III:

- prediction of future violence (cases include *Baxstrom v. Herold*, 1966)
- mitigation (cases include *Lockett v. Ohio*, 1978)
- juvenile sentencing (cases include *Miller v. Alabama*, 2012)
- sexually violent predators (cases include *Kansas v. Hendricks*, 1997)
- the death penalty for persons who have intellectual developmental disorder (IDD; cases include *Atkins v. Virginia*, 2002)
- competency to be executed (cases include *Ford v. Wainwright*, 1986).

These six issues are reviewed in Chapters 12 through 18. Where psychometric tests have been developed to assist in answering these questions, these tests are reviewed and evaluated.

DOI: 10.4324/9781003385028-14

12 Assessing risk of violence

Expert opinions regarding risk of future violence are sought in a variety of judicial and correctional contexts. Juvenile courts use predictions of future violence to determine sentencing (see Chapter 15) and transfer to adult court (see Chapter 11). Parole boards use predictions of dangerousness to determine whether prisoners can be released. Courts use predictions of violence to determine pardons, certificates of rehabilitation, expungement of records, and sentencing including capital punishment.

SUBJECTIVE EVALUATIONS BY MENTAL HEALTH PROFESSIONALS ARE NOT GOOD PREDICTORS OF VIOLENCE: *BAXSTROM V HEROLD* (U.S. 1966)

Johnnie Baxstrom was found guilty of assault and he was sentenced to 30 to 36 months in prison. While in prison he developed a mental illness and was transferred to Dannemora State Hospital, a maximum security prison hospital operated by the New York Department of Correction. When Baxstrom reached the end of his sentence on December 18, 1961, the New York Department of Correction believed that he still had a mental illness and they tried to transfer him to a civil hospital run by the New York Department of Mental Hygiene. The staff of the civil hospital did not consider Baxstrom suitable for commitment, and they did not accept him. The Department of Correction chose to keep Baxstrom at Dannemora rather than release him, even though he had completed his sentence.

Baxstrom argued that his right to liberty was being violated and he petitioned for his release. Not only did the U.S. Supreme Court decide to release Johnnie Baxstrom, but they also released 966 other inmates from Dannemora State Hospital. Those inmates who had not yet completed their sentences were returned to the general prison population. Those who had completed their sentences were returned to the community. Many of those prisoners had been at Dannemora for years.

DOI: 10.4324/9781003385028-15

Social scientists Henry Steadman and Joseph Cocozza (1974, 1978) knew a good research topic when they saw one. They perceived *Baxstrom* as a grand natural experiment in the ability of psychiatrists to predict violent behavior. They followed those 967 inmates for four years and found that 21 percent committed an assault either in prison or in the community. Twenty percent were re-arrested. Only 3 percent were deemed sufficiently violent to be returned to a maximum security institution. Only 2 percent were convicted of a new crime involving assault. The large majority of inmates who had been considered dangerous by the psychiatrists of Dannemora State Hospital did not go on to commit another act of violence. Apparently the U.S. Supreme Court was correct and the State of New York had put too much faith in the ability of psychiatrists to predict future violence.

THE MEEHL CONTROVERSY: CLINICAL VS. STATISTICAL PREDICTION

In what became known as "the Meehl controversy," psychologist Paul Meehl (1954) reported that actuarial predictions of human behavior are more accurate than subjective predictions by experts. Meehl's book stirred up considerable controversy and wounded a lot of professional egos. He later referred to it as "my disturbing little book" (Meehl, 1986). If a simple set of numbers consistently outperforms the work of experts with decades of training and experience, then what good is all that training and experience? It was the social science version of the folk legend about John Henry and the steam drill, and, if you know the legend, you know that things did not turn out well for John Henry.

Meehl in 1954 sampled predictions from a variety of educational, correctional, military, and vocational sources including success in elementary school, success on parole, success as an aircraft pilot, success in Electricians Mate's School, and adjustment of inmates in a reformatory. The science of predicting violent behavior took another step toward the use of actuarial methods in 1977 with the publication of John Monahan's book, *The Clinical Prediction of Violent Behavior*. Today actuarial methods for predicting violence are a permanent part of the landscape and are widely used in courts and corrections to render verdicts and to assign inmates to maximum, medium, or minimum security prisons.

In 2000, when Grove et al. revisited the topic of actuarial assessment, they were able to identify 136 studies that compared clinical vs. actuarial assessment. Eight of those studies favored clinical assessment, 63 favored actuarial assessment, and 65 showed no significant difference.

METHODS FOR ASSESSING RISK OF VIOLENCE

After professionally embarrassing moments like the *Baxstrom* decision and Meehl's "disturbing little book," social scientists began to seek methodologically sound ways to improve our predictions of violence. The movement toward standardized assessment was led by psychologist Saleem Shah in his role as director of the National Institute of Mental Health Center for Studies of Crime and Delinquency. With Dr. Shah's consultation, the first standardized assessments of violence risk appeared (as well as the first standardized assessments of competency to stand trial and comprehension of Miranda rights; see Rogers & Fiduccia, 2015). By 2008, mental health professionals had developed 457 instruments for assessing risk of violence (Guy, 2008). In this chapter we will review a handful of those instruments that have been most frequently used and studied in forensic assessment. (Other methods not discussed here are reviewed by Otto and Douglas, 2010. These include methods designed specifically for use with juveniles, violent adults, and adult sex offenders. See also Monahan et al., 2005, whose work with the MacArthur Foundation produced a risk assessment tool designed specifically for prediction of violence among offenders with mental illness.)

Risk assessment methods can be classified under three headings:

1 Clinical methods like the Psychopathy Checklist (PCL; Hare, 1980) and its progeny. The use of these instruments requires detailed administration by a trained mental health clinician.
2 Actuarial methods like the Violence Risk Appraisal Guide (VRAG; Quinsey et al., 1998); the Sex Offender Risk Appraisal Guide (SORAG; Quinsey et al., 1998); the Violence Risk Appraisal Guide-Revised (VRAG-R; Harris et al., 2015); the Rapid Risk Assessment for Sexual Offense Recidivism (RRASOR; Hanson, 1997); and the Static-99 (Hanson, 1997) and its progeny: the Static-99R, Static-2002, and Static-2002R (see Helmus et al., 2021). (The word "static" in this context refers to variables that do not change, like age of victim, gender of victim, and age at offense. Factors that change over time – for example, stress level – are called "dynamic" variables.)

   Some of the scoring of actuarial instruments requires the input of a trained mental health professional. Scoring the VRAG and SORAG requires a clinical diagnosis, if one exists, and a PCL score, which requires input from a trained clinician. Scoring the VRAG-R requires Facet 4 of the PCL-R, which must be administered by a trained clinician. Otherwise, the input, output, and analysis of these instruments can be performed by clerical personnel.
3 Structured Professional Judgments (SPJs) like the Historical Clinical Risk – 20 (HCR-20; Webster et al., 1997) and the Sexual Violence Risk – 20 (SVR-20; Boer et al., 1997).

   SPJs require interpretation by professional clinicians. The clinician using an SPJ considers an array of variables that have been demonstrated by research to be linked to violent behavior. These include static variables as well as situational and immediate variables that are dynamic. In this respect, they may represent the best of both worlds between clinical and actuarial prediction.

SPJs can be scored quantitatively, but these quantitative scores are used in research only. In clinical practice, the SPJs are interpreted qualitatively. The flexibility of their use is an important aspect of their utility. Risk of violence is not static, as it fluctuates over time. SPJs allow for fluid interpretation and may be preferred especially in the assessment of short-term risk of violence.

These methods for assessing risk of violence will be presented here in the chronological order in which they appeared. Before readers begin to think that risk assessment is a dry mathematical exercise, please allow me to point out that expert opinion regarding predictions of violence has been a matter of life and death in capital murder cases such as *Jurek v. Texas* (1976) and *Estelle v. Smith* (1981), both of which are discussed in Chapter 13.

The Hare Psychopathy Check List (PCL) and its progeny

An early method for assessing risk of violence – and one that is still widely used today in its revised form – is the Hare Psychopathy Checklist (PCL), developed in 1980 by Professor Robert Hare of the University of British Columbia. When it was first developed, the PCL was not intended to be used as a risk assessment tool but rather as a method for measuring psychopathy as it was described by psychiatrist Hervey Cleckley (1941/1988) of Augusta, Georgia. It was only after the PCL had been developed that it was appreciated for its utility in predicting violent behavior.

Scoring the PCL requires a review of the defendant's records. Because defendants tend to prevaricate, the PCL is not scored on the basis of a defendant's self-report alone. A clinical interview is not required, but it does help the clinician assess certain variables like glibness, superficial charm, and shallow affect.

The success of the PCL in measuring psychopathy and predicting violence has led to two revisions (PCL-R, Hare, 1991a; PCL-R second edition, Hare, 2003); an unpublished self-report version (Hare, 1991b); a condensed screening version (PCL:SV; Hart et al., 1995); a youth version (PDL:YV; Forth et al., 2003); a non-clinical assessment of psychopathic traits (P-SCAN; Hare & Hervé, 1999); and a screening test for children ages 6 to 13 (Antisocial Process Screening Device; APSD; Frick & Hare, 2001).

Factor analysis with the PCL has revealed a two-factor structure (Harpur et al., 1988, 1989). Factor 1 has been called the "Interpersonal/

Affective" factor and includes eight variables. Hare (2003) split these eight variables into Facet 1 (Interpersonal) and Facet 2 (Affective), as follows:

Facet 1: Interpersonal

- glibness/superficial charm
- grandiose sense of self worth
- pathological lying
- conning/manipulative

Facet 2: Affective

- lack of remorse or guilt
- shallow affect
- callous/lack of empathy
- failure to accept responsibility for own actions.

Factor 2 has been called "Social Deviance" and includes ten variables, which Hare (2003) split into Facets 3 (Lifestyle) and 4 (Antisocial) as follows:

Facet 3: Lifestyle

- need for stimulation/proneness to boredom
- parasitic lifestyle
- lack of realistic, long-term goals
- impulsivity
- irresponsibility.

Facet 4: Antisocial

- poor behavioral controls
- early behavioral problems
- juvenile delinquency
- revocation of conditional release
- criminal versatility.

Salekin et al.'s (1996) meta-analysis of 18 studies examined whether the PCL and PCL-R can predict recidivism. They reported a Cohen's d of 0.55 (moderate effect) for general recidivism and 0.79 (moderate effect) for violent recidivism. (Please see Appendix O for an introduction to the statistics that are used to evaluate psychometric tests.)

In a meta-analysis of 34 samples, Guy et al. (2010) reported an AUC of 0.69 ($d = 0.70$, moderate effect) for the PCL-R.

A meta-analysis of 32 samples ($N = 10,555$) by Kennealy et al. (2010) found that effect sizes were generally low but were higher for PCL-R

Factor 2 (Social Deviance; AUC = 0.61, *d* = 0.40, small effect) than for Factor 1 (Interpersonal/Affective; (AUC = 0.53, *d* = 0.11, negligible effect).

Singh et al. (2011) found the PCL-R to have a median AUC of .66 (moderate effect), which was the lowest AUC of the nine instruments analyzed in that study.

Schwalbe (2007) analyzed studies of the PCL:YV and found it to have an AUC of 0.70 (moderate effect).

In summary, the Hare Psychopathy Checklists in their various incarnations are an important feature of the assessment landscape. They are widely used and widely studied in the psychological assessment of defendants and in the prediction of criminal behavior. Also, a defendant's PCL-R score is used in a number of actuarial and SPJ assessments, such as the VRAG, VRAG-R, HCR-20, and SVR-20, all of which are considered below.

In 2020, in a series of four papers written by two opposing camps, the PCL-R came under intense scrutiny regarding the prediction of serious institutional violence in capital sentencing. This question is an important one, because serious institutional violence is a factor that courts consider when determining capital punishment. According to this reasoning, if a defendant is so immutably violent that they are likely to harm people even in prison, then they might as well receive the death penalty.

A position paper (a "Statement of Concerned Experts") by DeMatteo et al. (2020a) argued that the PCL-R is not robust enough to be used to predict serious violence in prisons. They based their arguments on (1) the low interrater reliability of the PCL-R (which is around .60 for violent offenders); (2) the effects of "adversarial allegiance" (i.e., experts hired by the prosecution generate higher PCL-R scores than experts hired by the defense); and (3) the limited ability of the PCL-R to predict future violence (with effect sizes of 0.30 to 0.35).

A second group of experts, Olver et al. (2020), questioned DeMatteo et al.'s (2020a) evaluation of the PCL-R's psychometric properties, presented new evidence, including a meta-analysis and a meta-meta-analysis, and argued against the assertion that the PCL-R cannot be used in high-stakes contexts.

The contest went back and forth with two more volleys. DeMatteo et al. (2020b) dismissed the concerns expressed by Olver et al. (2020), asserting that Olver et al. (2020) agreed with their main points, and arguing that the areas of disagreement were "of little consequence" (DeMatteo et al., 2020b, p. 512). In their opinion, Olver et al. had mischaracterized their statement and had failed to understand the law related to capital sentencing evaluations. Regarding Olver et al.'s meta-analysis and meta-meta-analysis, they argued that these analyses were not relevant because they included tests other than the PCL-R and outcome criteria other than serious institutional violence. Regarding the argument that they had not defined what level of "precision and accuracy" would be sufficient for a psychometric test, they pointed out that no specific threshold exists and that this threshold varies with context (e.g., the high stakes of capital sentencing; 2020, p. 514).

Hare et al. (2020) countered that DeMatteo et al.'s arguments underestimated the reliability and predictive validity of PCL–R ratings and overestimated the centrality of the PCL–R in sentencing decisions. They argued that DeMatteo et al. had based most of their arguments on mock trials, sexually violent predator hearings, and the prediction of general violence and therefore were not relevant to the question of capital punishment. Hare et al. concluded that there was insufficient basis for the bold statement that the PCL-R "cannot and should not be used" (DeMatteo et al., 2020b, p. 511) to predict serious institutional violence in capital sentencing.

The Violence Risk Appraisal Guide (VRAG), Sex Offender Risk Appraisal Guide (SORAG), and Violence Risk Appraisal Guide – Revised (VRAG-R)

The VRAG and SORAG were developed by Quinsey et al. (1998) at Queens University in Ontario. The VRAG consists of twelve items and the SORAG has fourteen items. There is an overlap of ten items between the two guides, which invited the question of whether they could be combined into a single instrument. This combination was accomplished in the third edition of their book (Harris et al., 2015) and was named the VRAG-R. The VRAG-R comprises twelve items which include Facet 4 (Antisocial) of the PCL-R. The twelve items are:

1 whether the subject lived with both biological parents until age 16
2 elementary school maladjustment
3 history of alcohol or drug problems
4 marital status at the time of the offense
5 criminal history for non-violent offenses (as scored by the Cormier-Lang system, Harris et al., 2015)
6 failure on conditional release
7 age at the offense
8 criminal history for violent offenses (as scored by the Cormier-Lang system; Harris et al., 2015)
9 number of prior admissions to correctional institutions
10 history of conduct disorder before age 15
11 sex offending history
12 Facet 4 (Antisocial) of the PCL-R.

Please note that the first eleven items of the VRAG-R are static. Facet 4 (Antisocial) of the PCL-R is a combination of static and dynamic factors: Early behavioral problems and history of juvenile delinquency are static by the time a defendant has reached adulthood; poor behavioral controls may fluctuate during the course of a defendant's lifetime.

AUC values for the VRAG have ranged from 0.60 (small effect; Rice & Harris, 1995) to 0.84 (large effect; Quinsey et al., 2006). Larger effect sizes have been obtained when larger samples were used, when cases with missing data were eliminated, and when the subject pool was restricted to include rapists only.

The VRAG-R was found to have a large effect size, with an AUC of .76 (Harris et al., 2015).

Structured professional judgments (SPJs)

Structured professional judgments (SPJs) allow the evaluator to consider an array of variables that empirical research has connected to violent behavior. SPJs typically combine static and dynamic factors. Quantitative scoring systems can be applied as if SPJs were actuarial instruments, and this has been accomplished in a number of research studies with variable results, as reviewed below. In the clinic, however, SPJs are not scored quantitatively but are interpreted qualitatively. This flexibility of individual interpretation and short-term prediction may make SPJs superior instruments for use in clinical practice.

Christopher Webster at Simon Fraser University, and his colleagues, published two well-known SPJs in 1997: the Historical Clinical and Risk Management – 20 (HCR-20; Webster et al., 1997) and the Sexual Violence Risk – 20 (SVR-20; Boer et al., 1997). The acronym "HCR" represents three categories of variables: "Historical," "Clinical," and "Risk Management." The ten Historical items of the HCR are based on past behavior and therefore are "static" variables.

The ten Historical factors of the HCR-20 are:

1 history of previous violence
2 age at first violent incident
3 relationship instability
4 employment problems
5 substance use problems
6 major mental illness
7 psychopathy (i.e., the score from the PCL-R or PCL:SV)
8 early maladjustment
9 personality disorder
10 history of supervision failure.

The five Clinical items and five Risk Management items are dynamic in nature. The five Clinical items of the HCR-20 are:

1 lack of insight
2 negative attitudes
3 active symptoms of major mental illness
4 impulsivity
5 unresponsiveness to treatment.

The five Risk Management items of the HCR-20 are:

1 feasibility of safety plan
2 exposure to destabilizers
3 lack of personal support
4 non-compliance with remediation attempts
5 stress.

By including highly fluid items like "stress" and "destabilizers," an SPJ can be more flexible than an actuarial method that relies almost entirely on static variables. Overwhelming stress can override a subject's defense mechanisms and may result in an act of violence. A subject's level of stress can change from moment to moment and can be essential in understanding their risk of violence, which can make SPJs more individualized and more useful than actuarial methods in the clinical assessment of short-term risk of violence.

- In a study of 97 incarcerated male offenders, HCR-20 scores yielded an AUC of 0.57 (small effect) for major institutional misconduct and an AUC of 0.62 (small effect) for violent recidivism after release (Kroner & Mills, 2001).
- A Dutch sample of treated sex offenders (de Vogel et al., 2004) found the SVR-20 to have an AUC = .80 (large effect) and the Static-99 to have an AUC = .71 (large effect).
- In a meta-analysis of 34 samples, Guy et al. (2010) reported an AUC of 0.69 ($d = 0.70$, moderate effect) for the HCR-20.
- Singh et al. (2011) found the SVR-20 to have a median AUC of .78, which is a large effect and was the highest AUC of the nine risk assessment instruments they studied.
- Researchers at a forensic psychiatric hospital in Denmark found the HCR-20 to have an AUC of 0.68 (moderate effect; Pedersen et al., 2012). Commenting on the moderate performance of the HCR-20 in their study, the authors observed that in their hospital setting high risk of violence resulted in "intensive" efforts to contain the violent

behavior, thereby confounding risk of violence with treatment efforts and possibly lowering the predictive validity of the HCR-20 (Pedersen et al., 2012, p. 742).

- Vojt et al. (2013) found the HCR-20 to have an AUC of 0.86 (large effect) in predicting serious incidents.
- Lofthouse et al. (2013) studied an SPJ that was designed to assess the risk of sexual re-offending among persons with intellectual disabilities – the Assessment of Risk and Manageability of Individuals with Developmental and Intellectual Limitations who Offend – Sexually (ARMIDILO-S) – and found it to have a large effect (AUC = 0.92) among a group of 64 adult males, outperforming the Static-99 (AUC = 0.75) and the VRAG (AUC = 0.58).

Summary: Evaluating risk assessment instruments

As reported above, studies of the receiver operating characteristics (ROCs) of risk assessment instruments have yielded effect sizes that range from large to negligible. The largest values – AUC $\geq$ .80 – have been found for the VRAG, SVR-20, and ARMADILO-S. Lower values have been found for the PCL-R, HCR-20, and Static-99. Whether these instruments are powerful enough to be used in court is a question for the judges who serve as gatekeepers in deciding whether to allow expert testimony into the courtroom (see *Daubert v. Merrell Dow Pharmaceuticals*, 1993, discussed in Chapter 3), and also a question for individual mental health professionals as they decide which tests to use, how to interpret them, and how much weight to give them in developing their opinions.

RISK OF VIOLENCE, SEVERE MENTAL ILLNESS, AND SUBSTANCE ABUSE

The long-standing impression among the general public has been that people who have a severe mental illness like schizophrenia are more dangerous than the rest of society. This impression is likely fueled by their extreme and unpredictable behavior, and by the salience of assassinations and assassination attempts against public figures. A number of these cases involving monarchs and other public figures are described in this book: *Hadfield* (see Chapter 20), *M'Naghten* (see Chapter 20), *White* (see Chapter 21), *Hinckley* (see Chapter 22), *Bellingham* (see Appendix H), and *Oxford* (see Appendix I).

In contrast to this public impression, the long-standing wisdom among mental health professionals was that people with mental illness were no more violent than the general public (Monahan, 1977/1995). The first empirical evidence that people who have schizophrenia are slightly more violent than the general public was published by Jeffrey Swanson of Duke

University, using data from the Epidemiological Catchment Area (ECA) study conducted by the National Institute of Mental Health. This was a large survey of mental health data collected between 1980 and 1985, drawn from 20,861 subjects in five states and spanning the country from north to south and east to west (Swanson et al., 1990). After Swanson et al. published the results of the ECA, Monahan publicly recanted and acknowledged that, as a group, people who have schizophrenia are slightly more violent than the rest of society.

Further epidemiological research by Bruce Link of Columbia University and his colleagues replicated this finding – the vast majority of people who have mental illness do not commit acts of violence, but as a group people who have severe mental illness are slightly more violent than the rest of society (Link et al., 1992; Link & Stueve, 1994; and Stueve & Link, 1997).

More recent research has continued to establish the connection between mental illness and violence. Silverstein et al. reviewed this literature in 2015 and found mixed results, but concluded that people who have schizophrenia are more likely to commit acts of violence due to the specific nature of their symptoms. They also concluded that risk of violence among persons with schizophrenia is increased by brain abnormalities, psychiatric comorbidities, and demographic factors not related to schizophrenia.

Roché et al. (2018) reviewed 63,572 intake records for evidence of violent ideation and behavior (VIB). These inpatients had a variety of conditions including serious mental illness (SMI, defined as schizophrenia, schizoaffective disorder, bipolar disorder, and unipolar depression), non-SMI psychopathology, and substance use disorders. Their analysis revealed that patients with SMI had higher rates of VIB than patients with non-SMI psychopathology and patients with substance use disorders only, and that patients who had both SMI and a substance use disorder were responsible for most of the VIB. Additional effects were found for age, race, and gender.

Further research has attempted to identify what it is about people with mental illness that makes them more violent. Work by Swanson et al. indicated that the positive symptoms of schizophrenia (like delusions of persecution) increase the risk of violence, whereas the negative symptoms of schizophrenia (like social withdrawal) actually decrease risk of violence (Swanson et al., 2006; see Chapter 26 for a discussion of the positive and negative symptoms of schizophrenia.)

Proper investigation into the links between mental illness and violence needs to include important third variables that are known to potentiate violence, including substance abuse and victimization. Eric Silver of Penn State University, and his colleagues, followed 1,136 psychiatric patients after their release from the hospital for one year and compared them with 519 community controls. They found a strong relationship between violence and substance abuse. The psychiatric patients who did not abuse substances were no more violent than the rest of the community. In both the psychiatric and non-psychiatric groups, however, substance abusers accounted for most of the acts of violence. Psychiatric patients were more likely to abuse substances (perhaps as a form of self-medication), which may help to explain why they were more violent (Silver et al., 1999; Steadman et al., 1998).

The link between violence and substance abuse is well-established. A meta-meta-analysis of thirty-two previous meta-analyses by Duke et al. (2018) – embracing several thousand studies published between 1985 and 2014 – demonstrated the strong connection between substance abuse and violence.

Research with the North Carolina segment of the ECA (N = 3,438) indicated that the connection between mental illness and violence is mediated by stressful life events and impaired social supports (Silver & Teasdale, 2005). Persons with severe mental illness lead stressful lives, and they are often victimized. Hiday et al. (1999) found that people with severe mental illness are 2.5 times more likely to be victims of violence than people who do not have severe mental illness (8.2 percent vs. 3.1 percent). Persons who have been victims of violence are more likely to become violent themselves (Widom, 1989).

Often persons with severe mental illness are cut off by their families and other social supports. Their families tend to "burn out" with them, stop communicating, and stop supporting them because of their erratic behaviors and impossible demands. The support given to these families by the rest of society is not sufficient. When a person with severe mental illness behaves violently, it may be reactive in nature, related to stress, and the relationship of their illness to their violence may be only indirect, mediated by the stressful nature of their lives.

A large study (Elbogen & Johnson, 2009; N = 34,653) conducted between 2001 and 2005 by the National Institute on Alcohol Abuse and Alcoholism indicated that mental illness itself did not contribute to violence. People who had severe mental illness did commit more acts of violence, but only if there was (1) co-occurring substance abuse and/or dependence; (2) a history of past violence, juvenile detention, physical abuse, or parental arrest record; (3) perceived threats to their own safety; or (4) contextual factors like divorce, unemployment, or victimization. People who have mental illness lead stressful lives and they were more likely to have these stress factors in their histories or in their current life circumstances.

These findings hold implications for prevention and rehabilitation. If we can find ways to reduce stress and increase social support for persons with mental illness – and their families – we may be able to prevent acts of violence. Treatment approaches that are designed to reduce the risk of violence among persons with mental illness were reviewed by Douglas et al. (2009), who listed a number of approaches deemed most promising on the basis of the limited research available.

PREDICTING RECIDIVISM AMONG CONVICTED SEX OFFENDERS

Psychometric methods for predicting risk of sexual violence include the SORAG, RRASOR, Static-99, SVR-20, and ARMADILO-S. These were discussed above in the review of risk assessment instruments. The following case history illustrates the use of the revised version of the Static-99.

Case study #10: Eli – pardoning a paroled sex offender

At the age of 39, Eli was questioned by the police and he admitted that he had several sexual encounters with an underage boy. He had not known that the boy was underage. The boy looked older than his real age, acted like an adult, already was sexually active, and had wanted the sexual contact with Eli. (Sexual relations with a minor who looks like an adult and who consents to the act is an example of a strict liability crime, i.e., a crime that does not entail mens rea; see Chapter 7.) The boy had been arrested on an unrelated charge, and while he was in police custody he had told the authorities about his sexual encounters with Eli. When Eli was questioned by police, he admitted his crime immediately. (This is almost unheard of in my experience with sex offenders, who generally deny all wrongdoing.) The detectives gave Eli the opportunity to turn himself in, and he did so. His prior criminal history consisted of a fraudulent check and driving on a suspended license.

Eli pleaded guilty to sex with a minor and spent the next 21 months in prison. After his release he had supervised parole for another 13 months. Upon his release from parole he sought a pardon from the governor of his state, and he retained me for a forensic mental health evaluation. If pardoned he would no longer be a felon, his name would come off the sex offender registry, and new opportunities would open up for him in terms of employment and his social life. In order to be pardoned by the governor, he first had to obtain a Certificate of Rehabilitation from a Superior Court judge, and according to the law of his state this required a forensic mental health evaluation.

This was Eli's second attempt at getting a Certificate of Rehabilitation. The Superior Court Judge had been critical of Eli's first mental health report because it had been written by an unlicensed psychologist (who had a doctoral degree in psychology but had not obtained a license) and because the first psychologist had not used any psychometric testing. (I was most gratified to see this judge's faith in professional licensing and psychometric testing!)

My evaluation of Eli covered the relevant facts of his life, his sexual history, the nature of the offense, his incarceration and sex offender treatment, and his conduct since his release. Eli, a Black male, never married and he has no children. He graduated from high school and took some college courses. He had a good work history for 20 years before he was arrested.

Eli had no relationship with his biological father. He was adopted by his maternal uncle and aunt while his mother lived elsewhere. From the ages of 6 to 17, he was sexually abused by several men. When he reached the age of majority he continued to have sex with men, but he was never comfortable with it (ego dystonia), and he stopped having sex with men when he was arrested.

Eli denied having any other history of sexual relations with underage partners. He denied having any history of sexual fantasies about children. I administered a battery of psychometric tests: the Minnesota Multiphasic Personality Inventory – 2 (MMPI-2), the Multiphasic Sex Inventory II (MSI II), and the Static-99R. Eli was depressed in mood and he suffered profound feelings of rejection, but he did not have any other history of mental health difficulties. Regarding his offense, it was my opinion that loneliness and depression had made him susceptible to attention from an attractive partner. I saw no indication that any of his sexual encounters had been predatory, malicious, or psychopathic in nature. The victim's statement to the police did not suggest any form of coercion. I had no reason to suspect that these encounters were anything but consensual. I recommended that Eli receive mental health services for depressed mood.

Because of research that followed a group of 466 convicted Black male sex offenders for five years (Lee et al., 2016), I was able to state in my report that Black male sex offenders had a low recidivism rate (6.4 percent). The penal code of Eli's state recognizes the Static-99R as the preferred method of sex offender risk assessment. Eli's score on the Static-99R was 2. I was able to include in my report that Lee et al. found that parolees of all races with a score of 2 (N = 1,198) had a five-year recidivism rate of only 2.1 percent. (This is the kind of risk assessment tool and statistic that were needed in the era of Johnnie Baxstrom but were not available at that time).

It is not surprising that Eli's risk of recidivism is so low. Ex-convicts do not want to return to prison, and sex offenders especially do not want to return to prison (where they are treated harshly by other inmates, many of whom were victims of child abuse themselves). The Superior Court judge granted Eli his Certificate of Rehabilitation. His petition went to the governor, where it awaits signature. Meanwhile, the law changed in Eli's state in 2021, and sex offenders are now classified as Tier 1, Tier 2, or Tier 3, based on the seriousness of their offense. As a Tier 1 sex offender, Eli was required to register for ten years, which he has completed. His name no longer appears on the sex offender registry.

In the course of preparing this chapter, I contacted Eli and obtained his permission to share his story. He told me that he is doing well but that his childhood experiences have left him with a profound sense of rejection, from which he is still recovering. He expects this healing to go on for the rest of his life.

(Please note that nothing in this section is intended to imply that gay men present a disproportionate risk to children. For a discussion of this topic, see Schlatter and Steinback, 2010.)

REFERENCES

Baxstrom v. Herold, 383 U.S. 107 (1966).

Boer, D. P., Hart, S. D., Kropp, P. R., & Webster, C. D. (1997). *Manual for the Sexual Violence Risk-20: Professional guidelines for assessing risk of sexual violence.* Vancouver, Canada: The Mental Health, Law, and Policy Institute, Simon Fraser University.

Cleckley, H. (1941/1988). *The mask of sanity. Fifth edition.* St. Louis, MI: Mosby.

Daubert v. Merrell Dow Pharmaceuticals, Inc., 509 U.S. 579 (1993).

de Vogel, V., de Ruiter, C., van Beek, D., & Mead, G. (2004). Predictive validity of the SVR-20 and Static-99 in a Dutch sample of treated sex offenders. *Law and Human Behavior*, 28(3), 235–251. doi: 10.1023/b:lahu.0000029137.41974.eb.

DeMatteo, D., Hart, S. D., Heilbrun, K., Boccaccini, M. T., Cunningham, M. D., Douglas, K. S., Dvoskin, J. A., Edens, J. F., Guy, L. S., Murrie, D. C., Otto, R. K., Packer, I. K., & Reidy, T. J. (2020a). Statement of concerned experts on the use of the Hare Psychopathy Checklist-Revised in capital sentencing to assess risk for institutional violence. *Psychology, Public Policy, and Law*, 26(2), 133–144. doi: 10.1037/law0000223.

DeMatteo, D., Hart, S. D., Heilbrun, K., Boccaccini, M. T., Cunningham, M. D., Douglas, K. S., Dvoskin, J. A., Edens, J. F., Guy, L. S., Murrie, D. C., Otto, R. K., Packer, I. K., & Reidy, T. J. (2020b). Death is different: Reply to Olver et al. (2020). *Psychology, Public Policy, and Law*, 26, 511–518. doi: 10.1037/law0000285.

Douglas, K. S., Nicholls, T. L., & Brink, J. (2009). Reducing the risk of violence among people with serious mental illness: A critical analysis of treatment approaches. In P. M. Kleespies (Ed.) *Behavioral emergencies: An evidence-based resource for evaluating and managing risk of suicide, violence, and victimization* (pp. 351–376). Washington, D.C.: American Psychological Association. doi:10.1037/11865-016.

Duke, A. A., Smith, K., Oberleitner, L. M. S., Westphal, A., & McKee, S. A. (2018). Alcohol, drugs, and violence: A meta-meta-analysis. *Psychology of Violence, 8*(2), 238–249. doi:10.1037/vio0000106.

Elbogen, E. B., & Johnson, S. C. (2009). The intricate link between violence and mental disorder: Results from the National Epidemiologic Survey on Alcohol and Related Conditions. *Archives of General Psychiatry, 66*(2), 152–161. doi:10.1001/archgenpsychiatry.2008.537.

Estelle v. Smith, 451 U.S. 454 (1981).

Forth, A. E., Kosson, D. S., & Hare, R. D. (2003). *The Hare Psychopathy Checklist: Youth Version.* Toronto: Multi-Health Systems.

Frick, P. J., & Hare, R. D. (2001). *Antisocial Process Screening Device.* Toronto: Multi-Health Systems.

Grove, W. M., Zald, D. H., Lebow, B. S., Snitz, B. E., & Nelson, C. (2000). Clinical versus mechanical prediction: A meta-analysis. *Psychological Assessment, 12*(1), 19–30. PMID: 10752360.

Guy, L. S. (2008). *Performance indicators of the structured professional judgement approach for assessing risk for violence to others: A meta-analytic survey.* Unpublished doctoral dissertation. Simon Fraser University, Burnaby, British Columbia, Canada.

Guy, L. S., Douglas, K. S., & Hendry, M. (2010). The role of psychopathic personality disorder in violence risk assessments using the HCR-20. *Journal of Personality Disorders, 24*(5), 551–580. doi:10.1521/pedi.2010.24.5.551.

Hanson, R. K. (1997). *The development of a brief actuarial risk scale for sexual offense recidivism.* User Report 97-04. Ottawa, ON, Canada. Department of the Solicitor General of Canada.

Hare, R. D. (1980). A research scale for the assessment of psychopathy in criminal populations. *Personality and Individual Differences, 1*(2), 111–119. doi:10.1016/0191-8869(80)90028-8.

Hare, R. D. (1991a). *The Hare Psychopathy Checklist – Revised.* Toronto: Multi-Health Systems.

Hare, R. D. (1991b). *The Self-Report Psychopathy Scale – II.* Unpublished test. University of British Columbia, Vancouver, British Columbia, Canada.

Hare, R. D. (2003). *The Hare Psychopathy Checklist – Revised. Second edition.* Toronto: Multi-Health Systems.

Hare, R. D., & Hervé, H. (1999). *Hare P-Scan: Research version.* Toronto: Multi-Health Systems.

Hare, R. D., Olver, M. E., Stockdale, K. C., Neumann, C. S., Mokros, A., Baskin-Sommers, A., Brand, E., Folino, J., Gacono, C., Gray, N. S., Kiehl, K., Knight, R., Leon-Mayer, E., Logan, M., Meloy, J. R., Roy, S., Salekin, R. T., Snowden, R. J., Thomson, N., Tillem, S., Vitacco, M., & Yoon, D. (2020). The PCL–R and capital sentencing: A commentary on "Death is different" DeMatteo et al. (2020a). *Psychology, Public Policy, and Law*, 26(4), 519–522. doi:10.1037/law0000290.

Harpur, T. J., Hakstian, A. R., & Hare, R. D. (1988). Factor structure of the Psychopathy Checklist. *Journal of Consulting and Clinical Psychology*, 56(5), 741–747. doi:10.1037/0022-006X.56.5.741.

Harpur, T. J., Hare, R. D., & Hakstian, A. R. (1989). Two-factor conceptualization of psychopathy: Construct validity and assessment implications. *Psychological Assessment: A Journal of Consulting and Clinical Psychology*, 1(1), 6–17. doi:10.1037/1040-3590.1.1.6.

Harris, G. T., Rice, M. E., Quinsey, V. L., & Cormier, C. A. (2015). *Violent offenders: Appraising and managing risk. Third edition.* Washington, D.C.: American Psychological Association.

Hart, S. D., Cox, D. N., & Hare, R. D. (1995). *The Hare Psychopathy Checklist: Screening Version.* Toronto: Multi-Health Systems.

Helmus, L. M., Lee, S. C., Phenix, A., Hanson, R. K., & Thornton, D. (2021). *Static-99R & Static-2002R evaluators' workbook.* Published by the Society for the Advancement of Actuarial Risk Need Assessment (SAARNA). https://saarna.org/static-2002r/.

Hiday, V. A., Swartz, M. S., Swanson, J. W., Borum, R., & Wagner, H. R. (1999). Criminal victimization of persons with severe mental illness. *Psychiatric Services*, 50(1), 62–68. doi:10.1176/ps.50.1.62.

Jurek v. Texas, 428 U.S. 262 (1976).

Kennealy, P. J., Skeem, J. L., Walters, G. D., & Camp, J. (2010). Do core interpersonal and affective traits of PCL-R psychopathy interact with antisocial behavior and disinhibition to predict violence? *Psychological Assessment*, 22(3), 569–580. doi:10.1037/a0019618.

Kroner, D. G., & Mills, J. F. (2001). The accuracy of five risk appraisal instruments in predicting institutional misconduct and new convictions. *Criminal Justice and Behavior*, 28(4), 471–489. doi:10.1177/009385480102800405.

Lee, S. C., Restrepo, A., Satariano, A., & Hanson, R. K. (2016). The predictive validity of Static-99R for sexual offenders in California: 2016 update. Retrieved 11/19/2019 from www.saratso.org.

Link, B. G., Elis, H., & Cullen, F. T. (1992). The violent and illegal behavior of mental patients reconsidered. *American Sociological Review*, 57(3), 275–292. doi:10.2307/2096235.

Link, B. G., & Stueve, A. (1994). Psychotic symptoms and the violent/illegal behavior of mental patients compared to community controls. In J. Monahan & H. J. Steadman (Eds.) *Violence and mental disorder: Developments in risk assessment* (pp. 137–160). Chicago, IL: University of Chicago Press.

Lofthouse, R. E., Lindsay, W. R., Totsika, V., Hastings, R. P., Boer, D. P., & Haaven, J. L. (2013). Prospective dynamic assessment of risk of sexual re-offending in individuals with an intellectual disability and a history of sexual offending behaviour. *Journal of Applied Research in Intellectual Disabilities*, 26(5), 394–403. doi:10.1111/jar.12029.

Meehl, P. E. (1954). *Clinical versus statistical prediction: A theoretical analysis and a review of the evidence.* Minneapolis: University of Minnesota Press.

Meehl, P. E. (1986). Causes and effects of my disturbing little book. *Journal of Personality Assessment, 50*(3), 370–375. doi:10.1207/s15327752jpa5003_6.

Monahan, J. (1977/1995). *The clinical prediction of violent behavior.* Lanham, MD: Jason Aronson, Inc.

Monahan, J., Steadman, H., Robbins, P., Appelbaum, P., Banks, S., Grisso, T., Heilbrun, K., Mulvey, E., Roth, L., & Silver, E. (2005). An actuarial model of violence risk assessment for persons with mental disorders. *Psychiatric Services, 56*(7), 810–815. doi:10.1176/appi.ps.56.7.810.

Olver, M. E., Stockdale, K. C., Neumann, C. S., Hare, R. D., Mokros, A., Baskin-Sommers, A., Brand, E., Folino, J., Gacono, C., Gray, N. S., Kiehl, K., Knight, R., Leon-Mayer, E., Logan, M., Meloy, J. R., Roy, S., Salekin, R. T., Snowden, R., Thomson, N., Tillem, S., Vitacco, M., & Yoon, D. (2020). Reliability and validity of the Psychopathy Checklist-Revised in the assessment of risk for institutional violence: A cautionary note on DeMatteo et al. (2020). *Psychology, Public Policy, and Law, 26*(4), 490–510. doi:10.1037/law0000256.

Otto, R. K., & Douglas, K. S. (2010). *Handbook of violence risk assessment.* New York: Routledge.

Pedersen, l., Rasmussen, K., & Elsass, P. (2012). HCR-20 violence risk assessments as a guide for treating and managing violence risk in a forensic psychiatric setting. *Psychology, Crime & Law, 18*(8), 733–743. doi:10.1080/1068316X.2010.548814.

Quinsey, V. L., Harris, G. T., Rice, M. E., & Cormier, C. A. (1998). *Violent offenders: Appraising and managing risk.* Washington, D.C.: American Psychological Association.

Quinsey, V. L., Harris, G. T., Rice, M. E., & Cormier, C. A. (2006). *Violent offenders: Appraising and managing risk. Second edition.* Washington, D.C.: American Psychological Association.

Rice, M. D., & Harris, G. T. (1995). Violent recidivism: Assessing predictive validity. *Journal of Consulting and Clinical Psychology, 63*(5), 737–748. doi:10.1037/0022-006X.63.5.737.

Roché, M. W., Boyle, D. J., Cheng, C.-C., Del Pozzo, J., Cherneski, L., Pascarella, J., Lukachko, A., & Silverstein, S. M. (2018). Prevalence and risk of violent ideation and behavior in serious mental illnesses: An analysis of 63,572 patient records. *Journal of Interpersonal Violence, 36*(5–6), 2732–2752. doi:10.1177/0886260518759976.

Rogers, R., & Fiduccia, C. E. (2015). Forensic assessment instruments. In B. L. Cutler & P. A. Zapf (Eds.) *APA handbook of forensic psychology. Volume 1: Individual and situational influences in criminal and civil contexts* (pp. 19–34). Washington, D.C.: American Psychological Association.

Salekin, R. T., Rogers, R., & Sewell, K. W. (1996). A review and meta-analysis of the Psychopathy Checklist and Psychopathy Checklist-Revised: Predictive validity of dangerousness. *Clinical Psychology: Science and Practice, 3*(3), 203–215. doi:10.1111/j.1468-2850.1996.tb00071.x.

Schlatter, E., & Steinback, R. (2010). 10 anti-gay myths debunked. Intelligence Report, (2010 Winter Issue). Retrieved 01/16/2023 from https://www.splcenter.org/intelligence-report?f%5B0%5D=field_intel_report_issue%3A11692.

Schwalbe, C. S. (2007). Risk assessment for juvenile justice: A meta-analysis. *Law and Human Behavior, 31*(5), 449–462. doi:10.1007/s10979-006-9071-7.

Silver, E., Mulvey, E. P., & Monahan, J. (1999). Assessing violence risk among discharged psychiatric patients: Toward an ecological approach. *Law and Human Behavior, 23*(2), 237–255. doi:10.1023/a:1022377003150.

Silver, E., & Teasdale, B. (2005). Mental disorder and violence: An examination of stressful life events and impaired social support. *Social Problems, 52*(1), 62–78. doi:10.1525/SP.2005.52.1.62.

Silverstein, S. M., Del Pozzo, J., Roché, M., Boyle, D., & Miskimen, T. (2015). Schizophrenia and violence: realities and recommendations. *Crime Psychology Review, 1*(1), 21–42. doi:10.1080/23744006.2015.1033154.

Singh, J. P., Grann, M., & Fazel, S. (2011). A comparative study of violence risk assessment tools: A systematic review and metaregression analysis of 68 studies involving 25,980 participants. *Clinical Psychology Review, 31*(3), 499–513. doi:10.1016/j.cpr.2010.11.009.

Steadman, H. J., & Cocozza, J. J. (1974). *Careers of the criminally insane: Excessive social control of deviance.* Lexington, MA: Lexington Books.

Steadman, H. J., & Cocozza, J. J. (1978). Psychiatry, dangerousness and the repetitively violent offender. *Journal of Criminal Law and Criminology, 69*(2), 226–231. doi:10.2307/1142396.

Steadman, H. J., Mulvey, E. P., Monahan, J., Robbins, P. C., Appelbaum, P. S., Grisso, T., Roth, L. H., & Silver, E. (1998). Violence by people discharged from acute psychiatric inpatient facilities and by others in the same neighborhoods. *Archives of General Psychiatry, 55*(5), 393–401. doi:10.1001/ARCHPSYC. 55.5.393.

Stueve, A., & Link, B. G. (1997). Violence and psychiatric disorders: Results from an epidemiological study of young adults in Israel. *Psychiatric Quarterly, 68*(4), 327–342. doi:10.1023/a:1025443014158.

Swanson, J. W., Holzer, C. E. III, Ganju, V. K., & Jono, R. T. (1990). Violence and psychiatric disorder in the community: Evidence from the Epidemiological Catchment Area surveys. *Hospital and Community Psychiatry, 41*(7), 761–770. doi:10.1176/ps.41.7.761.

Swanson, J. W., Swartz, M. S., Van Dorn, R. A., Elbogen, E. B., Wagner, H. R., Rosenheck, R. A., Stroup, T. S., McEvoy, J. P., & Lieberman, J. A. (2006). A national study of violent behavior in persons with schizophrenia. *Archives of General Psychiatry, 63*(5), 490–499. doi:10.1001/archpsyc.63.5.490.

Vojt, G., Thomson, L. D. G., & Marshall, L. A. (2013). The predictive validity of the HCR-20 following clinical implementation: Does it work in practice? *Journal of Forensic Psychiatry and Psychology, 24*, 371–385. doi:10.1080/ 14789949.2013.800894.

Webster, C. D., Douglas, K. S., Eaves, D., & Hart, S. D. (1997). *HCR-20: Assessing risk for violence (Version 2).* Burnaby, British Columbia, Canada: Simon Fraser University; Mental Health, Law, and Policy Institute.

Widom, C. S. (1989). Does violence beget violence? A critical examination of the literature. *Psychological Bulletin, 106*(1), 3–28. doi:10.1037/0033-2909.106.1.3.

13 Risk assessment and the death penalty

Expert opinions regarding risk of future violence are sought in a number of judicial contexts, including capital punishment. In death penalty trials, predictions of dangerousness are used to help the court determine whether a defendant is so dangerous they are likely to continue committing acts of violence even inside the confines of a prison, in which case a life sentence may be considered too risky to the safety of others and the death penalty may be considered the preferred alternative.

Risk assessment by forensic mental health professionals has been a matter of life and death in capital cases like *Jurek v. Texas* (1976) and *Estelle v. Smith* (1981). The essential backdrop to understanding these cases is the moratorium imposed on capital punishment by the U.S. Supreme Court decision in *Furman v. Georgia* (1972) and the subsequent efforts by state legislatures to reimpose the death penalty by making it more consistent and less discriminatory.

THE U.S. SUPREME COURT MORATORIUM ON THE DEATH PENALTY DUE TO ITS INCONSISTENCY AND DISCRIMINATION: *FURMAN V. GEORGIA* (U.S. 1972)

Although the prediction of violence was not an issue in *Furman v. Georgia* (1972), an understanding of this trial is essential to understanding the series of cases that followed. Opposition to the death penalty prevailed in 1972, when the U.S. Supreme Court ruled in *Furman* that capital punishment was not consistently applied in the United States and therefore was unconstitutional under the Eighth Amendment's provision regarding cruel and unusual punishment and the Fourteenth Amendment's provision regarding due process. It was not the death penalty itself that the Court found to be cruel and unusual, but rather the arbitrary and discriminatory manner in which it was applied.

William Henry Furman was convicted of murder in Georgia and he was sentenced to death. When his case came to the U.S. Supreme Court, it was combined with the cases of Lucious Jackson, Jr. (who had been convicted

DOI: 10.4324/9781003385028-16

and sentenced to death for rape in Georgia) and Elmer Branch (who had been convicted and sentenced to death for rape in Texas. These cases were heard prior to *Coker v. Georgia*, 1977, in which the U.S. Supreme Court held that a defendant cannot be sentenced to death for rape, due to lack of proportionality). All three defendants were Black.

Justice Douglas wrote in *Furman*,

> [It] is "cruel and unusual" to apply the death penalty – or any other penalty – selectively to minorities whose numbers are few, who are outcasts of society, and who are unpopular, but whom society is willing to see suffer though it would not countenance general application of the same penalty across the board. (*Furman v. Georgia*, 1972, at 245)

Justice Douglas quoted Goldberg and Dershowitz (1970): "A penalty therefore should be considered 'unusually' imposed if it is administered arbitrarily or discriminatorily" (at 249).

Because of the *Furman* decision, a moratorium was imposed on the death penalty in the United States that lasted until 1976. By then, several state legislatures had enacted laws intended to give more regularity and consistency to capital punishment and thereby provide a basis for bringing the death penalty before the U.S. Supreme Court once again. Death penalty cases that came before the U.S. Supreme Court in 1976 were *Gregg v. Georgia* (1976), *Proffitt v. Florida* (1976), and *Jurek v. Texas* (1976). All three defendants were White.

STATES REVISE THEIR DEATH PENALTY STATUTES: *JUREK V. TEXAS* (U.S. 1976)

Jerry Lane Jurek was 22 years old when he confessed to kidnaping a 10-year-old girl, forcibly raping her, strangling her, and drowning her in a river. One of the arresting officers was the victim's father. Texas had revised its criminal code during the moratorium imposed by the *Furman* decision. Texas now defined capital murder more narrowly and included only particularly heinous crimes. The new Texas Penal Code, which became effective on January 1, 1974, limited capital murder to intentional and knowing murders committed in one or more of five situations:

1 the murder of a peace officer or fireman
2 murder committed in the course of a kidnaping, burglary, robbery, forcible rape, or arson
3 murder for remuneration
4 murder committed while escaping or attempting to escape from a penal institution
5 murder committed by a prison inmate upon a prison employee.

The revised Texas Penal Code also required that all three of the following questions be answered in the affirmative beyond a reasonable doubt before the death penalty could be imposed:

1 whether the conduct of the defendant that caused the death of the deceased was committed deliberately and with the reasonable expectation that the death of the deceased or another would result
2 whether there is a probability that the defendant would commit criminal acts of violence that would constitute a continuing threat to society
3 if raised by the evidence, whether the conduct of the defendant in killing the deceased was unreasonable in response to the provocation, if any, by the deceased.

Item (2) above is the province of forensic mental health assessment. It is the kind of risk assessment that mental health professionals perform on a regular basis. The U.S. Supreme Court found these new procedures acceptable, and the death penalty was reinstated in Texas.

The U.S. Supreme Court would rule in each of the three above cases (*Jurek*, *Proffitt*, and *Gregg*) that Texas, Florida, and Georgia had developed valid procedures for imposing the death penalty, and capital punishment was reinstated in those jurisdictions. As of 2023, a total of twenty-seven states have the death penalty: Alabama, Arizona, Arkansas, California, Florida, Georgia, Idaho, Indiana, Kansas, Kentucky, Louisiana, Mississippi, Missouri, Montana, Nebraska, Nevada, North Carolina, Ohio, Oklahoma, Oregon, Pennsylvania, South Carolina, South Dakota, Tennessee, Texas, Utah, and Wyoming.

In four of those states – Arizona, California, Oregon, and Pennsylvania – the governors have declared a moratorium on executions. The federal government also has the death penalty, but also has declared a moratorium on executions. The U.S. military has the death penalty. The District of Columbia has abolished capital punishment (Death Penalty Information Center, 2023).

Jerry Jurek was convicted of murder under the new Texas law and was sentenced to death. His execution was set for January 19, 1977. Two days before his scheduled execution, he was granted a stay of execution and he petitioned for a writ of habeas corpus. Psychologists testified at his federal habeas corpus hearing "that Jurek had the sort of mental handicaps that made him particularly susceptible to the influence and suggestions of others" (*Jurek v. Estelle*, 1979, at 677). He had a verbal IQ of 66. He was, in the words of the court, "less likely to be able to understand his right to remain silent. He may also be unable to insist effectively that that right be observed" (at 677).

The police had questioned Jerry Jurek under suspicious circumstances. He had been arrested at 1:00 a.m. and had been removed from his home without a shirt or shoes. The police moved him from town to town (which is a known strategy for breaking down resistance). He was not allowed to see his parents for 42 hours. He was not allowed to see an attorney even though he asked for one. He was not taken before a magistrate until 21 hours had passed and he had given an incriminating statement, despite the fact that Texas law requires a defendant to be taken before a magistrate immediately and provides that a confession is not considered valid unless this is done. The U.S. Court of Appeals for the Fifth Circuit wrote,

> [The] reason is clear; a magistrate might help break the defendant's isolation and lift the psychological siege of the law enforcement authorities. Jurek received no such relief until the police had overcome his resistance and obtained an incriminating verbal statement from him. (*Jurek v. Estelle*, 1979, at 678)

Also, the statements used against Jurek and attributed to him "[Were] apparently not his own words. They are written in complete sentences, mostly grammatical, with even a touch of legalese" (at 677). For example, he was purported to have said, "In the statement that I gave him I did not tell the truth about the conversation I had with Wendy at the river and about the prior discussion about trying to find some girls to pick up and I now herein wish to correct that statement" (at fn. 5).

The U.S. Court of Appeals for the Fifth Circuit remanded Jurek for a new trial. In 1982, he pleaded guilty in exchange for a life sentence. Despite his guilty plea and his confession to the police, he continued to assert that he had not killed the girl (Chammah, 2021).

EGREGIOUS EXPERT TESTIMONY IN THE PREDICTION OF VIOLENCE: *ESTELLE V SMITH* (U.S. 1981)

Under the Texas Penal Code of 1974 – quoted in the last section – assessment for risk of violence is a necessary feature of capital proceedings. Substantive and procedural questions remained regarding what would constitute a valid assessment for risk of violence and how that testimony could be presented.

Ernest Benjamin Smith and an accomplice robbed a grocery store, and during that robbery Smith's accomplice shot and killed a clerk. Smith went on trial for capital murder.

The court ordered a competency evaluation, and this was conducted at the jail by psychiatrist James P. Grigson, who interviewed Smith for

90 minutes. Smith was found competent to stand trial and he was found guilty of murder. Death penalty trials are bifurcated, with a guilt phase and a penalty phase. The prosecution called Dr. Grigson during the penalty phase to testify regarding Smith's future dangerousness. The defense protested that Grigson had not been listed as an expert witness for the penalty phase. Grigson had been hired to assess competency to stand trial and not dangerousness. The judge allowed the testimony, and Dr. Grigson testified

> (a) that Smith "is a very severe sociopath"; (b) that "he will continue his previous behavior"; (c) that his sociopathic condition will "only get worse"; (d) that he has no "regard for another human being's property or for their life, regardless of who it may be"; (e) that "[t]here is no treatment, no medicine ... that in any way at all modifies or changes this behavior"; (f) that he "is going to go ahead and commit other similar or same criminal acts if given the opportunity to do so"; and (g) that he "has no remorse or sorrow for what he has done." (*Estelle v. Smith,* 1981, at 459–460)

The jury found that Smith was a danger to others, and he was sentenced to death.

Grigson's foundation for these sweeping claims about Smith's future dangerousness is questionable at best. Smith appealed to the U.S. District Court for the Northern District of Texas, and this court ruled that allowing Dr. Grigson's testimony at the penalty phase had been a constitutional error. That decision by the District Court was later upheld by the U.S. Supreme Court, who wrote,

> The court concluded that the death penalty had been imposed on Smith in violation of his Fifth and Fourteenth Amendment rights to due process and freedom from compelled self-incrimination, his Sixth Amendment right to the effective assistance of counsel, and his Eighth Amendment right to present complete evidence of mitigating circumstances. (1981, at 460)

Smith was resentenced to life in prison. Dr. Grigson later would be expelled from the American Psychiatric Association and from the Texas Association of Psychiatric Physicians for testifying regarding defendants he had not examined (e.g., in *Barefoot v. Estelle,* 1983) and for testifying that he could predict future violence with 100 percent certainty (Brakel & Brooks, 2001). In the court of public opinion, he acquired the nickname "Doctor Death."

REFERENCES

Barefoot v. Estelle, 463 U.S. 880 (1983).

Brakel, S. J., & Brooks, A. D. (2001). *Law and psychiatry in the criminal justice system*. Getzville, NY: William S. Hein.

Chammah, M. (2021). *Let the Lord sort them: The rise and fall of the death penalty*. New York: Crown.

Coker v. Georgia, 433 U.S. 584 (1977).

Death Penalty Information Center. (2023). *State by state*. Retrieved 03/16/2023 from https://deathpenaltyinfo.org/state-and-federal-info/state-by-state.

Estelle v. Smith, 451 U.S. 454 (1981).

Furman v. Georgia, 408 U.S. 238 (1972).

Goldberg, A. J., & Dershowitz, A. M. (1970). Declaring the death penalty unconstitutional. *Harvard Law Review*, 83, 1773–1819. https://www.jstor.org/stable/pdfplus/1339687.pdf.

Gregg v. Georgia, 428 U.S. 153 (1976).

Jurek v. Estelle, 593 F.2d 672 (1979).

Jurek v. Texas, 428 U.S. 262 (1976).

Proffitt v. Florida, 428 U.S. 242 (1976).

14 Mitigation testimony in capital sentencing has no limits

Lockett v. Ohio (U.S. 1978)

Capital proceedings are bifurcated jury trials: first a guilt phase during which a jury decides whether the defendant is guilty of the crime, and then a penalty phase during which the jury determines whether the defendant receives the death penalty. In *Ring v. Arizona*, 2002, the U.S. Supreme Court held that only a jury and not a judge can give the death penalty, based upon the defendant's Sixth Amendment right to a jury trial.

Sandra Lockett drove the getaway car in a robbery that resulted in the death of a pawn shop owner. Under Ohio law at that time, certain crimes required the death penalty, and only a few mitigating factors could be considered, namely:

1 whether the victim brought violence upon themselves
2 whether the offense was committed under duress or coercion
3 whether the crime was the product of mental deficiency.

Lockett was convicted of murder and was sentenced to death. She appealed her case to the U.S. Supreme Court, arguing that the Ohio law was unconstitutional in limiting the range of mitigating factors. In a 7–1 decision, the U.S. Supreme Court agreed with her and ruled that all mitigating factors must be considered in capital cases.

Mental health professionals may be employed in providing mitigation testimony, which is intended to help triers of fact understand the psychological circumstances surrounding a crime. Mitigation testimony has been effective in court at getting life sentences instead of the death penalty, even in the most horrific crimes (Stetler, 2008). Examples include:

- Zacarias Moussaoui, the "twentieth hijacker" of 9/11/2001, who is now serving life in prison without the possibility of parole at a Supermax federal prison in Florence, Colorado
- Lee Boyd Malvo, the "Beltway Sniper" of October 2002, who is currently serving multiple life sentences without the possibility of parole

DOI: 10.4324/9781003385028-17

at Red Onion State Prison near Pound, Virginia; his co-defendant John Allen Muhammad died by lethal injection at the Greensville Correctional Center near Jarratt, Virginia, on November 10, 2009

- Terry Nichol, co-defendant of domestic terrorist Timothy McVeigh, whose bombing of the Alfred P. Murrah Federal Building in Oklahoma City on April 19, 1995, caused the deaths of 168 people, including 19 children. Co-defendant McVeigh was executed by lethal injection at a federal prison in Terre Haute, Indiana, on June 11, 2001.

Justice Sandra Day O'Connor defined death penalty mitigation as "facts about the defendant's character or background, or the circumstances of the particular offense that may call for a penalty less than death" (*Franklin v. Lynaugh*, 1988, concurring opinion, at 188; *Franklin v. Lynaugh* was a Texas case that limited jury instructions regarding mitigation).

If I may be permitted a bold oversimplification, mitigation testimony is about showing the triers of fact that the defendant is a human being and not a sadistic monster. Juries have been amenable to the ideas that defendants may merit special consideration and may not deserve the harshest penalties if they (a) had relatively minor involvement in the crime (such as Sandra Lockett, who drove the getaway vehicle and did not pull the trigger), (b) were under the influence of a domineering co-defendant, (c) have histories of childhood abuse or neglect, (d) have problems with substance use, (e) were intoxicated at the time of the offense, (f) have a mental illness or low intelligence, or (g) behave well while in jail awaiting trial. The U.S. Supreme Court has ruled that positive prisoner adjustment can be introduced as a mitigating factor in capital sentencing (*Skipper v. South Carolina*, 1986). If a defendant can behave well during incarceration, then their incarceration may not pose a threat to the safety of prison staff and other prisoners, and they may elude the death penalty. Mitigation testimony prompts the triers of fact to ask themselves, "What would I have done in a similar situation?" or to say, "There but for the grace of God go I," as British cleric John Bradford (1510–1555) is reported to have said when he saw men being led to their executions. (In 1555 Bradford would be escorted to his own execution.) (The converse of mitigation testimony, if I may be permitted another gross oversimplification, is the insanity defense, in which the defense argues that this defendant is so unusual and so different from the rest of us that the laws which apply to other human beings do not apply to them.)

For a discussion of how post-traumatic stress disorder was used as mitigation in a death penalty proceeding, see Chapter 29. For recent texts with further information about mitigation testimony, see Ashford and Kupferberg (2013) and Silver (2021).

REFERENCES

Ashford, J. B., & Kupferberg, M. (2013). *Death penalty mitigation: A handbook for mitigation specialists, investigators, social scientists, and lawyers.* Oxford: Oxford University Press.

Franklin v. Lynaugh, 487 U.S. 164 (1988).

Lockett v. Ohio, 438 U.S. 586 (1978).

Ring v. Arizona, 536 U.S. 584 (2002).

Silver, M. S. (2021). *Handbook of mitigation in criminal and immigration forensics: Humanizing the client towards a better legal outcome. Seventh edition.* New York: Author.

Skipper v. South Carolina, 476 U.S. 1 (1986).

Stetler, R. (2008). The mystery of mitigation: What jurors need to make a reasoned moral response in capital sentencing. *University of Pennsylvania Journal of Law and Social Change, 11,* 237–264. SSRN: https://ssrn.com/abstract=1847065.

15   Juvenile sentencing

Juveniles who commit serious crimes can be transferred to adult court (see Chapter 11), but this does not mean that those juveniles should receive the harshest penalties that can be given to adult defendants; namely, capital punishment and life without parole. Our system of justice is based on the mind of the offender (see Chapter 7), and the juvenile and adult minds differ in ways that should be taken into account when juveniles are sentenced.

In *Roper v. Simmons* (2005), the U.S. Supreme Court ruled that convicted murderers cannot be executed for a murder committed before the age of 18. In *Graham v. Florida* (2010), the U.S. Supreme Court held that juveniles cannot be sentenced to life without parole for any offense other than homicide. *Miller v. Alabama* (2012), which concerned automatic sentences of life without parole for certain serious crimes, involved not just chronological age but psychological factors as well. Sentencing a juvenile to life without parole cannot be mandatory but must consider the individual defendant.

MILLER V. ALABAMA (U.S. 2012)

On a night in 2003, Evan Miller (age 14) and an accomplice were smoking marijuana and drinking alcohol in the trailer of a 52-year-old drug dealer. Miller's mother was one of the drug dealer's customers. When the dealer passed out, Miller and his accomplice stole $300 from his wallet. Miller was in the process of returning the wallet to the victim's pocket when the victim woke and grabbed him by the throat. Miller's friend struck the victim with a baseball bat. Miller took the bat and beat the man savagely. Then the boys set the trailer on fire. The drug dealer died of injuries and smoke inhalation. Miller's case was transferred to adult court, where he was convicted of "murder in the course of arson," a crime that carried a mandatory minimum sentence of life without parole in Alabama. The U.S. Supreme Court combined Miller's case with a 1999 case from Arkansas

DOI: 10.4324/9781003385028-18

involving another 14-year-old murderer, Kuntrell Jackson, and granted certiorari.

The court ruled 5–4 that mandatory life sentences without parole for juveniles are cruel and unusual punishment contrary to the Eighth Amendment. Severe sentencing for juveniles cannot be mandatory but must consider each defendant as a unique individual. The court based its decision on three psychosocial differences between the adult mind and the juvenile mind:

- Juveniles have "'an underdeveloped sense of 'responsibility,' leading to recklessness, impulsivity, and heedless risk-taking" (*Miller v. Alabama*, 2012, at 467).
- Juveniles are more susceptible "to negative influences and outside pressures," including pressures from peers and families. Minors lack the freedom of movement that adults have and therefore "lack the ability to extricate themselves from horrific, crime-producing settings" (at 467).
- Juveniles have years of development ahead of them and their characters are not yet fixed. Their actions are "less likely to be evidence of irretrievable depravity" (at 467).

The adage "once a criminal always a criminal" does not apply well to juvenile delinquents. More than half of adolescents engage in criminal activities like drug use and drunk driving (Arnett, 1992; Moffitt, 1993). However, most of them do not go on to become adult criminals. The "age-crime curve," which shows that crime decreases with age, is one of the most consistent findings across nations and across social groups (Arnett, 1992; Loeber et al., 2008; Moffitt, 1994; Monahan et al., 2009). Antisocial behavior, including violent crime, peaks at age 17 and then drops precipitously in young adulthood.

Even for serious crimes like murder, not all juvenile offenders go on to have criminal careers. Monahan et al. (2009) found that only 6 percent of serious juvenile offenders persisted in high levels of antisocial behavior during adulthood. The results of other longitudinal studies have been less sanguine. Kathleen Heide of the University of South Florida and her colleagues followed a group of 59 juveniles who were sentenced as adults to the Florida Department of Corrections for homicide or attempted homicide. In 2001, they published the results of 15 to 17 years of follow-up, and in 2016 they published the results of 30 years of follow-up. In 2001, more than two-thirds had been released from prison, and 60 percent of those released had returned to prison (Heide et al., 2001). Most of those who returned to prison did so in the first three years after release. At the 30-year follow-up, 88 percent of these juveniles had been re-arrested (Khachatryan et al., 2016).

Caudill and Trulson (2016) reported ten years of post-release follow-up on 221 juvenile homicide offenders who had been committed to a juvenile institution in Texas. More than half were re-arrested for another felony within ten years.

THE PSYCHOLOGY OF ADOLESCENCE ACCORDING TO *MILLER*

As Supreme Court Justice John Paul Stevens explained in *Thompson v. Oklahoma* (1988, at 835), the immaturity of youth is the very reason why society does not trust them with important privileges and responsibilities like driving, drinking, voting, marriage, and military service. Their immaturity is the same reason why their conduct is less morally reprehensible than that of adults.

The *Miller* court relied upon the work of psychologists Laurence Steinberg and Elizabeth Scott (2003), who in turn relied upon the work of legal scholars Sanford Kadish (1987) and Stephen Morse (1994) in identifying three categories of variables that reduce criminal culpability for all defendants, both juvenile and adult. For each of these three sources of mitigation, it can be argued that adolescents are less culpable than adults.

1 "Endogenous impairments or deficiencies in the actor's decision-making capacity" as may be caused by "mental illness, mental retardation, extreme emotional distress, or susceptibility to influence or domination" (Steinberg & Scott, 2003, p. 1011). Adolescents are immature and have low levels of cognitive and psychosocial development that make them less capable of competent decision making.
2 Compelling external factors like "duress, provocation, threatened injury, or extreme need" (Steinberg & Scott, 2003, p. 1011). Adolescents are more vulnerable to peer pressure or coercion in the form of provocation, threat, or duress.
3 Actions that are "out of character for the actor," i.e., are not the product of "bad character" (Steinberg & Scott, 2003, p. 1011). Adolescents are in the process of forming their personal identity. Their criminal behavior is less likely to reflect bad character.

The behavior of adolescents is driven by transitory influences. This is almost the definition of adolescence. The process of identity formation, which is a major psychological task of adolescence, involves exploration and experimentation. The "identity crisis" of middle adolescence is resolved as the chrysalis of the child metamorphoses into the developed self of late adolescence and early adulthood (Waterman, 1982). Often this experimentation involves risky, illegal, or dangerous behaviors like alcohol use, drug use, unsafe sex, and antisocial behavior. For most adolescents these behaviors occur within a relatively brief span of time. Only a small number develop entrenched patterns of antisocial behavior (Farrington, 1986; Moffitt, 1993). Much of juvenile crime stems, not from deep-seated moral deficiencies or "bad character," but from normal experimentation with risky behaviors within the contexts of peer pressure and self-discovery. The causes of most juvenile crimes – like immature reasoning and susceptibility to peer pressure – weaken and disappear as adolescents grow into adulthood. Adolescent offenders often lack this important component of culpability – the connection between bad behavior and bad character. When juveniles are tried in adult courts, their futures are placed at risk and they are in danger of spending the rest of their lives paying for a behavioral flaw that was transitory in nature.

As Justice Lewis F. Powell wrote in *Eddings v. Oklahoma* (1982, at 115), "[Youth] is more than a chronological fact. It is a time and condition of life when a person may be most susceptible to influence and to psychological damage."

Aggravating this already troubling situation is the fact that racial and ethnic biases affect perceptions of youthful offenders. Minority youth are more likely to be perceived as having solidified, criminal personalities (Bridges & Steen, 1998; Graham, 2002) and therefore are judged more harshly.

Steinberg and Scott (2003) went on to identify "four dimensions of psychosocial maturity" in which adolescents differ from adults (p. 1012):

a *Susceptibility to peer influence.* Between childhood and early adolescence, susceptibility to peer influence increases as juveniles break away from their parents. Susceptibility to peer influence peaks around age 14 and then declines through the high school years.

b *Attitudes toward and perception of risk.* A person's "risk-reward calculus" changes between adolescence and adulthood. Adolescents are less risk-aversive and more strongly oriented toward potential rewards. This shifts as adolescents enter adulthood. Adults give more thought to potential risks and are less persuaded by fantasies about potential rewards.

c *Future orientation.* Adolescents are less likely than adults to consider future consequences. This makes them less risk-aversive and more susceptible to duress. The amount of duress that is sufficient to influence a juvenile's behavior does not have the same effect on an adult, whose focus of attention is on a future goal and plan for their own life.

d *Capacity for self-management.* Adolescents typically have difficulty regulating their moods, impulses, and behaviors. Self-management skills grow and impulsivity declines during early, middle, and late adolescence.

THE *MILLER* BRIEF

An amici curiae brief in *Miller* was filed jointly by the American Psychological Association, the American Psychiatric Association, and the National Association of Social Workers (American Psychological Association, 2012). This brief sets out four reasons why juveniles should not be punished as severely as adults. While some of this material duplicates information that was reviewed in the previous section under the three factors employed by the U.S. Supreme Court in their decision in *Miller*, I will review this brief in its entirety here in order to preserve the integrity of this document.

1 Juveniles are less capable of mature judgment than adults.
2 Juveniles are more vulnerable to negative external influences.
3 Juveniles have a greater capacity for change and reform.
4 Juveniles' psychosocial immaturity is consistent with recent research regarding adolescent brain development.

Juveniles are less capable of mature judgment than adults

The immature judgment of adolescents contributes to their tendency to engage in risky and illegal behavior. An adolescent's judgment and decision making differ from those of an adult in four important respects:

1 Adolescents are less able to control their impulses.
2 Adolescents have a different view of risks and rewards.
3 Adolescents are less able to anticipate future consequences of their behavior.
4 Adolescents are less able to consider another person's perspective.

Adults make better decisions than adolescents because adults have developed their capacities to stay focused on long-term goals and to resist the pull of social and emotional influences (Albert & Steinberg, 2011; Galvan et al., 2007; Leshem & Glicksohn, 2007). Adolescents have not yet developed adult capacities to exercise self-restraint, to weigh risks and rewards, and to plan for the future (Cauffman & Steinberg, 2000; Halpern-Felsher & Cauffman, 2001). The most dramatic increase in psychosocial maturity occurs between the ages of 16 and 19. These changes have profound effects on the adolescent's ability to make consistently mature judgments. For adolescents to develop self-control, they need opportunities to make mistakes and learn from them. To expect an experienced-based self-control to exist before the age of 18 or 19 is "wishful thinking" (Zimring, 2000). If courts are going to think of adolescents as nothing more than miniature adults, then it will come as no surprise that courts will impose harsh penalties, because they will expect adolescents to remain impulsive and dangerous throughout their lives.

Juveniles are not free to change families, quit school, leave their neighborhoods, or run away from home. They are not free to remove themselves from the negative influences that may come from these environments.

Susceptibility to peer pressure to engage in antisocial behavior increases between childhood and early adolescence, peaks around age 14, and then declines during late adolescence, with relatively little change after age 18 (Berndt, 1979; Fagan, 2000; Scott & Steinberg, 2008; Steinberg & Silverberg, 1986).

Adolescents are far more likely than adults to commit crimes in groups (Scott & Steinberg, 2008). Fear of peer rejection and desire for peer approval affect the choices of adolescents even when no direct coercion takes place. Most juvenile offenses take place on a social stage, where the dominant motivation is the immediate approval of peers (Zimring, 2000).

Youth is a developmental stage that is distinct from adulthood, and juveniles should not be treated like little adults. Juveniles are more capable of change. The behavior of an adolescent is less likely to be a sign of "irretrievably depraved character" (quoting *Roper v. Simmons* at 570). For most persons, the process of identity formation is incomplete until at least their early twenties (Scott & Steinberg, 2008; Steinberg & Schwartz, 2000; Waterman, 1982). Features of immaturity like deficient self-regulation and susceptibility to peer pressure are likely to resolve as a mature identity emerges. In other words, juveniles are likely to "grow out of it." For most juveniles, antisocial behavior ends when maturity develops and individual identity emerges and then settles. Only a small number of adolescents who experiment with illegal activities go on to become adult criminals. The vast majority desist from crime (Moffitt, 1993; Monahan et al., 2009; Steinberg & Scott, 2003). Adolescent criminal conduct frequently results from experimentation with risky behavior and not from bad character (Arnett, 1992; Moffitt, 1993). It would be a mistake to think that all fleeting juvenile experiments are going to persist as lifelong patterns of behavior.

Juveniles' psychosocial immaturity is consistent with research on adolescent brain development

The adolescent brain differs in important ways, both from the child brain and from the adult brain (Wahlstrom et al., 2010). Significant development occurs throughout adolescence in the prefrontal cortex and in the connections between the prefrontal cortex and other brain structures.

These structures and their connections are critical in developing executive functions, which include:

- planning
- impulse control
- self-regulation
- motivation
- judgment
- decision making
- evaluating future consequences
- weighing risk and reward
- perceiving emotions
- controlling emotions
- processing and inhibiting impulses. (Casey et al., 2000; Damasio & Anderson, 2003; Goldberg, 2001; Sowell et al., 1999)

Middle adolescence is a time of heightened vulnerability to risky and reckless behaviors because of the temporal disjunction created by two processes: (1) the rapid rise in dopaminergic activity around the time of puberty, which leads to increased reward-seeking, and (2) the more gradual maturation of the prefrontal cortex and its connections, which leads eventually to improved cognitive control and the coordination of cognition with affect. Risk-taking declines as dopaminergic activity diminishes from its peak in early adolescence, and as self-regulatory systems mature (Somerville et al., 2010; Steinberg, 2010). Middle adolescence, roughly ages 14 to 17, is a period of especially heightened vulnerability to risky behavior, during which sensation-seeking is high and self-regulation is immature. The results are reckless behaviors such as reckless driving, unprotected sex, suicide attempts, and delinquent behavior (Steinberg, 2010). Adolescents mature as their brains change and they gain more control over their impulses.

To quote *Roper,* it is "the rare juvenile offender whose crime reflects irreparable corruption" (at 573).

To quote the *Miller* brief, "And, even in the case of the most serious offenses, there is no reliable way to distinguish the juvenile offender who might become a hardened criminal from the far more common offender whose crime is a product of the transient influences of adolescence itself" (American Psychological Association, 2012, p. 35).

Sowell et al. (1999) mapped the entire brain from adolescence to young adulthood and found patterns of brain development that were distinctly different from childhood development, with changes in the lenticular nuclei and in large areas of the dorsal, medial, and orbital frontal cortices, and relatively little change in any other area. Four related changes in the brain merit special attention.

THE INCENTIVE PROCESSING SYSTEM

Early adolescence, especially the period of time immediately after puberty, is characterized by major changes in the incentive processing system. This system includes the orbitofrontal cortex and the ventral striatum (which contains the nucleus accumbens). The incentive processing system influences decision making in terms of predicting and evaluating potential rewards (pleasures) and punishments. In the interval immediately following puberty, major changes take place in the incentive processing system involving dopamine and similar neurotransmitters (Albert & Steinberg, 2011; Chein et al., 2011; Ernst et al., 2009; Spear, 2010). Changes in the dopamine system result in heightened sensitivity to rewards (Spear, 2010). Reward-related regions of the brain and their neurocircuitry undergo marked changes (Doremus-Fitzwater et al., 2010; Steinberg, 2009). These pubertal changes have been linked to changes in reward-directed activity among adolescents, particularly in their willingness to engage in risky and socially motivated behaviors (Spear, 2010; Steinberg, 2010; Van Leijenhorst et al., 2010). Spikes in reward seeking, risk-taking, and peer influence during adolescence correlate with these aspects of normal adolescent brain development.

SYNAPTIC PRUNING

The paring away of unused synapses during childhood and early adolescence leads to more efficient neural connections. During adolescence, this pruning occurs particularly in the prefrontal cortex and is correlated with improved executive functioning. Most of the synaptic pruning during adolescence affects receptors for excitatory neurotransmitters like glutamate. By early adulthood, a shift has taken place and the brain has fewer excitatory synapses and more inhibitory synapses (Spear, 2000).

MYELINATION

The adolescent brain acquires a significant amount of myelin. This process goes on until age 25. Myelin improves connectivity within the prefrontal cortex and is important for higher-order functions like planning, inhibiting impulses, weighing risks and rewards, and considering multiple sources of information simultaneously (Casey et al., 2000; Sowell et al., 2001; Steinberg, 2009).

CORTICAL AND SUBCORTICAL INTERCONNECTIONS

Well into late adolescence there is an increase in connections, not only among cortical areas but also between cortical and subcortical regions. These connections, and their myelination, are especially important in developing emotional regulation (Eluvathingal et al., 2007; Somerville et al., 2010; Spear, 2010; Steinberg, 2009). Adolescents grow in their abilities to make mature judgments about risk and reward, and to control their emotional impulses, especially in situations that are socially charged (Chein et al., 2011; Spear, 2010; Steinberg, 2010).

PREDICTING JUVENILE VIOLENCE

If mental health professionals could determine which juveniles already have well-formed characters, and if we could predict which juveniles will become antisocial adults, then we could consult effectively to the courts in rendering behavioral predictions that are relevant to juvenile sentencing. The methodology for making such determinations is the topic of this section.

For three decades, researchers have been searching for variables that will predict which juvenile offenders will desist from crime and which will continue to commit crimes as juveniles and as adults. In the 1990s, the concept of psychopathy was borrowed from the adult literature and was applied to adolescents (Frick et al., 1994; Lynam, 1996, 1997).

Psychometric tools for assessing juvenile risk, recidivism, and psychopathy began to appear around 2002. These include:

- the Structured Assessment of Violence Risk in Youth (SAVRY; Borum et al., 2002, 2006)
- the Youth Level of Service/Case Management Inventory (YLC/CMI; Hoge & Andrews, 2002)
- the Psychopathy Checklist: Youth Version (PCL:YV; Forth et al., 2003).

A survey by Viljoen et al., (2010) indicated that these tools are widely used in mental health and juvenile justice settings.

The PCL:YV is a version of the Psychopathy Checklist-Revised (PCL-R; Hare, 2003), modified to suit the developmental level of adolescents. It consists of twenty items in two factors and four domains: Factor 1: Interpersonal-Affective (comprising Interpersonal and Affective domains), and Factor 2: Lifestyle-Antisocial (comprising Lifestyle and Antisocial domains).

The YLS/CMI is an actuarial instrument comprising forty-two variables and assessing eight categories of risk factors:

- prior and current offenses
- family circumstances/parenting
- education/employment
- peer associations

- substance abuse
- leisure/recreation
- personality/behavior
- attitudes/orientation.

The SAVRY is a structured professional judgment (SPJ; see Chapter 12 for a discussion of SPJs) of twenty-four items in three domains (historical risk factors, social/contextual risk factors, and individual risk factors).

Research with these instruments has yielded some encouraging results, suggesting that juvenile recidivism can be predicted. Three important research questions were asked:

- whether juvenile psychopathy exists as a stable feature of personality
- whether juveniles with psychopathic characteristics will go on to exhibit the same characteristics as adults
- whether juvenile behaviors predict juvenile recidivism and adult crime.

The first wave of research demonstrated that childhood psychopathy is indeed a reality (Lynam & Gudonis, 2005). Childhood psychopathy is a stable personality trait, with a stability coefficient of 0.80 for repeated assessments by the same parent across a span of four years (Frick et al., 2003). Also, a number of studies have demonstrated its convergent validity – measures of childhood psychopathy have correlated positively with measurements of aggression (Edens et al., 2001), number of charges (Salekin et al., 2004), and delinquency at a five- to seven-year follow-up (Piatigorsky & Hinshaw, 2004).

The second research question is whether childhood psychopathy predicts adult psychopathy. Research suggests that psychopathy is a relatively stable personality trait from childhood to young adulthood. Using a sample of 271 boys from the Pittsburgh Youth Study, Lynam et al., (2007) compared psychopathy at age 13 (assessed by using mothers' reports on the Childhood Psychopathy Scale; CPS; Lynam, 1997) with assessments at age 24 using the interviewer-rated Psychopathy Checklist: Screening Version (PCL:SV; Hart et al., 1995). Psychopathy proved to be relatively stable ($r = .31$). While this correlation is statistically significant ($p < .001$), and is of the magnitude that is generally found for significant relationships in social science research, please note that it explains only 9.6 percent of the variance.

When data from the Pittsburgh Youth Study (Lynam et al., 2007) were used to predict adult psychopathy from juvenile psychopathy, the false positive rate was unacceptably high. Table 15.1 presents these data in the form of an error matrix. (Error matrices are explained in Appendix O.) Please note that the PCL:SV has a cut score, but the CPS does not. The authors therefore created an arbitrary cut score for the CPS at the top quintile.

Table 15.1 Utility of the Childhood Psychopathy Scale (CPS) in predicting adult psychopathy as measured by the Psychopathy Checklist: Screening Version (PCL:SV)

	PCL:SV at age 24			
CPS at age 13	Psychopathic	Not psychopathic	Totals	
Top quintile	9	46	55	positive predictive value = .16
Bottom four quintiles	12	204	216	negative predictive value = .94
Totals	21	250	271	total predictive value = .79
	sensitivity = .43	specificity = .82		

Source: Data from Lynam et al. (2007).

Note
Rate of adult psychopathy: 7.7 percent.

As can be seen in Table 15.1, the CPS was accurate 79 percent of the time and wrong 21 percent of the time in predicting whether or not an adolescent with psychopathic features would continue to show psychopathy as a young adult. Breaking this answer into its two components, when the CPS predicted that a juvenile *was not* going to show psychopathy as an adult, it was accurate a very respectable 94 percent of the time and wrong only 6 percent of the time; however, when the CPS predicted that a juvenile *was* going to become an adult psychopath, it was right only 16 percent of the time and wrong a whopping 84 percent of the time. This true positive rate of 16 percent does not come close to the meaning of "more likely than not." It is consistent with the arguments presented in the joint amicus brief discussed above, that bad behavior by juveniles does not provide any reasonable degree of certainty in predicting adult psychopathy. Most juveniles outgrow their antisocial tendencies: even those in the top quintile of the CPS. As Lynam et al. concluded, "developmentally normative traits might masquerade as psychopathy" (2007, p. 162).

In 2001, Edens et al. argued that psychopathy measured during adolescence may not tap into stable and deviant personality features but rather may reflect irrelevant variance associated with normal and temporary characteristics of adolescent behavior. Mulvey and Cauffman wrote in the same year that the assessment of adolescents "presents the formidable challenge of trying to capture a rapidly changing process with few trustworthy markers" (p. 799). Trying to predict adult criminal behavior from juvenile behavior is like trying to hit a moving target.

As explained in Appendix O, this high false positive rate of 84 percent is related to the low base rate of adult psychopathy in this sample (7.7 percent). The false positive rate would be lower in a sample with a higher base rate of psychopathy. Other research reviewed below has been more encouraging about the ability of psychometric tests to predict juvenile recidivism and adult crime. This is the third research question: Does juvenile psychopathy predict crime? The results have been somewhat mixed, but when psychometric test data are analyzed with correlations and receiver operating characteristics (see Appendix O), the results are generally positive. That is, there are indications that adult crime can be predicted from juvenile behavior.

Catchpole and Gretton (2003) followed 74 young offenders for one year to see if psychometric tests could predict juvenile recidivism. They found the SAVRY to have a large effect (AUC = 0.81), the PCL:YV to have a large effect (AUC = 0.73), and the YLC/CMI to have a moderate effect (AUC = 0.64). (For an explanation of AUC, see Appendix O.)

Gretton et al. (2004) followed a group of 157 juvenile delinquents in British Columbia for ten years and found that adolescent psychopathy measured with the PCL:YV did predict violent recidivism. The point bi-serial correlation – using PCL:YV score as a continuous variable and recidivism as a "yes-or-no" dichotomous variable – was 0.32 (p < .001). The PCL:YV also was effective in predicting which offenders would be the first to re-offend. The largest of the correlations was between Factor 2 (Lifestyle-Antisocial) of the PCL:YV and time to first violent offense, which was an impressive r = –0.49, p < .001.

Olver et al. (2009) reported the results of a meta-analysis of forty-nine studies and 8,746 juveniles. General violence and re-offending were moderately correlated at r = 0.31 and 0.33 for the SAVRY, r = 0.29 and 0.32 for the YLS/CMI, and r = 0.25 for the PCL:YV. These are modest correlations that explain a small part of the variance (6.3 percent to 10.9 percent) and are at a level that is typically found among significant re-lationships in social science research.

Shaffer et al. (2022) followed a group of 156 adjudicated juvenile delinquents in Vancouver, British Columbia, for four years. Predictions of general re-offending and violent re-offending were equally good, with AUC = 0.75 and 0.71 for the SAVRY, AUC = 0.75 and 0.72 for the YLS/CMI, and AUC = 0.76 and 0.71 for the PCL:YV. These AUC values all indicate large effect sizes.

Other research has had less encouraging results. Edens and Cahill (2007) followed a group of 75 male juvenile offenders for ten years and found that assessment of psychopathy with the PCL:YV did not predict either general recidivism or violent recidivism.

When we look retrospectively at the lives of juvenile delinquents, we often find that they have certain features in common. For example, they tend to come from broken homes and bad neighborhoods. But when we look at their lives prospectively, we do not find that these features nec-essarily lead to further delinquent behavior. These negative factors tend not to predict whether a particular juvenile will re-offend. While many adult criminals share common features from their childhoods, the great majority of juvenile offenders who have those same characteristics do not go on to become adult offenders.

For example, the Pittsburgh Youth Study (Loeber & Farrington, 2011) of 3,436 boys found that homicide offenders tended to come from broken families and bad neighborhoods. However, when those authors used these characteristics to predict who would commit homicide, they obtained an unacceptably high false positive rate of 87 percent (similar to that reported by Lynam et al. 2007; see above). When Loeber and Farrington (2011) restricted their sample to boys who already had committed an act of violence, the false positive rate did not decrease, but in fact rose slightly to 89 percent.

According to Piquero et al. (2012), most juveniles who are violent as adolescents have stopped being violent by their late teens or early twenties. Trying to predict which of these juveniles will be violent recidivists is virtually impossible. These and other researchers, including Monahan et al. (2009), have concluded that the behavior of those who will and those who will not become adult criminals is "often indistinguishable during adolescence" (p. 1655). Loeber et al. (2008) drew attention to the "danger that policy makers will start to use less than good predictions as a rationale for harsh punishments and severe legal sanctions" (p. 333).

The good news is that most juvenile offenders do not go on to become adult criminals. This is true even among juveniles who commit the most serious crimes (Loeber et al., 2008). The bad news – i.e., posing conceptual difficulties for the courts that must decide their futures – is that our ability to predict their future criminality is quite limited. The capacity of juveniles to change does not excuse their bad behavior, but it does argue against imposing the harshest penalties.

MILLER AND THE FOUR GOALS OF SENTENCING

The *Miller* court went on to address the four goals of sentencing (which are the subject of Chapter 6).

- *Retribution*: "Because '[t]he] heart of the retribution rationale' relates to an offender's blameworthiness, 'the case for retribution is not as strong with a minor as with an adult'" (*Miller*, at 472; quoting *Graham v. Florida* (2010) at 71, *Tison v. Arizona* (1987) at 149, and *Roper v. Simmons* (2005) at 571).
- *Deterrence*: "Nor can deterrence do the work in this context, because '"the same characteristics that render juveniles less culpable than adults"'—their immaturity, recklessness, and impetuosity—make them less likely to consider potential punishment." (*Miller*, at 472; quoting *Graham* at 72 and *Roper* at 571).
- *Incapacitation*: "Similarly, incapacitation could not support the life-without-parole sentence in *Graham*: Deciding that a 'juvenile offender forever will be a danger to society' would require 'mak[ing] a judgment that [he] is incorrigible'—but '"incorrigibility is inconsistent with youth."'" (*Miller*, at 472–473; quoting *Graham* at 73 and *Workman v. Commonwealth*, 1968, at 378).
- *Rehabilitation*: "And for the same reason, rehabilitation could not justify that sentence. Life without parole 'forswears altogether the rehabilitative ideal.' It reflects 'an irrevocable judgment about that

person's value and place in society,' at odds with a child's capacity for change." (*Miller*, at 473; quoting *Graham* at 74).

IMPLICATIONS OF THE *MILLER* DECISION

The position taken by the U.S. Supreme Court in *Miller* is that a sentence of life in prison without the possibility of parole is so severe a deprivation of liberty that it cannot be given to juveniles automatically based on the nature of their crime. Juvenile sentencing at this level of severity must take individual factors into account. As the court wrote in *Miller,* mandatory sentences of life without parole disregard the facts about a juvenile's immaturity, impetuosity, and failure to appreciate risks and consequences. Mandatory sentences preclude consideration of the juvenile's family and home environments from which they cannot extricate themselves. Mandatory sentencing overlooks the circumstances of their offense, which may include their degree of participation in the crime. It ignores the possibility that they may have been convicted of lesser offenses if not for certain incompetencies that are typical of youth, such as limitations in their capacity to assist their attorneys and inability to cope with police officers and prosecutors (such as may occur during plea negotiations). "[The] features that distinguish juveniles from adults also put them at a significant disadvantage in criminal proceedings" (*Miller* at 474; quoting *J. D. B. v. North Carolina*, 2011).

Miller opened the gateway for mental health professionals to participate in legal proceedings by investigating a juvenile's

- immaturity
- impulse control
- appreciation of risks and consequences
- home environment
- offense circumstances, including degree of participation
- competencies in dealing with the juvenile justice system.

For a recent text on mental health evaluation in juvenile sentencing, see Kavanaugh and Grisso (2020).

JONES V. MISSISSIPPI (U.S. 2021): A DOOR CLOSES ON MILLER

Nine years after individualized sentencing for juveniles became the law in *Miller*, the U.S. Supreme Court decided, in a 6–3 decision, that juveniles are not entitled to a finding of incorrigibility before they are sentenced to life without parole. In other words, judges can now sentence juveniles to life without parole without first having to conclude that this juvenile is not likely to be rehabilitated in the juvenile justice system. The *Jones* decision thereby closed one of the doors (likelihood of rehabilitation) that *Kent* and *Miller* had opened for juvenile defendants.

Justice Sotomayor wrote in her dissent that this decision "guts *Miller v. Alabama*" (at 1328). The good intentions of *Miller* are ineffectual if juvenile court judges are not required to act upon them.

REFERENCES

Albert, D., & Steinberg, L. (2011). Judgment and decision making in adolescence. *Journal of Research on Adolescence, 21*(1), 211–224. doi:10.1111/j.1532-7795.2010.00724.x.

American Psychological Association. (2012). Brief for the American Psychological Association, American Psychiatric Association, and National Association of Social Workers as *amici curiae* in support of petitioners Evan Miller and Kuntrell Jackson, in the Supreme Court of the United States. Retrieved 11/27/2022 from www.apa.org/about/offices/ogc/amicus/miller-hobbs.pdf.

Arnett, J. (1992). Reckless behavior in adolescence: A developmental perspective. *Developmental Review, 12*(4), 339–373. doi:10.1016/0273-2297(92)90013-R.

Berndt, T. (1979). Developmental changes in conformity to peers and parents. *Developmental Psychology, 15*(6), 608–616. doi:10.1037/0012-1649.15.6.608.

Borum, R., Bartel, P., & Forth, A. (2002). *Manual for the Structured Assessment of Violence Risk in Youth: Consultation version*. Tampa: University of South Florida, Florida Mental Health Institute.

Borum, R., Bartel, P., & Forth, A. (2006). *SAVRY: Structured Assessment of Violence Risk in Youth: Professional manual*. Lutz, FL: Psychological Assessment Resources.

Bridges, G., & Steen, S. (1998). Racial disparities in official assessments of juvenile offenders: Attributional stereotypes as mediating mechanisms. *American Sociological Review, 63*(4), 554–570. doi:10.2307/2657267.

Casey, B. J., Giedd, J. N., & Thomas, K. M. (2000). Structural and functional brain development and its relation to cognitive development. *Biological Psychiatry, 54*(1–3), 241–257. doi:10.1016/s0301-0511(00)00058-2.

Catchpole, R. E. H., & Gretton, H. M. (2003). The predictive validity of risk assessment with violent young offenders: A 1-year examination of criminal outcome. *Criminal Justice and Behavior, 30*(6), 688–708. doi:10.1177/0093854803256455.

Caudill, J. W., & Trulson, C. R. (2016). The hazards of premature release: Recidivism outcomes of blended-sentence juvenile homicide offenders. *Journal of Criminal Justice, 46*, 219–227. doi:10.1016/j.jcrimjus.2016.05.009.

Cauffman, E., & Steinberg, L. (2000). (Im)maturity of judgement in adolescence: Why adolescents may be less culpable than adults. *Behavioral Sciences and the Law, 18*(6), 741–760. doi:10.1002/bsl.416.

Chein, J., Albert, D., O'Brien, L., Uckert, K., & Steinberg, L. (2011). Peers increase adolescent risk taking by enhancing activity in the brain's reward circuitry. *Developmental Science, 14*(2), F1–F10. doi:10.1111/j.1467-7687.2010.01035.x.

Damasio, A., & Anderson, S. (2003). The frontal lobes. In K. Heilman & E. Valenstein (Eds.) *Clinical Neuropsychology. Fourth edition* (pp. 404–446). Oxford: Oxford University Press.

Doremus-Fitzwater, T. L., Varlinskaya, E. I., & Spear, L. P. (2010). Motivational systems in adolescence: Possible implications for age differences in substance abuse and other risk-taking behaviors. *Brain and Cognition, 72*(1), 114–123. doi:10.1016/j.bandc.2009.08.008.

Edens, J. F., & Cahill, M. (2007). Psychopathy in adolescence and criminal recidivism in young adulthood: Longitudinal results from a multiethnic sample of youthful offenders. *Assessment, 14*(1), 57–64. doi:10.1177/1073191106290711.

Edens, J. F., Skeem, J. L., Cruise, K. R., & Cauffman, E. (2001). Assessment of "juvenile psychopathy" and its association with violence: A critical review. *Behavioral Sciences and the Law, 19*(1), 53–80. doi:10.1002/bsl.425.

Eddings v. Oklahoma, 455 U.S. 104 (1982).

Eluvathingal, T. J., Hasan, K. M., Kramer, L., Fletcher, J. M., & Ewing-Cobbs, L. (2007). Quantitative diffusion tensor tractography of association and projection fibers in normally developing children and adolescents. *Cerebral Cortex, 17*(12), 2760–2768. doi:10.1093/CERCOR/BHM003.

Ernst, M., Romero, R. D., & Andersen, S. L. (2009). Neurobiology of the development of motivated behaviors in adolescence: A window into a neural systems model. *Pharmacology, Biochemistry, and Behavior, 93*(3), 199–211. doi:10.1016/j.pbb.2008.12.013.

Fagan, J. (2000). Contexts of choice by adolescents in criminal events. In T. Grisso & R. Schwartz (Eds.), *Youth on trial: A developmental perspective on juvenile justice* (pp. 371–401). Chicago: University of Chicago Press.

Farrington, D. (1986). Age and crime. In M. Tonry & N. Morris (Eds.) *Crime and justice: An annual review of research* (pp. 189–217). Chicago: University of Chicago Press.

Forth, A. E., Kosson, D. S., & Hare, R. D. (2003). *The Hare Psychopathy Checklist: Youth Version.* Toronto: Multi-Health Systems.

Frick, P. J., Kimonis, E. R., Dandreaux, D. M., & Farell, J. M. (2003). The 4 year stability of psychopathic traits in non-referred youth. *Behavioral Sciences and the Law, 21*(6), 713–736. doi:10.1002/bsl.568.

Frick, P. J., O'Brien, B. S., Wootton, J. M., & McBurnett, K. (1994). Psychopathy and conduct problems in children. *Journal of Abnormal Psychology, 103*(4), 700–707. doi:10.1037//0021-843x.103.4.700.

Galvan, A., Hare, T., Voss, H., Glover, G., & Casey, B. J. (2007). Risk-taking and the adolescent brain: Who is at risk? *Developmental Science, 10*(2), 8–14. doi:10.1111/j.1467-7687.2006.00579.x

Goldberg, E. (2001). *The executive brain: Frontal lobes and the civilized mind.* Oxford: Oxford University Press.

Graham, S. (March 2002). Racial stereotypes in the juvenile justice system. Paper presented at the biennial meeting of the American Psychology-Law Society, Austin, TX.

Graham v. Florida, 560 U.S. 48 (2010).

Gretton, H. M., Hare, R. D., & Catchpole, R. E. (2004). Psychopathy and offending from adolescence to adulthood: A 10-year follow-up. *Journal of Consulting and Clinical Psychology, 72*(4), 636–645. doi:10.1037/0022-006X.72.4.636.

Halpern-Felsher, B., & Cauffman, E. (2001). Costs and benefits of a decision: Decision-making competence in adolescents and adults. *Journal of Applied Developmental Psychology, 22*(3), 257–273. doi:10.1016/S0193-3973(01)00083-1.

Hare, R. D. (2003). *The Hare Psychopathy Checklist – Revised. Second edition.* Toronto: Multi-Health Systems.

Hart, S. D., Cox, D. N., & Hare, R. D. (1995). *The Hare Psychopathy Checklist: Screening Version.* Toronto: Multi-Health Systems.

Heide, K. M., Spencer, E., Thompson, A., & Solomon, E. P. (2001). Who's in, who's out, and who's back: Follow-up data on 59 juveniles incarcerated in adult prison for murder or attempted murder in the early 1980s. *Behavioral Sciences and the Law, 19*(1), 97–108. doi:10.1002/bsl.423.

Hoge, R., & Andrews, D. (2002). *The Youth Level of Service/Case Management Inventory manual and scoring key.* Toronto: Multi-Health Systems.

J. D. B. v. North Carolina, 564 U. S. 261 (2011).

Jones v. Mississippi, 593 U.S. ____, 141 S. Ct. 1307 (2021).

Kadish, S. (1987). Excusing crime. *California Law Review, 75*(1), 257–296. doi:10.2307/3480580.

Kavanaugh, A., & Grisso, T. (2020). *Evaluations for sentencing of juveniles in criminal court.* Oxford: Oxford University Press.

Khachatryan, N., Heide, K. M., & Hummel, E. V. (2016) Recidivism patterns among two types of juvenile homicide offenders: A 30-year follow-up study. *International Journal of Offender Therapy and Comparative Criminology.* doi:10.1177/0306624xX16657052.

Leshem, R., & Glicksohn, J. (2007). The construct of impulsivity revisited. *Personality and Individual Differences, 43*(4), 68–691. doi:10.1016/J.PAID.2007.01/015.

Loeber, R., & Farrington, D. P. (2011). *Young homicide offenders and victims: Risk factors, prediction, and prevention from childhood.* New York: Springer.

Loeber, R., Farrington, D. P., Stouthamer-Loeber, M., & White, H. R. (Eds.) (2008). *Violence and serious theft: Development and prediction from childhood to adulthood.* New York: Taylor and Francis Group, LLC.

Lynam, D. R. (1996). Early identification of chronic offenders: Who is the fledgling psychopath? *Psychological Bulletin, 120*(2), 209–234. doi:10.1037/0033-2909.120.2.209.

Lynam, D. R. (1997). Pursuing the psychopath: Capturing the fledgling psychopath in a nomological net. *Journal of Abnormal Psychology, 106*(3), 425–438. doi:10.1037//0021-843x.106.3.425.

Lynam, D. R., Caspi, A., Moffitt, T. E., Loeber, R., & Stouthamer-Loeber, M. (2007). Longitudinal evidence that psychopathy scores in early adolescence predict adult psychopathy. *Journal of Abnormal Psychology, 116*(1), 155–165. doi:10.1037/0021-843X.116.1.155.

Lynam, D. R., & Gudonis, L. (2005). The development of psychopathy. *Annual Review of Clinical Psychology, 1*, 381–407. doi:10.1146/ANNUREV.CLINPSY. 1.102803.144019.

Miller v. Alabama, 567 U.S. 460 (2012).

Moffitt, T. (1993). Adolescence-limited and life-course-persistent antisocial behavior: A developmental taxonomy. *Psychological Review, 100*(4), 674–701. doi:10.1037/0033-295X.100.4.674.

Moffitt, T. (1994). Natural histories of delinquency. In E. G. M. Weitekamp & H. J. Kerner (Eds.) *Cross-national longitudinal research on human development and criminal behavior* (pp. 3–61). New York: Springer.

Monahan, K. C., Steinberg, L., Cauffman, E., & Mulvey, E. P. (2009). Trajectories of antisocial behavior and psychosocial maturity from adolescence to young adulthood. *Developmental Psychology, 45*(6), 1654–1668. doi:10.1037/a0015862.

Morse, S. (1994). Culpability and control. *University of Pennsylvania Law Review, 142*(5), 1587–1660. https://scholarship.law.upenn.edu/penn_law_review/vol142/iss5/7.

Mulvey, E., & Cauffman, E. (2001). The inherent limits of predicting school violence. *American Psychologist, 56*(10), 797–802. doi:10.1037//0003-066x. 56.10.797.

Olver, M. E., Stockdale, K. C., & Wormith, J. S. (2009). Risk assessment with young offenders: A meta-analysis of three assessment measures. *Criminal Justice and Behavior, 36*(4), 329–353. doi:10.1177/0093854809331457.

Piatigorsky, A., & Hinshaw, S. P. (2004). Psychopathic traits in boys with and without attention-deficit/hyperactivity disorder: Concurrent and longitudinal correlates. *Journal of Abnormal Child Psychology, 32*(5), 535–550. doi:10. 1023/B:JACP.0000037782.28482.6b.

Piquero, A. R., Jennings, W. G., & Barnes, J. C. (2012). Violence in criminal careers: A review of the literature from a developmental life-course perspective. *Aggression and Violent Behavior, 17*(3), 171–179. doi:10.1016/j.avb.2012.02.008.

Roper v. Simmons, 543 U.S. 551 (2005).

Salekin, R. T., Leistico, A. M., Neumann, C. S., DiCicco, T. M., & Duros, R. L. (2004). Psychopathy and comorbidity in a young offender sample: Taking a closer look at psychopathy's potential importance over disruptive behavior disorders. *Journal of Abnormal Psychology, 113*(3), 416–427. doi:10.1037/ 0021-843X.113.3.416.

Scott, E., & Steinberg, L. (2008). *Rethinking juvenile justice*. Cambridge, MA: Harvard University Press.

Shaffer, C. S., Viljoen, J. L., & Douglas, K. S. (2022). Predictive validity of the SAVRY, YLS/CMI, and PCL:YV is poor for intimate partner violence perpetration among adolescent offenders. *Law and Human Behavior, 46*(3), 189–200. doi:10.1037/1hb0000483.

Somerville, L. H., Jones, R. M., & Casey, B. J. (2010). A time of change: Behavioral and neural correlates of adolescent sensitivity to appetitive and aversive environmental cues. *Brain and Cognition, 72*(1), 124–133. doi:10.1016/j.bandc.2009.07.003.

Sowell, E. R., Thompson, P. M., Holmes, C. J., Jernigan, T. L., & Toga, A. W. (1999). *In vivo* evidence for post-adolescent brain maturation in frontal and striatal regions. *Nature Neuroscience, 2*(10), 859–861. doi:10.1038/13154.

Sowell, E. R., Thompson, P. M., Tessner, K. D., & Toga, A. W. (2001). Mapping continued brain growth and gray matter density reduction in dorsal frontal cortex: Inverse relationships during postadolescent brain maturation. *Journal of Neuroscience: The official journal of the Society for Neuroscience, 21*(22), 8819–8829. doi:10.1523/JNEUROSCI.21-22-08819.2001.

Spear, L. P. (2000). The adolescent brain and age-related behavioral manifestations. *Neuroscience and Biobehavioral Reviews, 24*(4), 417–463. doi:10.1016/s0149-7634(00)00014-2.

Spear, L. P. (2010). *The behavioral neuroscience of adolescence.* New York: Norton.

Steinberg, L. (2009). Should the science of adolescent brain development inform public policy? *American Psychologist, 64*(8), 739–750. doi:10.1037/0003-066X.64.8.739.

Steinberg, L. (2010). A behavioral scientist looks at the science of adolescent brain development. *Brain and Cognition, 72*(1), 160–164. doi:10.1016/j.bandc.2009.11.003.

Steinberg, L., & Schwartz, R. (2000). Developmental psychology goes to court. In T. Grisso & R. Schwartz (Eds.) *Youth on trial: A developmental perspective on juvenile justice* (pp. 9–31). Chicago, IL: University of Chicago Press.

Steinberg, L., & Scott, E. S. (2003). Less guilty by reason of adolescence: Developmental immaturity, diminished responsibility, and the juvenile death penalty. *American Psychologist, 58*(12), 1009–1018. doi:10.1037/0003-066X.58.12.1009.

Steinberg, L., & Silverberg, S. B. (1986). The vicissitudes of autonomy in early adolescence. *Child Development, 57*(4), 841–851. doi:10.2307/1130361.

Thompson v. Oklahoma, 487 U.S. 815 (1988).

Tison v. Arizona, 481 U.S. 137 (1987).

Van Leijenhorst, L., Zanolie, K., Van Meel, C. S., Westenberg, P. M., Rombouts, S. A. R. B., & Crone, E. A. (2010). What motivates the adolescent? Brain regions mediating reward sensitivity across adolescence. *Cerebral Cortex, 20*(1), 61–69. doi:10.1093/cercor/bhp078.

Viljoen, J. L., McLachlan, K., & Vincent, G. M. (2010). Assessing violence risk and psychopathy in juvenile and adult offenders: A survey of clinical practices. *Assessment, 17*(3), 377–395. doi:10.1177/1073191109359587.

Wahlstrom, D., Collins, P., White, T., & Luciana, M. (2010). Developmental changes in dopamine neurotransmission in adolescence: Behavioral implications and issues in assessment. *Brain and Cognition, 72*(1), 146–159. doi:10.1016/j.bandc.2009.10.013.

Waterman, A. (1982). Identity development from adolescence to adulthood: An extension of theory and a review of research. *Developmental Psychology, 18*(3), 341–358. doi:10.1037/0012-1649.18.3.341.

Workman v. Commonwealth, 429 S. W. 2d 374 (Kentucky App. 1968).

Zimring, F. (2000). Penal proportionality for the young offender. In T. Grisso, & R. Schwartz (Eds.) *Youth on Trial* (pp. 271–289). Chicago, IL: University of Chicago Press.

16 Civil commitment of sexually violent predators (SVPs)

Kansas v. Hendricks (U.S. 1997)

Sex offenders who are released from prison are not likely to recidivate. Sex offenders are treated harshly by other inmates, many of whom are child abuse victims themselves, who act out their anger and revenge on incarcerated sex offenders. No ex-convict wants to return to prison, but this is especially true of sex offenders.

Among adult sex offenders, recidivism rates range from about 3 percent after three years to about 24 percent after 15 years (Przybylski, 2015). Recidivism rates among juvenile sex offenders range from about 7 to 13 percent after five years (Lobanov-Rostovsky, 2015). These figures are low compared to general recidivism, which is around 66 percent after three years and 82 percent after ten years (Antenangeli & Durose, 2021).

A large study by the Bureau of Justice Statistics (Alper & Ducrose, 2019) followed 20,195 sex offenders released from state prisons in 30 states for nine years. Of those, 67 percent were re-arrested within nine years, but most of them were arrested for other crimes. Only 8 percent were arrested for another sexual assault or rape. In other words, sex offenders may return to prison for other crimes, but they are not likely to return to prison for another sex crime.

In short, a relatively small number of sex offenders released from prison continue to pose a threat to public safety in terms of sexual re-offending. The challenges to our courts, correctional systems, and mental health professions are to identify those sex offenders who continue to pose a risk and then to adjudicate, incapacitate, and treat them appropriately.

SVPS WHO POSE A THREAT TO PUBLIC SAFETY AT THE TIME OF THEIR RELEASE CAN BE CIVILLY COMMITTED: *KANSAS V. HENDRICKS* (U.S. 1997)

Leroy Hendricks was a repeat child molester. He agreed with the mental health professionals who examined him that he was a pedophile. His career of sexually abusing children began at the age of 21 in 1955, when

DOI: 10.4324/9781003385028-19

he exposed his genitals to two young girls. He pleaded guilty to indecent exposure. Then, in 1957, he was found guilty of lewdness toward a young girl and he served a brief jail sentence. In 1960, he molested two young boys while he was working at a carnival. He served two years and was paroled. Then he molested a 7-year-old girl. He was treated for sexual deviance at a state psychiatric hospital, and in 1965 was discharged as being "safe to be at large." Shortly thereafter he performed oral sex on an 8-year-old girl and fondled the penis of an 11-year-old boy. He was imprisoned again in 1967, where he refused to participate in sex offender treatment and therefore remained in prison until 1972. Shortly after his parole, he began sexually abusing his stepson and stepdaughter; this abuse continued for four years. Then he attempted to fondle two adolescent boys and he was returned to prison. He was eligible for release in 1994.

By Hendricks' own testimony, he had an uncontrollable urge to molest children whenever he felt "stressed out." He said that "treatment is bullshit," and that the only time his criminal behavior would end would be when he died. Kansas had to decide what to do with this repeat and recalcitrant child molester. Hendricks was the first offender committed under Kansas' Sexually Violent Predator Act (SVPA). Under the Kansas law, when a sex offender has served their sentence, the state can initiate commitment proceedings, keep them incapacitated, and thereby continue to protect the public. This law is consistent with one of the general principles of civil commitment; namely, to incapacitate persons with mental illness who are a danger to others. Kansas Statute 59-29a02 allows for the "involuntary detention or commitment" of a person

a … who suffers from a mental abnormality or personality disorder which makes the person likely to engage in repeat acts of sexual violence.

b "Mental abnormality" means a congenital or acquired condition affecting the emotional or volitional capacity which predisposes the person to commit sexually violent offenses in a degree constituting such person a menace to the health and safety of others.

It is essential in SVP laws that they mention mental illness and lack of self-control (volitional incapacity). Otherwise, SVP proceedings could be misused as a means of committing any unpopular defendant who has committed a sex offense. In the words of the U.S. Supreme Court, these provisions are "necessary lest 'civil commitment' become a 'mechanism for retribution or general deterrence'" (*Kansas v. Crane*, 2002, at 407, quoting *Kansas v. Hendricks*, 1997, at 372–373).

Please notice that the Kansas law mentions "personality disorder" in paragraph (a), which sets forth the grounds for commitment, but omits it from paragraph (b), which entails "emotional or volitional capacity." That is, there is no assumption under the Kansas law that personality disorder involves loss of capacity, yet personality disorder can serve as grounds for commitment. (We will return shortly to this matter of the inclusion of personality disorder in SVP laws.)

A jury unanimously found beyond a reasonable doubt that Leroy Hendricks was a sexually violent predator. He was held in prison past his release date. Hendricks appealed this decision, arguing that his continued confinement violated the due process, double jeopardy, and ex post facto protections of the U.S. Constitution. The U.S. Supreme Court disagreed with him and upheld the Kansas decision to keep him incapacitated. However, the U.S. Supreme Court clarified that Hendricks was not facing any new charges, and therefore his commitment was civil and not criminal. This distinction has two important outcomes – the defendant goes to a hospital and not to a prison, and the distinction between emotional and volitional incapacity is void (see the discussion below of *Kansas v. Crane*, 2002).

At the present time, the federal government, the District of Columbia, and nineteen states have SVP laws: Arizona, California, Florida, Illinois, Kansas, Massachusetts, Minnesota, Missouri, Nebraska, New Hampshire, New Jersey, New York, North Dakota, Pennsylvania, South Carolina, Texas, Virginia, Washington, and Wisconsin.

In 1994, Leroy Hendricks was transferred from prison to Larned State Hospital, where he participated in sex offender treatment. In 2005, he was moved to Osawatomie State Hospital in preparation for transfer to a private facility, which was consistent with his progress in therapy. In 2005, at age 70 and confined to a wheelchair, he was moved to a private facility in a rural, residential area near Linwood, Kansas. A Kansas couple planned to establish a group home for sexual predators at that site. Kansas agreed to pay the couple $278,000 to house Hendricks and maintain 24-hour surveillance for 15 months. However, the couple had failed to obtain a special use permit before moving Hendricks to the facility, and he was returned to Osawatomie State Hospital within a matter of days (Scheller, 2006). He died in custody in 2010.

LOSS OF VOLITIONAL CONTROL DOES NOT HAVE TO BE COMPLETE: *KANSAS V. CRANE* (U.S. 2002)

On January 6, 1993, Michael T. Crane (age 31) exposed himself to an attendant at a tanning salon. Then, thirty minutes later, he attacked a clerk at a video store. He waited until the store was empty, and then he grabbed the clerk from behind. With his genitals exposed, he lifted her, pushed her, and squeezed her neck with his hands. He ordered her to perform oral sex and said he was going to rape her. The attack ended suddenly when Crane simply stopped and ran out of the store. He had a history of being sexually inappropriate on other occasions.

Crane's behavior suggested a mixture of volitional elements. The fact that he assaulted two women in the space of thirty minutes suggests that he was in the grip of a powerful compulsion that he was not able to control. The fact that he stopped and ran away suggests that he had some degree of volitional control.

Crane was convicted of lewd and lascivious behavior for the incident at the tanning salon. He was convicted of kidnaping, attempted rape, and attempted aggravated criminal sodomy for his behavior in the video store. He was sentenced to 35 years to life. Because of procedural errors by the prosecution which involved failure to file appropriate information within designated time limits, his conviction was overturned. He pleaded guilty to aggravated sexual battery for the assault in the video store and his sentence was reduced to three to ten years. After a little more than four years, he was scheduled for release. Kansas authorities sought to have him committed as an SVP. The psychologist who evaluated him diagnosed him with exhibitionism (a paraphilic disorder) and antisocial personality disorder. In the psychologist's opinion, Crane was a sexually violent predator. The psychologist noted the "increasing frequency" and "increasing intensity" of these incidents, as well as Crane's "increasing disregard for the rights of others and his increasing daring and aggressiveness" (*Kansas v. Crane*, at 417).

Also, Crane claimed "to have been in a blackout state during the video store incident." Another psychologist examined him regarding that claim and did not believe him (*In re Care and Treatment of Michael T. Crane*, 2000).

Crane was committed as an SVP by the Kansas District Court. The Kansas Supreme Court disagreed, reversed, and remanded for a new trial, because

> the jury ... was not instructed to make a finding as to Crane's inability to control his behavior. Since we hold that such a finding is required, the failure to so instruct the jury was error and requires that we reverse and remand for a new trial. (*In re Care and Treatment of Michael T. Crane*, 2000)

Crane was held in custody while the State of Kansas appealed this decision to the U.S. Supreme Court. The U.S. Supreme Court agreed that *Kansas v. Hendricks* "requires a finding that the defendant cannot control his dangerous behavior ... And the trial court made no such finding" (*Kansas v. Crane*, at 407).

The U.S. Supreme Court went on to clarify what their ruling in *Hendricks* does not require.

Hendricks set forth no requirement of *total* or *complete* lack of control, but the Constitution does not permit commitment of the type of dangerous sexual offender considered in *Hendricks* without *any* lack-of-control determination. *Hendricks* referred to the Act as requiring an abnormality or disorder that makes it *"difficult*, if not impossible, for the [dangerous] person to control his dangerous behavior." *Id.*, at 358 (emphasis added). The word "difficult" indicates that the lack of control was not absolute. Indeed, an absolutist approach is unworkable and would risk barring the civil commitment of highly dangerous persons suffering severe mental abnormalities. Yet a distinction between a dangerous sexual offender subject to civil commitment and "other dangerous persons who are perhaps more properly dealt with exclusively through criminal proceedings," *id.*, at 360, is necessary lest "civil commitment" become a "mechanism for retribution or general deterrence," *id.*, at 372–373. In *Hendricks*, this Court did not give "lack of control" a particularly narrow or technical meaning, and in cases where it is at issue, "inability to control behavior" will not be demonstrable with mathematical precision. It is enough to say that there must be proof of serious difficulty in controlling behavior. The Constitution's liberty safeguards in the area of mental illness are not always best enforced through precise bright-line rules. States retain considerable leeway in defining the mental abnormalities and personality disorders that make an individual eligible for commitment; and psychiatry, which informs but does not control ultimate legal determinations, is an ever advancing science, whose distinctions do not seek precisely to mirror those of the law. Consequently, the Court has sought to provide constitutional guidance in this area by proceeding deliberately and contextually, elaborating generally stated constitutional standards and objectives as specific circumstances require, the approach embodied in *Hendricks*. That *Hendricks* limited its discussion to volitional disabilities is not surprising, as the case involved pedophilia – a mental abnormality involving what a lay person might describe as a lack of control. But when considering civil commitment, the Court has not ordinarily distinguished for constitutional purposes between volitional, emotional, and cognitive impairments. See, *e.g.*, *Jones* v. *United States*, 463 U.S. 354. The Court in *Hendricks* had no occasion to consider whether confinement based solely on "emotional" abnormality would be constitutional, and has no occasion to do so here. Pp. 410–415. (*Kansas v. Crane*, at 407–408)

The U.S. Supreme Court vacated the decision by the Kansas Supreme Court and remanded the case back to the Kansas courts for further deliberation.

Please note that in the passage above the U.S. Supreme Court condoned the use of personality disorder as a diagnosis in commitment proceedings. If I may be allowed to paraphrase:

> States will be allowed to decide who they commit, but they cannot commit just any defendant. There must be some determination by a court that the defendant is not able to control their own behavior. The Constitution does not allow commitment unless it is determined that the defendant lacks self-control. This lack of self-control need not be complete, but "there must be proof of serious difficulty in controlling behavior" (*Kansas v. Crane*, at 407). The court thereby defines a class of sex offenders for whom civil commitment is appropriate, so that the civil commitment of sex offenders does not become a mechanism for retribution or general deterrence. (Retribution and general deterrence are goals of sentencing in criminal trials and not in civil commitment proceedings. The goals of civil commitment proceedings are to protect the public and the individual.) Because Crane was involved in a civil commitment and not a criminal proceeding, the Court did not need to distinguish whether his impairment was cognitive, emotional, or volitional.

Michael Crane remained in custody for more than three years after he completed his sentence. It took that long for his case to work its way through the courts. He was released in January 2002 – the same month that the U.S. Supreme Court vacated the decision by the Kansas Supreme Court – after his doctors concluded that his condition had changed and that he was no longer a threat to the public.

Crane was re-arrested 14 months after his release for attacking a woman in her car. DNA from the semen at that crime matched his DNA, which is kept in a database of convicted felons. He faced a possible life sentence at that time (Associated Press, 2003). However, the Kansas prisoner locator shows that he was released in 2003.

DIAGNOSTIC CONTROVERSIES AT SVP HEARINGS

As noted above, paragraph (a) of the Kansas statute includes "personality disorder" alongside "mental abnormality." Similar laws are found in other states. Only New York and the federal government have rejected this use of the diagnosis of personality disorder (see Sreenivasan et al., 2020, who compiled two tables that list the statutory and case law regarding SVPs in every jurisdiction).

The inclusion of personality disorder as a mental disorder makes SVP laws unique among all areas of the law. Other procedures preclude consideration of persons whose only evidence of abnormality is repeated criminal acts (which applies to the diagnoses of conduct disorder and antisocial personality disorder). Antisocial personality disorder (ASPD) cannot be used to argue insanity. The Model Penal Code (Section 401.(2)) specifically omits from the insanity defense "an abnormality manifested only by repeated criminal or otherwise antisocial conduct." ASPD does not make a person eligible for disability benefits. It cannot be used to obtain mental health treatment services in prison. It cannot be used in civil commitment proceedings. In *Foucha v. Louisiana* (1992) – a case regarding the commitment of an insanity acquittee – the U.S. Supreme Court ruled that ASPD is not a mental illness. Ambiguity over whether ASPD is a mental disorder led to the infamous "weekend flip flop case" (*In re Rosenfield*, 1957; see Chapter 19), which proved embarrassing to the mental health profession.

The most common DSM diagnosis among SVPs is "other specified paraphilia, nonconsent." This diagnosis is often given mistakenly, because clinicians fail to understand the nature of paraphilia (Frances, 2020). Paraphilia is denoted by "intense and persistent sexual interest" (American Psychiatric Association, 2022, p. 779). Rape and molestation are crimes, but they are not paraphilias unless the defendant has an "intense and persistent sexual interest" in those behaviors. The American Psychiatric Association, when drafting the various iterations of the DSM, consistently rejected the idea that rape could be considered a form of paraphilia (where it might be called "coercive paraphilia" or "paraphilia, nonconsent"), because "Rape is always, or almost always, just a simple crime; it is never, or very rarely, related to a paraphilic arousal pattern" (Frances, 2020, p. 193). Experts who give the wrong diagnosis at an SVP hearing because they fail to understand the DSM criteria may face cross-examination regarding the proper use of the diagnosis.

Certain crimes are so horrific, senseless, and repulsive that it is tempting to imagine that the perpetrator must have a mental illness, but this is not always the case. In order to receive a diagnosis of a mental illness, the DSM usually requires that there be some indication other than the antisocial behavior itself; for example, a disorder of thought, mood, or interest. Exceptions to this rule are the diagnoses of conduct disorder (which can be given to juveniles and to adults; American Psychiatric Association, 2022, pp. 530–537) and ASPD (American Psychiatric Association, 2022, pp. 748–752). ASPD can involve features other than antisocial behavior – namely, impulsivity, failure to plan ahead, irritability, irresponsibility, lack of remorse, indifference, and rationalization – but the diagnosis also can be given when none of these features are present and the only signs of the disorder are a series of antisocial acts.

This is a double standard. The diagnosis of ASPD is used to commit SVPs, but it is not used in any other legal context. The profession of psychiatry is divided on this issue. Sreenivasan et al. (2020) found this use of the diagnosis to be acceptable. Frances (2020), on the other hand, pointed out the logical inconsistency of using a diagnosis to incapacitate a person when that same diagnosis cannot be used to help them avoid prison with an insanity defense:

> The DSM-5 definition of ASPD is mostly a cataloging of criminal behaviors, making ASPD extremely common among rapists and not useful in distinguishing between rape as part of common criminality and rape arising from mental abnormality, which is a distinction clearly required by the Supreme Court in justifying the constitutionality of SVP statutes. Because ASPD does not allow an offender to avoid prison, it should not later justify his psychiatric incarceration; it is inconsistent to rule that the ASPD offender had sufficient volitional control to be held responsible for his crimes (resulting in his receiving the prison sentence), and then to rule years later that he is now no longer in volitional control (and therefore can be forced involuntarily into a hospital). (Frances. 2020, p. 193)

This double standard in the use of a diagnosis does not reflect upon the scientific nature of psychiatry but rather on the politics of protecting the public from dangerous sex offenders. The criminal justice system, rightly or wrongly, has shown that it is flexible enough to use a psychiatric diagnosis in one context that does not justify special treatment in any other context. Psychiatric diagnosis is not only scientific but also is political in nature (see, for example, Caplan & Cosgrove, 2004).

The same argument about a double standard can be applied to the diagnosis of paraphilic disorders if there is resistance to considering them worthy of the insanity defense. Malin and Saleh (2007) reported that paraphilic disorder has occasionally prevailed as a diagnosis in the insanity defense.

REFERENCES

Alper, M., & Ducrose, M. R. (2019). Recidivism of sex offenders released from state prison: A 9-year follow-up (2005-14). Retrieved 11/29/2022 from https://bjs.ojp.gov/content/pub/pdf/rsorsp9yfu0514.pdf.

American Psychiatric Association. (2022). *Diagnostic and Statistical Manual of Mental Disorders. Fifth edition. Text revision.* Washington, D.C.: American Psychiatric Association.

Antenangeli, L., & Durose, M. R. (2021). Recidivism of prisoners released in 24 states in 2008: A 10-year follow-up period (2008–2018). Bureau of Justice Statistics. Retrieved 06/17/2022 from https://bjs.ojp.gov/library/publications/recidivism-prisoners-released-24-states-2008-10-year-follow-period-2008-2018.

Associated Press. (June 22, 2003). Sex offender in predator case held in rape after his release. Retrieved 08/18/2022 from www.nytimes.com/2003/06/22/us/sex-offender-in-predator-case-held-in-rape-after-his-release.html.

Caplan, P. J., & Cosgrove, L. (Eds.) (2004). *Bias in psychiatric diagnosis*. Lanham, MD: Jason Aronson.

Foucha v. Louisiana, 504 U.S. 71 (1992).

Frances, A. (June 2020). Misuse of Diagnostic and Statistical Manual diagnosis in sexually violent predator cases. *Journal of the American Academy of Psychiatry and the Law*, 48(2), 191–194. doi:10.29158/JAAPL.200020-20.

In re Care and Treatment of Michael T. Crane. Supreme Court of Kansas. No. 82,080 (2000).

In re Rosenfield, 157 F. Supp. 18 (D.D.C. 1957).

Kansas v. Crane, 534 U.S. 407 (2002).

Kansas v. Hendricks, 521 U.S. 346 (1997).

Lobanov-Rostovsky, C. (2015). Recidivism of juveniles who commit sex offenses. U.S. Department of Justice. Office of Justice Programs. Retrieved 07/17/2022 from https://smart.ojp.gov/sites/g/files/xyckuh231/files/media/document/juvenilerecidivism.pdf.

Malin, H. M., & Saleh, F. M. (April 15, 2007). Paraphilias: Clinical and forensic considerations. *Psychiatric Times*, 24(5). Retrieved 11/29/2022 from www.psychiatrictimes.com/view/paraphilias-clinical-and-forensic-considerations.

Przybylski, R. (2015). Recidivism of adult sexual offenders. U.S. Department of Justice. Office of Justice Programs. Retrieved June 17, 2022 from www.ojp.gov/ncjrs/virtual-library/abstracts/recidivism-adult-sexual-offenders.

Scheller, L. (April 8, 2006). Sexual predator Leroy Hendricks won't be returned to Leavenworth County: Kansas Supreme Court upholds land-use decision. Retrieved 11/29/2022 from www.tonganoxiemirror.com/news/2006/apr/28/sexual_predator_leroy/.

Sreenivasan, S., Rokop, J., DiCiro, M., Colley, J., & Weinberger, L. E. (2020). Case law considerations in the use of ASPD in SVP/SDP evaluations. *Journal of the American Academy of Psychiatry and the Law*, 48(2), 181–190. doi:10.29158/JAAPL.003915-20.

17 Executing persons who have intellectual developmental disorder (IDD)

Atkins v. Virginia (U.S. 2002)

The relationship between IDD and murder is not like the other psycholegal relationships discussed in this book (with the possible exception of the relationship between dissociative identity disorder and insanity in federal courts; see the discussion of *United States v. Denny-Shaffer* in Chapter 30), as forensic examiners need only demonstrate that IDD exists in order to trigger the appropriate mollification from the courts. The forensic examiner does not have to demonstrate, for example, that a particular defendant's IDD caused them to interpret facts incorrectly, or to show poor judgment, or to acquiesce inappropriately to the suggestions of others. The same latitude is not found with other diagnoses and other psycholegal questions. For example, in questions of insanity and incompetency to stand trial, a forensic examiner must not only demonstrate that a mental disorder or defect of sufficient severity exists, but also that this defect or disorder renders the defendant incapable of understanding the case against them, incapable of cooperating with their attorney (see Chapter 10), or incapable cognitively, morally, or volitionally (see Chapter 19). In the relationship between IDD and murder, a forensic examiner need only demonstrate that the condition exists in order to elicit the proper response from the courts. (Therefore the "Cautionary Statement for Forensic Use of DSM-5" [American Psychiatric Association, 2022, p. 29], which points out some of the differences between clinical and forensic uses of diagnosis, does not apply to cases of IDD and murder.) Perhaps because IDD is such a globally debilitating condition, the courts have not parsed it into sets of incapacities as they have with the other disorders and psycholegal questions. (They might do so in the future, however. Conceivably, a court of the future may require a forensic examiner to demonstrate not only that a defendant has IDD but also to show how the features of IDD such as concrete thinking, poor judgment, low memory skills, low levels of adaptive functioning, and susceptibility to influence affected the behavior of a particular defendant.)

IDD occurs in about 1 percent of the population (American Psychiatric Association, 2022; p. 43). A review by Blume et al. (2014) indicated that

DOI: 10.4324/9781003385028-20

the claim of IDD was presented in 7.7 percent of death penalty cases nationwide and prevailed in 55 percent of those cases. The success of the claim varies with the standard of evidence in that jurisdiction, as will be explained below.

A PERSON WHO HAS IDD CANNOT BE CONDEMNED TO DEATH: *ATKINS V. VIRGINIA* (U.S. 2002)

Daryl Atkins (age 18) and a co-defendant spent the day of August 16, 1996, drinking alcohol and smoking marijuana. That night they walked to a convenience store, where they robbed an 18-year-old airman from nearby Langley Air Force Base. Not satisfied with the $60.00 he had on his person, they drove him to an ATM, where he withdrew another $200.00. Then they drove him to an isolated location, where they shot him eight times with a semi-automatic pistol. Atkins and his co-defendant were easily identified from the ATM camera and they were soon apprehended. (Readers can view this photograph at https://th.bing.com/th/id/R.7e33ce60493d0d4d2a3a2 eff36a14b76?rik=%2b8x1DPuhwRH%2f3A&riu=http%3a%2f%2fwww. murderpedia.org%2fmale.A%2fimages%2fatkins_daryl%2f001.jpg&ehk= nrPItHsz2lpFpFhdCXNFvPkKBxinPXkLtGRI8qintiU%3d&risl=&pid= ImgRaw&r=0.) Both defendants said the other man was the shooter. The co-defendant negotiated a plea bargain for life in prison in exchange for his testimony against Atkins. Atkins' cellmate at the jail also testified against him, saying that Atkins had confessed to the killing. The jury, presented with two versions of the offense, found the co-defendant's version to be more credible. Atkins was convicted of murder and sentenced to death. His IQ was 59.

The U.S. Supreme Court would rule that a defendant who has IDD cannot be put to death. The State of Virginia never conceded that Daryl Atkins has IDD, and they continued to pursue the death penalty. On January 17, 2008, his sentence was commuted to life in prison due to prosecutorial misconduct (coaching a witness, namely, Atkins' co-defendant; Liptak, 2008). Evidence of prosecutorial misconduct included 15 minutes that were missing from a recorded interview with Atkins' co-defendant as well as testimony from that man's defense attorney. Daryl Atkins is currently a resident of the Nottoway Correctional Center in Burkeville, Virginia.

The *McCarver* brief

As part of Atkins' appeal, the American Psychological Association, together with the American Psychiatric Association and the American Academy of Psychiatry and Law, filed an amici curiae brief advocating for persons with IDD. This brief had been filed previously in the death penalty trial of *McCarver v. North Carolina* (2001). In 2001, the U.S. Supreme Court had dismissed *McCarver* as moot because North Carolina had passed a law that made it illegal to execute persons who have IDD. In *Atkins*, however, the U.S. Supreme Court granted certiorari. This brief argues

> that such persons are substantially less capable of both abstract reasoning and practical or adaptive functioning than nonretarded adults. These very real and serious impairments are reflected in diminished capacities to understand basic facts, foresee the moral consequences of actions, learn from one's mistakes, and grasp the feelings, thoughts, and reactions of other people. (American Psychological Association, 2001, p. 2)

Therefore, the brief argues, persons who have IDD are not capable of the high level of moral blameworthiness that warrants capital punishment. The brief goes on to argue that

> A blanket prohibition against the execution of individuals with mental retardation is workable, because mental retardation can be identified using time-tested instruments and protocols with proven validity and reliability ... [Independent] professionals undertaking separate assessments should reach the same conclusion. (p. 3)

And,

> individuals with mental retardation form a well-demarcated group ... Two qualified mental retardation professionals separately administering these diagnostic tests should reach the same conclusion concerning whether an individual has mental retardation. As a result, a blanket rule against execution of persons with mental retardation should not result in new "battles of experts" concerning whether a defendant, in fact, has mental retardation. (p. 14)

The *McCarver* brief lists eight "diminished capacities" of persons who have IDD that reduce their blameworthiness. (I have added numerals for clarity.) These are the capacities:

1 to understand and process facts and information;
2 to learn from mistakes and from experience generally;
3 to generalize and to engage in logical if-then reasoning;
4 to control impulses;
5 to communicate;
6 to understand the moral implications of actions and to engage in moral reasoning; and

7 to recognize and understand the feelings, thoughts, and reactions of other people.

8 Moreover, people with mental retardation are often especially eager to please others, a characteristic obviously susceptible to manipulation. (American Psychological Association, 2001, pp. 8–9)

The *Atkins* decision

In *Gregg v. Georgia* (1976), the U.S. Supreme Court had analyzed the goals of sentencing as they apply to capital punishment and had concluded that only two of the four goals apply: retribution and deterrence of others (also known as "general deterrence"). Their reasoning becomes clear if we take a moment to examine all four goals of sentencing as they apply to the death penalty. (For a general discussion of the four goals of sentencing, see Chapter 6.) There is nothing about capital punishment that rehabilitates a defendant or deters them from future misbehavior. As for the goal of incapacitation, if we want to incapacitate a defendant we send them to prison and we do not execute them. The remaining two goals are retribution and general deterrence. The *Atkins* court ruled that executing persons with IDD does not serve either of these goals. Therefore the execution of persons with IDD is cruel and unusual punishment, prohibited by the Eighth Amendment.

Executing persons who have IDD does not deter crime

The goal of deterrence breaks into two parts (see Chapter 6): (1) deterring defendants from committing future crimes (specific deterrence) and (2) deterring others who might be tempted to commit the same type of crime (general deterrence). With regards to IDD, the discussion of general deterrence breaks into two further parts: (1) deterring persons who have IDD and (2) deterring people who do not have IDD.

The U.S. Supreme Court wrote in *Enmund v. Florida* (1982) that "capital punishment can serve as a deterrent only when murder is the result of premeditation and deliberation" (at 799). In *Atkins*, the Court ruled that persons who have IDD are less capable of premeditation and deliberation. Therefore, the court reasoned, they are less likely to be deterred. Quoting *Enmund*, the court concluded that the goal of deterrence is not served by executing offenders who have IDD (*Atkins*, at 319). The *Atkins* court noted further that persons who have IDD

have diminished capacities to understand and process information, to communicate, to abstract from mistakes and learn from experience, to engage in logical reasoning, to control impulses, and to understand the reactions of others. (at 318)

They wrote:

> Exempting the mentally retarded from that punishment will not affect the "cold calculus that precedes the decision" of other potential murderers. *Gregg v. Georgia* (1976), 428 U.S., at 186. Indeed, that sort of calculus is at the opposite end of the spectrum from behavior of mentally retarded offenders. The theory of deterrence in capital sentencing is predicated upon the notion that the increased severity of the punishment will inhibit criminal actors from carrying out murderous conduct. Yet it is the same cognitive and behavioral impairments that make these defendants less morally culpable – for example, the diminished ability to understand and process information, to learn from experience, to engage in logical reasoning, or to control impulses – that also make it less likely that they can process the information of the possibility of execution as a penalty and, as a result, control their conduct based upon that information. (*Atkins*, at 319–320)

With regard to murders committed by persons who do not have IDD, the court concluded that executing persons with IDD will not deter them:

> Nor will exempting the mentally retarded from execution lessen the deterrent effect of the death penalty with respect to offenders who are not mentally retarded. Such individuals are unprotected by the exemption and will continue to face the threat of execution. Thus, executing the mentally retarded will not measurably further the goal of deterrence. (at 320)

Executing persons who have IDD does not serve the goal of retribution

In a system of retributive justice, the severity of the punishment must coincide with the culpability of the offender. The *Atkins* court concluded that executing persons with IDD therefore does not serve the goal of retribution. Execution is the ultimate punishment and must be reserved for

> a narrow category of the most serious crimes ... If the culpability of the average murderer is insufficient to justify the most extreme sanction available to the State, the lesser culpability of the mentally retarded offender surely does not merit that form of retribution. Thus, pursuant to our narrowing jurisprudence, which seeks to ensure that only the most deserving of execution are put to death, an exclusion for the mentally retarded is appropriate. (*Atkins*, at 319)

DIFFICULTIES IN PROVING IDD

With all due respect to the authors of the *McCarver* brief, the diagnosis of IDD is not as simple and straightforward as they made it seem. Investigating adaptive living skills requires relying upon archival and collateral information, and these are subject to threats to their validity, as outlined below. Furthermore, a variety of definitions of IDD can be found in the various iterations of the Diagnostic and Statistical Manuals (DSMs) published by the American Psychiatric Association (APA) and in the publications of the American Association on Intellectual and Developmental Disabilities (AAIDD; formerly known as the American Association on Mental Retardation, or AAMR). (See, for example, American Association on Mental Retardation, 1992; American Psychiatric Association, 2013, 2022; Schalock et al., 2021.) These various definitions have important elements in common. They all agree that IDD is comprised of three factors:

- intellectual deficits
- deficits in adaptive functioning
- onset during the developmental period.

The *Atkins* decision brought an end to the execution of persons who have IDD, but the debates did not stop there. Courtroom arguments shifted to the difficulties of determining who has IDD, and the types of crimes that might be committed by persons who have IDD.

The authors of the joint brief, as reported above, blithely assumed that the diagnosis of IDD would be a simple and straightforward matter, but this is not the case. Those authors failed to appreciate five factors about the diagnosis of IDD and the way that evidence is used in court:

1 State courts and legislatures are not accustomed to letting mental health professionals define their legal terms and concepts, and (until the U.S. Supreme Court decision in *Moore v. Texas*, 2019; see below) they defined IDD in ways that suited themselves.
2 The diagnosis of IDD relies upon information that the forensic examiner cannot obtain firsthand in an examination room. This includes information about the defendant's childhood and the defendant's adaptive functioning across a variety of contexts. The forensic examiner is required to rely on written records and the testimony of witnesses, and these are subject to the ambiguities, inconsistencies, contradictions, omissions, and biases that are typical of such evidence. Forensic examiners are likely to find themselves in the position of explaining which records and which witnesses they believe and which they do not believe, and then explaining why. Given these

inconsistencies, ambiguities, and contradictions, disagreements between opposing sides are inevitable.

3 The stakes are high (as high as can be), and defendants are likely to malinger. The accurate diagnosis of IDD varies with the examiner's skill at detecting malingering and the quality of the detection methods employed. Because some methods of detecting malingering rely on assessments of the defendant's cognition, and because cognition is compromised in persons who have IDD, the utility of these measures can be questioned.

4 Standard of evidence is crucial. In Georgia, where the standard of evidence is "beyond a reasonable doubt," no defendant accused of malice murder has been found by a jury to have IDD (see below).

5 An attorney can keep a trial from turning into a "battle of the expert" simply by not calling an expert witness of their own. The attorney then proceeds to impeach the testimony of the lonely expert, who must carry the burden of proof by themselves. The "battle," in such a trial, then takes place between the prosecutor and the defense expert, and the expert witness may be at a disadvantage. The prosecutor may be better prepared for this type of combat, because the defense expert is trained in science and mathematics and may have little interest in verbal combat. The prose-cutor, on the other hand, is trained in verbal combat, and the "battle" takes place in front of a naïve jury who does not understand the science, the mathematics, or the strategic advantage that the prosecution has gained simply by not hiring their own expert. Impeachment is not difficult in retrospective assessments like the diagnosis of IDD, because records and informants tend to be vague, ambiguous, inconsistent, contradictory, self-contradictory, biased, or missing, as explained above.

With *Atkins*, the U.S. Supreme Court ended the execution of persons with IDD, and they left it up to the states to develop their own procedures for administering this decision. Some states took it upon themselves not only to administer the decision but also to define IDD for themselves. In the series of cases that followed, the issue at hand was who would define IDD: the mental health professionals or the states.

No bright line at 70: *Cherry v. State* (Fla. 2007) and *Hall v. Florida* (U.S. 2014)

The standard error of measurement (SEm), which might otherwise seem like a dry mathematical calculation (see Appendix O), becomes literally a matter of life and death in capital trials when a defendant's IQ score is in the low 70s. This occurred in two Florida cases: *Cherry v. State* (2007) and *Hall v. Florida* (2014).

Roger Lee Cherry was convicted of two murders. His IQ was 72. The Florida Supreme Court ignored the role of SEm in interpreting test scores and ruled that the diagnosis of IDD cannot be made if the IQ score is above 70.

Freddie Lee Hall had been on death row for murder in Florida for 30 years when he appealed, based on the *Atkins* decision. His IQ was 71.

The U.S. Supreme Court disagreed with Florida's interpretation of IQ scores. As Justice Kennedy wrote in the majority of a 6–3 decision, Florida's neglect of the SEm was not consistent with clinical practice, and a state is not free to define IDD in a manner that is not consistent with clinical practice. Justice Kennedy wrote, "Intellectual disability is a condition, not a number" (*Hall v. Florida*, 2014, at 2001).

Point estimation is not used to interpret the scores of psychometric tests because these tests have a degree of error. Interval estimation must be used when making important determinations like the diagnosis of IDD (see Tassé & Blume, 2018). When a murder defendant has an IQ in the low 70s, the SEm can save their life. (For further discussion of SEm, confidence intervals, and their use in the diagnosis of IDD, see Appendix O.)

The mental health professions and not the states define IDD: *Moore v. Texas* (U.S. 2017, 2019)

Bobby James Moore (age 20) and two accomplices robbed a supermarket in Houston, Texas, on April 25, 1980. A female employee screamed, and Moore shot and killed her 70-year-old co-worker. Moore was found guilty of murder and he was condemned to death. His IQ was 74.

Moore's academic skills and adaptive behaviors were deficient. As a child he had been slow in speech, reading, and writing. He could not keep up with his lessons in school. In the sixth grade he struggled to read at a second-grade level. Often he was separated from the rest of the class and was told to draw pictures instead of being allowed to read with the other children. At age 13, he lacked a basic understanding of the days of the week and the months and seasons of the year. He could scarcely tell time or comprehend basic measurements. He could barely understand the principle that subtraction is the reverse of addition. He did not always understand the conversations of family members. He did not always answer to his own name. After failing every subject in the ninth grade, he dropped out of school, mowed lawns, worked as a field hand, and bet on pool games. He lived on the street, ate out of dumpsters, and twice got food poisoning.

As Moore's appeal worked its way toward the U.S. Supreme Court, there was considerable disagreement in Texas courts regarding his adaptive deficits. As might be expected, the prosecution highlighted his strengths and Moore's defense attorneys highlighted his deficits. The U.S. Supreme Court summarized this process as follows:

> The CCA (Texas Court of Criminal Appeals) overemphasized Moore's perceived adaptive strengths – living on the streets, mowing lawns, and playing pool for money – when the medical community focuses the adaptive functioning inquiry on adaptive *deficits*. (*Moore v. Texas*, 2017, at 3; italics in the original)

Persons with IDD show adaptive strengths, as do all living things. It is not unusual for an adult with IDD to drive a car, have a job, read a newspaper, make plans, play cards, have friends, tell lies, and have romantic relationships. A brief filed by the American Psychological Association (2017) quoted a recent article by Ellenkamp et al. (2016) of an international literature review (United States, Hong Kong, Canada, Spain, Japan, Australia, and New Zealand), which reported that between 9 percent and 40 percent of persons with IDD held some form of paid employment.

IDD is a "Swiss cheese" diagnosis. The prosecution can always point to the strengths, and the defense can point to the holes. The U.S. Supreme Court ruled that the professional community and not the states will be the ones to define IDD:

> While our decisions in "*Atkins* and *Hall* left to the States 'the task of developing appropriate ways to enforce' the restriction on executing the intellectually disabled," 581 U. S., at ___ (slip op., at 9) (quoting *Hall*, 572 U.S., at 719), a court's intellectual disability determination "must be 'informed by the medical community's diagnostic framework,'" 581 U. S., at ___ (slip op., at 9) (quoting *Hall*, 572 U.S., at 721).

In other words, the court had left it up to the states to determine how to administer the death penalty, but the definition of IDD is the province of the medical profession.

The U.S. Supreme Court decided *Moore v. Texas* twice – once in 2017 and again in 2019. After the 2017 ruling, the Texas Court of Criminal Appeals issued a new decision, but they failed to apply the Supreme Court's reasoning on the question of IDD. They again found that Bobby James Moore did not have IDD by the Texas definition and again sentenced him to death. Then, in 2019, the U.S. Supreme Court heard the case a second time. In a rare decision – rare because the U.S. Supreme Court does not often make decisions about individual defendants (it makes decisions about principles of justice and then sends those decisions back to the states for their own deliberations) – the court concluded that Moore had IDD, and therefore under *Atkins* he could not be put to death.

(We might assume that the U.S. Supreme Court did not want to hear the case a third time.) Associate Justices Alito, Thomas, and Gorsuch dissented and argued that issuing a decision about an individual defendant and not a principle of law usurped the "factfinding" mission of the Texas courts.

Texas had no choice but to commute Moore's sentence. He was paroled on June 8, 2020, after spending nearly 40 years on death row (CBS News, 2019; Feldman, 2020).

Crime does not indicate level of adaptive functioning

Prosecutors have attempted to deflate claims of IDD by pointing out the degrees of planning, preparation, deception, and skill that went into the commission of crimes, and then arguing that the defendant must not have IDD because they were capable of such behavior. This is a "strength-based" approach to defining IDD which attempts to disprove its existence by pointing out the defendant's strengths. The definitions of ID and IDD by the mental health professions, on the other hand, take a "deficit-based" approach and define it on the basis of a person's weaknesses. To assume that a defendant who has IDD cannot be capable of planning, preparation, deception, and skill is to ignore their personal capabilities and to perpetuate a false stereotype of persons who have IDD. The mental health professions define ID or IDD on the basis of (1) intellectual deficits, (2) adaptive deficits, and (3) onset during the developmental period. This is the full extent of the diagnostic criteria. There is no fourth criterion that says, "Also this person must be incapable of committing a crime." When we look at the lives of people who have IDD, we may find a number of personal capabilities, as some of them hold jobs, drive cars, start families, read newspapers, and commit crimes.

Experts on IDD including the leaders of professional associations have responded to this type of cross-examination by replying that there is no science regarding the types of crimes that are committed by persons who have IDD. Robert J. McCaffrey, President of the American Board of Professional Neuropsychology, wrote to the Texas legislature:

> As clinical practitioners, we believe the issue of the presence of properly diagnosed mental retardation and the facts of a specific crime are now and should be independent ... The diagnosis of mental retardation thus is based on objective diagnostic criteria that direct the clinician to well studied, standardized, and objective measures of function. The presence or absence of a criminal act and its facts have no true bearing on such a diagnosis and we believe their consideration in this context would only distract a clinician or other fact-finder from the task at hand – the determination of the presence or absence of mental retardation. (McCaffrey, letter to the Texas legislature, March 19, 2003)

Leslie D. Rosenstein of the National Academy of Neuropsychology wrote for their Board of Directors as follows:

[We] recommend that the determination of mental retardation be made independent of the facts of the crime ... We support legislation that maintains the separation of the issue of mental retardation and any facts of a crime that may prejudice the fact finder ... Facts of a criminal case do not have a bearing on the determination of mental retardation ... Such facts can only serve to introduce bias into the determination of mental retardation when it is put before a lay jury. Moreover, such issues are not consistent with established clinical and scientific procedures for the diagnosis of mental retardation ... In summary, we strongly recommend that the determination of mental retardation be made independent of the facts of the crime. (Rosenstein, letter to the Texas legislature, March 18, 2003)

The AAIDD wrote in their definition manual of 2009 that "There is not enough available information, and there is a lack of normative information" regarding crime. Experts are not able to determine whether the abilities and actions a person displayed in committing a crime represent subaverage adaptive functioning (Schalock et al., 2009, p. 102).

Greenspan and Switzky (2006) wrote,

The first reason has to do with the fact that not enough information is typically available (on a precise microlevel) regarding the exact situational demands and the level of cognitive skills required to navigate those demands ... The second reason is that we simply do not possess normative information, adaptive behavior scales notwithstanding, about whether someone with MR (mental retardation) can fire a gun, drive a car, case out a crime scene, or assert his will on victims. One of the lessons of the "support revolution" is that people with MR can do many things, including aspects of work and independent living, that previously one would not have thought they could do. (Greenspan & Switzky, 2006, p. 287)

There may be no science regarding the types of crimes that are committed by persons who have IDD, but testifying experts are advised to take a reasonable approach to this topic. For example, if a defendant who claims to have IDD were to commit a very sophisticated crime like a securities fraud (and this might be presented as a hypothetical by a prosecuting attorney during cross-examination), it may be more reasonable to answer that this could raise questions about the validity of the diagnosis and the possibility of malingering than to answer flatly that there is no science regarding crime and IDD, and thereby risk losing credibility in the eyes of the triers of fact.

Proof beyond a reasonable doubt (BRD) is required to establish IDD in Georgia

Georgia is the only state in the Union that requires proof of IDD beyond a reasonable doubt (BRD) in criminal proceedings. No other state has ever required such a high standard of evidence. Probably because of this high standard of evidence, no jury in Georgia has ever found a defendant accused of malice murder to have IDD.

This author has testified five times regarding murder and IDD in Georgia. The reader may never be called upon to consult on a murder trial in Georgia. Nevertheless, this section is included here because it sheds light on a number of themes of this book, including the role of standards of evidence and the nature of forensic mental health assessment.

Ironically, Georgia was the first state to recognize that defendants who have IDD should not be put to death. Perhaps the fact that this law has become an anomaly (requiring proof beyond a reasonable doubt) reflects the problem with going first. No other state has ever required proof of IDD beyond a reasonable doubt.

Georgia passed their law in 1988, 14 years before *Atkins*. The history of this law begins in 1986, when Georgia executed Jerome Bowden, who had an IQ of 65 and could not count to ten. The backlash from disability advocates and state legislators resulted in the nation's first law prohibiting the execution of persons who have IDD. In its current iteration, Georgia Code § 17-7-131(j)(2) states that defendants in capital proceedings who are found "guilty but with intellectual disability" are not executed but are sent to the Georgia Department of Corrections for life.

The BRD standard of evidence exists to protect citizens from governmental overreach. However, the Georgia law twists it into something unrecognizable that has made it very difficult for defendants with IDD to elude the death penalty. And it happened by mistake – the result of careless drafting. Testimony obtained in 2013 indicated that, when the new law was drafted in 1988, the standard of evidence for a guilty verdict was set at BRD (which is consistent with other jurisdictions), but the phrase "mentally retarded" was tacked on at the end of a sentence, inadvertently imposing the BRD standard of evidence on the issue of IDD (Lucas, 2017, p. 9). This sentence reads,

> The defendant may be found "guilty but with intellectual disability" if the jury, or court acting as trier of facts, finds beyond a reasonable doubt that the defendant is guilty of the crime charged and is with intellectual disability. (Georgia Code § 17-7-131(c)(3))

Readers may perceive the ambiguity of this sentence. Georgia Courts have interpreted it to mean that IDD must be proved beyond a reasonable doubt.

At the time of Lucas's article, the death penalty was in use by the federal government, military courts, and thirty-one states. The *Atkins* decision in 2002 required all of these jurisdictions to make special provisions for IDD. Only Georgia applied the BRD standard.

In three states, the lower "clear and convincing" standard was applied: Arizona, Colorado, and Florida.

In twenty states, the even lower "preponderance of the evidence" standard was applied: Alabama, Arkansas, California, Idaho, Indiana, Kentucky, Louisiana, Mississippi, Missouri, Nebraska, Nevada, Ohio, Pennsylvania, South Carolina, South Dakota, Tennessee, Texas, Utah, Virginia, and Washington.

Two states – North Carolina and Oklahoma – used "clear and convincing evidence" at pre-trial hearings and "preponderance of the evidence" at the sentencing phase.

Five states had not defined a standard of evidence for IDD: Kansas, Montana, New Hampshire, Oregon, and Wyoming.

IDD can be a difficult diagnosis to make, for reasons explained above. Defendants, like all living creatures, have both strengths and weaknesses. Informants, witnesses, and written records may be inconsistent and contradict themselves and each other. When a defendant goes to trial, the defense will point out the deficits, and the prosecution will point out the strengths of the individual and the inconsistencies in the record. When the standard of evidence is BRD, a prosecutor need only create reasonable doubt in order to prevail. In a complicated, retrospective diagnosis like IDD, reasonable doubt is easily accomplished, and prosecutors in the state of Georgia have succeeded in creating reasonable doubt in every trial that went before a jury.

The question of whether IDD is a strength-based diagnosis as defined by the states or a deficit-based diagnosis as defined by mental health professionals was settled by the U.S. Supreme Court in *Moore v. Texas* (2019; see above). This is not to say that courts do not retain oversight regarding mental health testimony. Triers of fact still have the duty and authority to weigh evidence, to confirm that testifying experts have arrived at the proper conclusions, and to determine whether the evidence meets the proper standard. In Georgia, where the standard of evidence is BRD, this has proved to be an impossible hurdle in every jury trial.

In *Hill v. Humphrey* (2011), the U.S. Court of Appeals, Eleventh Circuit, did not accept defendant Warren Lee Hill's claim that he had IDD, and thereby affirmed his death penalty. Justice Rosemary Barkett (Figure 17.1) wrote a dissenting opinion that reflects her keen understanding of these issues.

Barkett was born in Mexico to Syrian immigrants trying to enter the United States. She became a nun, then decided to study law, and became

Figure 17.1 Justice Rosemary Barkett (1939–) of the U.S. Court of Appeals, Eleventh Circuit, who argued in a dissenting opinion that "beyond a reasonable doubt" is an unreasonable standard for determining intellectual developmental disorder (IDD) that will lead inevitably to the unlawful execution of defendants who have IDD.

the first female Justice and first female Chief Justice of the Florida Supreme Court. Later she was appointed to serve on the Iran-United States Claims Tribunal in The Hague. While she served on the U.S. Court of Appeals, Eleventh Circuit, her dissenting opinion in *Hill v. Humphrey* (2011) reflects her accurate perception of the nature of mental health testimony and the difficulties in applying the BRD standard to IDD. She wrote:

> Requiring the mentally retarded to prove their mental retardation beyond any reasonable doubt will inevitably lead, through the rule's natural operation, to the frequent execution of mentally retarded individuals, thus depriving the mentally retarded of their constitutional right "to procedures which are adequate to safeguard against" their execution. See *Speiser v. Randall* (1958) at 521 ... This is so because placing this highest of standards of proof upon such offenders places upon them practically all of the risk of an erroneous determination. The risk is compounded here because the fact of mental retardation has to be based on a psychiatric diagnosis, "the subtleties and nuances" of which the Supreme Court has recognized "render certainties beyond reach in most situations." *Addington v. Texas* (1979) at 430 ... Thus, mental retardation is almost never provable beyond a reasonable doubt (at least where contested), and the "risk" of an erroneous determination resulting in a wrongful execution approaches a near certainty. (*Hill v. Humphrey*, 2011, at 1370–1371)
>
> Mental retardation is a medical condition that is diagnosed only through, among other things, a subjective standard that requires experts to assess intellectual functioning and to interpret the meaning of behavior long into the offender's past. Given the imprecise nature of the mental retardation determination, "the possibility of mistaken factfinding inherent in all litigation," [*Speiser v. Randall* (1958) at 526] ... becomes a near-certainty in this context. (at 1372)
>
> "The subtleties and nuances of psychiatric diagnosis render certainties virtually beyond reach in most situations" (quoting *Addington v. Texas*, 1979, at 429–30). (at 1372–1373)
>
> A clinician conducting this retrospective diagnosis must assess a "thorough social history" of the individual, including "investigat[ing] and organiz[ing]... all relevant information about the person's life," and "explor[ing]... possible reasons for absence of data or differences in data"; she must also "[conduct] a thorough review of school records," and contact teachers and peers from the subject's adolescence, looking for evidence of deficits in cognitive, adaptive, or social skills. (quoting AAIDD User's Guide, at 17–20) [Author's note: The document that Justice Barkett referred to as "AAIDD User's Guide" is referenced below as Schalock, 2007.]

Where the proof must be beyond a reasonable doubt, common sense tells us that requiring reliance on these unavoidably incomplete and subjective sources of information renders the *Atkins* claimant's job a near-impossible task. (at 1373–1374)

Moreover, with respect to adaptive skills, most mentally retarded individuals, especially those whose mental retardation is mild, "present a mixed competence profile." AAIDD User's Guide, at 16. Individuals with mild mental retardation may "manifest subtle limitations that are frequently difficult to detect, especially in academic skills, planning, problem solving, and decision making, and social understanding and judgment." (at 1375)

These adaptive abilities are frequently mischaracterized by judicial factfinders as evidence that the individual is not retarded. Indeed, this Court and the Fifth Circuit have recognized that mildly mentally retarded individuals are capable of holding jobs, driving cars, paying bills, taking care of their families, and so forth … Therefore, the existence of the fact of mental retardation, especially in the case of mild mental retardation, will almost always be open to some doubt. (at 1375)

Justice Barkett identified twenty-two Georgia murder trials in which defendants claimed to have IDD since the passage of their law in 1988. Only two defendants (9 percent) – Christopher Lewis and Vernessa Marshall – were found to have IDD, which is far below the national average of 55 percent of defendants whose claims of IDD prevail in death penalty proceedings (see Blume et al., 2014). Both Lewis and Marshall were adjudicated under special circumstances. Lewis was found to have IDD not by a jury but by a judge during post-conviction proceedings. As Blume et al. (2014) pointed out, judges deal with crime every day and may be more objective than juries about horrible crimes.

Georgia defendant Vernessa Marshall (*State v. Marshall*, 1999) was found to have IDD beyond a reasonable doubt, but her charge had been downgraded from malice murder to felony murder (i.e., without intent to kill).

Lucas (2017) summarized these facts by writing that "Georgia defendants have been unable to overcome the very high burden of establishing intellectual disability before a jury at the guilt phase of a capital trial – a finding that has never occurred in a case of intentional murder" (p. 577).

Before Warren Lee Hill was executed, the Georgia Board of Pardons and Paroles received a request for clemency from the executive director of the AAIDD. The Board also received requests for clemency from several members of the victim's family, several jurors from Hill's trial, the president of the American Bar Association, former President of the United States and former Georgia Governor Jimmy Carter, and former first lady Rosalynn Carter. Despite these requests for clemency, Hill was executed on January 27, 2015, at the Jackson County State Prison (Georgia Resource Center, 2022).

In 2021, attorneys for Rodney Renia Young petitioned the U.S. Supreme Court for a writ of certiorari on the question of whether BRD is an unreasonably high standard of evidence for IDD, contrary to the "cruel and unusual punishments" clause of the Eighth Amendment and the "due process" clause of the Fourteenth Amendment. The U.S. Supreme Court denied certiorari (*Young v. Georgia*, 2022).

REFERENCES

Addington v. Texas, 441 U.S. 418, 99 S.Ct. 1804 (1979).

American Association on Mental Retardation (AAMR). (1992). *Mental retardation: Definitions, classification, and systems of support.* Washington, D.C.: American Association on Mental Retardation.

American Psychiatric Association. (2013). *Diagnostic and Statistical Manual of Mental Disorders. Fifth edition.* Arlington, VA: American Psychiatric Publishing.

American Psychiatric Association. (2022). *Diagnostic and Statistical Manual of Mental Disorders. Fifth edition. Text Revision.* Washington, D.C.: American Psychiatric Association.

American Psychological Association. (2001). Brief of the American Psychological Association, American Psychiatric Association, and the American Academy of Psychiatry and Law as *amici curiae* in support of petitioner Ernest Paul McCarver, in the Supreme Court of the United States. Retrieved 11/29/2022 from www.apa.org/about/offices/ogc/amicus/mccarver.pdf.

American Psychological Association. (2017). Brief of *amici curiae* American Psychological Association, American Psychiatric Association, American Academy of Psychiatry and the Law, National Association of Social Workers, and National Association of Social Workers Texas Chapter in support of petitioner Bobby James Moore, in the Supreme Court of the United States. Retrieved 11/29/2022 from www.apa.org/about/offices/ogc/amicus/moore.pdf.

Atkins v. Virginia, 536 U.S. 304 (2002).

Blume, J. H., Johnson, S. L., Marcus, P., & Paavola, E. C. (2014). A tale of two (and possibly three) *Atkins*: Intellectual disability and capital punishment twelve years after the Supreme Court's creation of a categorical bar. *William & Mary Bill of Rights Journal*, 23, 393–414. Available at http://ssrn.com/abstract=2549737.

CBS News. (November 6, 2019). Texas Appeals Court commutes death sentence of convicted killer Bobby James Moore. Retrieved 05/13/2022 from www.cbsnews.com/dfw/news/texas-appeals-court-commutes-death-sentence-of-convicted-killer-bobby-james-moore/.

Cherry v. State, 959 So. 2d. 702 (Florida, 2007).

Ellenkamp, J. J. H., Brouwers, E. P. M., Embregts, P. J. C. M., Joosen, M. C. W., & van Weeghel, J. (2016). Work environment-related factors in obtaining and maintaining work in a competitive employment setting for employees with intellectual disabilities: A systematic review. *Journal of Occupational Rehabilitation*, 26(1), 56–69. doi:10.1007/s10926-015-9586-1.

Enmund v. Florida, 458 U.S. 782 (1982).

Feldman, K. (June 9, 2020). Intellectually disabled Texas inmate granted parole after almost 40 years on death row. *New York Daily News*. Retrieved 05/13/2022 from www.nydailynews.com/news/national/ny-texas-inmate-parole-death-row-20200609-sxu4zol6yvapzgjk4rzkxeomoq-story.html.

Georgia Resource Center. (2022). Warren Lee Hill: The execution of a man with intellectual disability. Retrieved 08/19/2022 from www.garesource.org/cases/warren-lee-hill/.

Greenspan, S., & Switzky, H. N. (2006). *Lessons from the* Atkins *decision for the next AAMR manual.* In H. N. Switzky & S. Greenspan (Eds.) *What is mental retardation? Ideas for an evolving disability in the 21st century.* Washington, D.C.: American Association on Mental Retardation.

Gregg v. Georgia, 428 U.S. 153 (1976).

Hall v. Florida, 134 U.S. 1986 (2014).

Hill v. Humphrey, 662 F.3d 1335 (11th Cir. 2011).

Liptak, A. (January 19, 2008). Lawyer reveals secret, toppling death sentence. *New York Times*. Retrieved 01/07/2023 from www.nytimes.com/2008/01/19/us/19death.html.

Lucas, L. S. (2017). An empirical assessment of Georgia's beyond a reasonable doubt standard to determine intellectual disability in capital cases. *Georgia State University Law Review, 33*(3), 553–608. Retrieved 05/11/2022 from https://readingroom.law.gsu.edu/gsulr/vol33/iss3/1.

McCarver v. North Carolina, 533 U.S. 975 (2001).

Moore v. Texas, 581 U.S. 1039, 137 S. Ct. 1039 (2017).

Moore v. Texas, 586 U.S. 666 (2019).

Schalock, R. L. (2007). *User's guide: Mental retardation: Definition, classification and systems of supports. Tenth edition: Applications for clinicians, educators, disability program managers, and policy makers.* Washington, D.C.: American Association on Mental Retardation.

Schalock, R. L., Borthwick-Duffy, S. A., Buntinx, W. H. E., Coulter, D. L., & Craig, E. M. (2009). *Intellectual disability: Definition, classification, and systems of supports. Eleventh edition.* Washington, D.C.: American Association on Intellectual and Developmental Disabilities.

Schalock, R. L., Luckasson, R., & Tassé, M. J. (2021). *Intellectual disability: Definition, diagnosis, classification, and systems of supports. Twelfth edition.* Washington, D.C.: American Association on Intellectual and Developmental Disabilities.

Speiser v. Randall, 357 U.S. 513, 78 S.Ct. 1332 (1958).

State v. Marshall, No. 98-CR-0290-J (Georgia Superior Court, Athens-Clarke County. September 22, 1999).

Tassé, M. J., & Blume, J. H. (2018). *Intellectual disability and the death penalty: Current issues and controversies.* Santa Barbara, CA: Praeger.

Young v. Georgia, cert. denied, 142 S.Ct. 1206 (Mem) (Feb. 28, 2022).

18   Competency to be executed

Ford v. Wainwright (U.S. 1986)

On July 21, 1974, Alvin Ford (age 20) allegedly murdered a helpless, wounded police officer by shooting him in the back of the head at close range. Ford denied the execution style of the murder and said that he had fired at the officer when the officer had drawn his own weapon. Ford was found guilty of murder and was condemned to death.

Ford began to show signs of mental illness in 1982. He developed a number of delusional beliefs which expanded as time went on. He believed that he was the victim of a conspiracy. He believed that the correctional officers at the prison were conspiring with the Ku Klux Klan to drive him to commit suicide. He believed that the same people who were tormenting him at the prison had also made hostages of members of his family. He believed that women in his family were being held somewhere inside the prison, where they were being tortured and sexually abused. He believed that correctional officers at the prison were killing prisoners and placing their bodies in the concrete slabs that were used for beds. He believed that 135 people were being held hostage at the prison, including his family, friends, "senators, Senator Kennedy, and many other leaders" (*Ford v. Wainwright*, 1986, at 476).

Ford believed he was the only person who could save them. In 1983, he wrote a letter to the Attorney General of Florida, assuming authority for ending this "crisis" and claiming to have fired a number of prison officials. He began to call himself "Pope John Paul III," and he claimed to have appointed nine new Justices to the Florida Supreme Court.

Ford's attorneys had him evaluated by a psychiatrist, who wrote "that Ford suffered from 'a severe, uncontrollable, mental disease which closely resembles Paranoid Schizophrenia With Suicide Potential' – a 'major mental disorder ... severe enough to substantially affect Mr. Ford's present ability to assist in the defense of his life'" (at 476–477). Ford believed that this psychiatrist had joined the conspiracy against him, and he refused to see him again.

DOI: 10.4324/9781003385028-21

Ford's attorneys subsequently sent another psychiatrist, who wrote that Ford spoke in "long streams of seemingly unrelated thoughts in rapid succession" (at 477). Among his ramblings, Ford told the psychiatrist that he knew "there is some sort of death penalty," but that he was

> "free to go whenever I want, because it would be illegal and the executioner would be executed." When asked if he would be executed, Ford replied: "I can't be executed because of the landmark case. I won. Ford v. State will prevent executions all over." (at 477)

The psychiatrist

> concluded that Ford had no understanding of why he was being executed, made no connection between the homicide of which he had been convicted and the death penalty, and indeed sincerely believed that he would not be executed because he owned the prisons and could control the Governor through mind waves. (at 477)

Pursuant to Florida law, the Governor appointed a panel of three psychiatrists, who interviewed Ford as a group for about 30 minutes and concluded that he had a mental illness but that he was sane and understood his situation. On April 30, 1984, the Governor signed a death warrant for Ford's execution. Ford's attorneys filed a petition for habeas corpus, and the U.S. Supreme Court granted certiorari. At issue was the important question of whether executing a person with severe mental illness violates the Eighth Amendment's provision against cruel and unusual punishment. This issue had become ripe for the Supreme Court, because by 1986 the Eighth Amendment had been incorporated (i.e., it was being applied to decisions in State courts).

The English common-law tradition regarding what we now call "competency" and "sanity" is expressed in this passage from Blackstone's *Commentaries* (1765–1769/2016):

> [Idiots] and lunatics are not chargeable for their own acts, if committed when under these incapacities: no, not even for treason itself. Also, if a man in his sound memory commits a capital offence, and before arraignment for it, he becomes mad, he ought not to be arraigned for it: because he is not able to plead to it with that advice and caution that he ought. And if, after he has pleaded, the prisoner becomes mad, he shall not be tried: for how can he make his defence? If, after he be tried and found guilty, he loses his senses before judgment, judgment shall not be pronounced; and if, after judgment, he becomes of nonsane

memory, execution shall be stayed: for peradventure, says the humanity of the English law, had the prisoner been of sound memory, he might have alleged something in stay of judgment or execution. (Book IV, Chapter 2, p. 24)

In this passage, Blackstone recognizes several important features that are consistent with our modern understanding of mental illness – that mental illness can occur unpredictably, that it can occur at any age, that it can be debilitating, and that it can interfere with a defendant's legal capacities. As Blackstone perceived, and as the case of Alvin Ford demonstrates, there are no time limits on incompetency. If a person loses their competency, then the proceedings against them must stop, no matter what stage of the process has been reached. Mental health professionals can be employed at every step of the process when a defendant shows signs of incompetency.

The U.S. Supreme Court ruled in *Ford v. Wainwright* (1986) that defendants are entitled to an examination of their competency before they are executed, and that sentencing an incompetent person to death is cruel and unusual punishment, contrary to the Eighth Amendment. Justice Thurgood Marshall wrote in the majority opinion:

Today, no State in the Union permits the execution of the insane. It is clear that the ancient and humane limitation upon the State's ability to execute its sentences has as firm a hold upon the jurisprudence of today as it had centuries ago in England. The various reasons put forth in support of the common law restriction have no less logical, moral, and practical force than they did when first voiced. For today, no less than before, we may seriously question the retributive value of executing a person who has no comprehension of why he has been singled out and stripped of his fundamental right to life ... Similarly, the natural abhorrence civilized societies feel at killing one who has no capacity to come to grips with his own conscience or deity is still vivid today. And the intuition that such an execution simply offends humanity is evidently shared across this Nation. Faced with such widespread evidence of a restriction upon sovereign power, this Court is compelled to conclude that the Eighth Amendment prohibits a State from carrying out a sentence of death upon a prisoner who is insane. Whether its aim be to protect the condemned from fear and pain without comfort of understanding, or to protect the dignity of society itself from *the barbarity of exacting mindless vengeance*, the restriction finds enforcement in the Eighth Amendment. (at 408–410; italics added)

The court remanded Ford to the state of Florida to develop a new disposition more suitable for a person who has a serious mental illness. Alvin Ford died in prison of natural causes on February 26, 1991, at the age of 37.

REFERENCES

Blackstone, W. (1765–1769/2016). *Commentaries on the laws of England. 4 volumes*. Oxford: Clarendon Press.
Ford v. Wainwright, 477 U.S. 399 (1986).

Part IV

The insanity defense

Issues related to insanity are addressed at trial. This is such a large topic that the entirety of Part IV is devoted to it.

Chapter 19 introduces the four definitions of insanity that are used in U.S. courts:

- cognitive incapacity
- moral incapacity
- volitional incapacity
- the product test.

Chapter 20 presents a series of foundational cases from the United Kingdom. These include *Rex v. Hadfield* (1800), which is the pivotal case in the history of the insanity defense because it led to innovations in the law and in the housing of acquittees with mental illness. Also included in this discussion is *Regina v. M'Naghten* (1843), which is remembered as the iconic decision in the history of the insanity defense because it identified the cognitive and moral incapacities as the substance of insanity. The judicial reasoning used in *M'Naghten* continues to be highly influential in the United States to this day.

Chapter 21 is not, technically speaking, a chapter on the insanity defense, as it focuses on a set of pleas and defenses that are not insanity but which are related to mental illness and extreme emotional states. These pleas and arguments include "guilty but mentally ill" (GBMI) and the "diminishment" defenses, which go by several names – "diminished responsibility," "diminished capacity," "diminished actuality."

Chapter 22 reviews three U.S. cases that narrowed the scope of the insanity defense:

- *Leland v. Oregon* (1952), in which the U.S. Supreme Court held that states are not required to have the defense of volitional incapacity.

DOI: 10.4324/9781003385028-22

- *United States v. Hinckley* (1981), heard in the U.S. District Court for the District of Columbia, regarding defendant John Hinckley, Jr., who shot President Ronald Reagan. Hinckley's acquittal by reason of insanity was so unpopular with the public that it prompted Congress to pass the first federal law on the insanity defense, known as the Insanity Defense Reform Act of 1984. In this law, Congress abolished volitional incapacity from federal law. The public demanded change, and the defense of volitional incapacity happened to be the low-hanging fruit.
- *Clark v. Arizona* (2006), in which the U.S. Supreme Court ruled that states are not required to have the defense of cognitive incapacity.

Chapter 23 is devoted to a discussion of the trial of James W. Wilson (*State v. Wilson*, 1992), a school shooter with schizophrenia in Greenwood, South Carolina. Wilson is, to my knowledge, the only defendant in the United States who is on death row despite the fact that the trial judge found him to be so severely mentally ill that he could not control his own behavior (volitional incapacity). His trial is perhaps the most unique in the history of volitional incapacity.

Chapter 24 reviews the history of states' efforts to abolish the insanity defense during the 20th century. In four states – Louisiana, Mississippi, Nevada, and Washington – those laws were quickly struck down by their own supreme courts. In four other states – Idaho, Kansas, Montana, and Utah – those laws have persisted, and today those states do not have the insanity defense. The U.S. Supreme Court in *Kahler v. Kansas* (2020) held that the states are not required to have an insanity defense. *Kahler* is the last case discussed in this book, and it is a fitting climax, because with that decision the U.S. Supreme Court ended five centuries of tradition in Anglo-American law.

REFERENCES

Clark v. Arizona, 548 U.S. 735 (2006).
Kahler v. Kansas, 589 U.S. ____ (2020).
Leland v. Oregon, 343 U.S. 790 (1952).
Regina v. M'Naghten, 10 Clark & Fin. 200, 8 Eng. Rep. 718 (1843).
Rex v. Hadfield, 27 Howell's State Trials, 1281 (1800).
State v. Wilson, 306 S.C. 498, 413 S.E.2d 19 (South Carolina, 1992).
United States v. Hinckley, 525 F. Supp. 1342 (D.D.C. 1981).

19　The three incapacities

When a court finds that a defendant is not guilty by reason of insanity (NGRI), the court is saying that the defendant was not responsible for their behavior because of a mental disorder.

The idea that persons with mental illness lack moral responsibility can be traced back more than 2,000 years through Greek and Roman philosophy and law (Platt & Diamond, 1966; Walker, 1985). Aristotle wrote around 350 BCE that mental illness can be a condition that excuses people for their behavior (see Appendix C). Walker (1985) considers Aristotle's philosophy to have been "ahead of his time" (p. 26). Walker dates the first laws regarding insanity to the Justinian Digest of 53 CE. According to Moran (1985), the first recorded insanity acquittal in English common law occurred in 1505. (For more information about the early history of the insanity defense in English common law, see Appendix E.)

The abstractions about the insanity defense that will be discussed in this chapter did not emerge from the ether but are based upon the actual trials of people who committed acts of violence. I have "put the cart before the horse," so to speak, in this chapter by addressing the abstractions before I review the cases themselves. I hope that this will help to put the cases in their proper context when we address them in Chapters 20 through 24.

The best way I have found to understand the insanity defense as it is practiced today is to skip 2,000 years of Western jurisprudence and go directly to the taxonomy that was set forth by the U.S. Supreme Court in *Clark v. Arizona* (2006). The *Clark* court identified three fundamental standards:

- cognitive incapacity
- moral incapacity
- volitional incapacity.

This tripartite formulation – cognitive, moral, and volitional incapacities – demonstrates an implicit theory of human nature in terms of three

DOI: 10.4324/9781003385028-23

fundamental capacities that we expect all sane people always to have with them:

- People are *cognitive* beings who perceive the world and invent theories about it. Because reality is a shared social construct, it is proper to say that what we expect of defendants is that they know what they are doing and that they perceive and understand the world in roughly the same terms as the triers of fact (e.g., free of pseudohallucination). When a defendant does not comprehend reality in the same way as the triers of fact, the defendant may be found not guilty by reason of insanity. Of the defendant with cognitive incapacity, we might say, "They did not know what they were doing" or "They thought they were doing something else."
- People are *moral* beings who make judgments about right and wrong. Because morality is a shared social construct, it is proper to say that what we expect of defendants is that they comprehend right and wrong in a manner that is consistent with the moral values held by the triers of fact (e.g., free of delusion). Of the defendant with moral incapacity we might say, "They did not know it was wrong" or "They thought they were doing the right thing."
- People are *volitional* beings who have preferences, set goals, form intentions, make choices, initiate behaviors, and stick to their plans. We expect people to be able to make right choices and adhere to them. Of the defendant with volitional incapacity, we might say, "They could not control what they were doing."

When one or more of these capacities is disturbed by a mental disorder, the defendant may be found not guilty by reason of insanity (depending on the laws of their jurisdiction, as will be explained in this chapter).

COGNITIVE INCAPACITY

Defendants who have cognitive incapacity do not know what they are doing. Their perception of reality is unique and is not shared by the triers of fact.

This form of insanity is uncommon. People generally know what they are doing, even when they have a severe mental illness. Case examples and hypotheticals of cognitive incapacity tend to be awkward and may require a stretch of the imagination.

Examples given by Thomas Erskine during his arguments in *Rex v. Hadfield* (1800; see Chapter 20) are of a man who commits homicide believing that he is killing "any brute animal, or an inanimate being (and such cases have existed)," or who believes "the man he had destroyed to have been a potter's vessel" (quoted in Murray, 1959, p. 139).

Two examples offered by Judge Sir James Fitzjames Stephen (1863/2017) are given without names or citations and may be imaginary – a man wounds someone when he thinks he is breaking a jar, and a man strangles someone when he thinks he is squeezing an orange (cited in Walker, 1968, p. 115).

A hypothetical given by Justice Stephen Breyer in his dissenting opinion in *Kahler v. Kansas* (2020) is that of a defendant who kills a human being while believing that he is killing a dog.

A tentative draft of the Model Penal Code (§ 4.01, Comment 2 [Tent. Draft No. 4, 1955]) presented the hypothetical of a man who strangles his wife believing that he is squeezing a lemon. Ultimately the American Law Institute dropped the cognitive prong from the 1985 version of the Model Penal Code for being redundant with the moral prong – if a defendant does not know what they are doing, then they do not know that what they are doing is wrong. When the State of Arizona dropped the cognitive prong from their insanity defense, this was upheld by the U.S. Supreme Court in *Clark v. Arizona* (2006; see Chapter 22).

Rogers and Shuman (2005, p. 198) suggested the following questions (paraphrased) to evaluate cognitive incapacity:

- Is the defendant's account consistent with the physical evidence? (This question evaluates the extent to which the defendant may have been out of touch with reality.)
- Can the defendant describe their actions chronologically?
- Did the defendant appear to understand the immediate consequences of their actions?
- Did the defendant engage in purposeful behavior before the act?
- What did the defendant hope to gain (i.e., motive)?

To reprise our parking lot example from the discussion of mens rea in Chapter 7, imagine that Driver C (for "cognitive incapacity") has a mental disorder that involves pseudohallucination (i.e., he perceives things as different from what they are). He runs over the little boy, believing that he is hitting a paper bag blowing in the wind. He may be not guilty by reason of insanity due to cognitive incapacity.

MORAL INCAPACITY

When a defendant is insane due to moral incapacity, they may or may not have known what they were doing (i.e., cognitive capacity), but they did not know that what they were doing was wrong. Many insanity acquittals involve moral incapacity related to delusional beliefs. Moral incapacity is far more common than cognitive incapacity, and examples can be provided that do not stretch the imagination. In many cases, the defendant acted according to a motive (such as self-defense) that would have exonerated them if only their belief about the situation had been accurate and not delusional. In such cases, the defendant with a delusional belief and moral incapacity feels justified in doing what they did because their action would have been justified if their interpretation of reality were correct. (For illustrations from my own practice, see the case of William, presented below, and the case of Betty, presented in Chapter 26.)

Rogers and Shuman (2005, p. 198) suggested the following questions (paraphrased) when evaluating moral incapacity:

- Did the defendant believe they were acting in self-defense?
- Did the defendant believe they were carrying out the orders of a government agent?
- Did the defendant believe they were preventing or minimizing a greater harm?
- Did the defendant believe they were obeying commands from a divine authority (i.e., the "divine imperative")?

Returning to our parking lot example, Driver M (for "moral incapacity") runs down the little boy playing a videogame, believing that he is preventing an invasion of earth by extraterrestrials who are communicating with hand-held devices. In the mind of Driver M, hitting the little boy is the right thing to do because he is saving planet Earth.

Because human beings are capable of moral reasoning on multiple levels, some defendants have broken the law in the interest of a greater good. For example, during unpopular wars there have been cases of civil disobedience like tax resistance and draft resistance. When the alleged crime is related to a delusional belief, the defendant's thinking may reflect varying levels of moral reasoning about good and evil. (I am careful to write "alleged crime," because if the defendant is not guilty by reason of insanity, then no crime was committed.) Two famous examples of moral incapacity that are discussed in Chapters 20 and 22 are James Hadfield, who fired a pistol over the head of King George III in 1800, and John Hinckley, Jr., who shot President Ronald Reagan in the chest in 1981. Both men knew that their actions were wrong on one level, but both men believed that their actions were the right thing to do. Hadfield, in fact, expected to be killed for what he had done. Hinckley expected to lose "my freedom and possibly my life." Hadfield's delusional belief was that he was "ordained to die, and to die as Jesus Christ did." Hinckley believed that shooting President Reagan would bring love into his life. Hadfield and Hinckley both knew what they were doing (i.e., both had sufficient cognitive capacity), and both knew that it would get them in serious trouble (i.e., that people would think it was wrong), but both believed that pulling the trigger was the right thing for them to do in that moment. Hadfield and Hinckley are both examples of moral incapacity.

Case study #11: William – a case of moral incapacity

William was a Black man 34 years of age who was my patient at a forensic hospital. He had a long history of schizophrenia. On the day he was arrested for homicide, he had tried to have sexual relations with his girlfriend but he was unable to maintain an erection. Intensely frustrated and seething with anger, he blamed all White men for his emasculation. He loaded his shotgun and went out into the street in broad daylight, vowing that he would kill the first White man he saw. The first White man he saw was the hapless postman who was delivering mail in his neighborhood. William shot him down without further provocation.

William felt justified in his action. He believed that he was doing the right thing because he believed in his delusion that all White men were responsible for his emasculation, and he believed that this had to be avenged. My opinion was that he had a severe mental illness and was not responsible for his behavior due to moral incapacity. Volitional incapacity was also suggested by the urgency with which he had carried out his mission.

William was incompetent to stand trial due to his inability to reason clearly and his inability to cooperate with an attorney. He was kept in the hospital for many months while staff attempted to restore his competency through anti-psychotic medication and educational classes on competency. I left for another job before he was discharged so, unfortunately, I have no follow-up on the outcome of the charge against him.

VOLITIONAL INCAPACITY

Insanity due to volitional incapacity has a more complex and convoluted history than the first two incapacities addressed here, and much of the remainder of this chapter will be devoted to its discussion.

Defendants who have volitional incapacity are unable to control their behavior because of a mental disorder. The defendant may or may not know what they are doing (i.e., cognitive capacity), and they may or may not believe that what they are doing is right (i.e., moral capacity), but they are not able to control themselves.

The concept of "volition" assumes that people have mental functions that guide their decisions and actions. Questions about volition lead to a discussion of human decision making and free will, which is beyond the scope of this book. The nature and even the existence of free will is a topic that leads people into fundamental disagreements. For an introduction to the philosophy of free will, I recommend Kane (2002). An individual's belief about free will may be a matter of intuition and not proof. If forensic mental health professionals would evaluate defendants regarding their volitional capacity, I recommend that they study the philosophy of free will and decide for themselves what they believe about the nature of human volition.

The compulsive handkerchief thief described by Krafft-Ebing (1886/ 1926; see Chapter 35) is a good example of volitional incapacity. His illegal behavior persisted for over a decade despite repeated arrests and incarcerations, and this, plus the nature of his internal experience, indicated his inability to control his behavior.

Another example of volitional incapacity is school shooter Jamie Wilson, who is the topic of Chapter 23 and who is, to my knowledge, the only defendant in the U.S. who is on death row after a trial judge found him to have volitional incapacity.

Returning to our parking lot example, Driver V (for "volitional incapacity") has a mental illness, knows he is about to hit the little boy, and knows it is the wrong thing to do, but he cannot stop himself. Because this may seem an unlikely occurrence, allow me to develop a hypothetical scenario. Imagine that Driver V hears a voice telling him what to do (command auditory hallucination). If he cannot resist the voice, then his is a case of volitional incapacity. If he believes that obeying the voice is the right thing to do, then his insanity may be a combination of moral and volitional incapacities. Driver V has lost control of his behavior. He may be found not guilty by reason of insanity due to volitional incapacity (if the parking lot happens to be in one of the jurisdictions that recognizes the defense of volitional incapacity; see Table 22.1).

Volitional incapacity has a more complex history than the other two incapacities of insanity, and we will take more time to review it.

Irresistible impulse

The theory of "irresistible impulse" took root in Scottish courts during the nineteenth century and – both in Scotland and in the United States – became an important "third prong" of the insanity defense (along with cognitive and moral incapacities).

The phrase "irresistible impulse" first appeared, in a very different context, in the book, *An Essay on the Nature and Immutability of Truth, in Opposition to Sophistry and Scepticism,* by Scottish philosopher James Beattie (1770/2005). Beattie's book was very popular and it sold well in Scotland (which reportedly infuriated David Hume). Beattie coined the phrase "irresistible impulse" when he referred to the process by which people comprehend common-sense, self-evident truths. By the mid-nineteenth century the phrase was being used in Scottish courts to describe volitional incapacity. This usage of the phrase caught on and has been used widely in legal decisions since that time.

"Irresistible impulse" is a nice alliteration, which appeals to a culture that values poetry. As a legal term it leaves much to be desired. It is an example of the lyrical but imprecise language that we inherited from centuries of common law. The phrase "irresistible impulse" unfortunately refers only to the weaker edge of a two-edged sword. The other edge of the sword is the defendant's weak volitional control, and this is what we are most likely to encounter in defendants who have mental illness. While it is conceivable that some defendants who have mental illness are prepossessed by over-powering impulses, it is more likely that they have normal but inappropriate impulses and that their ability to resist these impulses is weak. The range of normal human impulses is very wide indeed. One need only watch movies or read graphic novels to know that this is true. What keeps our inappropriate impulses in check is our good volitional controls. Conceivably there may be some impulses that are unique to persons who have mental illness, and these may sometimes be so powerful that they cannot be controlled, but what is more likely is that the defendant has a normal but inappropriate impulse and their volitional controls have failed.

The "policeman at the elbow" test

A rule of thumb that has been used by some courts and forensic examiners in the evaluation of volitional incapacity is known as the "policeman at the elbow" test. It might be stated as follows: "Would this defendant have committed the act if a policeman had been standing at their elbow?" If they would have committed the act even when a policeman was at their elbow, then they can be said to lack volitional capacity, according to this test.

The origin of this test has been attributed to Lord Bromwell, who heard testimony that a defendant lacked volitional capacity because he once killed a cat. "His lordship asked if he thought he would have killed the cat if a policeman had been present. The witness answered, 'No.' His lordship then said he supposed the impulse was irresistible only in the absence of a policeman" (quoted in *People v. Hubert*, 1897, pp. 223–224).

Morse (1994, 2002) described the "policeman at the elbow" test in its most extreme form when he wrote that anyone can resist a supposedly irresistible impulse if they have a gun to their head. (Morse's version does not apply to all impulses – for example, the impulses to breathe or to micturate – but more importantly it does not fit our ordinary social reality. We do not go about with guns to our heads or policemen at our elbows. Assessments of volitional capacity are more persuasive when they are gauged to the reality of a defendant's life and not to an unrealistic hypothetical.)

Furthermore, if a defendant has a gun to their head or a policeman at their elbow, then volition is not the issue. These are examples of duress, not volition. In situations of duress, a defendant's behavior is caused not by their own volition but by the person who brings the duress (i.e., by the person who holds the gun or by the policeman). This has been recognized since the time of Aristotle (see Appendix C). Duress is a situation in which a person's volition and responsibility are overwhelmed by another. A defendant's behavior while they are under duress is not a valid measure of their volitional capacity.

The "policeman at the elbow" test was held to be the only test of volitional incapacity in a military court (*United States v. Kunak*, 1954). Civilian courts have been more willing to recognize that there are defendants who can restrain themselves when a policeman is present but who nevertheless lack volitional capacity (*People v. Jackson*, 2001). The relevant issue is not whether a defendant can be controlled by another person, but whether they have sufficient internal resources to control their own behavior.

The murder trial of Archie Brawner (*United States v. Brawner*, D.C. Cir. 1972) is the case in which the District of Columbia Court of Appeals embraced the defense of volitional incapacity and dropped the product test of insanity. (The product test of insanity is addressed later in this chapter.) Judge Leventhal wrote:

> The question is not properly put in terms of whether he would have capacity to conform in some untypical restraining situation – as with an attendant or policeman at his elbow. The issue is whether he was able to conform in the unstructured condition of life in an open society, and whether the result of his abnormal mental condition was a lack of substantial internal controls. (*United States v. Brawner*, D.C. Cir. 1972, at 991)

The "can't/won't" distinction

An abiding question in arguments about volitional incapacity has been whether a defendant *could not have resisted* the impulse or merely *chose not to resist* the impulse. Moore (2016) called this the "can't/won't distinction." If a defendant who has mental illness *can't resist* the impulse, then their volitional capacity was overwhelmed by the mental illness and they are not responsible for their behavior. If on the other hand the defendant simply *chose not to resist* the impulse, then their volitional capacity was intact and they are responsible for their behavior.

This question was articulated as early as 1855 by Judge Sir James Fitzjames Stephen (1829–1894), who wrote – at the precocious age of 26 – "There may have been many instances of irresistible impulse of this kind, although I fear

Figure 19.1 Judge Sir James Fitzjames Stephen (1829–1894), who codified English
　　law, appreciated the nature of volitional incapacity, and chastised his
　　colleagues on the bench for their "sarcasm and ridicule" of mental
　　health professionals.

there is a disposition to confound them with unresisted impulses" (quoted in Walker, 1968, p. 105). Judge Stephen later was more convinced about the reality of volitional incapacity in the 1870s, when he embarked on a codification of English criminal law. He was convinced that the law should exempt a defendant who was "prevented either by defective mental power or by any disease affecting his mind from controlling his own conduct" (quoted in Walker, 1968, p. 106).

A number of judges, legislators, and commentators have argued that it is not possible to make the "can't/won't" distinction. They have argued that – because of the alleged inability to make the "can't/won't" distinction – the loss of volitional capacity can never be proved. This argument has been used to eliminate volitional incapacity from the law in many jurisdictions, including 18 U.S.C. §17, known as the federal Insanity Defense Reform Act of 1984, discussed further in Chapter 22.

This alleged inability to make the "can't/won't" distinction is one of the reasons why the American Medical Association and the American Psychiatric Association recommended that the volitional prong be dropped from legal tests of insanity (American Medical Association & American Psychiatric Association, 1985; American Psychiatric Association, 1983). It is the reasoning that the U.S. Court of Appeals, Fifth Circuit, applied in *United States v. Lyons* (1984) when they rejected defendant Robert Lyons' claim of volitional incapacity. It is fair to say that this idea that the "can't/won't" distinction cannot be made was one of the most influential ideas in mental health law during the last half of the 20th century. However, I find this reasoning to be inadequate, as I will explain shortly. The laws of seventeen states continue to recognize the defense of volitional incapacity (see Table 22.1), which means that the legislatures of those states trust their triers of fact to make the "can't/won't" distinction when they are called upon to do so.

I can identify six reasons for doubting this notion that the "can't/won't" distinction cannot be made.

1 To demand such clarity from the "can't/won't" distinction begs the question of the existence of free will. That is, the "won't" half of the "can't/won't" distinction presupposes the existence of free will, and I would argue that the existence of free will cannot be proved because an alternative, deterministic explanation can always be found for any human behavior. (The existence of free will can, however, be intuited.) To say that the "can't/won't" distinction cannot be made is simply to restate that the existence of free will cannot be proved.

2 Triers of fact must be allowed to have their own intuitions. If jurors must be allowed to have their own intuitions, and if they are capable of discerning for themselves whether or not they believe in the existence of

free will, then, I would argue, they must be allowed to intuit for themselves whether free will existed for this particular defendant or whether this defendant lacked free will because of a severe mental illness.

At a trial, it matters little what the army of philosophers, legal scholars, and legislators think about the "can't/won't" distinction and matters only what the triers of fact conclude. The ultimate decision about volitional incapacity is left up to the triers of fact in those seventeen states that recognize volitional incapacity as a form of insanity (see Table 22.1). The legislatures of those states trust their juries to discern for themselves when a defendant does or does not have volitional incapacity.

Legal authorities have expressed deep differences of opinion regarding the capacity of jurors to make difficult distinctions about insanity. In the oral arguments in *Kahler v. Kansas* (2020), for example (see Chapter 24), Associate Justice Brett Kavanaugh questioned whether it is feasible to expect jurors to grasp the concepts involved in the insanity defense. Professor Sarah Schrup, representing defendant James Kahler, answered that jurors *are capable* of making decisions about insanity, and that jurors make judgments about "reasonableness" all the time (oral arguments in *Kahler v. Kansas*, 2020, at 24).

3 Juries do not need to reach complete certainty on any question that is set before them, and this includes questions of insanity. The law recognizes – when it sets forth standards of evidence (see Chapter 5) – that total certainty is not a realistic expectation. The standard of evidence for insanity – depending on the jurisdiction – is either "clear and convincing evidence" or "preponderance of the evidence." When someone argues that the "can't/won't" distinction cannot be made, we must remember that total certainty is not required. The question is more properly phrased, "Can we make the 'can't/won't' distinction to a clear and convincing level of certainty or by a preponderance of the evidence?"

4 To reject the defense of volitional incapacity because of the alleged inability to make the "can't/won't" distinction is to present a one-sided argument that reflects (to borrow a term from Moore, 2016, p. 190) an "ultra-conservative" bias. Critics who reject the defense of volitional incapacity on these grounds do not go on to assert that – because we cannot tell the "can'ts" from the "won'ts" – therefore all defendants who claim volitional incapacity are "can'ts" who are not responsible for their behavior. Rather, these critics take the position that all defendants who claim volitional incapacity should be treated like "won'ts" (or they take the compatibilist position that the distinction between "can't" and "won't" is not relevant in determining moral responsibility). They take the position that the defendant should be held accountable for their behavior and should go to prison. The argument that the "can't/won't" distinction cannot be made may sound logical on the surface, but it subserves an ultra-conservative agenda.

5 A subset of defendants who claim to be "can'ts" but who actually are "won'ts" are malingerers pretending to have a serious mental illness. Debates about the "can't/won't" distinction have proceeded without an appreciation for the advances that have been made in the detection of malingering (see, for example, Boone, 2021; Rogers & Bender, 2018; Rubenzer, 2018). When malingerers can be identified and eliminated from the pool of defendants claiming volitional incapacity, then negotiating the "can't/won't" distinction becomes a bit more manageable.

6 Despite the contention that the "can't/won't" distinction cannot be made, methods have been developed that assess volitional incapacity. These are based largely on the work of psychologist Richard Rogers, and they are the topic of the next section.

Assessing volitional capacity

Rogers (1987) and Rogers and Shuman (2000) identified seven criteria (paraphrased below) by which to assess volitional incapacity:

- loss of capacity to choose between alternatives
- impulse that cannot be satisfied by any available alternative
- incapacity for extended or indefinite delay (i.e., a sense of urgency)
- disregard for apprehension
- foreseeability and avoidability (i.e., is the defendant aware of situations in which they have lost control in the past and do they avoid those situations?)
- the behavior is the result of a mental disorder of sufficient severity
- the alleged loss of volitional capacity has a sustained, negative effect on the defendant's day-to-day living (i.e., it is not persuasive for a defendant to argue lack of volitional capacity when the only evidence for this alleged incapacity is the crime itself).

Translating these seven factors into actionable terms, the defendant who has a robust volitional capacity and who purposely and knowingly chooses to commit a crime is a person who:

- perceives a range of options and chooses to commit the crime
- perceives at least one course of action *other* than the crime and *chooses not* to follow it
- plans, prepares, and selects an advantageous time and place for the crime (i.e., is capable of delay)
- conceals evidence or evades arrest
- is aware of situations in which they have lost control in the past and then avoids those situations

- does not have a mental disorder of sufficient severity
- shows good volitional capacity in all other areas of life.

Defendants who suffer in any of these seven areas may lack volitional capacity.

Rogers and Shuman (2005, p. 204) suggested the following questions (paraphrased below) to evaluate volitional incapacity:

1 Could the defendant have withheld, delayed, or discontinued the behavior?
2 Was the defendant overpowered by a need to perform the behavior? Did it come as a sudden impulse?
3 Did it pass the "policeman at the elbow" test (i.e., was it done without regard for apprehension)?
4 What options did the defendant perceive?
5 What efforts did the defendant make to resist the impulse?
6 Did the defendant choose to be in circumstances where their loss of control was foreseeable?
7 Why did loss of volitional control occur at this particular time?
8 Is loss of control evident in other areas of the defendant's life?

In addition to the eight questions developed by Rogers and Shuman, I would suggest three more (which are not separate from Rogers and Shuman's questions but which overlap them):

- Was the defendant responding to a command auditory hallucination?
- Did the defendant experience thought insertion, thought withdrawal (two of Kurt Schneider's first-rank symptoms of schizophrenia), or thought control, i.e., the experience that someone outside themselves was inserting thoughts into their mind, stealing their thoughts away, or controlling their thoughts?
- Did the defendant have a developmental history that was characterized by lack of opportunity to develop sufficient volitional control?

The individual envisioned in this last question is someone who did not have appropriate opportunity or encouragement at home, at school, or in their community to develop normal volitional controls. These defendants include school shooter Jamie Wilson, who is the subject of Chapter 23. Wilson was a withdrawn and unusual child who was the victim of physical, emotional, and sexual abuse. He did not participate in athletic, academic, or other competitions. When he became unmanageable at home, his parents took him to a hospital, motel, or the home of a relative, or they gave him the antipsychotic medication that had been prescribed for his grandmother, thereby depriving him of opportunities to develop volitional controls by

(1) isolating him; (2) removing him from potentially effective attachment, role modeling, and verbal instruction; (3) negatively reinforcing him for loss of control; and (4) altering his cognition with medication so that he could not process information effectively and learn important lessons about self-monitoring and self-regulation. Furthermore, violence was the norm in his family and community. When Wilson became psychotic in his teenage years, he responded to command auditory hallucinations and shot eleven people at an elementary school. He was arrested and tried for murder. The judge found him incapable of conforming his conduct to the requirements of the law (which is another way of saying "volitional incapacity").

Defendants who have failed to develop appropriate volitional controls may have been abused as children. They may experience learned helplessness (Peterson et al., 1993), in which case they may have never developed a proper sense of agency. They may have had no opportunity to participate in sports, academics, or other competitive activities where they might have developed a personal sense of agency and good volitional controls. The "fair opportunity conception" of responsibility (Brink, 2021) argues that individuals who have less opportunity to participate in normal life bear less responsibility for their actions.

Defendants' abilities to control their behavior are likely to vary with their developmental experiences. Experiences that may contribute to the development of appropriate volitional controls include (1) effective modeling of self-control by people in their environment, including adults, siblings, neighbors, and peers; (2) effective social institutions including a well-functioning educational system; and (3) a rewarding environment that positively reinforces the individual for the proper exercise of self-control. Conversely, experiences that probably contribute to poor impulse control and lack of volitional capacity include (1) insufficient modeling of impulse control by persons in their environment, including adults, siblings, neighbors, and peers; (2) harsh treatment, including child abuse; (3) harsh or ineffective social institutions, such as inadequate schools, foster care, child protection, and correctional systems where children are mistreated or are returned to abusive families without proper investigation and treatment; (4) reinforcement (positive or negative) for loss of impulse control; (5) the use of medications and intoxicants that alter a child's consciousness during important developmental events when the child could be learning effective methods of impulse regulation; and (6) trauma and illness, including mental illness, which interferes with the development of normal self-control.

A disability model of volitional incapacity

Insanity is a form of mental disability and it makes sense to conceptualize volitional incapacity from the perspective of the disability model. The disability model helps us to avoid absolutist thinking about mental illness and instead to think of volitional incapacity in terms of the psychic cost that a defendant would have to pay in order to conform their conduct to the requirements of the law.

The disability model entails the concept of cost. For example, when a physician assesses a back injury and says that a person cannot lift 40 lb., the physician is not saying that this person is never capable under any circumstances of lifting 40 lb. The physician is saying that this person would pay an inordinate cost for doing so. We can conceptualize volitional incapacity in the same terms. When a person with a mental disorder resists an impulse, they may pay an unreasonable cost in terms of overwhelming anxiety. An example can be found among the paraphilic disorders, such as Krafft-Ebing's handkerchief thief discussed in Chapter 35. Krafft-Ebing (1886/1926) wrote, "If he could not gain possession of the handkerchief he desired, he would become painfully excited, tremble and sweat all over" (p. 258). By indulging in his paraphilia and stealing women's handkerchiefs, the thief avoided crippling levels of anxiety. Repeated arrests and incarcerations did not deter him. He risked (and suffered) jail time and ignominy rather than endure the overwhelming anxiety caused by resisting his impulse to steal handkerchiefs.

When a psychotic killer is overcome with fear and rage and their volitional controls fail them, we may ask what cost they would have paid in terms of further decompensation had they attempted the Herculean task of exerting self-control in that moment.

Volitional incapacity as "low-hanging fruit"

Chapters 22 through 24 discuss seven occasions when judges and legislators have either diminished the significance of volitional incapacity or have eliminated it altogether: (1) the U.S. Supreme Court decision in *Leland v. Oregon* (1952); (2) the federal Insanity Defense Reform Act of 1984 (18 U.S.C. §17); (3) the laws of eight states (now only four) that abolished the insanity defense in the twentieth century; (4) the laws of twenty-nine states that have an insanity defense but do not consider volitional incapacity to be a form of insanity; (5) the "guilty but mentally ill" (GBMI) verdicts in Delaware, Pennsylvania, and South Carolina, in which volitional incapacity is not recognized as a form of insanity but is, or can be, a form of GBMI; (6) the South Carolina law that made volitional incapacity a mitigating factor and not a form of insanity; and (7) the death penalty for school shooter Jamie Wilson (*State v. Wilson*, 1992), who to my knowledge is the only defendant in the U.S. who is condemned to death despite the fact that a trial judge found him to have volitional incapacity.

The defense of volitional incapacity has long been the low-hanging fruit of the insanity defense, and it has proved to be susceptible to diminution or removal by its political opponents. The defense of volitional incapacity was accepted in Scottish courts, but it never became a mainstream idea in England. In fact, it was deemed "a most dangerous doctrine" in *Regina v. Burton* (1863), and it succumbed to the judicial and legislative attacks that are reviewed in Chapters 22 through 24.

The iconic case in the definition of insanity in Anglo-American law is *Regina v. M'Naghten* (1843; see Chapter 20). As judge Sir James Fitzjames Stephen (1883/2015) pointed out, volitional incapacity was not a defense used in *M'Naghten* and therefore was not considered in the development of the M'Naghten Rules. If M'Naghten's attorneys had argued for volitional incapacity, history may have been different.

Public interest in the insanity defense was aroused in 1981, when John Hinckley, Jr., shot President Ronald Reagan and was acquitted by reason of insanity in District Court in the District of Columbia (*United States v. Hinckley*, 1981; see Chapter 22). An outraged public demanded change, believing that Hinckley should be punished and not acquitted. This resulted in the first comprehensive federal legislation on the insanity defense, known as the federal Insanity Defense Reform Act of 1984 (18 U.S.C. §17), and it does not include volitional incapacity. The prevailing forces in psychiatry accepted the idea that volitional incapacity cannot be assessed and recommended that volitional incapacity be removed from legal tests of insanity (American Psychiatric Association, 1983).

The irony is that this change in the federal law probably would not have changed the outcome of Hinckley's trial. Although the defense argued volitional incapacity at Hinckley's trial, they also argued for moral incapacity, and indeed the evidence of moral incapacity was stronger. (For a further discussion of *Hinckley* and its aftermath, see Chapter 22). When Hinckley was acquitted by reason of insanity, the public demanded change, and volitional incapacity happened to be the low-hanging fruit.

The political opponents of the insanity defense – i.e., those who would narrow its scope or eliminate it altogether – seek to protect the public from dangerous people who have mental illness. It is a worthy motive, but they seek to accomplish it by convicting persons who have serious mental illness, sending them to prisons instead of hospitals, imprisoning them for long periods of time, and even condemning them to death. The risk to their civil liberties is dire when you consider that mental illness is real, insanity is real, and defendants who are insane deserve special treatment by the courts.

THE "DURHAM RULE" OR "PRODUCT TEST" OF INSANITY: *DURHAM V. UNITED STATES* (D.C. CIR. 1954)

A fourth standard by which insanity is adjudicated in the United States is known as the "product test." According to this test, a defendant is not guilty by reason of insanity if it can be demonstrated that their behavior was the product of a mental illness.

The product test was championed in the District of Columbia Court of Appeals by Judge David L. Bazelon (1909–1993), where it was known as the "Durham Rule" after that Court's decision in *Durham v. United States* (1954). Judge Bazelon thought that the product test would be a good solution to the problem of insanity because he believed that the three incapacities – cognitive, moral, and volitional – were too narrow in scope and did not account for advances made by the profession of psychiatry (Brooks, 1974).

Perhaps a stronger argument for the product test is "that a precise definition of insanity is impossible" (Goldstein, 1967, p. 87). The form that insanity takes can be idiosyncratic, and we may expect to find defendants in our courtrooms who do not fit any of the pre-defined categories of *Clark* but who nevertheless have serious mental illness and deserve special consideration by the courts.

The logic behind the product test was appealing, but the test itself proved to be too unwieldly in its administration. It relied too heavily on the opinions of expert witnesses. Trials turned into courtroom battles between opposing experts, who "frequently" gave opinions regarding a defendant's state of mind that contradicted the observations of eye-witnesses and contradicted the defendant's own words and actions at the time of the offense (*In re Rosenfield*, 1957, p. 21).

Also, the political nature (as opposed to the scientific nature) of psychiatric diagnosis was troubling and proved to be embarrassing to the mental health profession. The infamous "weekend flip flop case" – *In re Rosenfield* – involved a psychiatrist from St. Elizabeths Hospital who testified on a Friday afternoon that defendant Milton Rosenfeld did not have a mental disorder because he had a "psychopathic or sociopathic personality," which at that time was not considered to be a mental disorder. Over the weekend, "psychopathic or sociopathic personality" was redefined by an administrator at St. Elizabeths Hospital as being a mental disorder:

> a formal announcement was made by the acting head of that institution that thereafter members of the staff would express the opinion that such a mental state is in fact a mental disease. In other words, the concept was changed overnight by the psychiatrists themselves. (*In Re Rosenfield*, 1957, at 21, quoted in *United States v. Brawner*, D.C. Cir. 1972, at 978)

The question of whether "psychopathic or sociopathic personality" is a mental illness is an enduring and recurring problem (see the discussion in Chapter 16 regarding sexually violent predators).

Monte Durham himself was tried three times, and at his third trial he pleaded guilty, "thus admitting by necessary implication that he was sane at the time of the crime." (*In re Rosenfield*, 1957, n. 2). District Judge Alexander Holtzoff summarized, "psychiatry is far from an exact science, much less so than other branches of medicine" (*In re Rosenfield*, 1957, at 20–21).

The product test lost credibility. Even Judge Bazelon lost faith in it. He complained that the Durham Rule did not do "nearly enough to eliminate the experts' stranglehold on the process" (quoted in Huckabee, 1980, p. 17). The District of Columbia Court of Appeals ultimately laid it to rest in *United States v. Brawner* (D.C. Cir. 1972), at which time they adopted the standard of insanity advocated by the American Law Institute in the Model Penal Code, i.e., the combination of moral and volitional incapacities (see below).

At the present time the product test is used only in the state of New Hampshire, where it has been the law since *State v. Jones* (1871; see also New Hampshire Revised Statutes Section 628:2). To cite an example, the jury instructions in *Abbott v. Cunningham* (1991) are reproduced below. These jury instructions make it clear that, in the state of New Hampshire, a jury has the discretion to decide whether a defendant is sane or insane, without the encumbrance of laws that would restrict their decision:

> There is no simple test to use in deciding whether Mr. Abbott was insane at the time of the offense. Insanity is merely a question of fact to be decided by you based on all of the evidence. You may consider the testimony of both expert psychiatrists and the testimony of lay persons who were in a position to observe Mr. Abbott around that period of time. You may consider a variety of other factors, including the presence or absence of a previous mental illness, whether Mr. Abbott was suffering from delusions or hallucinations, whether Mr. Abbott acted impulsively or acted with cunning and plan in committing the acts. None of these is by itself a test for insanity, but each of these is an example of the type of factors that you may consider in reaching your decision on whether it was more likely or not that Mr. Abbott was insane at the time he committed the acts. (*Abbott v. Cunningham*, 1991, at 1220)

Defendant George Abbott's jury found him to be sane and guilty of murder.

THE MODEL PENAL CODE (MPC) OF 1985 OF THE AMERICAN LAW INSTITUTE (ALI)

The Model Penal Code (MPC) of 1985 combined the moral prong of the M'Naghten Rule with volitional incapacity. The MPC rejected cognitive incapacity as being redundant with moral incapacity – if a defendant does not know what they are doing (cognitive incapacity), then they do not know that what they are doing is wrong (moral incapacity).

The ALI proposals regarding the insanity defense are found in Section 4 of the MPC. Section 4.01, "Mental disease or defect excluding responsibility," reads as follows:

1 A person is not responsible for criminal conduct if at the time of such conduct as a result of mental disease or defect he lacks substantial capacity either to appreciate the criminality [wrongfulness] of his conduct or to conform his conduct to the requirements of law.
2 As used in the Article, the terms "mental disease or defect" do not include an abnormality manifested only by repeated criminal or otherwise antisocial conduct.

Please notice that the phrase "substantial capacity" in item (1) softens the total lack of capacity that was required by the M'Naghten Rule of 1843 (see Chapter 20). Please notice also item (2) eliminates from consideration the defendant whose only signs of "mental disease or defect" are "repeated criminal or otherwise antisocial conduct." This refers to the DSM-5-TR diagnoses of conduct disorder and antisocial personality disorder, as reviewed in Chapter 16. Whereas the DSM-5-TR diagnosis of antisocial personality disorder may involve other features – namely, impulsivity, failure to plan ahead, irritability, irresponsibility, lack of remorse, indifference, and rationalization – this diagnosis also can be given when the only sign of the disorder is "repeated criminal or otherwise antisocial conduct" (MPC Section 4.01(2)). DSM diagnoses that meet the MPC criteria have additional features like aberrations of thought, mood, perception, or interest, or other unusual behavior.

EVALUATING INSANITY: THE ROGERS CRIMINAL RESPONSIBILITY ASSESSMENT SCALES (R-CRAS)

Rogers (1984) developed a structured professional judgment (SPJ) for assessing criminal responsibility (see Chapter 12 for a discussion of structured professional judgments). A survey by Borum and Grisso (1995) indicated that the R-CRAS was the most frequently used instrument of its kind.

Rogers embraced the two-pronged ALI standard of moral and volitional incapacities as well as a diminished capacity or "guilty but mentally ill" (GBMI) standard to assess the criminal responsibility of individual defendants. Thirty variables are considered regarding a defendant's status and behavior during the commission of an alleged crime. These include:

- brain damage or disease
- intellectual disability
- intoxication
- bizarre behavior
- anxiety
- amnesia
- delusions
- hallucinations
- depressed mood
- elevated or expansive mood
- verbal coherence
- intensity and appropriateness of affect
- thought disorder
- planning and preparation
- awareness of criminality
- focal victim
- level of activity
- self-reported sense of agency
- impaired judgment
- impaired reality testing
- capacity for self-care
- awareness of right and wrong
- malingering.

Variables are rated on four-, five-, or six-point scales. Assessment of these and other variables concludes with a pair of tables that summarize whether the defendant may be considered insane or GBMI.

Interrater agreement on the ultimate conclusion was a very respectable 97 percent. Agreement on moral incapacity was 87 percent, and on volitional incapacity it was 89 percent. (In the R-CRAS, these are labeled "cognitive control" and "behavioral control," respectively.) Regarding malingering, the experts agreed with each other 85 percent of the time.

Factor analysis by Rogers et al. (1981) yielded three categories of results:

- bizarre behavior: with delusions and lack of awareness
- high activity: with inappropriate, intense affect
- high anxiety: with unreliable self-reports and the likelihood of malingering.

Table 19.1 Predicting verdicts (guilty vs. insane) with the R-CRAS

R-CRAS	Verdict			
	Insane	Guilty	Totals	
Insane	22	8	30	positive predictive value = .733
Sane	3	60	63	negative predictive value = .952
Totals	25	68	93	total predictive value = .882
	sensitivity = .880	specificity = .882		

Source: Adapted and reproduced by special permission of the Publisher, Psychological Assessment Resources, Inc., 16204 North Florida Avenue, Lutz, Florida 33549, from the Rogers Criminal Responsibility Assessment Scales by Richard Rogers, Ph.D. Copyright 1984 by PAR. Further reproduction is prohibited without permission of PAR.

Note:
Base rate of insanity (by verdict) was 26.9 percent.

These are the three outcomes that can be expected as most likely when defendants are evaluated with the R-CRAS. (From their description, they appear to correspond to diagnoses of schizophrenia, mania, and malingering, respectively.)

Verdicts reached by the courts agreed with the R-CRAS 88.2 percent of the time, based on a study of 93 defendants at the Isaac Ray Center in Chicago, Illinois, and the Court Diagnostic and Treatment Center in Toledo, Ohio. These data are presented in the form of an error matrix in Table 19.1. (See Appendix O for a discussion of the error matrix.)

In Appendix O we introduce a *Daubert*-style examination question regarding the assessment of error: "Doctor, how often are you wrong?" For Table 19.1, we might rephrase this question as, "Doctor, how often does the R-CRAS fail to predict the verdict?" The answer to that question, for these samples from Chicago and Toledo, is a respectable 11.8 percent. Breaking that into its two component parts: (1) when the R-CRAS said that a defendant was insane, the court agreed with the R-CRAS 73.3 percent of the time and disagreed 26.7 percent of the time; and (2) when the R-CRAS said that a defendant was sane, the court agreed 95.2 percent of the time and disagreed only 4.8 percent of the time (Rogers, 1984). The difference between 73.3 percent and 95.2 percent is rather large, but is at least partly a function of the base rate. Only 26.9 percent of these defendants were found by the courts to be insane. A higher base rate of insanity would have yielded a higher positive predictive value (see the discussion of base rate in Appendix O).

REFERENCES

Abbott v. Cunningham, 766 F. Supp. 1218 (D.N.H. 1991).

American Medical Association and American Psychiatric Association. (1985). Joint statement of the American Medical Association and the American Psychiatric Association regarding the insanity defense. *American Journal of Psychiatry*, 142(9), 1135–1136. doi:10.1176/ajp.142.9.1135.

American Psychiatric Association. (1983). Statement on the insanity defense. *American Journal of Psychiatry*, 140(6), 681–688. doi:10.1176/ajp.140.6.681.

Aristotle. (350 BCE/1998). *The Nicomachean ethics*. New York: Dover Publications.

Beattie, J. (1770/2005). *An essay on the nature and immutability of truth, in opposition to sophistry and scepticism*. (1770 edition): Edinburgh: A. Kincaid & J. Bell. (2005 edition): Chestnut Hill, MA: Adamant Media Corporation.

Boone, K. B. (Ed.) (2021). *Assessment of feigned cognitive impairment: A neuropsychological perspective. Second edition*. New York: Guilford Press.

Borum, R., & Grisso, T. (1995). Psychological test use in criminal forensic evaluations. *Professional Psychology: Research and Practice*, 26(5), 465–473. doi:10.1037/0735-7028.26.5.465.

Brink, D. O. (2021). *Fair opportunity and responsibility.* Oxford: Oxford University Press.

Brooks, A. D. (1974). *Law, psychiatry, and the mental health system.* Boston: Little, Brown.

Clark v. Arizona, 548 U.S. 735 (2006).

Durham v. United States, 214 F.2d 862 (D.C. Cir. 1954).

Goldstein, A. S. (1967). *The insanity defense.* New Haven, CN: Yale University Press.

Huckabee, H. M. (1980). *Lawyers, psychiatrists, and criminal law: Cooperation or chaos?* Springfield, IL: Thomas.

In re Rosenfield, 157 F. Supp. 18 (D.D.C. 1957).

Kahler v. Kansas, 589 U.S. ____, 140 S. Ct. 1021 (2020).

Krafft-Ebing, R. V. (1886/1926). *Psychopathia sexualis.* New York: Physicians and Surgeons Book Company.

Leland v. Oregon, 343 U.S. 790 (1952).

Moore, M. S. (2016). The neuroscience of volitional excuse. In D. Patterson & M. S. Pardo (Eds.) *Philosophical foundations of law and neuroscience* (pp. 179–230). Oxford: Oxford University Press.

Moran, R. (1985). The origin of insanity as a special verdict: The trial for treason of James Hadfield (1800). *Law & Society Review, 19*(3), 487–519. doi:10.2307/3053574.

Morse, S. (1994). Culpability and control. *University of Pennsylvania Law Review, 142*(5), 1587–1660. https://scholarship.law.upenn.edu/penn_law_review/vol142/iss5/7.

Morse, S. (2002). Uncontrollable urges and irrational people. *Virginia Law Review, 88*, 1025–1078. https://scholarship.law.upenn.edu/faculty_scholarship/1375.

Murray, W. S. (1959). Regicide in Drury Lane. *North Dakota Law Review, 35*(2), 137–145. https://commons.und.edu/ndlr/vol35/iss2/4.

People v. Hubert, 119 Cal. 216, 51 P. 329 (California, 1897).

People v. Jackson, 627 N.W.2d 11, 245 Mich. App. 17 (Michigan, 2001).

Peterson, C., Maier, S. F., & Seligman, M. E. P. (1993). *Learned helplessness: A theory for the age of personal control.* Oxford: Oxford University Press.

Platt, A., & Diamond, B. L. (1966). The origins of the "Right and Wrong" test of criminal responsibility and its subsequent development in the United States: An historical survey. *California Law Review, 54*(3), 1227–1260. doi:10.15779/Z38GX9T.

Regina v. Burton, 3 F. & F. 772, 176 Eng. Rep. 354 (1863).

Regina v. M'Naghten, 10 Clark & Fin. 200, 8 Eng. Rep. 718 (1843).

Rex v. Hadfield, 27 Howell's State Trials, 1281 (1800).

Rogers, R. (1984). *Rogers Criminal Responsibility Assessment Scales (R-CRAS).* Odessa, FL: Psychological Assessment Resources, Inc.

Rogers, R. (1987). The APA position on the insanity defense: Empiricism vs. emotionalism. *American Psychologist, 42*(9), 840–848. doi:10.1037//0003-066x.42.9.840.

Rogers, R., & Bender, S. (Eds.) (2018). *Clinical assessment of malingering and deception. Fourth edition.* New York: Guilford Press.

Rogers, R., Dolmetsch, R., & Cavanaugh, J. (1981). An empirical approach to insanity evaluations. *Journal of Clinical Psychology, 37*(3), 683–687. doi:10.1002/1097-4679(198107)37:3<683::aid-jclp2270370343>3.0.co;2-f.

Rogers, R., & Shuman, D. W. (2000). *Conducting insanity evaluations. Second edition.* New York: Guilford Press.

Rogers, R., & Shuman, D. W. (2005). *Fundamentals of forensic practice.* New York: Springer.

Rubenzer, S. (2018). *Assessing negative response bias in competency to stand trial evaluations.* Oxford: Oxford University Press.

State v. Jones, 50 N.H. 369 (New Hampshire, 1871).

State v. Wilson, 306 S.C. 498, 413 S.E.2d 19 (South Carolina, 1992).

Stephen, J. F. (1863/2017). *A general view of the criminal law of England.* (2017 version): Miami, FL: HardPress.

Stephen, J. F. (1883/2015). *A history of the criminal law of England. In three volumes.* (2015 version): London: Forgotten Books.

United States v. Brawner, Appellant, 471 F.2d 969, D.C. Cir. (1972).

United States v. Hinckley, 525 F. Supp. 1342 (D.D.C. 1981).

United States v. Kunak, 5 USCMA 346, 17 CMR 346 (1954).

United States v. Lyons, 731 F.2d 243, 739 F2d 994 (5th Cir. 1984).

Walker, N. (1968). *Crime and insanity in England. Volume 1: The historical perspective.* Edinburgh: University of Edinburgh Press.

Walker, N. (1985). The insanity defense before 1800. *Annals of the American Academy of Political and Social Science, 477*(1), 25–30. doi:10.1177/0002716285477001003.

20 Foundational cases in the United Kingdom from *Rex v. Edward Arnold* (1724) to *Regina v. M'Naghten* (1843)

The earliest recorded acquittal by reason of insanity in English common law occurred in the year 1505 (Moran, 1985). The earliest trial for which we have a complete record is *Rex v. Edward Arnold* (1724).

THE FIRST COMPLETE RECORD: *REX V. EDWARD ARNOLD* (1724)

Edward Arnold was a frankly delusional defendant who went on trial for the attempted murder of Lord Onslow. Arnold testified in court that he had fired a pistol at Lord Onslow because Onslow had bewitched him and had sent into his "chamber devils and imps" who had "invaded his bosom such that he could not sleep." Arnold's family testified that Edward was delusional.

Mr. Justice Tracy instructed the jury that, in deciding whether to acquit Arnold,

> A man must be totally deprived of his understanding and memory, so as not to know what he is doing, no more than an infant, a brute, or a wild beast.

Please notice that this was a purely cognitive standard, with no mention of Arnold's capacity to appreciate right and wrong, or of his ability to control his own behavior. It was a standard based solely on Arnold's "understanding and memory." To modern eyes, this is not a reasonable standard for insanity. Most people, even those with the most severe mental illnesses, retain some "understanding and memory." Rarely is a sentient human being "totally deprived" of these faculties. In cases of insanity, the issue is not that "understanding and memory" are absent but that the "understanding and memory" are insane (i.e., characterized by cognitive, moral, or volitional incapacities).

Despite the severity of his mental illness, Arnold was found guilty (perhaps in relation to those unreasonable jury instructions). Arnold was

DOI: 10.4324/9781003385028-24

sentenced to death. In a remarkable act of forgiveness, Lord Onslow asked the court not to execute Edward Arnold, and this request was granted (Walker, 1968).

As the modern era evolved, courts would eschew the figurative language of common law (e.g., "wild beast") and would find more practical ideas and expressions that better suit our modern sensibilities.

A DELUSIONAL COMBAT VETERAN: *REX V. JAMES HADFIELD* (1800)

The trial of this brain-injured combat veteran who fired a pistol over the head of King George III is arguably the pivotal case in the history of Anglo-American mental health law. Because of Hadfield, insanity was redefined in English courts, and sweeping reforms came about in criminal procedures and in the disposition of defendants who have mental illness. Before *Hadfield,* insanity acquittees generally were sent home, often to their families. A few were chained to the walls of churches or other public buildings. Because these verdicts were acquittals, the defendants could not be sent to prisons. Moran (1985) has explained that this is why the standard for insanity was set so high in English courts before 1800. Even a severely delusional man like Edward Arnold (see the previous section) could not get an insanity acquittal in an English court, because it would mean that he would be set free and could present a serious risk to public safety. The special verdict of "not guilty by reason of insanity" – by which a defendant could be sent to a hospital for an indefinite period of time – did not exist before Hadfield and was created because of him. Because of Hadfield, the House of Lords passed legislation that (1) created the special verdict of "not guilty by reason of insanity," (2) made it possible for hospitals to hold insanity acquittees for indefinite periods of time, and (3) created the first formal process for finding a defendant incompetent to stand trial. Soon a secure facility for insanity acquittees was built at Bethlem Royal Hospital in London. A second facility, Broadmoor Hospital, was built in Crowthorne in 1863.

Hadfield's case is remarkable for the amount of documentation that is available to historians. He fired his pistol in a theater full of witnesses. There were also witnesses to the prelude and aftermath of this event. Furthermore, these events occurred at a time when court proceedings in the United Kingdom were being recorded in full. Also, a number of periodicals were flourishing which were eager to publish news about the man who had fired a pistol over the head of King George III. As a result, historians have available an extraordinary amount of detail regarding James Hadfield and his trial.

James Hadfield (1771–1841) was a combat veteran who had suffered a life-altering brain injury. In 1793, British forces led by the King's nephew,

Figure 20.1 James Hadfield (c. 1771–1841), a combat veteran with a severe brain injury who, on May 15, 1800, fired a pistol over the head of King George III. His trial for treason resulted in profound changes to the law.

the Duke of York, tried to invade France but were stopped by the French army in Flanders. Hadfield was one of the Duke's orderlies. In action at Lincelles, Hadfield received a blow from a sword that almost beheaded him. His helmet was knocked off his head. Another blow caused a

Figure 20.2 Thomas Erskine (1750–1823), attorney who defended James Hadfield in 1800. Erskine went on to serve as Lord High Chancellor of Great Britain from 1806 to 1807.

depressed skull fracture. In total, Hadfield received eight saber wounds to his head and face, and his wrist was fractured by shot. He lost a piece of his skull and the "membrane" of his brain (presumably the dura mater) was exposed. He was left for dead on the battlefield, but he survived and spent the next four years in a French camp for prisoners of war.

When Hadfield returned to England, he was given a small military pension (a Chelsea pension), and he found employment making spoons for a silversmith. Meanwhile, he heard the voice of God speaking to him, and he believed that the world was about to end. He joined a millenarist cult, i.e., a group who believe that the world is about to undergo a profound transformation. (As this was the decade of the French Revolution, this belief was not implausible.) Hadfield befriended Bannister Truelock, a shoemaker from Islington, who believed that he (Truelock) was the son of God and who reportedly told Hadfield to kill the King. A witness – a clerk to the silversmith who employed Hadfield – testified at trial that he heard Truelock tell Hadfield: "it was a shame there should be any soldiers; that Jesus Christ was coming; and we should have neither King nor soldiers."

On the evening of May 15, 1800, at the Theatre Royal in Drury Lane, the audience rose as the orchestra played "God Save the King." George III in his royal box began to bow when Hadfield, standing on a seat in the second row, fired a horse pistol over the King's head. The ball flew about twelve inches over the King's head and pierced a hollow pilaster.

Commentators have differed as to whether they believe Hadfield was trying to assassinate the King. Hadfield himself said that he had "not attempted to kill the King," that he could have killed him if he wanted to, and that he was "as good a shot as any in England." Indeed, Hadfield was so concerned about matters of sin and the afterlife that it does not seem likely he would have wanted to enter the hereafter with murder and treason on his soul.

Hadfield dropped the pistol after firing. A Bow Street officer (i.e., an officer who did not belong to a single precinct but who could enforce the law throughout London) seized Hadfield and, together with musicians from the orchestra, lifted him over the orchestra rail and carried him down into the musicians' anteroom below the stage. The King was unperturbed and watched these events transpire through an opera glass. The orchestra began "God Save the King" a second time, and the audience stood and sang in full chorus. This song includes the lyrics:

From every latent foe
From the assassins blow
God save the King.

A number of officials were summoned to the theater, including the Duke of York, who had been Hadfield's commander in Flanders. The Duke was a member of the Privy Council, which processed crimes against the King. He questioned Hadfield for forty-five minutes. Meanwhile, the play went on overhead.

The Duke thought that he recognized Hadfield, and he (Hadfield) reminded the Duke that he had been his orderly in Flanders. The Duke later would testify at trial that Hadfield told him "he was tired of life, that he thought he should certainly be killed if he were to make an attempt upon his majesty's life." According to a story published in *Bell's Weekly Messenger*, Hadfield had said that "he wished for death, but not to die by his own hand." He had hoped that the crowd at Drury Lane would fall upon him and kill him on the spot.

The shoemaker Bannister Truelock was brought before the Privy Council. He told the Council, inter alia, that he was "a true descendant of God," and that he had "resolved to destroy this world in the course of three days." Truelock was taken into custody and was committed to Bethlem Royal Hospital. No criminal charges were brought against him. He was kept isolated from other prisoners because of his seditious ideas. He continued to make shoes. He spent the last thirty years of his life at Bethlem, except for a brief period in 1821 during which he escaped, visited a girlfriend, and tried in vain to find a publisher for his prophesies. He returned to Bethlem of his own accord and died there at the age of 80.

Hadfield's trial began six weeks after the shooting. In England at that time, a defendant generally received little assistance from counsel. An attorney could help a defendant understand the law and could cross-examine witnesses, but generally defense attorneys were not allowed to address the court. Because Hadfield's target had been a royal, the charge was treason and he was entitled to a number of privileges, the most important of which was the assistance of counsel who could address the court. Hadfield requested the assistance of Thomas Erskine, who happened to be in the courtroom at the time. Erskine was the leading barrister of his day and became Lord High Chancellor in 1806. Erskine was known for defending unpopular defendants, including Tom Paine and members of the London Corresponding Society (which had agitated for democratic reform of Parliament).

Hadfield pleaded insanity. The Attorney General, Sir John Mitford, argued that Hadfield should be found guilty because he had shown intention: (1) he had purchased the pistol, (2) he went to the theater, and (3) he fired in the direction of the King. Mitford argued that these behaviors demonstrated Hadfield's competence and his intention to kill the King, i.e., mens rea. (Please notice Mitford's emphasis on the sufficiency of intention as indicating that a crime has been committed and that the defendant merits conviction. This is the position that Moore [2016] called "ultraconservative.")

Mitford explained the legal standard for insanity to the jury by quoting Lord Chief Justice Edward Coke (1552–1634). In *Pleas of the Crown*, Coke (1628/2003) had written that, in order for a defendant to be found not guilty by reason of insanity, there must be "absolute madness, and a total deprivation of memory."

Figure 20.3 Sir Edward Coke (1552–1634), Chief Justice of the King's Bench from 1613 to 1616. Along with Bracton, Hale, and Blackstone, he is considered one of the four great scholars of English common law.

Mitford cited *Rex v. Arnold* (1724; see above) and explained that there was little doubt that defendant Arnold had been deranged, but he was able "to form a steady and resolute design," and therefore he was found guilty of the charge against him. As quoted above, Mr. Justice Tracy had said in *Arnold,*

A man must be totally deprived of his understanding and memory, so as not to know what he is doing, no more than an infant, a brute, or a wild beast.

Mitford told the jury that this was still the definition of insanity in England.

When the Duke of York entered the courtroom, Hadfield leaped to his feet and yelled, "God Almighty, bless his good soul, I love him dearly." After Hadfield was quieted, the Duke testified regarding the interview he had held with Hadfield in the musicians' anteroom immediately after the shooting. Hadfield had told him that he was tired of life, that he had not intended to kill the King, and that he thought he would be killed for firing the pistol. The Duke testified that Hadfield had been "perfectly collected" during questioning and had understood the consequences of his action, i.e., that his life would be forfeited. When asked if Hadfield had shown any "derangement of understanding," the Duke answered, "Not the least: on the contrary, he appeared to speak as connectedly as could possibly be … He was as much collected as possible."

Thomas Erskine spoke in Hadfield's defense. He found fault with Coke's description of insanity as "total deprivation of memory and understanding" and told the jury that they should not take this description literally, because "no such madness ever existed in the world." Even the most severe form of mental illness does not deprive a person totally of their memory and understanding. Not only was James Hadfield on trial, but so was the English definition of insanity.

Erskine argued that a person may know when something is wrong yet do it in accordance with a delusion (i.e., moral incapacity). Erskine demonstrated a modern understanding of these issues and argued that the test of insanity is not whether a defendant lacks understanding but whether their understanding is delusional.

Erskine addressed the testimony by the Duke of York regarding Hadfield's "perfectly collected" manner and argued that a person with a severe mental illness is not necessarily a raving madman but that delusion "unaccompanied by frenzy or raving madness [was] the true character of insanity."

Erskine produced a series of effective witnesses, including an officer from Hadfield's former regiment who testified that Hadfield had been an excellent soldier until his head injury and afterwards was incoherent with "manifest symptoms of derangement." (Indeed, we can be assured that Hadfield was an excellent soldier, because he had become orderly to the Duke of York.)

The regimental surgeon testified that Hadfield had been so disruptive that he had him tied to his bed for a fortnight. Hadfield's brother and sisters-in-law testified that he was subject to terrifying fits of madness and that two days before the incident at Drury Lane he had threatened to kill his own beloved 8-month-old son because God told him to do so, and then he could not remember saying that.

Erskine pointed out to the jurors Hadfield's disfiguring head wounds, and invited them to look into Hadfield's skull and see the exposed membrane of his brain. (The record does not reflect whether any of the jurors took Erskine up on this offer.)

A physician from Bethlem Royal Hospital, Dr. Creighton, had examined Hadfield at Newgate Gaol and testified that Hadfield's behavior was unremarkable until it came "to the subject of his lunacy," at which time he answered "irrationally ... It requires that the thoughts which have relation to his madness should be awakened in his mind, in order to make him act unreasonably." Dr. Creighton testified that Hadfield believed "he was ordained to die, and to die as Jesus Christ did."

After Hadfield's landlady testified, Chief Justice Lord Kenyon apparently had heard all he needed. He asked Erskine if he were almost finished, and Erskine replied that he had twenty more witnesses. The judge then brought the trial to a close and directed the jury to acquit Hadfield by reason of insanity. The jury delivered this verdict without leaving the box. The trial lasted less than six hours.

James Hadfield was acquitted by reason of insanity and the problem now remained of what to do with him. Under British law at that time, there was no option but to release him, because he had been acquitted, but clearly he was a dangerous person and could not be released. Lord Kenyon said, "the prisoner, for his own sake, and for the sake of society at large, must not be discharged." There were no suitable alternatives, so Lord Kenyon returned Hadfield to Newgate Gaol, even though this was contrary to the law. Parliament quickly passed the Criminal Lunatics Act of 1800, which made an insanity acquittee subject to automatic confinement for an indefinite period of time. Hadfield later was confined at Bethlem Royal Hospital. He escaped in 1802 but was captured at Dover while awaiting a boat to France. He was housed at Newgate Gaol until the new, secure wing for "criminal lunatics" was completed at Bethlem. He spent the last forty-one years of his life in a locked cell and died of tuberculosis in 1841 (Moran, 1985; Murray, 1959; Walker, 1968).

In summary, Hadfield had a mental illness of sufficient severity to warrant a verdict of insanity. He had suffered a traumatic brain injury in combat, he heard the voice of God telling him what to do (command auditory hallucination with a divine imperative), and he had been a danger to others on two occasions. In terms of the three incapacities – cognitive, moral, and volitional – his behavior was complex. He did not lack cognitive capacity, as he knew that he was firing a pistol in the direction of the

King. He may have lacked volitional capacity – i.e., ability to control his behavior – but this defense was not offered at his trial. He did not lack moral capacity in the sense that he knew it was wrong; in fact, he expected to be killed for it. Moral capacity can be complex – as it was in the case of James Hadfield – and can reflect the multilayered moral reasoning of which human beings are capable. People may perform actions they know to be wrong or illegal and do them for a higher purpose. When this involves a logical argument, as in cases of draft resistance and tax resistance during unpopular wars, it does not suggest mental illness or insanity. When it involves a delusion, as in *Rex v. Hadfield*, it is evidence of moral incapacity. According to the testimony of Dr. Creighton, Hadfield believed that he was "ordained to die, and to die as Jesus Christ did." His belief was delusional, and his insanity was a case of moral incapacity.

INSANITY IS DEFINED AS COGNITIVE INCAPACITY AND/OR MORAL INCAPACITY: *REGINA V. M'NAGHTEN* (1843)

Daniel M'Naghten's name is spelled variously in the legal literature as "M'Naghten" and "M'Naughton." His trial is remembered as the iconic case of insanity in Anglo-American law because of its clear definition of "insanity" in modern terminology.

The *M'Naghten* court defined insanity as having two prongs: cognitive and moral incapacity. While this definition has been modified in most U.S. jurisdictions and in the Model Penal Code, it remains a highly influential decision. In the United States, it is the standard used in federal courts and in twenty-one states (see Table 22.1).

Daniel M'Naghten (1813–1865) was a woodworker from Glasgow. On January 20, 1843, he planned to kill the Tory Prime Minister of England, Sir Robert Peel. M'Naghten waited outside Peel's house with a loaded pistol, but the man who came out of Peel's house was Peel's secretary, Edward Drummond. M'Naghten followed Drummond and shot him once in the back, killing him. M'Naghten was arrested at the scene.

M'Naghten said at his arraignment,

> The Tories in my native city have compelled me to do this. They followed me and persecuted me where ever I go and have entirely destroyed my peace of mind ... They have accused me of crimes which I am not guilty; in fact, they wish to murder me. (quoted in Quen, 1981, pp. 4–5)

M'Naghten's trial began on February 20, 1843. His father testified that M'Naghten had suffered delusions of persecution as a teenager. Doctors who examined M'Naghten in prison testified that he was delusional and

Figure 20.4 Daniel M'Naghten (1813–1865), a woodworker from Glasgow, Scotland, who murdered Edward Drummond in a case of mistaken identity on January 20, 1843. His trial produced the iconic definition of insanity in Anglo-American law.

insane. One doctor testified that his delusions "operated to the extent of depriving M'Naghten of all self-control." A total of nine doctors testified to his insanity.

Lord Chief Justice Tindal instructed the jury, saying,

> [The] question to be determined is, whether at the time the act in question was committed, the prisoner had or had not the use of his understanding, so as to know that he was doing a wrong or wicked act ... To establish a defence on the ground of insanity, it must clearly be proved that, at the time of the committing of the act, the party accused was labouring under such a defect of reason, from disease of the mind, as

not to know the nature and quality of the act he was doing; or if he did
know it, that he did not know he was doing what was wrong. (*Regina v.
M'Naghten*, 1843, 10 Clark & Fin. at 210, 8 Eng. Rep. at 722)

Please notice that Tindal's jury instructions were a combination of
cognitive and moral incapacity: "as not to know the nature and quality of
the act he was doing; or if he did know it, that he did not know he was
doing what was wrong." The jury acquitted M'Naghten by reason of
insanity and he was committed to a mental institution, where he spent the
remainder of his life (Goldstein, 1967; Perlin, 1994; Walker, 1968;
Weiner, 1985).

The *M'Naghten* verdict was not popular with the British public or with
their Queen. Public opinion was that M'Naghten had gotten away with
murder. In England until 1964, the punishment for murder was death by
hanging. Victoria – after the acquittals of John Goode in 1837 (see below)
and Edward Oxford in 1840 (see Appendix I) – was outraged by the
insanity defense and she demanded change. Victoria did not get the change
she wanted, but she did receive clarity from Parliament. In March 1843,
the Lord Chancellor, John Singleton Copley, First Baron Lyndhurst,
opened a debate in the House of Lords on the subject of criminal
responsibility. A panel of fifteen judges responded to questions about the
insanity defense. Included in the panel was Lord Chief Justice Tindal, who
had presided over M'Naghten's trial. The panel endorsed the definition of
insanity expressed in Lord Tindal's jury instructions at M'Naghten's trial
and quoted above. This formula embraces the two standards or "prongs"
of cognitive incapacity and moral incapacity. These are known as the
"M'Naghten Rules" (Simon, 1967).

The M'Naghten Rules were needed at that point in history and they
were effective for several reasons: (1) they defined insanity in realistic and
practical terms; (2) they eschewed the vague and poetic language of
English common law (e.g., "wild beast test") which may have communi-
cated meaningfully to judges and juries in centuries past but by 1843 was
too imprecise to be practicable; and (3) their language is clear and
straightforward enough to be understood by all parties, including
defendants, attorneys, judges, juries, mental health professionals, and the
press. In this regard the M'Naghten Rules were a success and they have
stood the test of time, existing in one form or another for the past 180
years. Perhaps their major failing is the omission of the "third prong" of
insanity: volitional incapacity (see Chapter 19).

In time the cognitive incapacity prong was dropped in many jurisdictions (and in the Model Penal Code of 1985) as being redundant with
moral incapacity, as explained above. If someone does not know what
they are doing, then they do not know that what they are doing is wrong.

QUEEN VICTORIA AND THE INSANITY DEFENSE

As stated above, the acquittal by reason of insanity of Daniel M'Naghten was not popular with the British public or with their Queen. Victoria took a personal interest in the outcome. She was infuriated and she was outspoken about her dissatisfaction. Her interests in the insanity defense and the disposition of homicidal defendants is understandable, given that eight attempts were made against her life (Charles, 2012). Would-be assassins numbers one (Edward Oxford in 1840; see Appendix I) and seven (Roderick MacLean in 1882) were acquitted by reason of insanity. Also acquitted by reason of insanity was Captain John Goode, a former army officer, who approached her carriage in 1837 – just a few months after her ascension to the throne – shook his fist at her, called her a "usurper," and said, "I'll have you off the throne this day week." Goode claimed to be the son of King George IV and he carried a card with the name "King John II" (*Regina v. Goode*, 1837). Victoria, in fact, during the first two years of her reign had multiple encounters with subjects who had serious mental illness (Walker, 1968, p. 80). Would-be assassins numbers five and six (Robert Pate in 1850 and Arthur O'Connor in 1872) probably also had severe mental illness but were found guilty (Charles, 2012).

Victoria was convinced that all of these men knew what they were doing. (She probably was right about this, because cognitive incapacity is rare. All but a few defendants know what they are doing, even if they have serious mental illness and are insane.) She thought that Edward Oxford should have been hanged. She believed in the power of deterrence – even the deterrence of madmen. On April 23, 1882 – after Roderick McLean tried to shoot her on a railway platform, was acquitted by reason of insanity, and was sent to Broadmoor Hospital – she wrote to Prime Minister William Gladstone that the criminally insane should not be sent to hospitals but to prisons:

> Punishment deters not only sane men but also eccentric men, whose supposed involuntary acts are really produced by a diseased brain capable of being acted upon by external influence. A knowledge that they would be protected by an acquittal on the grounds of insanity will encourage these men to commit desperate acts, while on the other hand certainty that they will not escape punishment will terrify them into a peaceful attitude towards others. (quoted in Walker, 1968, p. 189)

Victoria's belief that "eccentric men" can be deterred is hard to justify with our modern understanding of mental illness. In order to be deterred, a person must have the cognitive capacity to understand the law, the moral reasoning to know right from wrong, and the volitional capacity to obey.

Figure 20.5 Queen Victoria (1819–1901). Eight assassination attempts – including two that resulted in verdicts of not guilty by reason of insanity – left her with a strong opinion against the insanity defense.

According to our modern sensibility regarding mental illness, we do not imagine that people who have cognitive, moral, or volitional incapacities can be deterred.

In 1883, Parliament passed the Trial of Lunatics Act, which re-affirmed the authority of juries regarding the special verdict of "not guilty by reason of insanity." Queen Victoria was not pleased, and she asked that the verdict be changed to "guilty but insane." Despite her wishes, the special verdict remained in place and defendants who were found not guilty by reason of insanity continued to go to hospitals and not prisons. (Victoria's preference for a verdict by which defendants with mental illness would be sent to prisons instead of hospitals was to become a reality in the state of Michigan in 1975; see Chapter 4.)

REFERENCES

Charles, B. (2012). *Kill the Queen! The eight assassination attempts on Queen Victoria*. Stroud, Gloucestershire, UK: Amberley Publishing.

Coke, E. (1628/2003). Steve Sheppard (ed.), *The Selected Writings and Speeches of Sir Edward Coke. 3 volumes*. Indianapolis, IN: Liberty Fund.

Goldstein, A. S. (1967). *The insanity defense*. New Haven, CN: Yale University Press.

Moore, M. S. (2016). The neuroscience of volitional excuse. In D. Patterson & M. S. Pardo (Eds.) *Philosophical foundations of law and neuroscience* (pp. 179–230). Oxford: Oxford University Press.

Moran, R. (1985). The origin of insanity as a special verdict: The trial for treason of James Hadfield (1800). *Law & Society Review*, 19(3), 487–519. doi:10.2307/3053574

Murray, W. S. (1959). Regicide in Drury Lane. *North Dakota Law Review*, 35(2), 137–142. https://commons.und.edu/ndlr/vol35/iss2/4.

Perlin, M. L. (1994). *The jurisprudence of the insanity defense*. Durham, NC: Carolina Academic Press.

Quen, J. M. (1981). Anglo American concepts of criminal responsibility. In S. J. Hucker, C. D. Webster, & M. H. Ben-Aron (Eds.) *Mental disorder and criminal responsibility* (pp. 1–10). Toronto: Butterworth.

Regina v. Goode, 7 Ad. & El. 536 (1837).

Regina v. M'Naghten, 10 Clark & Fin. 200, 8 Eng. Rep. 718 (1843).

Rex v. Arnold, 16 Howell's State Trials, 765 (1724).

Rex v. Hadfield, 27 State Trials 1281 (1800).

Simon, R. A. (1967). *The jury and the defense of insanity*. Boston, MA: Little, Brown.

Walker, N. (1968). *Crime and insanity in England. Volume 1: The historical perspective*. Edinburgh: University of Edinburgh Press.

Weiner, B. A. (1985). Insanity evaluation. In S. J. Brakel, J. Parry, & B. A. Weiner (Eds.) *Mentally disabled and the law* (pp. 707–734). Chicago, IL: American Bar Association.

21 Diminished responsibility and its progeny as a "middle road" of the insanity defense

The concept of "diminished responsibility" for defendants who have mental illness was introduced by the 17th-century Dutch legal writer Antonius Matthaeus (1601–1654). The use of this defense in the U.K. was foreshadowed by Sir Matthew Hale (1609–1676, who, along with Henry de Bracton, Sir Edward Coke, and Sir William Blackstone, is considered one of the four great scholars of English common law). Hale wrote,

> [It] is very difficult to define the invisible line that divides perfect and partial insanity, but it must rest on circumstances duly to be weighed and considered by the jury, lest on the one side there be a kind of inhumanity towards the defects of human nature, or, on the other side, too great an indulgence given to crimes. (quoted in Parry, 1902, p. 433)

By 1678, the concept of diminished responsibility was being argued in a Scottish court by the King's prosecutor, Sir George Mackenzie:

> It may be argued that since the law grants a total impunity to such as are absolutely furious therefore it should by the rule of proportions lessen and moderate the punishments of such, as though they are not absolutely mad, are Hypochondrick and Melancholy to such a degree, that it clouds their reason. (quoted in Walker, 1968, p. 139)

Walker called diminished responsibility "the Scottish expedient" (p. 147).

DIMINISHED RESPONSIBILITY PREVAILS IN A SCOTTISH MURDER TRIAL: *H.M. ADVOCATE V. DINGWALL* (1867)

The concept of diminished responsibility was put to the test before a Scottish jury in an 1867 murder trial: *H.M. Advocate v. Dingwall* (see Loughman, 2012). Diminished responsibility gave the jury a third option – "culpable homicide" – which was intended to be a middle-of-the-road

DOI: 10.4324/9781003385028-25

Figure 21.1 Sir Matthew Hale (1609–1676), Chief Justice of the King's Bench from 1671 to 1676. Along with Bracton, Coke, and Blackstone, he is remembered as one of the four great scholars of English common law.

verdict between the all-or-nothing alternatives of guilty of murder or not guilty by reason of insanity.

Alex Dingwall was dependent on alcohol. He apparently had suffered sunstroke in India. He confessed to killing his wife with a carving knife after she hid his alcohol and money on Hogmanay (New Year's Eve). Lord Deas, who presided over the trial, was pivotal in bringing the diminished responsibility defense into Scottish courts. Deas justified the verdict of diminished responsibility in *Dingwall* by noting (1) the "unpremeditated and sudden nature of the attack," (2) "the prisoner's habitual kindness to his wife," (3) the fact that "there was only one stab wound," and (4) the "prisoner appeared not only to have been peculiar in his mental constitution but to have had his mind weakened by successive attacks of disease" possibly caused by "a stroke of the sun in India" (*Dingwall*, 1867, at 479). Deas concluded by saying that "the state of the mind of a prisoner ... might ... be an extenuating circumstance, although not such as to warrant an acquittal on the ground of insanity" (*Dingwall*, at 480). The jury followed Deas' lead and found Dingwall guilty of culpable homicide. He was sentenced to ten years of penal servitude. (The usual sentence for murder in the United Kingdom at that time was death by hanging.)

English courts did not consider using the diminished responsibility defense until the Royal Commission on Capital Punishment (1949–1953). By 1949, it also was an established feature in California courts, where it went by the name "diminished capacity."

THE DIMINISHED CAPACITY DEFENSE IN CALIFORNIA

For three decades, state courts in California heard evidence regarding diminished capacity, beginning in 1949 with *People v. Wells*.

Wesley Robert Wells, an inmate at Folsom State Prison, severely injured a correctional officer by throwing a cuspidor made of heavy crockery. In the act of swinging the cuspidor, Wells struck two other correctional officers who were standing behind him and trying to stop him. Because Wells was already serving a life sentence, assault on a correctional officer was a capital offense. At his trial, Wells tried to introduce the testimony of psychiatrist Bernard L. Diamond, who was prepared to say that Wells "was in a state of nervous tension and subject to abnormal fears from slight stimuli." However, the trial court would not allow the psychiatrist's testimony. Upon appeal, the Supreme Court of California ruled that the psychiatric testimony should have been heard, but they ruled that this was a harmless error, and they affirmed the judgment against Wells.

The significance of *Wells* was that it opened the door to testimony by mental health professionals regarding diminished capacity, that is, the effect of mental states other than the "either-or" decision between sanity and insanity. The *Wells* court wrote, "That there are several states of mind, other than insanity, which render a person incapable of committing crime" (1949, at 348). (For a discussion of the discrete, binary thinking of the law and how it differs from the continuous variables considered by mental health professions, see Appendix N.)

Bernard L. Diamond, M.D., (1912–1990), the psychiatrist who would have testified at Wells' trial, was a professor of law and psychiatry at the University of California, Berkeley. Professor Diamond is also remembered for his evaluations of Sirhan Sirhan (who assassinated Presidential candidate Robert F. Kennedy in 1968) and Mark David Chapman (who assassinated John Lennon in 1980). Ten years after *Wells*, Professor Diamond testified in *People v. Gorshen* (1959), which was the second major case on diminished capacity in California. Diminished capacity became known as the "Wells-Gorshen" Rule.

Diminished capacity: *People v. Gorshen* (Cal. 1959)

Nicholas Gorshen, a longshoreman, came to work drunk one day. His foreman told him to go home, but Gorshen refused to leave. The two men struggled and the foreman knocked Gorshen to the ground. Gorshen said that he was going to go home, get his gun, and come back and kill the foreman. Gorshen went home, cleaned and loaded his gun, returned to the docks, and shot the foreman once in the abdomen, killing him. (This was a clear failure of the "policeman at the elbow" test, because the police had been summoned and they were in the room at the time.) He was charged with first degree murder.

The *Gorshen* court referred to the decision in *Wells* that allowed expert testimony on diminished capacity,

> In so doing, we opened the door for diminished capacity, since we permitted expert evidence not as a "complete defense" negating capacity to commit any crime but as a "partial defense" negating [a] specific mental state essential to a particular crime. (at 727)

At Gorshen's trial, his defense introduced evidence regarding his intoxication and presented the testimony of Professor Diamond, who said that Gorshen had been suffering from a mental disease at the time of the shooting. Professor Diamond testified that Gorshen did "not have the mental state which is required for malice aforethought or premeditation or anything which implies intention, deliberation or premeditation" (at 723).

(We might question Professor Diamond's conclusions. Gorshen verbally threatened the foreman, cleaned and loaded his weapon, and brought the weapon to the scene of the homicide. This provides evidence of intention, deliberation, premeditation, and malice aforethought. Failing the "policeman at the elbow" test, on the other hand, does suggest volitional incapacity.)

The trial court found that there was malice aforethought and found Gorshen guilty, but they used the psychiatric testimony to reduce his crime to second degree murder. (This was an atypical trial in which malice aforethought did not define first degree murder.)

Professor Diamond, in his testimony in *Gorshen*, referred to the work of Sigmund Freud and said, "what we call free will or voluntary choice is merely the conscious rationalization of a chain of unconsciously determined processes." (Apparently Professor Diamond was a determinist. If nobody has agent-causal free will, then its absence in defendant Gorshen was nothing extraordinary. The court, by finding Gorshen guilty, apparently did not consider the lack of agent-causal free will to be exculpatory.)

The Supreme Court of California would write in *People v. Henderson* (1963),

> It can no longer be doubted that the defense of mental illness not amounting to legal insanity is a "significant issue" in any case in which it is raised by substantial evidence. Its purpose and effect are to ameliorate the law governing criminal responsibility prescribed by the M'Naughton rule ... Under that rule a defendant is not insane in the eyes of the law if at the time of the crime he knew what he was doing and that it was wrong. Under the Wells-Gorshen rule of diminished responsibility even though a defendant be legally sane according to the M'Naughton test, if he was suffering from a mental illness that prevented his acting with malice aforethought or with premeditation and deliberation, he cannot be convicted of murder of the first degree. This policy is now firmly established in the law of California. (at 490–491)

Then, in 1978, Daniel White shot and killed San Francisco Mayor George Moscone and District 5 Supervisor Harvey Milk. Three years later John Hinckley, Jr., shot President (and former governor of California) Ronald Reagan (see *United States v. Hinckley*, 1981). The era of diminished capacity in California came to an end.

The end of diminished capacity in California: *People v. White* (Cal. App. 1981)

Daniel James White, age 32, had been a sergeant in the 101st Airborne Division and had served in Vietnam. After leaving the military he joined the San Francisco Police Department. While in that job, he saw another officer beat a handcuffed prisoner. He reported this to his superiors and then resigned from the SFPD. He joined the San Francisco Fire Department, where he rescued a woman and her baby from a seventh-floor apartment and got his name in the papers.

White was a Roman Catholic Irish-American who was known to have a rigid set of values. He was subject to periodic bouts of depression. He was not well suited to a life in politics. He was elected to the San Francisco Board of Supervisors in 1977 and resigned on November 10, 1978, giving as his reasons the corruption of city politics and his inability to support his wife and child on the meager salary of a city supervisor ($9,600).

Mayor Moscone stated publicly that if White changed his mind he could have his job back. Five days after resigning – having been entreated by neighbors, police officers, and firefighters – White asked for his job back, but it was too late. A coalition of liberal supervisors led by Harvey Milk had prevailed upon Mayor Moscone to appoint a liberal supervisor.

White felt betrayed. He was depressed in the days leading up to the homicides. He lost interest in social contacts and he shunned his wife. He quit shaving and lost interest in his personal appearance. Whereas he had been health-conscious, he lost interest in eating a healthy diet and he subsisted on junk food, which made him feel even worse, crave more junk food, and binge-eat on junk foods like Twinkies.

On November 27, 1978, White sneaked into City Hall with a loaded .38 caliber revolver and ten extra rounds. He avoided a metal detector by climbing through a first-floor window. He went to Moscone's office and pleaded for his job. When Moscone refused, White shot him four times: twice in the head, once in the chest, and once in the shoulder. He walked to the other side of the building, reloaded his pistol, and shot Harvey Milk five times.

White was charged with capital murder but ultimately was convicted of voluntary manslaughter. Several psychiatrists "testified that at the time of the killings he lacked the capacity to deliberate, premeditate, harbor malice, or to form intent" (*People v. White,* 1981).

(As with *Gorshen,* we might question this testimony. White's behavior did suggest deliberation, premeditation, malice, and intent. He had brought a loaded pistol and ten extra rounds to City Hall. He circumvented the metal detector and entered the building in relative safety by sneaking through a window on the first floor. He reloaded his weapon. He did not wander aimlessly through the building, but walked from one side to the other to reach his second victim.)

White was found guilty of voluntary manslaughter and was sentenced to 7 years and 8 months in prison. With good behavior he would be out in 5 years, 1 month, and 9 days. The public was outraged. Rioters stormed City Hall and set fire to police cars. The junk food issue was blown out of proportion in the press and the diminished capacity arguments that were put forward by White's lawyers were ridiculed as "the Twinkie defense." The psychiatrist who testified about Twinkies and had given his most sincere and rational testimony has complained that he will never live it down.

The irony is that White's verdict and his lenient sentence probably had less to do with his alleged mental illness than with the politics that surround the death penalty qualification of jurors. Pursuant to *Witherspoon*

Figure 21.2 Harvey Milk (1930–1978), America's first widely recognized openly gay politician, shown here walking with supporters, on his way to be sworn in as Supervisor at San Francisco City Hall on January 8, 1978. His assassination by Daniel James White on November 27, 1978, and White's lenient sentence, led Californians to abolish the defense of diminished capacity.

v. Illinois (1968), potential jurors in capital trials can be asked during voir dire if they are prepared to give the death penalty. If a potential juror says, "No," then they need not be seated on the jury. What may have saved Dan White from a capital murder conviction was the death penalty qualification of his jury, because jurors who are prepared to give the death penalty tend to be politically conservative. White's jury had no Blacks and no gays. It was comprised mostly of women, many of whom had children White's age. When this politically conservative jury was asked to give the death penalty to this young, conservative, Christian father, veteran, police officer, fireman, and hero who had killed the nation's first widely recognized openly gay politician, the verdict was voluntary manslaughter and not capital murder, and his sentence was 7 years and 8 months instead of death. Moscone's press secretary Corey Busch commented, "If White had just murdered the mayor, I think the outcome of the trial would have been very different" (Pogash, 2003). The same might be said if the District Attorney had not pursued the death penalty, in which case the jury would not have been death-penalty-qualified and may not have been as politically conservative. This is not meant to imply that jury deliberations went smoothly. Bystanders heard the jurors yelling at each other, and at one point the jury was escorted to the roof of the building so they could "cool off."

White served five years at the Correctional Training Facility in Soledad and was paroled on January 7, 1984. He was paroled to Los Angeles instead of his home in San Francisco, out of concerns that returning him to San Francisco would provoke further destruction of civic property. He completed his one year of probation and returned to San Francisco, where he tried to reunite with his wife, but his marriage ended shortly thereafter. He committed suicide by carbon monoxide poisoning in his garage on October 21, 1985.

Diminished actuality in California after *People v. White* (Cal. App. 1981) and after *United States v. Hinckley* (D.D.C. 1981)

Public outrage over the lenient sentence of Daniel White – and over Hinckley's verdict of not guilty by reason of insanity (see Chapter 22), both events occurring in 1981 – resulted in voter and legislative initiatives that eliminated the diminished capacity defense in California. The law that went into effect on January 1, 1982 (1981 Cal. Stat. ch. 404), abolished the defense of diminished capacity. The pivotal word in that last sentence is "capacity." California switched from a *diminished capacity* standard to a *diminished actuality* standard. Testimony regarding "intoxication, trauma, mental illness, disease, or defect" would still be permitted, but such testimony would not be allowed to address the issue of "capacity." Defendants who hope to use a mental state in their defense must demonstrate that their mental state *actually interfered* with their criminal responsibility. They cannot merely assert that they lacked "capacity."

This was a time of great experimentation and rapid change in the law. Proposition 8, known as the Victim's Bill of Rights, was approved by California voters on June 8, 1982. It contained provisions about diminished capacity and a guarantee that convicted defendants would get appropriately harsh sentences (Krausz, 1983). Proposition 8 added Section 25(a) to the California Penal Code, which reads as follows:

> The defense of diminished capacity is hereby abolished. In a criminal action, as well as any juvenile court proceeding, evidence concerning an accused person's intoxication, trauma, mental illness, disease, or defect shall not be admissible to show or negate capacity to form the particular purpose, intent, motive, malice aforethought, knowledge, or other mental state required for the commission of the crime charged. (California Penal Code, Section 25(a))

Again, the pivotal word in this passage is "capacity." Expert testimony addressing mental states in California must show that the mental state *actually did interfere* with criminal responsibility and not merely assert that the defendant lacked "capacity."

California prosecutors were alarmed by the 1982 law, because it permitted mental abnormality to negate criminal responsibility for any crime whatsoever. California prosecutors predicted that dangerous people would be acquitted unfairly, and the law was changed again, this time defining the range of crimes to which it applied. On January 1, 1983, a new law went into effect (1982 Cal. Stat. ch. 893, which amended four sections of the California Penal Code, including Section 28), based upon the distinction between specific intent crimes and general intent crimes. Mental abnormality was allowed to negate mens rea in specific intent crimes but not in general intent crimes. (The distinction between specific intent crimes and general intent crimes is complex, and a thorough discussion is beyond the scope of this book. When applied to actual cases the distinction may in fact be an illusion. See Morse, 1984. For our purposes we can adopt the formula used by Kadish et al., 1983, which defines specific intent crimes as those that are done *purposely* and *knowingly* and general intent crimes as those that are done *recklessly* or *negligently*. For a discussion of these levels of mens rea, see Chapter 7.)

California Penal Code Section 28(a) now reads:

> Evidence of mental disease, mental defect, or mental disorder shall not be admitted to show or negate the capacity to form any mental state, including, but not limited to, purpose, intent, knowledge, premeditation,

deliberation, or malice aforethought, with which the accused committed the act. Evidence of mental disease, mental defect, or mental disorder is admissible solely on the issue of whether or not the accused *actually formed* a required specific intent, premeditated, deliberated, or harbored malice aforethought, when a specific intent crime is charged. (italics added)

Again, the key word in the law is "capacity." Actuality has replaced capacity in California law.

REFERENCES

H.M. Advocate v. Dingwall, 5 Irvine 466 (1867).

Kadish, S. H., Schulhofer, S. J., & Paulsen, W. (1983). *Criminal law and its processes. Fourth edition.* New York: Aspen Publishers.

Krausz, F. (1983). The relevance of innocence: Proposition 8 and the diminished capacity defense. *California Law Review*, 71(4), 1197–1215. doi:10.2307/34 80197.

Loughman, A. (2012). *Manifest madness: Mental incapacity in the criminal law.* Oxford: Oxford University Press.

Morse, S. J. (1984). Undiminished confusion in diminished capacity. *Journal of Criminal Law and Criminology*, 75(1), 1–55. 10.2307/1143205.

Parry, W. H. (November 1902). Insanity in criminal cases. *Albany Law Journal*, 63(12), 429–441.

People v. Gorshen, 51 Cal.2d 716, 336 P.2d 492 (California, 1959).

People v. Henderson, 60 Cal.2d 482 (California, 1963).

People v. Wells, 33 Cal 2d 330 (California, 1949).

People v. White, 117 Cal. App. 3d 270, 172 Cal. Rptr. 612 (California, 1981).

Pogash, C. (2003). Myth of the "Twinkie defense"/The verdict in the Dan White case wasn't based on his ingestion of junk food. Retrieved 12/05/2022 from www.sfgate.com/health/article/Myth-of-the-Twinkie-defense-The-verdict-in-2511152.php.

United States v. Hinckley, 525 F. Supp. 1342 (D.D.C. 1981).

Walker, N. (1968). *Crime and insanity in England. Volume 1: The historical perspective.* Edinburgh: University of Edinburgh Press.

Witherspoon v. Illinois, 391 U.S. 510 (1968).

22 U.S. cases that narrowed the insanity defense

Leland v. Oregon (1952) was mentioned above in Chapter 5 in our discussion of "beyond a reasonable doubt." It also is a landmark case in the history of volitional incapacity as the missing third prong of the insanity defense.

Morris Leland – who was described by people who knew him as "slender" and "sullen-faced" – started getting into trouble with the law when he was a teenager. He had a history of arrests for robbery, auto theft, and sexual assault, and for a while he had been confined in a state psychiatric hospital. At the age of 22, he was arrested for the homicide of a 15-year-old girl. He said, "It would have been better if they had kept me in the hospital and not turned me loose" (Perry, 2018).

At 4:15 on the morning of Friday, August 5, 1949, a 15-year-old girl was standing with her lunch pail on a street in Portland, Oregon, waiting for the bus that would take her to the fields to pick beans. Ex-convict Morris Leland, age 22, saw her and persuaded her to go with him to an isolated spot under the St. Johns Bridge on the east bank of the Willamette River. There he tried to have sex with her, but she was a virgin, and Leland stopped when he saw that he was causing her pain.

Leland was armed with a long knife that he carried in a scabbard on his belt. At some point in the day he picked up a bar of steel eighteen inches long and one-half inch in diameter. He admitted in his confession that, a day before the murder, he began to think about using this steel bar to kill her.

They spent the day and night together. They slept in a clump of trees on the riverbank. The next morning, he killed her by hitting her over the head several times with the steel bar and stabbing her twice with the knife. He covered her body with driftwood, threw the knife and steel bar into the river, disposed of his cigarette butts, and wiped his fingerprints off her lunch pail.

DOI: 10.4324/9781003385028-26

Five days later, Leland was arrested for stealing a car and he was brought to the Portland police station. He told the sergeant that he wanted to speak to a homicide officer because he had killed a girl. A full confession was recorded by a stenographer, and Leland signed it. He led the police to the scene of the crime and pointed out the location of her body. At his own request he made another confession in his own handwriting (*Leland v. Oregon*, 1952). He told police that he had to kill her "because she was a good girl and might tell" (Perry, 2018).

At trial he pleaded not guilty by reason of insanity. His lawyers urged the court to consider a defense of irresistible impulse, but Oregon law at that time recognized only cognitive and moral incapacity as the tests of insanity (i.e., the M'Naghten Rules). Consistent with Oregon law, the trial judge did not instruct the jury regarding volitional incapacity. The jury found Leland guilty of murder in the first degree and did not recommend a life sentence, which meant that he was sentenced to death.

The U.S. Supreme Court affirmed Leland's conviction and sentence. Regarding irresistible impulse, the court quoted the Oregon statute that "morbid propensity to commit prohibited acts, existing in the mind of a person who is not shown to have been incapable of knowing the wrongfulness of such acts, forms no defense to a prosecution therefor" (*Leland v. Oregon*, at 800). That is, there was no provision for volitional incapacity in Oregon.

The U.S. Supreme Court concluded, "The 'irresistible impulse' test of legal sanity is not 'implicit in the concept of ordered liberty' (a phrase borrowed from *Palko v. Connecticut*, 1937, at 325); and due process does not require the State to adopt that test, rather than the 'right and wrong' test" (*Leland v. Oregon*, at 791).

Morris Leland died by asphyxiation in a gas chamber on January 9, 1953. Oregon later would adopt the definition of insanity that is used in the Model Penal Code, i.e., moral and volitional incapacities. Oregon voters abolished the death penalty in 1964 and then reinstated it in 1978. On December 13, 2022, Oregon had seventeen inmates on death row when Governor Kate Brown in her last month in office commuted all their sentences to life in prison without the possibility of parole (Selsky, 2022).

The significance of *Leland* for our discussion lies in its erosion of the insanity defense. This decision by the U.S. Supreme Court meant that a defendant who has mental illness, depending on the laws of their local jurisdiction, does not have a constitutional right to a defense of volitional incapacity.

Morris Leland's crime showed planning, preparation, premeditation, a degree of self-control (when he interrupted the sex act), and awareness that he had done something wrong (when he concealed evidence). He brought the murder weapons to the scene. He began to think about killing the victim a day before the murder. He hid evidence and, as he told the police, his motive for the murder was an attempt to conceal a crime. Although Leland had a history of psychiatric hospitalization, the facts of his behavior do not suggest volitional incapacity or any other form of insanity or lack of mens rea.

AN INSANITY ACQUITTAL SPURS REFORM OF THE FEDERAL INSANITY DEFENSE: *UNITED STATES V. HINCKLEY* (D.D.C. 1981)

On March 30, 1981 – in a political climate characterized by (1) fear of people with mental illness (related to events such as those that occurred in Michigan in 1975 and led to the creation of the GBMI verdict; see Chapter 4); (2) calls to abolish the insanity defense (see Gerber, 1975); and (3) the desire to incapacitate these individuals with long prison sentences – John Hinckley, Jr., shot President Ronald Reagan.

President Reagan was leaving the Washington Hilton Hotel where he had just given a speech to the leaders of the Building and Trades Union. He was on the sidewalk walking toward his limousine when Hinckley fired a spray of six bullets from a .22 caliber automatic pistol. Four people were injured. One bullet ricocheted off the limousine and hit Reagan in the chest. Another bullet hit press secretary James Brady in the head. Brady survived but was permanently disabled. Other bullets struck a police officer and a Secret Service agent. Hinckley was taken down by a 67-year-old labor union official, who struck him in the head and pulled him to the ground.

John Hinckley, Jr., was 25 years old and the son of a wealthy Texas family. He had attended Texas Tech University in Lubbock, off and on, from 1974 to 1980, and then he had dropped out. He was under a doctor's care for emotional difficulties. Antidepressant and tranquilizing medication had been prescribed.

In 1975, he moved to Los Angeles and sought a career as a songwriter. He returned to his parents' home the following year. He purchased a number of weapons and practiced with them. He was obsessed with the 1976 film *Taxi Driver* and its co-star Jodie Foster. When Ms. Foster entered Yale University, Hinckley moved to New Haven, Connecticut, to be near her. He enrolled in a writing class at Yale, telephoned Ms. Foster repeatedly, and slipped poems and messages under her door. He fantasized about getting her attention by hijacking an airplane, committing suicide, or assassinating President Jimmy Carter. He followed Carter from state to state and was arrested in Nashville, Tennessee, on a firearms charge. He returned home to Texas, where he collected information about the Kennedy assassination. He thought of Lee Harvey Oswald as a role model. He was treated for depression, but he did not improve.

Figure 22.1 John W. Hinckley, Jr. (1955–), shot President Ronald Reagan on March 30, 1981. He was found not guilty by reason of insanity and was confined at St. Elizabeths Hospital. He was released from government supervision on June 15, 2022, after 41 years.

On December 31, 1980 (23 days after John Lennon was murdered in the archway of the Dakota), Hinckley spoke into a tape recorder:

> John Lennon is dead. The world is over. Forget it ... I still think about Jodie all the time. That's all I think about really. That, and John Lennon's death. They were sorta binded together ... I hate New Haven with a mortal passion. I've been up there many times, not stalking her really, but just looking after her ... I was going to take her away for a while there, but I don't know. I am so sick I can't even do that ... It'll be total suicide city. I mean, I couldn't care less. Jodie is the only thing that matters now. Anything I might do in 1981 would be solely for Jodie Foster's sake ... I wouldn't want to stay here on earth without her.

On March 29, 1981, the day before the shooting, Hinckley penned a letter to Ms. Foster and left it in his room at the Park Central Hotel:

> Dear Jodie,
>
> There is a definite possibility that I will be killed in my attempt to get Reagan. It is for this very reason that I am writing you this letter now.
>
> As you well know by now I love you very much. Over the past seven months I've left you dozens of poems, letters and love messages in the faint hope that you could develop an interest in me. Although we talked on the phone a couple of times I never had the nerve to simply approach you and introduce myself. Besides my shyness, I honestly did not wish to bother you with my constant presence. I know the many messages left at your door and in your mailbox were a nuisance, but I felt that it was the most painless way for me to express my love for you.
>
> I feel very good about the fact that you at least know my name and know how I feel about you.
>
> And by hanging around your dormitory, I've come to realize that I'm the topic of more than a little conversation, however full of ridicule it may be. At least you know that I'll always love you.
>
> Jodie, I would abandon this idea of getting Reagan in a second if I could only win your heart and live out the rest of my life with you, whether it be in total obscurity or whatever.
>
> I will admit to you that the reason I'm going ahead with this attempt now is because I just cannot wait any longer to impress you. I've got to do something now to make you understand, in no uncertain terms, that I am doing all of this for your sake! By sacrificing my freedom and possibly my life, I hope to change your mind about me.
>
> This letter is being written only an hour before I leave for the Hilton Hotel. Jodie, I'm asking you to please look into your heart and at least

give me the chance, with this historical deed, to gain your respect and love.

I love you forever,
John Hinckley

Hinckley's delusional belief was that he could win Foster's love by shooting Ronald Reagan. He knew what he was doing, which means that he did not experience cognitive incapacity. His moral reasoning reflects the multiple levels of which human beings are capable – he knew that what he was doing was illegal and that he would lose his freedom or even his life (much like James Hadfield in 1800; see Chapter 20). However, he believed it was the right thing to do because it would bring love into his life.

Hinckley's trial began thirteen months after the shooting and lasted seven weeks. He pleaded not guilty by reason of insanity. Four mental health experts testified. Expert testimony presented by his defense argued that he had schizophrenia and was insane at the time of the shooting. Expert testimony presented by the prosecution (Park Dietz, M.D.) argued that Hinckley had a narcissistic personality disorder, schizoid personality disorder, and dysthymia with borderline and passive-aggressive features, and that Hinckley had been sane at the time of the shooting (Bonnie et al., 2000; Low, 1986).

The defense presented testimony supporting both moral and volitional incapacities. The evidence for moral incapacity was stronger and included Hinckley's delusional belief that shooting Ronald Reagan would win the love of Jodie Foster. The evidence presented for volitional incapacity was not as strong and consisted of the "driven" and "frantic" qualities of his behavior, his determination to end his own life, and a lack of "the two anchors" in his life – psychiatric help and the support of his parents. Because of these problems, his actions were "extensively determined by his inner state" (Bonnie et al., 2000, p. 67). The prosecution was able to point out a number of problems with this theory: Hinckley planned the crime in advance, chose a concealable handgun, purchased Devastator exploding ammunition, concealed his plans from his family and psychiatrist, knew Reagan's itinerary, chose a time and place, waited for an opportunity, and debated with himself whether or not to go through with it. Earlier, when Hinckley had stalked President Jimmy Carter, he had left his gun behind while finding out how close he could get to the President. All of these features indicate planning and deliberation and do not suggest loss of volitional control.

In federal courts at that time, the burden was on the prosecution to demonstrate beyond a reasonable doubt that Hinckley was sane. The jury deliberated for three days and found him not guilty by reason of insanity. Given that burden of proof (on the prosecution) and that standard of evidence (beyond a reasonable doubt), there was little else they could have decided. After his trial, Hinckley wrote that shooting Ronald Reagan was "the greatest love offering in the history of the world."

Two months after the trial, Hinckley was transferred from the Federal Bureau of Prisons to St. Elizabeths Hospital in Washington, D.C. In 1987 the hospital petitioned the court to grant him an unsupervised Easter visit with his family. In support of this request, the hospital pointed out that Hinckley was no longer taking antipsychotic medication, was allowed to travel unaccompanied to and from his work assignment, had not been obsessed with Ms. Foster "for at least three years," and had developed an apparently healthy romantic relationship with Leslie deVeau (a former patient of St. Elizabeths: a woman 12 years his senior who had a psychotic disorder, had killed her 10-year-old daughter, and then shot herself with a shotgun). Ms. deVeau later would become Hinckley's fiancée (Walsh, 1999).

In opposition to the hospital's request, the prosecution produced a 1982 letter from Hinckley to a friend, in which he asked the friend to (1) mail him a pistol so that he could escape, or (2) go to New Haven and kill Jodie Foster, or (3) hijack an airplane and demand that Hinckley be released and Foster be brought to him.

Testimony presented at this hearing indicated that Hinckley had corresponded with serial killer Ted Bundy and had written to Lynette "Squeaky" Fromme asking for Charles Manson's address. (Among Manson's many crimes, he had inspired Fromme to attempt the assassination of President Gerald Ford in 1975.) These revelations prompted the judge to order that Hinckley's room be searched, that all of Hinckley's possessions be inventoried, and that "any and all writings, documents, notes, letters, post cards, correspondence and poems of any description" be delivered to the court. In contrast to the psychiatrist's testimony that Hinckley was no longer obsessed with Jodie Foster, the search of his room located fifty-seven photographs of her. The hospital withdrew its request for an unsupervised visit (Bonnie et al., 2000, pp. 143–144).

Beginning in 1999, Hinckley was allowed supervised visits with his parents. In 2005, a conditional release hearing was held at which all the experts, including the government's experts, testified that his psychosis and depression were in full remission and that the terms of his conditional release could be expanded. His parents were allowed to supervise his visits to their home in Williamsburg, Virginia. In 2016, he was released from the hospital and was allowed to live with his mother with a strict set of conditions, namely:

- He had to live at his mother's home.
- He was not allowed to drink alcohol.
- He was not allowed to possess any firearms, ammunition, or other weapons.
- He was not allowed to possess any photos, magazine articles, or memorabilia of Ms. Foster.

- He was not allowed to contact Ms. Foster or her agent.
- He was not allowed to contact any of his victims' families.
- He was not allowed to visit the homes, past homes, or graves of the current president, past presidents, or certain past or present government officials.
- He was not allowed to watch or listen to any violent movies, television shows, or compact discs.
- He was not allowed to access any violent movies, television shows, music, novels, or magazines online.
- He was not allowed to view any printed or online pornography.
- He was not allowed to erase his web browser's history.
- He was required to make a record of his web browser's history.
- He was not allowed to speak to the press.
- He was not allowed to drive more than 50 miles from his mother's home if attended, or more than 30 miles from her home if unattended.
- He was required to work at least three days a week.
- He was required to leave immediately if he found himself approaching any prohibited places.

In 2018, Hinckley was allowed to move out of his mother's home and live on his own. He was released unconditionally on June 15, 2022, after 41 years of government supervision (Rabinowitz & Mizelle, 2022).

The insanity defense before and after *United States v. Hinckley* (D.D.C. 1981)

Before 1954, federal courts in the District of Columbia used all three incapacities – cognitive, moral, and volitional – in adjudicating the insanity defense. In 1954, that court adopted the Durham Rule (also known as the "product test"; see *Durham v. United States* [1954], discussed in Chapter 19). The Durham Rule prevailed in the District of Columbia until 1972, when, in *United States v. Brawner* (1972), it was replaced by the formula used in the Model Penal Code written by the American Law Institute, which was a combination of moral and volitional incapacities (see Chapter 19). Hinckley's defense presented expert testimony supporting both moral and volitional incapacities, and the jury found him not guilty by reason of insanity (see Bonnie et al., 2000).

The public was outraged by Hinckley's insanity acquittal. Ninety percent of Americans favored abolishing the insanity defense (Mickenberg, 1987, pp. 946–947). Within a month after Hinckley's trial, both the House and Senate held hearings on the insanity defense. These efforts produced the first comprehensive federal legislation on the insanity defense: the Insanity Defense Reform Act of 1984 (18 U.S.C. §17), which does not include the volitional prong. This section of the U.S. Code is reproduced here for the reader's convenience:

---

18 U.S.C. §17

a Affirmative Defense. It is an affirmative defense to a prosecution under any Federal statute that, at the time of the commission of the acts constituting the offense, the defendant, as a result of a severe mental disease or defect, was unable to appreciate the nature and quality or the wrongfulness of his acts. Mental disease or defect does not otherwise constitute a defense.
b Burden of Proof. The defendant has the burden of proving the defense of insanity by clear and convincing evidence.

The phrase "unable to appreciate the nature and quality or the wrong-fulness of his acts" in 18 U.S.C. §17 indicates the cognitive and moral incapacities. The volitional prong has been excluded. The prevailing forces in psychiatry went along with eliminating the volitional prong. The American Psychiatric Association (1983) issued a statement recommending that volitional incapacity be dropped from legal tests of insanity. Bonnie (1983) expressed this opinion as follows:

> Unfortunately, however, there is no scientific basis for measuring a person's capacity for self-control or for calibrating the impairment of that capacity. There is, in short, no objective basis for distinguishing between offenders who were undeterrable and those who were merely undeterred, between the impulse that was irresistible and the impulse not resisted, or between substantial impairment of capacity and some lesser impairment. Whatever the precise terms of the volitional test, the question is unanswerable, or it can be answered only by "moral guesses." To ask it at all invites fabricated claims, undermines equal administration of the penal law, and compromises its deterrent effect. (p. 196)

Bonnie's goals are admirable: to discourage fabricated claims, support the equal administration of justice, enhance its deterrent effect, and eliminate "moral guesses." Who could find fault with these noble aims? But his argument implies that the criminal justice system is not otherwise riddled with imprecise methods, fabricated claims, moral guesses, and threats to equality and deterrence. I would argue that anyone who has encountered the criminal justice system in any context is likely to have seen these problems. The very act of sending someone to prison, for example, involves the "moral guess" that this is a better solution than giving them a second chance in their community. If we were to eliminate from the criminal justice system all the problems that Bonnie identifies, we would erase the entire system. Why single out volitional incapacity for criticisms that apply to the whole structure? Bonnie's arguments cover familiar territory – for example, the idea that the "can't/won't" distinction cannot be made (see Chapter 19) – but he would transmute forensic mental health into something with the certainty of laboratory science, and that is not going to happen. I would argue that criminal justice is not improved by removing from consideration an entire category of human behavior, namely, the phenomenon of volitional incapacity among persons with severe mental illness.

The irony of eliminating the volitional prong from federal law is that this change may not have affected the outcome of Hinckley's trial. Although his defense presented testimony supporting both moral and volitional incapacities, the evidence for moral incapacity was stronger. Hinckley believed that shooting Ronald Reagan was the right thing to do because he thought it would win the love of Jodie Foster. The evidence for volitional incapacity was weaker (as reviewed above), but for Congress the defense of volitional incapacity was low-hanging fruit, and it was plucked.

The Insanity Defense Reform Act of 1984 also (1) eliminated the defense of diminished capacity; (2) created a special verdict of "not guilty only by reason of insanity," which triggers a commitment hearing; (3) placed the burden of proof on the defense to establish insanity by clear and convincing evidence; (4) provided commitment for persons who become insane after they are found guilty in a federal court or while serving a sentence in a federal prison; and (5) curtailed the scope of expert testimony (see Rule 704, discussed in Chapter 8). Experts who testify in federal courts can no longer address the ultimate issue of insanity. Testifying experts can present facts and certain limited opinions (for example, we can report a defendant's diagnosis, or we can describe a defendant's delusions), but we cannot address the ultimate issue of whether a defendant was sane or insane at the time of the crime. To do so would usurp the authority that belongs to the trier of fact. (The same restriction regarding ultimate issue testimony by expert witnesses became law in California after Daniel White assassinated San Francisco Mayor George Moscone and City Supervisor Harvey Milk; see Chapter 21). Because of these changes in the law, a trial like that of John Hinckley, Jr., will not happen again. The outcome for Hinckley, however, may have been the same: His actions involved primarily moral incapacity, and his lawyers may have been able to convince a jury of his insanity by clear and convincing evidence.

Nearly half the states restricted their insanity defense around the same time. Many of these changes included (1) adopting the *M'Naghten* standard instead of the ALI standard (thereby eliminating the volitional prong), (2) shifting the burden of proof from the prosecution to the defense, and (3) introducing the verdict of guilty but mentally ill (GBMI) by which defendants with mental illness are found guilty and go to prisons instead of hospitals (see Chapter 4). By 2006, only seventeen states still recognized the defense of volitional incapacity (see Table 22.1).

Table 22.1 The three incapacities of insanity

Jurisdiction	Cognitive incapacity	Moral incapacity	Volitional incapacity
Alabama	*	*	
Alaska	*		
Arizona		*	
Arkansas		*	*
California	*	*	
Colorado	*	*	
Connecticut		*	*
Delaware		*	
District of Columbia		*	*
Federal	*	*	
Florida	*	*	
Georgia		*	*
Hawaii		*	*
Idaho			
Illinois		*	
Indiana		*	
Iowa	*	*	
Kansas			
Kentucky		*	*
Louisiana		*	
Maine		*	
Maryland		*	*
Massachusetts		*	*
Michigan	*	*	*
Minnesota	*	*	
Mississippi	*	*	
Missouri	*	*	
Montana			
Nebraska	*	*	
Nevada	*	*	
New Hampshire			
New Jersey	*	*	
New Mexico	*	*	*
New York	*	*	
North Carolina	*	*	
North Dakota	*	*	
Ohio		*	
Oklahoma	*	*	
Oregon		*	*
Pennsylvania	*	*	
Rhode Island		*	*
South Carolina		*	
South Dakota		*	
Tennessee	*	*	
Texas		*	
Utah			

(Continued)

Table 22.1 (Continued)

Jurisdiction	Cognitive incapacity	Moral incapacity	Volitional incapacity
Vermont		*	*
Virginia	*	*	*
Washington	*	*	
West Virginia		*	*
Wisconsin		*	*
Wyoming		*	*

Source: Survey by the U.S. Supreme Court for their decision in *Clark v. Arizona* (2006).

A more radical approach – that of abolishing the insanity defense entirely – has been accomplished by four states. Two of these states abolished the insanity defense in the wake of *Hinckley*: Idaho in 1982 and Utah in 1983. These were preceded by Montana in 1979 and followed by Kansas in 1995. More specifically, these states eliminated moral and volitional incapacity from the law and folded cognitive capacity into mens rea. This narrow use of mental health testimony was upheld by the U.S. Supreme Court in *Kahler v. Kansas* (2020). The abolition of the insanity defense is the topic of Chapter 24 and Appendix M.

An even more radical approach to volitional incapacity, which so far has been applied to only one defendant – school shooter Jamie Wilson of South Carolina – was to find a defendant GBMI due to volitional incapacity and then condemn him to death. This extraordinary trial, *State v. Wilson* (1992), is the subject of Chapter 23.

STATES ARE NOT REQUIRED TO HAVE A DEFENSE OF COGNITIVE INCAPACITY: *CLARK V. ARIZONA* (U.S. 2006)

The Arizona state legislature in 1993 adopted a truncated *M'Naghten* standard that eliminated the cognitive prong and defined insanity solely as moral incapacity. The U.S. Supreme Court affirmed this version of the insanity defense in 2006. The U.S. Supreme Court decision in *Clark v. Arizona* is worth studying if for no other reasons than its concise taxonomy of the three incapacities of insanity (described in Chapter 19) and its review of the status of the insanity defense in every jurisdiction (see Table 22.1).

In the early hours of June 21, 2000, citizens of a residential block in Flagstaff, Arizona, complained that a pickup truck was driving in circles around their block with loud music blaring from the speakers. The driver, Eric Michael Clark (age 17), stopped his truck when a marked police car drove up with siren blaring and emergency lights flashing. A uniformed police officer stepped out of the vehicle. Clark shot and killed him.

Clark had paranoid schizophrenia. No one questioned the reality of his mental illness. He was found incompetent to stand trial, and his trial was delayed for two years while his competency was restored. The question for the court was whether his illness had affected his behavior during the commission of this homicide, and in what way.

Clark's defense presented the testimony of his family, classmates, school officials, and a psychiatrist. These witnesses described his delusional beliefs and increasingly bizarre behavior in the year leading up to the homicide. He believed that aliens were trying to kill him. He had rigged his home with fishing line, beads, and wind chimes to warn him of possible intruders. He kept a bird in his truck to warn him of airborne poisons. He believed that aliens had inhabited the bodies of local citizens – including government agents – and that the only way to stop them was "with bullets." One night shortly before the homicide, Clark watched repeatedly a film about aliens masquerading as government agents, and he told people that this was a true story. Clark's parents testified that in the days leading up to the homicide he had called them "aliens." Two months after the homicide, he told his parents that Flagstaff was inhabited mostly by aliens, that the aliens had to be stopped, and that the only way to stop them was "with bullets."

The psychiatrist for the defense testified that Clark was insane at the time of the shooting and did not know right from wrong. A psychiatrist for the state disagreed and pointed out the degree of control that Clark had demonstrated over his behavior. He had circled the block with loud music blaring in the early morning hours as if to lure a victim. He had hidden the gun. He evaded the police after the shooting. (Hiding and evasion indicate that Clark knew he was in trouble.) What is not clear from the record is whether the prosecution's expert considered the possibility that luring a victim, hiding the gun, and evading the police are all consistent with moral incapacity if you believe that the police are aliens and it is your duty to save the world by killing them.

Also, the prosecution argued that Clark had recognized and had responded to the authority of the police officer by stopping his truck, which indicates that he knew the victim was a police officer. Other testimony for the prosecution indicated that Clark had been telling people for several weeks before the homicide that he wanted to shoot police officers. (Again, these arguments do not negate moral incapacity if Clark believed that police officers are dangerous aliens. The record in *Clark* does not allow us to draw any conclusions about this.)

Clark claimed that he did not know the man he shot was a police officer. If this were true, his claim might have helped him argue insanity under the cognitive prong of the M'Naghten Rule, but Arizona law did not have a cognitive prong, having dispensed with it in their 1993 revision of the law.

Clark waived his right to a jury trial. The trial judge ruled that Clark had not proved his alleged insanity. Clark was found guilty except insane of first degree murder, and he was sentenced to 25 years to life.

Clark believed that he was entitled to the defense of cognitive incapacity, and he took the matter to the U.S. Supreme Court. His petition to the U.S. Supreme Court argued, inter alia, that when Arizona eliminated cognitive incapacity from the insanity defense it had violated his right to due process. The U.S. Supreme Court disagreed and upheld his conviction. The Court recognized the power of each state to develop their own laws regarding insanity. Justice Souter in providing the majority opinion wrote,

> The alternatives are multiplied further by variations in the prescribed insanity verdict.... With this varied background, it is clear that no particular formulation has evolved into a baseline for due process, and that the insanity rule, like the conceptualization of criminal offenses, is substantially open to state choice. (at 745)

THE INSANITY DEFENSE BY JURISDICTION

In the *Clark* decision, the U.S. Supreme Court identified the four traditional strains of the insanity defense: cognitive incapacity, moral incapacity, volitional incapacity, and the product test (see Chapter 19). The court surveyed all fifty-two jurisdictions regarding their laws on the insanity defense and reported the data that are summarized in Table 22.1.

As can be seen in Table 22.1, only three states – Michigan, New Mexico, and Virginia – recognize all three incapacities as forms of insanity. The Model Penal Code – which recognizes only moral and volitional incapacities – is the law in thirteen states and in the District of Columbia. Four states have no insanity defense: Idaho, Kansas, Montana, and Utah. New Hampshire alone applies the product test of insanity.

Table 22.1 simplifies the many permutations of rules and definitions that abound in the fifty-two jurisdictions. Each jurisdiction has its own unique history and experience with mental illness, and each jurisdiction has developed its own set of rules. The U.S. Supreme Court has recognized the importance of allowing each state to develop their own procedures and has consistently resisted efforts to set a standard that might apply to every jurisdiction (see *Leland v. Oregon*, 1952; *Powell v. Texas*, 1968; and *Kahler v. Kansas*, 2020). Associate Justice David Souter wrote in the majority opinion in *Clark* that "due process imposes no single canonical formulation of legal insanity." Therefore, Arizona has no constitutional duty to include the defense of cognitive incapacity. Add to these complexities the evolving nature of mental health concepts and diagnoses, as well as the variety of psychological and psychiatric methods that are used to evaluate defendants and arrive at these determinations, and you have what Justice Souter pejoratively referred to as "fodder."

A more sympathetic tone was adopted by Judge Sir James Fitzjames Stephen when he wrote in 1883,

> Sarcasm and ridicule are out of place on the bench in almost all conceivable cases, but particularly when they are directed against a gentleman and a man of science who ... is attempting to state unfamiliar and in many ways unwelcome doctrines, to which he attaches high importance. (Stephen, 1883/2015, p. 125, quoted in McGuire, 1966, p. 103)

Justice Souter, in another comment that is likely to rankle every forensic psychologist, wrote that "the concepts of psychology ... are devised for thinking about treatment," and therefore it requires a leap "to the concepts of legal sanity, which are devised for thinking about criminal responsibility" (*Clark v. Arizona*, 2006, at 771). Justice Souter apparently was not familiar with the profession of forensic psychology and the ways in which it differs from the clinical practice of psychology. (For an introduction to this topic, see articles by Greenberg and Shuman [1997, 2007], and Strasburger et al. [1997].)

The majority in *Clark* also held that the cognitive incapacity test is duplicative and adds nothing to the moral incapacity test (thereby adopting the position taken by the American Law Institute) – if a person is so mentally ill that they do not know what they are doing, then they do not know that what they are doing is wrong.

> In practical terms, if a defendant did not know what he was doing when he acted, he could not have known that he was performing the wrongful act charged as a crime. (*Clark v. Arizona,* at 747)

Combining the decisions in *Leland*, *Clark*, and *Kahler* (see Chapter 24), the U.S. Supreme Court has ruled that Americans who have mental illness and who get into trouble with the law do not have a constitutional right to a defense based on volitional incapacity, cognitive incapacity, moral incapacity, or any form of insanity defense. The question of whether these defendants may claim an insanity defense is left up to the legislatures in the jurisdictions where they reside.

REFERENCES

American Psychiatric Association. (1983). Statement on the insanity defense. *American Journal of Psychiatry*, 140(6), 681–688. doi:10.1176/ajp.140.6.681.
Bonnie, R. (1983). The moral basis of the insanity defense. *American Bar Association Journal*, 69(2), 194–197. www.jstor.org/stable/20755324.

Bonnie, R. J., Jeffries, Jr., J. C., & Low, P. W. (2000). *A case study in the insanity defense: The trial of John W. Hinckley, Jr. Second edition.* New York: Foundation Press.

Clark v. Arizona, 548 U.S. 735 (U.S. 2006).

Durham v. United States, 214 F.2d 862 (D.C. Cir. 1954).

Gerber, R. J. (1975). Is the insanity test insane? *American Journal of Jurisprudence*, 20(1), 111–140. doi:10.1093/ajj/20.1.111.

Greenberg, S. A., & Shuman, D. W. (1997). Irreconcilable conflict between therapeutic and forensic roles. *Professional Psychology: Research and Practice*, 28(1), 50–57. doi:10.1037/0735-7028.28.1.50.

Greenberg, S. A., & Shuman, D. W. (2007). When worlds collide: Therapeutic and forensic roles. *Professional Psychology: Research and Practice*, 38(2), 129–132. doi:10.1037/0735-7028.38.2.129.

Kahler v. Kansas, 589 U.S. ____, 140 S. Ct. 1021 (2020).

Leland v. Oregon, 343 U.S. 790 (1952).

Low, P. W. (1986). *The trial of John W. Hinckley, Jr.: A case study in the insanity defense.* New York: Foundation Press.

McGuire, T. K. (1966). Integration of the insanity defense and mens rea: A suggested accommodation of medical and legal views in criminal responsibility of the mentally ill. *Issues in Criminology*, 2(1), 103–110. Retrieved 12/07/2022 from www.jstor.org/stable/42909552.

Mickenberg, I. (1987). A pleasant surprise: The guilty but mentally ill verdict has both succeeded in its own right and successfully preserved the traditional role of the insanity defense. *University of Cincinnati Law Review*, 55(4), 943–973.

Palko v. Connecticut, 302 U.S. 319 (1937).

Perry, D. (2018). "The most cold-blooded, cowardly treachery": 22 murder cases that rocked Oregon. Retrieved 07/25/2022 from www.oregonlive.com/history/2018/01/the_most_cold-blooded_cowardly.html.

Powell v. Texas, 392 U.S. 514, 88 S.Ct. 2145, 20 L.Ed.2d 1254 (1968).

Rabinowitz, H., & Mizelle, S. (2022). John Hinckley Jr. freed from all court oversight decades after Reagan assassination attempt. Retrieved 07/16/2022 from www.cnn.com/2022/06/15/politics/john-hinckley-full-court-release-reagan-assassination-attempt/index.html.

Selsky, A. (2022). *Oregon governor commutes all 17 of state's death sentences.* Associated Press. Retrieved 12/14/2022 from https://existsupporttest.z13.web.core.windows.net.

State v. Wilson, 306 S.C. 498, 413 S.E.2d 19 (South Carolina, 1992).

Stephen, J. F. (1883/2015). *A history of the criminal law of England. In three volumes.* (2015 version): London: Forgotten Books.

Strasburger, L. H., Gutheil, T. G., & Brodsky, A. (1997). On wearing two hats: Role conflict in serving as both psychotherapist and expert witness. *American Journal of Psychiatry*, 154(4), 448–456. doi:10.1176/ajp.154.4.448.

United States v. Brawner, Appellant, 471 F.2d 969, D.C. Cir. (1972).

United States v. Hinckley, 525 F. Supp. 1342 (D.D.C. 1981).

Walsh, E. (1999). Strange love: The woman who wanted to start a new life with Ronald Reagan's would-be assassin. *New Yorker Magazine.* www.newyorker.com/magazine/1999/04/05/strange-love.

23 Case study #12: the death penalty for a defendant with serious mental illness and volitional incapacity

State v. Wilson (S.C. 1992)

Many people in our society have violent fantasies. If they never act on these fantasies, then there is no actus reus, nobody gets hurt, their ideas stay in the realm of harmless fantasy, and they are not a threat to society. If, on the other hand, they have a severe mental illness and lack control over their own behavior, then they pose a threat to public safety. The challenges to a civilized society are to identify these individuals, to find humane methods by which to prevent their acting out, and, when people get hurt, to adjudicate fairly in the criminal justice system.

The capital trial of Jamie Wilson for murder in 1989 is arguably the most unique trial concerning volitional capacity in United States history. Wilson is the only inmate on death row in the United States who was found by a trial judge to be so severely mentally ill that he could not control his own behavior (i.e., volitional incapacity). His case is presented here, not because the reader is likely to encounter another Jamie Wilson, but to elucidate the nature of volitional incapacity, the behavior of persons who have severe mental illness, and how these factors play out in court.

The crux of the philosophical problem in *State v. Wilson* (1992) lies in the juxtaposition of two statements: (1) that Wilson was so mentally ill that he could not control his own behavior, and (2) that Wilson is completely culpable and responsible for his crimes. If you have no difficulty accepting the juxtaposition of these two statements, then you agree with the majority of the South Carolina Supreme Court. If, on the other hand, you find this juxtaposition to be incongruous, then you agree with the sole dissenting voice on that bench, Justice Ernest A. Finney, Jr. (see below).

Also at issue is the execution of persons who have severe mental illness – something which most of the world finds abhorrent (see the United Nations Commission on Human Rights, April 26, 2000) but which is legal in the United States under certain conditions.

DOI: 10.4324/9781003385028-27

JAMIE WILSON

Monday, September 26, 1988, was a school day in Greenwood, South Carolina.

A local resident had recently murdered his sister. This resident happened to have a neighbor, Jamie Wilson (age 19), who had severe mental illness and had a history of losing control of his own behavior. Wilson spent the weekend of September 24–25 in the throes of a turbulent psychosis. The murder of his neighbor had thrown him into an obsessional reverie about homicide. On Monday morning he was hearing voices telling him what to do (command auditory hallucinations), and he obeyed the voices. He drove to the home of his maternal grandmother, who kept a nine-shot, .22 caliber revolver on her mantelpiece. He took the pistol and drove to a discount store, where he purchased hollow-point long rifle bullets, a more destructive type of ammunition than his grandmother kept in her pistol. He emptied his grandmother's pistol and loaded it with the more destructive ammunition. Then he drove to the Oakland Elementary School. By then it was lunchtime. He walked into the school cafeteria and stood quietly for a moment. Then he took out the pistol and began firing, apparently choosing his victims at random. Witnesses commented on the "look of hatred and rage" on his face (*Wilson v. Ozmint*, 2004). Wilson put the pistol against the temple of a little boy and fired. (The boy survived.) He shot a female first-grade teacher twice: once in the shoulder and once in the hand. The bullet traveled through her hand and went into her throat. (The teacher survived.) He fired until the gun was empty. Then he walked into a lavatory, where he reloaded. He walked into a classroom and again started firing and again fired until the pistol was empty. Then he threw the gun down and stepped outside through a window. A teacher told him to stand still with his hands in the air, and he complied. When the police arrived, he handed them his library card. He had fired eighteen rounds had shot eleven people, and had killed two 8-year-old girls.

Wilson's life was characterized by poverty, child abuse, violence, and neglectful parents who had mental illness themselves. Four generations of his family had members who were hospitalized and medicated for mental illness. His maternal grandmother (who owned the pistol) was being treated with antipsychotic medication and had odd habits like putting pieces of aluminum foil around her yard.

Both of Wilson's parents and both of his paternal grandparents had physically abused him. His father had been physically abused by both of his parents. When Wilson was a child, his father used to pull a gun out and point it at him. Wilson's paternal grandfather was known to be a violent man. He would point guns at people, was a member of the Ku Klux Klan, and was rumored to have killed Black people. Alcohol and drug abuse – particularly misuse of prescription drugs – was common on both sides of the family and had been for several generations.

Wilson stuttered at the age of 5. He yelled obscenities in church. At age 8, he was very upset about germs, washed his hands compulsively, and had compulsions about bathing. He had elaborate rituals for preparing food and he refused to drink from anything but a Dixie cup. He would not allow his sisters to touch the refrigerator door. He would open doors only with a handkerchief. He was fascinated with the dark and he refused to let anyone open the drapes or turn on the dining room lights. He stopped attending church at age 13, because he thought people were staring at him. He became physically aggressive toward his mother, his grandparents, and other children. At age 13, when he became violent or difficult, his family gave him the antipsychotic medication that had been prescribed for his grandmother (which altered his consciousness and thereby deprived him of important opportunities to learn internalized mechanisms of control). Later, when Wilson was prescribed his own psychotropic medication, he abused it, and, when he ran out, his grandmother helped him get more.

Suicidal gestures began around age 13. At age 14, he developed a habit of spitting compulsively. His behavior in school grew increasingly odd. In the tenth grade, he clucked like a chicken in class. Around age 17 or 18, he lost his obsession with germs and lost interest in his personal hygiene. When his behavior at home became intolerable, his family would seek hospitalization, would move him to the home of another family member, or would move him to a motel room (which negatively reinforced his loss of control and further deprived him of opportunities to develop good internal controls). His only relationship outside the family was with a 42-year-old man who traded him drugs for sex.

He had a "splinter skill" that was unusual but was consistent with his cultural background. He could recite from memory – rapidly and in order – the titles of all the books of the Old and New Testaments.

By the time of the shooting Wilson had been hospitalized seven times. He was hospitalized three times at the ages of 14 and 15. His family did not follow through with recommendations for day hospital and outpatient treatment. He was hospitalized four times between the ages of 17 and 19. He was diagnosed with paranoia and borderline personality disorder. Neuroimaging of his brain conducted for his defense showed a greatly enlarged left lateral ventricle (which indicates a shrunken left cerebral hemisphere). Such a brain abnormality can be expected to result in language deficits, including a poverty of internal verbal rules by which to govern one's behavior.

Five months before the shooting, Wilson was discharged from the local private hospital because his father's insurance had run out. Shortly before the murders, Wilson sought hospitalization again, but he was no longer covered by his father's insurance, and the hospital denied him admission.

In the months leading up to the shooting, Wilson was sleeping days and awake nights. He spent his time watching television and staring into space (a negative symptom of schizophrenia). He refused to let people into the house. He was obsessed with books about murder. He was obsessed with Alfred Hitchcock's *Psycho* (1960; known as the world's first "slasher" movie). He watched *Psycho* over and over again and he became a joke at the local videotape club because he kept returning the movie and then renting it again. (Please note the compulsive nature of this behavior, suggesting a lack of internal control.)

The stutter which had appeared at age 5 and then disappeared now returned. He began to hear voices. He talked to himself and he talked to people who were not there. He thought that people were "out to get him" (*Wilson v. Ozmint*, 2004). He threatened his parents and grandparents. His family could see that his mental condition was getting worse.

His grandfather died around this time and Wilson did not show grief (i.e., flat affect: a negative symptom of schizophrenia). At first he refused to attend his grandfather's funeral, but when his family prevailed upon him he went, inappropriately dressed in blue jeans. At the funeral, he showed abnormal affect, alternating between moments of inappropriate, mildly elevated mood and moments in which he was out of contact with others (another negative symptom of schizophrenia). As mentioned above, Wilson was obsessed with the fact that a neighbor recently murdered his (the neighbor's) sister.

I first met Jamie Wilson two days after the shootings, in my capacity as a forensic psychologist at a local mental hospital. I continued to work on his appeal for another sixteen years.

At our first meeting, Wilson sat in a group interview room with myself and the other members of the evaluation team. He was soft, overweight, and deconditioned. He showed little concern for his personal appearance. His thin hair was short and uniform, as if someone had simply run clippers over his head. His facial expression was blank and he gave no sign of emotion (a negative symptom of schizophrenia). He did not make eye contact. He did not look up, down, right, or left, but looked straight ahead and did not focus on anyone or anything. He said very little. He was in his private world and he did not let us in. Our efforts to communicate were not important to him. When he responded at all, his answers were short and vague. His face was impassive and unchanging, except for an occasional twitch or shudder that ran through his face and body, as if he were

responding to internal stimuli. He gave no indication that he understood he was in a life-or-death situation or that it made any difference
to him.

Wilson's self-report was that he was obeying command auditory hallucinations at the time of the shooting, suggesting volitional incapacity. If
he believed that obeying the voices was the right thing to do, this also
would indicate moral incapacity. His attorneys entered a plea of guilty but
mentally ill (GBMI), which in South Carolina is the equivalent of volitional incapacity (i.e., inability to conform your conduct to the requirements of the law, because of mental illness). The defense presented
testimony by two members of our evaluation team who testified that
Wilson had schizophrenia and was unable to control his behavior at the
time of the shooting. Two additional mental health experts hired by the
defense also testified and essentially agreed with our team (although one
psychologist diagnosed Wilson with schizotypal personality disorder and
not schizophrenia). Today the diagnoses of schizophrenia and schizotypal
personality disorder are recognized as two points on the schizophrenia
spectrum; American Psychiatric Association, 2022.

Park Dietz, M.D., a well-known forensic psychiatrist, testified for the
prosecution without ever examining Wilson. Dietz testified that Wilson
had a borderline personality disorder and may have had a transient
psychotic episode during the offense, but he disagreed with the defense
experts and testified that Wilson had not experienced volitional
incapacity.

Wilson's actions on the day of the shootings were purposeful and did
not suggest lack of mens rea. He drove his car to a logical sequence of
locations, took his grandmother's pistol from her home, purchased a more
deadly type of ammunition, replaced his grandmother's ammunition,
brought the weapon to the school, went from one room to another, and
reloaded the weapon between rooms. There could be no question that he
had behaved intentionally. Opinions regarding volitional incapacity were
supported by his command auditory hallucinations during the crime and
by the compulsive nature of his behavior – he fired the gun until it was
empty, walked into another room, reloaded, and again fired until the gun
was empty. He had several opportunities in which he could have stopped
this destructive course of action if he had possessed normal volitional
controls. If free will consists of the ability to do otherwise, and if Wilson's
behavior was so compulsive that he could not stop himself, then he did not
exercise free will during these events.

The prosecution sought the death penalty. In May 1989, Wilson's
defense attorneys opted for a bench trial – that is, they waived Wilson's
right to a jury trial; his verdict and sentence would be decided by a judge

and not a jury. Wilson pleaded guilty but mentally ill (GBMI; the reader may remember from our discussion of pleas in Chapter 4 that GBMI is not a form of insanity). Testimony was heard from the five mental health professionals. The judge accepted Wilson's plea of GBMI, thereby accepting that Wilson had been so severely mentally ill during the commission of these crimes that he had been unable to control his behavior. Then, in an unexpected move, the judge sentenced Wilson to death. This sentence was unexpected for several reasons:

1 It is rare for any court in any state to impose the death penalty on a defendant who is GBMI.
2 Imposing the death penalty on a defendant with volitional incapacity is unprecedented.
3 Executing persons who have severe mental illness – while it is legal in the United States under certain conditions – is abhorrent to most of the world (see the United Nations resolution calling upon the nations of the world to stop executing persons who have mental illness: "The Commission urged States parties ... not to impose the death penalty on a person suffering from any form of mental disorder or to execute any such person"; United Nations Commission on Human Rights, April 26, 2000. The U.S. voted against this resolution. See also the decision in *Coker v. Georgia*, 1977, discussed below, in which the U.S. Supreme Court condemned the execution of persons who have mental illness).
4 As one of Wilson's attorneys would testify at Wilson's post-conviction relief hearing, the trial judge had told him that he would not impose the death penalty if Wilson would plead GBMI.

South Carolina Code of Laws Section 16-3-20 lists the aggravating and mitigating circumstances that a court can use when deciding whether to impose the death penalty. Wilson's trial judge analyzed these statutory factors as follows:

Aggravating circumstances

1 two or more persons murdered pursuant to one act or scheme
2 the murder of a child eleven years of age or under.

Mitigating circumstances

1 no significant history of prior violent crime conviction
2 Wilson's age or mentality at the time of the crime
3 the murders were committed under the influence of a mental or emotional disturbance

4 Wilson's capacity to appreciate the criminality of his conduct or conform his conduct to the requirements of law was substantially impaired.

By the trial judge's calculus, the actus-reus-oriented aggravating factors of number and age of victims were more dispositive than the mentality-oriented mitigating factors of Wilson's age, lack of criminal record, mental illness, and volitional incapacity.

In a sad and poignant moment immediately after the trial, one of the psychiatrists who had testified for the defense changed his mind and said that Wilson did in fact meet the criteria for insanity. Insanity could have been a better plea for Wilson because defendants who are not guilty by reason of insanity (NGRI) go to hospitals instead of prisons, and they are not eligible for the death penalty. This psychiatrist asked if he could go back on the witness stand, but it was too late. The trial was over, the verdict was in, and he had missed his opportunity. The fact that this psychiatrist had changed his mind was brought up during Wilson's appeal, but the appeals court did not find this to be persuasive.

Defendants who act in response to command auditory hallucination may have both moral and volitional incapacities. If they obey the voice, then they may have volitional incapacity. If they believe that obeying the voice is the right thing to do, then they may have moral incapacity. South Carolina recognizes only moral incapacity in its definition of insanity.

Few defendants in the United States who have been found GBMI have been sentenced to death. Emanuel (1989) – in an article which argues that the death penalty is disproportional for defendants who are GBMI – identified only three other GBMI defendants who were sentenced to death: William Crews of Illinois (*People v. Crews*, 1988); James Allen Harris of Indiana (*Harris v. State*, 1986); and Reginald Sanders of Delaware (*Sanders v. State*, 1990). None of these cases are identical to *Wilson*, because GBMI does not necessarily entail volitional incapacity in those other states (see 720 Illinois Compiled Statutes Section 6-4 and Indiana Code Title 35 Section 35). In Delaware, volitional incapacity is one of the possible defenses that *could*, but not necessarily *does*, lead to a verdict of GBMI (see 11 Delaware Code Section 401(b)). Reginald Sanders of Delaware was sentenced to death by a jury in 1986, but he appealed successfully to the Delaware Supreme Court in 1990, because the jury had not been informed that mental illness is a mitigating factor in death penalty determinations. Sanders' capital sentence was vacated and he currently resides in the Delaware Department of Corrections. The Delaware Supreme Court ruled the death penalty unconstitutional in 2016, and legislative efforts to reinstate it have not succeeded.

Jamie Wilson's tragedy is multi-leveled and includes the fact that he committed these homicides in a state that does not recognize volitional incapacity as a form of insanity. In seventeen other states (see Table 22.1), his volitional incapacity would have resulted in a verdict of not guilty by reason of insanity (NGRI), in which case he would have gone to a hospital and not a prison, and he could not have been given the death penalty. In South Carolina, volitional incapacity is not a form of insanity – it is the sole justification for a verdict of GBMI, and it is a mitigating factor in capital sentencing, which a judge can either emphasize or diminish, as was seen at Wilson's trial.

Wilson's lawyers appealed to the South Carolina Supreme Court in 1992. In a 4–1 decision the court accepted the trial judge's reasoning and affirmed the death penalty. The court relied upon some familiar territory, including the alleged inability to make the "can't/won't" distinction (see Chapter 19). The court wrote,

> It has been suggested that it is impossible to say that an impulse was irresistible rather than unsuccessfully resisted, or to distinguish between the uncontrollable impulse and the impulse that is not controlled ... [The] irresistible impulse test is plagued by internal debate over its validity within the profession of psychiatry. The federal insanity defense was recently amended to delete the irresistible impulse or "volitional prong." "A primary reason that the definition of insanity was altered by the (federal) Insanity Reform Act (to delete the irresistible impulse test) is that psychiatrists themselves are unable to agree upon the meaning of an 'irresistible impulse.'" *United States v. Freeman*, 804 F. (2d) 1574, 1576 (11th Cir. 1986) (citing S. Rep. 225, 98th Cong. (2d) Sess. 226-29, reprinted in 1984 U.S. Code Cong. & Ad. News 3182, 3408-11). (*State v. Wilson*, 1992, at 506)

However, it was not Wilson's verdict of GBMI, but rather his sentence of death, that was the issue before the court at that time. Wilson was not asking the court to make the "can't/won't" distinction. The trial judge implicitly indicated that he *could* make the "can't/won't" distinction when he accepted Wilson's plea of GBMI.

The South Carolina Supreme Court relied upon the U.S. Supreme Court decision in *Leland v. Oregon* (1952; see Chapter 22) and the federal Insanity Defense Reform Act of 1984, both of which diminished or eliminated the defense of volitional incapacity. The court concluded,

> Therefore, South Carolina has rejected the irresistible impulse test for insanity. (*State v. Wilson*, 1992, at 507)

The court also wrote,

> Our penal system was developed to punish those who refuse to act reasonably, and to deter those who can be deterred from acting unreasonably. (*State v. Wilson*, at 507)

However, this does not apply to Wilson. He did not "refuse to act reasonably." He was not capable of making such decisions, as the trial judge tacitly agreed when he accepted Wilson's plea of GBMI. Furthermore, Wilson has a severe mental illness and he was not capable of being deterred. To regard him like any other defendant is to overlook the reality of his mental illness.

The South Carolina Supreme Court wrote further:

> South Carolina does not recognize that one acting under an irresistible impulse is somehow less culpable … As stated earlier, under South Carolina law, Wilson is just as culpable as any other guilty defendant. Hence, there is no diminishment in his "personal responsibility and moral guilt." For similar reasons, we decline to accept Wilson's argument that no penological justification for his sentence exists. We hold that the penological goal of retribution is served by this sentence, as, under South Carolina law, Wilson is completely culpable and responsible for his crimes. (*State v. Wilson*, at 508–509)

These four members of the South Carolina Supreme Court adopted the legal and philosophical position that volitional incapacity is not a consideration in assigning moral responsibility. These four members of the court ruled that Wilson was "responsible for his crimes," and the fact that he lacked volitional incapacity was not important to them.

The sole dissenting voice in *State v. Wilson* was Justice Ernest A. Finney (1931–2017). Finney was the only Black justice on the court, and in fact was the first Black justice on the South Carolina Supreme Court since the Reconstruction. He earned his reputation as a young attorney in 1961, when he defended the Friendship Nine – a group of Black junior college students who were arrested in a lunch-counter protest in Rock Hill, South Carolina. Finney was the only member of the South Carolina Supreme Court who found Wilson's volitional incapacity to be meaningful. He wrote:

> In my view, imposition of the death penalty upon a defendant found 'guilty but mentally ill' is violative of the Cruel and Unusual Punishment Clause of the Eighth Amendment of the United States Constitution … Mental illness is a mitigating factor which must be considered in death penalty cases … This may be the only instance in South Carolina and

Figure 23.1 Justice Ernest Adolphus Finney (1931–2017), first Black justice of the South Carolina Supreme Court since the Reconstruction. Justice Finney was the only dissenting vote in *State v. Wilson* (1992), when he argued that a defendant who is too mentally ill to control their own behavior should not be condemned to death.

indeed, according to my research, in the entire nation where the death penalty has been imposed after a factual determination that mental illness deprived the offender of sufficient capacity to conform his conduct to the standard required by law ... Society's "evolving standards of decency" (quoting *Trop v. Dulles*, 1958, at 101) imposes a presumption against execution of persons lacking sufficient capacity to conform their conduct to the standards of the law. The natural abhorrence civilized societies feel at killing one who has no capacity to come to grips with his own conscience or deity is still valid today. (*State v. Wilson*, at 515–517)

Justice Finney's dissent expresses his belief that a defendant who has volitional incapacity should not be put to death.

As mentioned above, one of the philosophical problems in *State v. Wilson* is the juxtaposition of two statements: (1) that Wilson was so mentally ill that "he lacked sufficient capacity to conform his conduct to the requirements of the law" (quoting the definition of "Guilty But Mentally Ill" in the South Carolina Code of Laws Section 17-24-20); and (2) that "Wilson is completely culpable and responsible for his crimes" (*State v. Wilson*, 1992, at 509). If you can utter these two statements in a single breath, then you agree with the majority of the South Carolina Supreme Court. If, on the other hand, you find these two statements to be incongruous, then you may regard *State v. Wilson* as the odd sort of reasoning that can occur when the law does not recognize volitional incapacity as a form of insanity. Perhaps you agree with the legislatures of seventeen states where volitional incapacity is a form of insanity (see Table 22.1), and with Immanuel Kant, who wrote that freedom "must be the foundation of all moral laws ... without which no moral law and no moral imputation are possible" (1788/1873, pp. 226–227).

Wilson's attorneys John Blume and Sheri Lynn Johnson summarized,

At the very least, it is counterintuitive to kill someone for behavior he was powerless to avoid ... [No] other defendant – in South Carolina or in any other state – has ever been sentenced to death after the factfinder determined that he lacked volitional control. (Blume & Johnson, 2003, p. 95)

[Only] South Carolina law affirmatively sanctions execution of a defendant for conduct he was unable to control. (2003, p. 114)

Jamie Wilson is "responsible" for his behavior in the sense that it was he and not another person who pulled the trigger, but to a libertarian like Immanuel Kant this does not establish moral responsibility. To a libertarian, an agent who does not act with agent-causal free will does not bear moral responsibility.

Professor Stephen Morse (2008) of the University of Pennsylvania offered a compatibilist formula by which defendants can be prosecuted on the basis of their intentions and not on the basis of free will. Professor Michael Moore (2016) of the University of Illinois has called this the "ultraconservative" position. Certainly Jamie Wilson showed intention. He took his grandmother's pistol; drove to the store; purchased ammunition; unloaded, loaded, and reloaded; brought the weapon to the school; pointed the weapon; and pulled the trigger. The problem with the ultraconservative position is that Wilson has a severe mental illness and his intentions were beyond his control.

No higher court is likely to contravene South Carolina's GBMI statute, especially after the U.S. Supreme Court decision in *Kahler v. Kansas* (2020; see Chapter 24) that states are not required to have an insanity defense.

The tragedy of Jamie Wilson is multi-dimensional, and it is his own tragedy as well as that of the victims and their families. A psychotic young man had enough insight to seek mental health treatment shortly before these crimes, but he was turned away because he was no longer covered by his father's insurance. His psychotic grandmother was allowed to own a pistol. She kept it on her mantelpiece, where her dangerous grandson was able to steal it. A store sold him ammunition. Eleven people were shot and two precious lives were lost. All of this happened in a state where volitional incapacity is not a form of insanity, and the only state of the Union that sanctions the death penalty for a defendant who was so severely mentally ill that he could not control his behavior. Executing Wilson would compound the tragedy with another pointless loss of life – something that his attorneys have been working to prevent for the past 35 years. As Wilson's attorneys Blume and Johnson (2003) have argued, when a sentence applies to only one defendant in the country, then surely it is an "unusual punishment."

STATE V. WILSON AND THE FOUR GOALS OF SENTENCING: "EXACTING MINDLESS VENGEANCE"

The U.S. Supreme Court in *Gregg v. Georgia* (1976) wrote that capital punishment has two goals: deterrence and retribution. The other two goals of sentencing – incapacitation and rehabilitation – are not served by the death penalty. The reasoning is clear. If we want to incapacitate offenders, we keep them in prison and do not kill them. If we want to rehabilitate them, we keep them alive and we work with them.

In *Coker v. Georgia,* the U.S. Supreme Court wrote that executing a person with severe mental illness is "nothing more than the purposeless and needless imposition of pain and suffering" (*Coker v. Georgia,* 1977, at 592).

In *Enmund v. Florida* (1982) the Court wrote,

> Unless the death penalty when applied to those in (the defendant's) position measurably contributes to one or both of these goals (deterrence and retribution), it "is nothing more than the purposeless and needless imposition of pain and suffering," and hence an unconstitutional punishment. (at 798, quoting *Coker v. Georgia,* 1977, at 592)

The Court expressed similar ideas regarding the death penalty for Alvin Ford, who had severe psychosis and delusional beliefs (see Chapter 18):

> [It] provides no example to others, and thus contributes nothing to whatever deterrence value is intended to be served by capital punishment ... Other commentators postulate religious underpinnings: that it is uncharitable to dispatch an offender "into another world, when he is not of a capacity to fit himself for it" ... It is also said that execution serves no purpose in these cases because madness is its own punishment: *furiosus solo furore punitur* [Blackstone]. More recent commentators opine that the community's quest for "retribution" – the need to offset a criminal act by a punishment of equivalent "moral quality" – is not served by execution of an insane person, which has a "lesser value" than that of the crime for which he is to be punished. (quoting Hazard & Louisell, 1962, p. 387). (*Ford v. Wainwright,* 1986, at 476–477)

Executing a defendant with severe mental illness would be no more than the "exacting [of] mindless vengeance" (*Ford v. Wainwright,* 1986, at 410).

The execution of Jamie Wilson would not satisfy the goal of deterrence, because we cannot deter people who have no volitional control. Deterrence assumes that the person who is the object of deterrence is able to understand the law and able to conform their behavior to the requirements of the law (see Morse, 1994).

Whether you believe that executing Jamie Wilson serves the goal of retribution depends on whether you agree with South Carolina, twenty-eight other states, and the four states that do not have the insanity defense that volitional incapacity is not a form of insanity. If you do not recognize volitional incapacity as a form of insanity, then the fact that a defendant is unable to control their own behavior is no particular problem in terms of their culpability, responsibility, and blameworthiness; and putting them to death serves the goal of retribution. If, on the other hand, you agree with the seventeen states that accept volitional incapacity as a form of insanity, then Jamie Wilson was not responsible for his behavior, and executing him does not serve the goal of retribution.

JAMIE WILSON IN FEDERAL COURT

Wilson's efforts to find relief in federal court have not succeeded. He was granted a writ of habeas corpus by the federal district court, but this judgment was vacated by the U.S. Court of Appeals for the Fourth Circuit on the grounds that the district court had not sufficiently reviewed the facts. Those facts included that Wilson had been warned "no less than five times" that he could receive the death penalty if he pleaded guilty, and each time he indicated that he understood (*Wilson v. Ozmint*, 2004).

JAMIE WILSON IN PRISON

Thirty-five years after the tragedy at Oakland Elementary School, Wilson remains on death row at Kirkland Correctional Institution in Columbia, South Carolina. I first met him in 1988, two days after the shooting. I continued to work on his appeal for sixteen years. I visited him on death row many times.

As Wilson adjusted to prison life and responded to antipsychotic medication, his affect changed from flat to inappropriately jovial, cheerful, and silly. He joked and grinned and he enjoyed my visits in the way that a child enjoys receiving attention. He showed no interest in his personal appearance or hygiene. His teeth rotted away and had to be pulled. He came to our interviews with feces on his trousers. When I looked in on him in his cell, I saw him lying on his back staring at the ceiling (a negative symptom of schizophrenia). His cell was the barest I have seen in thirty-four years of visiting prisons. He had given all of his possessions away to other prisoners, including his television. The only thing in his cell was a stack of magazines that had been brought by the prison librarian, and they sat untouched in the middle of the floor.

I last interviewed Wilson in 2004, after which I moved to another state. Since that time, his lawyer has told me, his language skills have continued to decline. This can be expected of someone who has a deteriorating left cerebral hemisphere. I have been told that Wilson has not uttered an intelligible sentence since 2016. Although he remains on death row, it does not seem likely that mental health experts will consider him competent to be executed. The standard for competency to be executed was established by the U.S. Supreme Court in *Ford v. Wainwright* (1986; see Chapter 18). The *Ford* decision suggests that, before a defendant can be executed, they must demonstrate that they know they are being executed and why they are being executed. In addition, South Carolina law requires that a person must be competent to rationally and factually assist counsel during legal proceedings. If Wilson were asked a *Ford*-style question like "Why are you being executed?" and his answer was gibberish, it does not seem likely that a mental health expert would consider him to be competent.

A hearing regarding Wilson's competency to be executed was held in July 2011, and five mental health experts testified that Wilson was not competent. (Two expert witnesses from the South Carolina Department of Mental Health testified that they had no opinion, because they could not rule out the possibility of malingering.) As of this writing, there has been no ruling on this matter, and Wilson's mental condition continues to decline.

REFERENCES

American Psychiatric Association. (2022). *Diagnostic and Statistical Manual of Mental Disorders. Fifth edition. Text revision.* Washington, D.C.: American Psychiatric Association.

Blume, J. H., & Johnson, S. L. (2003). Killing the non-willing: Atkins, the volitionally incapacitated, and the death penalty. *Cornell Law Faculty Publications.* Paper 233. Retrieved 07/04/2020 from http://scholarship.law.cornell.edu/facpub/233.

Coker v. Georgia, 433 U.S. 584 (1977).

Emanuel, A. S. (1989). Guilty but mentally ill verdicts and the death penalty: An Eighth Amendment analysis. *North Carolina Law Review*, 68(1), 37–67. https://scholarship.law.unc.edu/nclr/vol68/iss1/9.

Enmund v. Florida, 458 U.S. 782 (1982).

Ford v. Wainwright, 477 U.S. 399 (1986).

Gregg v. Georgia, 428 U.S. 153 (1976).

Harris v. State, 499 N.E.2d 723 (Indiana, 1986).

Hazard, G. C., & Louisell, D. W. (1962). Death, the state, and the insane: Stay of execution. *UCLA Law Review*, 9, 381–405. Corpus ID: 152323763.

Kahler v. Kansas, 589 U.S. ____, 140 S. Ct. 1021 (2020).

Kant, I. (1788/1873). *The critique of practical reason.* New York: Longmans, Green and Company.

Leland v. Oregon, 343 U.S. 790 (1952).

Moore, M. S. (2016). The neuroscience of volitional excuse. In D. S. Patterson & M. S. Pardo (Eds.) *Philosophical foundations of law and neuroscience* (pp. 179–230). New York: Oxford University Press.

Morse, S. (1994). Culpability and control. *University of Pennsylvania Law Review, 142*, 1587–1660. https://scholarship.law.upenn.edu/penn_law_review/vol142/iss5/7.

Morse, S. J. (2008). Determinism and the death of folk psychology: Two challenges to responsibility from neuroscience. *Minnesota Journal of Law, Science and Technology*, 9(1), 1–36. https://scholarship.law.umn.edu/mjlst/vol9/iss1/3.

People v. Crews, 122 Il1. 2d 266, 522 N.E.2d 1167 (Illinois, 1988).
Sanders v. State, 585 A.2d 117 (Delaware, 1990).
State v. Wilson, 306 S.C. 498, 413 S.E.2d 19 (South Carolina, 1992).
Trop v. Dulles, 356 U.S. 86 (1958).
Wilson v. Ozmint, 352 F.3d 847 (4th Cir. 2004).

24   The abolitionist states

During the course of the twentieth century, eight states attempted the bold experiment of abolishing the insanity defense. Four states – Washington, Louisiana, Mississippi, and Nevada – abolished the insanity defense briefly, only to have those laws struck down by their own state supreme courts (*State v. Strasburg,* Washington, 1910; *State v. Lange,* Louisiana, 1929; *Sinclair v. State,* Mississippi, 1931; *Finger v. State,* Nevada, 2001). Four other states – Montana (1979), Idaho (1982), Utah (1983), and Kansas (1995) – abolished the insanity defense in the last quarter of the 20th century and have no insanity defense at this time. (For an analysis of the laws in each of these four states, see Appendix M.) The laws of these states allow mental health testimony to be used to negate mens rea and during sentencing, but they do not allow mental health testimony to address the question of insanity. The U.S. Supreme Court found this to be acceptable in *Kahler v. Kansas* (2020), which is the last case reviewed in this chapter and is a fitting climax, because with this decision the court ended five centuries of Anglo-American jurisprudence regarding the insanity defense.

The four "abolitionist" states employ a bifurcated process. First a defendant is found either guilty or not guilty, and then if found guilty the defendant is sent either to prison or to a hospital, depending on their treatment needs. Three of these states – Idaho, Montana, and Utah – have the special verdict of "guilty but insane," which allows a defendant to go to a hospital instead of a prison.

DELLING V. IDAHO (U.S. 2012), CERT. DENIED

Low-level government employees like myself have to see every defendant who comes through the door. The U.S. Supreme Court, on the other hand, gets to choose which cases they will hear. The process is known as certiorari. When a petition for a writ of certiorari arrives at the U.S. Supreme Court, the justices decide whether or not they will hear the case. The

DOI: 10.4324/9781003385028-28

decision is made according to the "rule of four," whereby if four justices believe that the case should be heard, the entire court hears the case. When fewer than four justices think the case should be heard, certiorari is denied. The U.S. Supreme Court is the highest court in the land, and when they deny a writ of certiorari the petitioner has no further recourse.

In deciding which cases to hear, the Court relies upon the principle of "ripeness." When an issue has been "ripening" in the country, perhaps with trials in multiple jurisdictions, then the Court may select a representative case or group of cases and grant a writ of certiorari. In the case of the four abolitionist states, the Court denied certiorari in *Delling v. Idaho* (2012), a case that had strong evidence of severe mental illness, and then granted certiorari in *Kahler v. Kansas* (2020), a case with weak evidence of mental illness. Observers like myself were concerned that the court had selected a weak case and would find it easy to reject Kahler's arguments.

John Joseph Delling

The two murders committed by John Joseph Delling in 2007 illustrate how a defendant with delusional thinking can retain their cognitive capacity while losing their moral capacity. Delling knew that he was killing people. He knew who he was killing. He believed that killing them was the right thing to do because he thought that this was the way to save his own life. He believed he was acting in self-defense, and self-defense is an affirmative defense to homicide, but Delling's actions were not justifiable, because his alleged "self-defense" was the product of his paranoid delusion. This tends to be the case with moral incapacity, as the violence might have been justified if the circumstances had been real and not the product of delusional beliefs. Delling had the misfortune of committing homicide in a state that had abolished the insanity defense.

At the age of 21, John Delling was living with his parents in Antelope, California. He believed that certain people were "stealing his powers," and that this was going to cost him his life. One day he asked his brother, "Do you think David [Boss] is the one stealing my powers?" He wrote a list of seven names of people he believed he had to kill in order to save himself.

Delling grew increasingly agitated and unstable. His family took away his firearms. He damaged his parents' bathroom. His family called local law enforcement, who told Delling to leave the house.

Delling had attended Timberline High School in Boise, Idaho, along with two of his victims: David Boss and Jacob Thompson. His third victim, Bradly Morse, had attended school in nearby Meridian, Idaho.

Delling had been violent in high school. At age 17, he pleaded guilty to battery in juvenile court after he beat a classmate with the anti-car-theft device known as "The Club." Witnesses heard Delling say that he wanted to kill this student in return for ruining his life. Delling was held in custody for three days and then spent ten weeks in home detention. He changed schools.

One day, at age 19, Delling began yelling at a 13-year-old boy in the parking lot of a grocery store. He spat at the boy and rammed him with the front tire of his motorcycle. The boy suffered some scratches but no other injury. Delling was convicted of misdemeanor battery.

In 2005, Delling was a student at the University of Idaho in Moscow, from which he was expelled for threatening dormitory residents. He was cited for misdemeanor disturbing the peace. Also in 2005, he was seen stalking three men in Boise. He was seen outside their home several times a day, often on his motorcycle. He pleaded guilty to stalking and was ordered to have no further contact with these men.

In February 2007, police told Delling (then age 21) to leave his parents' home because of his disruptive behavior. Over the next four weeks he drove 6,500 miles through Oregon, Washington, Idaho, Nevada, Utah, and Arizona. On March 20, 2007, he arrived in Tucson, Arizona, at the home of former classmate and University of Arizona student Jacob Thompson (age 23).

Thompson was at home when he heard a man tapping on his window and telling him to move his truck. When Thompson moved his truck, he saw a man sitting on a bicycle, and he asked if he were the person who wanted him to move his truck. The man on the bicycle approached the truck and fired five times at the driver's-side door. Thompson was hit three times: in his face, chest, and arm. He survived and later identified Delling in a photo lineup.

Delling drove to Idaho, where, on March 31, 2007, he met former classmate and University of Idaho student David Boss (age 21) at his off-campus apartment and killed him with two gunshot wounds to the head.

On the morning of April 3, 2007, the body of Bradly Morse (age 25), then a student at Boise State University, was found shot and killed in the park where Morse had been working as a janitor for the Idaho Department of Parks and Recreation.

Ada County Lt. Scott Johnson said of Delling, "He wasn't so much an outcast as he just wasn't really in with the in crowd ... We just don't know if he had any close friends. By some accounts, the two people he shot were the nicest to him" (Boone, 2007).

Defense counsel motioned for a competency evaluation. On February 27, 2008, Delling was found incompetent to stand trial and he was committed to a state hospital. It was almost a year before he returned to court with his competency restored. Delling filed pre-trial motions indicating (1) that he would present evidence that he was incapable of forming the required mens rea, and (2) that Idaho had violated his due process rights by abolishing the insanity defense and that this was unconstitutional under the Fifth, Sixth, Eighth, and Fourteenth Amendments. The district court judge denied the latter motion and ruled that:

> Simply because Idaho does not recognize an insanity defense does not mean that mentally ill offenders are deprived of any right recognized under either the United States Constitution or the Idaho Constitution. (*Idaho v. Delling*, 2011, at 2)

Delling pleaded guilty to two counts of second degree murder in exchange for the prosecutor's recommendation of concurrent sentences (2011, at 13). He was sentenced to two determinate life sentences (i.e., life without the possibility of parole). The district court judge wrote:

> [Unfortunately], the facts in this case are ... that the defendant unquestionably suffers from a very serious mental illness. He suffers from paranoid schizophrenia. It played a direct role in his conduct in this case, and it is most certainly a central issue in sentencing ... There is evidence of enormous premeditation around the deaths of these two young men, and the very serious attempt on the life of Jacob. And there's also evidence of the fact that there were four other people on a list who were also marked for death as a result of the defendant's deeply held delusions that other people were trying to steal his powers, and that their actions in his delusional thinking would result in his death. I don't question that that's how he frames it in his own mind, but my function here is to protect society ... In terms of 19-2523 factors, there is no question he is mentally ill. He suffers from paranoid schizophrenia. He is profoundly ill. The degree of his functional impairment in terms of his delusional thinking is quite strong. Unfortunately – and I think it is unfortunate – his ability to plan intelligently and rationally is not likewise impaired. So considerable intelligence, considerable ability to plan and premeditate is unimpaired by the illness that he suffers from. The prognosis for improvement or rehabilitation is at best speculative ... Because of the seriousness of his illness and the extraordinary risk of danger that it presents for the public, treatment in his situation has to be in a structured institutional setting ... [The] inability of a person convicted of a crime to appreciate the wrongfulness of their conduct does not make that person less of a threat to society ... [It] is essential that he be provided treatment. (2011, at 14–16)

The district court judge's analysis points out the problem with laws that allow only a mens rea defense while disallowing the insanity defense. The defendant who has a mental illness but nevertheless is cool, calculating, and capable of forming an intention has no defense in an abolitionist state, despite their severe mental illness and delusional beliefs.

As the district court judge noted, Delling's behavior indicated premeditation and intent. He had written a list of victims. He drove great distances to get to them. He carried a gun. He succeeded in luring a victim out of his home by a ruse. He may have learned how to kill effectively from his failure to kill his first victim, so that he succeeded in killing his second and third victims. John Delling is an example of a person with a serious mental illness who is capable of forming intentions and making plans. He had the requisite mens rea. No disrespect to the district court judge, the "unfortunate" part of Delling's history is not that he could form an intention. Intention is almost universal in human behavior, even among those who have serious mental illness. The challenge to society is how to manage the people who have severe mental illness. Delling's sentence means that he spends the rest of his life confined "in a structured institutional setting," whether or not his illness goes into remission (as it did for John Hinckley, Jr.; see Chapter 22). In addition to spending his life in prison, Delling now carries the stigma of two felony convictions. In a jurisdiction with an insanity defense, he may have been acquitted by reason of insanity, in which case he would not have a record of convictions.

Delling appealed his conviction to the Supreme Court of the State of Idaho, arguing "that Idaho's abolition of the insanity defense is unconstitutional" (*Idaho v. Delling*, 2011, at 1). The Supreme Court of the State of Idaho disagreed, upheld Delling's convictions, and affirmed his sentence.

Delling appealed to the U.S. Supreme Court for a writ of certiorari (*Delling v. Idaho*, 2012). Only three justices – Breyer, Ginsburg, and Sotomayor – were willing to grant the writ, and it takes four justices to grant a writ of certiorari. Justice Breyer wrote in his dissenting opinion,

> The law has long recognized that criminal punishment is not appropriate for those who, by reason of insanity, cannot tell right from wrong. (slip opinion, at 1)

Breyer cited Blackstone's *Commentaries on the Laws of England* (1769), *Regina v. M'Naghten* (1843), and *Clark v. Arizona* (2006) in support of the insanity defense. He offered two hypotheticals that illustrate the important difference between moral incapacity and a mens rea defense:

> Idaho law would distinguish the following two cases. *Case One*: The defendant, due to insanity, believes that the victim is a wolf. He shoots and kills the victim. *Case Two*: The defendant, due to insanity, believes that a

wolf, a supernatural figure, has ordered him to kill the victim. In *Case One*, the defendant does not know he has killed a human being, and his insanity negates a mental element necessary to commit the crime ... In *Case Two*, the defendant has intentionally killed a victim whom he knows is a human being; he possesses the necessary *mens rea*. In both cases the defendant is unable, due to insanity, to appreciate the true quality of his act, and therefore unable to perceive that it is wrong. But in Idaho, the defendant in *Case One* could defend the charge by arguing that he lacked the *mens rea*, whereas the defendant in *Case Two* would not be able to raise a defense based on his mental illness. (slip opinion, at 2–3)

The defendants in both of Justice Breyer's hypotheticals have psychotic disorders that result in homicide. In a state that has the insanity defense, both defendants could plead not guilty by reason of insanity. In an abolitionist state like Idaho, however, only the defendant in Case One could argue that his mentality interfered with his behavior. The defendant in Case Two has no defense, even though he has a severe mental illness. Justice Breyer argued that this is not consistent with due process. He would have granted certiorari.

Observers like myself who were watching this process unfold were concerned when the Court denied certiorari to Delling (who showed strong evidence of mental illness and moral incapacity), but then granted certiorari to James Kahler, a defendant with weak evidence of mental illness.

KAHLER V. KANSAS (U.S. 2020)

The abolition of the insanity defense was approved by the U.S. Supreme Court on March 23, 2020, when they upheld the Kansas statute.

James Kraig Kahler (age 48) murdered his wife (age 44), mother-in-law (age 89), and two daughters (ages 16 and 18) on Thanksgiving weekend 2009. He did not kill his son (age 10), because he did not think his son was siding against him. He was found guilty and sentenced to death. The death penalty was affirmed by the Kansas Supreme Court. Kahler appealed to the U.S. Supreme Court, arguing that Kansas had violated his constitutional rights when they abolished their insanity defense.

As reviewed above, Kansas law permits mental health testimony only (1) to negate mens rea (by proving cognitive incapacity and lack of intention) and (2) for sentencing. Kansas, like the other abolitionist states, has a bifurcated process – a first hearing to determine whether the defendant committed a crime (which includes a finding of mens rea) and a second hearing to determine whether the defendant goes to prison or a hospital.

The oral arguments in *Kahler v. Kansas*: October 7, 2019

Anyone with access to the internet can call up the live audio recordings of the U.S. Supreme Court in their oral arguments. On October 7, 2019, the U.S. Supreme Court heard oral arguments in *Kahler v. Kansas*. Kahler was represented by Sarah Schrup, Associate Professor at Northwestern University and founder and director of Northwestern's Appellate Advocacy Center. The state of Kansas was represented by Toby Crouse, Solicitor General of Kansas, and by Elizabeth Prelogar of the U.S. Department of Justice.

Associate Justice Ruth Bader Ginsburg (who voted in the minority) asked Professor Schrup whether Kansas' bifurcated process violates due process (at 5). Professor Schrup answered that it does, because of the stigma that is attached to a criminal conviction (at 8). The bifurcated process means that a defendant is found guilty before the question of mental illness can be addressed. Furthermore, although the guilt and sentencing phases of bifurcated proceedings are separate, the reality is that jurors make up their minds about sentencing during the guilt phase of a trial (at 19).

Associate Justice Sonia Sotomayor (who also voted with the minority) echoed this concern about the stigmatizing effect of criminal conviction. She pointed out that traditionally in the United States evidence of mental illness is used not to determine sentencing but to decide acquittal by reason of insanity (at 33–34).

Associate Justice Brett Kavanaugh (who voted with the majority) said that a debate has been going on for decades, questioning whether a jury can understand the issues involved in the insanity defense (at 20). He questioned how it would violate due process "to take this away from the jury as a separate defense, put it into *mens rea* and then, as Justice Ginsburg points out, have it considered at sentencing?" (at 20). Justice Kavanaugh suggested that issues related to insanity can be folded

> into a *mens rea* defense as Kansas has done, in part because the concept as a separate defense was too confusing for jurors ... They have funneled it into *mens rea* and then said that it can be considered at sentencing as well. (at 21)

Professor Schrup countered that jurors *are capable* of making decisions about insanity and that jurors make judgments about "reasonableness" all the time (at 24).

Professor Schrup argued further that the Eighth Amendment "was intended as a check on sovereign power" and that "states are simply not free to legislatively redefine culpability in a way that is inconsistent with history and long-standing practice" (at 25).

Associate Justice Elena Kagan (who wrote the majority opinion) argued that the United States does not have to adhere to a law just because it is a time-honored "law of olden times." She pointed out two examples of laws that have become archaic, namely, laws regarding sodomy and the marital exception to rape (at 13).

Several questions posed by the majority appear to have been attempts to minimize the seriousness of the problem.

Associate Justice Samuel Alito, Jr. (who voted with the majority), asked Professor Schrup if every diagnosis in the DSM should be considered the basis for insanity. He said that all 60 million people in the United States who have mental disorders could argue in front of a jury that they lacked the capacity to know right from wrong (at 11).

Professor Schrup answered, "Justice Alito, they should be given the opportunity to at least try. This shouldn't be legislatively cut off at the knees" (at 12).

Associate Justice Neil Gorsuch (who voted with the majority) asked if the insanity defense should be made available to all homicides, all felonies, or even misdemeanors.

Professor Schrup answered that the insanity defense should be available in all crimes (at 23; to my understanding, her answer is consistent with current law).

Chief Justice John Roberts (who voted with the majority) said that "underlying a lot of the debate" was the slim evidence that James Kahler's crime was related to a mental illness (at 15).

Justice Roberts was correct in this, and in fact this is exactly what some commentators feared when the Court denied certiorari in *Delling* but then granted certiorari in *Kahler*. Had the Court granted certiorari in *Delling*, they would have had to deal with a much stronger set of facts regarding severe mental illness and moral incapacity. The reality of Delling's mental illness and his insanity would have been hard to ignore. *Kahler*, on the other hand, presented a weak set of facts.

Associate Justice Alito argued that the facts in *Kahler* do not suggest the presence of mental illness:

[This] is an intelligent man, and he sneaked up on the house where his wife and her mother and his children were staying. He killed his ex-wife. He killed ... her mother. He executed his two teen-age daughters. One of them is heard on the tape crying. He, nevertheless, shot her to death. He spared the son, because he didn't think the son was siding with the mother. And then he ran away and turned himself in the next day. Now, this is the stuff from which you're going to make a defense he didn't know what he was doing was morally wrong, much less he didn't know what he was doing was legally wrong? (at 18–19)

Indeed, the case for insanity in *Kahler* is weak. James Kahler did not have a psychosis. He had a major depressive disorder (at 16). Major depressive disorder is so common that it is sometimes referred to as "the common cold of mental health." The great majority of defendants who have major depressive disorder are fully responsible for their actions.

Some of the evidence that was put forward to indicate that Kahler had a mental illness was that he "was described by some as a tightwad who would, for example, borrow rather than purchase tools" and that he "thrived on self-importance, community prestige, and being perceived as having an ideal or perfect marriage" (at 15–16). These are not features that necessarily suggest the presence of mental illness.

Kahler's mental health expert stated that "he couldn't rule out short-term disassociation" (at 17). Apparently the defense expert did not have a fully developed opinion regarding dissociation.

The facts that Kahler approached the house surreptitiously and that he ran away indicated that he knew he was doing something wrong. Sparing his son indicates that he was not acting on blind impulse or without volitional control but was selectively exercising judgment and choosing his victims.

Associate Justice Kagan asked how often the insanity plea is applied.

Professor Schrup answered correctly that the insanity plea is sought in less than 1 percent of criminal cases and prevails in about 25 percent of those (at 22–24). This literature was reviewed by Melton et al. (2018, p. 200). This is an area where public perception differs sharply from reality. A survey by Pasewark et al. (1981) indicated that the public believes the insanity defense is raised in 43 percent of criminal cases. In actuality, the highest rates occurred in Montana and ranged from 5.5 to 8 percent between 1976 and 1979 (the year Montana abolished its insanity defense; Steadman et al. [1982]. See the discussion in Appendix M, explaining why Montana had such a high rate of insanity claims at that time.)

Toby Crouse, Solicitor General for the state of Kansas, argued that the insanity defense is "not deeply rooted. The right vs. wrong test is a relatively recent vintage. The historical basis for it started somewhere around the 1800s; and, therefore, it's not deeply rooted" (see Appendix M).

With all due respect to Solicitor General Crouse, his remarks are hard to justify. According to Moran (1985), the first recorded acquittal by reason of insanity under English common law occurred in 1505. According to Oxford University historian Nigel Walker (1968), 14th-century jurist Henry Spigurnel (?1263–1328) used a child's understanding of good and evil to judge the child's maturity. At that time a child at the age of 7 could be hanged or burned (Walker, 1968, p. 28). The earliest use of the "right-wrong test" among persons with mental illness is found in a handbook, *The Country Justice,* by Justice Michael Dalton, first published in 1618 (Walker, 1968, p. 40-41). Sir Matthew Hale (1609–1676) advocated using the "discretion to discern between good and evil" to evaluate children and the insane in his *Historia Placitorum Coronae* of 1736 (Walker, 1968, p. 41).

Professor Schrup said in rebuttal,

[It's] just not right to say that the right and wrong principle is a 19th Century invention. There is a wall of cases and authorities starting in the 1500s and continuing, uninterrupted, all the way through until 1843 when *M'Naghten* was formed. There's literally scores of cases, here and in England, applying the right and wrong principle.

Associate Justice Alito said, "There wasn't even any such thing as psychiatry in 1791 and it was in its infancy in 1868" (at 67).

With all respect to Associate Justice Alito, historian Edwin Shorter (1997) – using the phrase "birth of psychiatry" – placed this event in 1751, when Dr. William Battie established St. Luke's Hospital for Lunatics in London. Dr. Battie was a governor at Bethlem ("Bedlam") Royal Hospital and was so dissatisfied with their treatment of patients that he established his own hospital.

"Infancy" is the term used by historian Albert Deutsch (1949, p. 194), who placed the infancy of psychiatry in 1844 at the first meeting of the Association of Medical Superintendents (an organization that in 1921 would change its name to the American Psychiatric Association). In 1791 psychiatry was an "infant" who was 40 years old, and in 1868 was 117 years old.

Associate Justice Kavanaugh quoted Justice Thurgood Marshall's opinion in *Powell v. Texas* (1968), "Nothing could be less fruitful than for this Court to be impelled into finding some sort of insanity defense – or insanity test in constitutional terms" (at 1256; *Kahler* oral arguments, at 26). That is, the states must be allowed to define insanity as they see fit.

Professor Schrup countered that *Powell* did not involve abolishing the insanity defense. It may be up to each state to define their own version of insanity, but every state should have at least *some form* of insanity defense.

At issue in *Kahler* is the important question of the difference between insanity and mens rea. If cognitive incapacity were the only variant of insanity, then it might be possible to fold insanity into mens rea, but cognitive incapacity is not the only type of insanity. Cognitive incapacity, in fact, accounts for a small number of cases. Defendants who have moral and volitional incapacities far outnumber the defendants who have cognitive incapacity.

Associate Justice Sotomayor pointed out the "lunatics" of the fifteenth century who heard voices telling them what to do and had "no volition to fight back" (at 31). Some of these "lunatics" committed homicide. Yet they had mens rea:

> They absolutely know they're killing someone; they just have no ability to say no … You could know something is against the law and still not have the ability to conform your conduct. If I make a moral choice I could say … I don't wish to do it because of my morality. Could I physically stop myself? Yes. Someone who is insane can't even physically stop themselves. (at 53)

Associate Justice Stephen Breyer shared the fact that his law clerk had identified forty cases "going back to Bracton" that disagree with the Kansas law.

Breyer simplified (and, in my opinion, improved upon) his hypothetical of the wolf that he first put forth in *Delling v. Idaho* (see above):

> [Imagine] two defendants … The first defendant shoots and kills Smith. The second defendant shoots and kills Jones. The first defendant thinks that Smith is a dog. The second defendant knows it's a person but thinks the dog told him to do it. (2012, at 38)

Both defendants are "crazy," but Kansas law considers the first defendant not guilty and the second defendant guilty. Breyer's hypothetical goes to the heart of the matter. The defendant who thinks they are killing a dog does not know the nature of their action. They have not formed the intention to kill a human being. They lack cognitive capacity and they lack mens rea. They may be subject to civil commitment, but they are not guilty of a crime in Kansas. The second defendant in Breyer's hypothetical is equally disturbed, but *did form* an intention to kill a human being and therefore had the necessary mens rea and in the state of Kansas they can be convicted of a crime. In Breyer's view, both defendants should be considered insane. Breyer's hypothetical points out the problem with the Kansas statute, as it makes a false distinction between varieties of insanity that does not match the reality of mental illness.

The *Kahler* decision

Ultimately, the court declined to set a standard for the state of Kansas. In a 6–3 decision, the court agreed with Kansas that due process does not require an insanity defense.

Traditionally, the U.S. Supreme Court has been reluctant to tell states what they should or should not do with the insanity defense. In *Leland v. Oregon* (1952), *Powell v. Texas* (1968), and *Clark v. Arizona* (2006), the

Court declined to instruct the states regarding the insanity defense. The realities of crime, mental illness, and expert testimony are so complex that each state has its own set of experiences and each has developed its own set of procedures. As Justice Marshall wrote in *Powell*:

> [This] court has never articulated a general constitutional doctrine of *mens rea*. We cannot cast aside the centuries-long evolution of the collection of interlocking and overlapping concepts which the common law has utilized to assess the moral accountability of an individual for his antisocial deeds. The doctrines of *actus reus*, *mens rea*, insanity, mistake, justification, and duress have historically provided the tools for a constantly shifting adjustment of the tension between the evolving aims of the criminal law and changing religious, moral, philosophical, and medical views of the nature of man. This process of adjustment has always been thought to be the province of the States. (1968, at 1269)

Folding insanity into mens rea, as the abolitionist states have done, raises the question of whether having the capacity to form an intention (i.e., mens rea) is the legal equivalent of having the capacities to know the nature of your actions, to know right from wrong, and to conform your conduct to the right. Justices Breyer, Ginsburg, and Sotomayor argued that it is not.

Associate Justice Kagan, who wrote the majority opinion, pointed out that the question of mens rea vs. moral incapacity has been around for almost 300 years in cases like *Rex v. Arnold* (1724; see Chapter 20) and *Rex v. Bellingham* (1812; see Appendix H). Regarding defendants Arnold and Bellingham, the English courts may have considered their capacity to understand the wrongfulness of their actions (i.e., their moral capacity), but both men clearly had the intent to kill. This would not be unusual, as almost all human behavior is done with intention, even among people with the most severe mental illness (for a rare exception, consider the question of automatism, discussed in Chapter 8).

Associate Justice Kagan neglects to mention that *Arnold* (see Chapter 20) was decided at a time when insanity acquittees were generally sent home to their families. *Arnold* was decided seventy-six years before *Rex v. Hadfield* (1800) and the construction of the first hospital ward for the criminally insane in England. The *Arnold* court had important, practical reasons for finding him guilty and sane – reasons that would disappear in the next century.

Associate Justice Kagan also neglects to mention that Bellingham was executed a mere seven days after he shot and killed the Prime Minister, in a whirlwind miscarriage of justice, lacking in due process, which was recognized as an embarrassment to the English justice system (see Appendix H).

Regarding the principle of moral incapacity, Justice Breyer wrote in his dissent, "This principle remained embedded in the law even as social mores shifted and medical understandings of mental illness evolved" (at 4)

If James Kahler had committed these murders in any of the forty-eight jurisdictions that have the insanity defense, he could have argued (depending on the jurisdiction) (1) that mental illness had interfered with his capacity to know what he was doing (i.e., cognitive incapacity), (2) that mental illness had interfered with his capacity to know right from wrong (moral incapacity), (3) that mental illness had interfered with his capacity to conform his conduct to the requirements of the law (volitional incapacity), or (4) that his crime had been the product of mental illness (the "product test"). Kansas law allows consideration only of whether his mental illness interfered with his capacity to form an intention. This is a very low hurdle, and not a test of insanity but of mens rea. The majority of the U.S. Supreme Court found this to be sufficient. The *Kahler* court found the Kansas law to be constitutional, and five centuries of Western jurisprudence regarding the insanity defense came to an end.

REFERENCES

Blackstone, W. (1765–1769/2016). *Commentaries on the laws of England. 4 volumes.* Oxford: Clarendon Press.

Boone, R. (April 11, 2007). Classmate slaying suspect called erratic. *Washington Post.* www.washingtonpost.com/wp-dyn/content/article/2007/04/11/AR2007041101994.html.

Clark v. Arizona, 548 U.S. 735 (2006).

Delling v. Idaho, 568 U.S. 1038 (2012) cert. denied.

Deutsch, A. (1949). *The mentally ill in America: A history of their care and treatment from colonial times. Second edition.* New York: Columbia University Press.

Finger v. State, 117 Nev. 548, 29 P.3d 66 (Nevada, 2001).

Idaho v. Delling, Supreme Court of the State of Idaho, 2011 Opinion No. 128.

Kahler v. Kansas, 589 U.S. ____, 140 S. Ct. 1021 (2020).

Leland v. Oregon, 343 U.S. 790 (1952).

Melton, G. B., Petrila, J., Poythress, N. G., Slobogin, C., Otto, R. K., Mossman, D., & Condie, L. O. (2018). *Psychological evaluations for the courts: A handbook for mental health professionals and lawyers. Fourth edition.* New York: Guilford Press.

Moran, R. (1985). The origin of insanity as a special verdict: The trial for treason of James Hadfield (1800). *Law & Society Review, 19*(3), 487–519. doi:10.2307/3053574.

Pasewark, R. A., Seidenzahl, D., & Pantle, M. A. (1981). Opinions about the insanity plea. *Journal of Forensic Psychiatry, 8*(1), 63–72. NCJ Number 79482.

Powell v. Texas, 392 U.S. 514, 88 S.Ct. 2145, 20 L.Ed.2d 1254 (1968).

Regina v. M'Naghten, 10 Clark & Fin. 200, 8 Eng. Rep. 718 (1843).

Rex v. Arnold, 16 Howell's State Trials, 765 (1724).

Rex v. Bellingham. O.B.S.P. case 433 (1812).

Rex v. Hadfield, 27 Howell's State Trials, 1281 (1800).

Shorter, E. (1997). *A history of psychiatry: From the era of the asylum to the age of Prozac*. Hoboken, NJ: Wiley.

Sinclair v. State, 161 Miss. 142, 132 So. 581 (Mississippi, 1931).

State v. Lange, 168 La. 958, 123 So. 639 (Louisiana, 1929).

State v. Strasburg, 60 Wash. 106, 110 P. 1020 (Washington, 1910).

Steadman, H. J., Monahan, J., Hartstone, E., Davis, S. K., & Robbins, P. C. (1982). Mentally disordered offenders: A national survey of patients and facilities. *Law and Human Behavior*, 6(1), 31–38. doi:10.1007/BF01049311.

Walker, N. (1968). *Crime and insanity in England. Volume 1: The historical perspective*. Edinburgh: University of Edinburgh Press.

Part V

Mental disorders and crime

This book reviews the relationships between mental disorders and crime, using the most recent version of the diagnostic system developed by the American Psychiatric Association (2022). Part V goes through this system in sequence as they are presented in the DSM-5-TR. The code numbers in parentheses by each diagnosis are the numbers that are used in the DSM-5-TR and are taken from the ICD-10-CM (the clinical modification of the International Classification of Diseases, adopted by the World Health Organization in 2015).

The DSMs published by the American Psychiatric Association have a long and substantial history. The first version was published in 1952. Since then there have been four editions, one revision (R), and two text revisions (TRs). The publication history of the DSM is as follows:

- DSM-I: 1952
- DSM-II: 1968
- DSM-III: 1980
- DSM-III-R: 1987
- DSM-IV: 1994
- DSM-IV-TR: 2000
- DSM-5: 2013
- DSM-5-TR: 2022.

Of the many changes that took place over these seven decades, the major shift took place between the DSM-II and DSM-III. DSM-I and DSM-II lacked specific criteria for each entity and they were criticized as lacking reliability. The DSM-III therefore introduced a set of specific criteria for each diagnostic entity, and reliability improved.

The relationship between the two fields of mental health and criminal justice includes the manner in which information about these disorders is used by the courts. This includes, for example, determinations regarding insanity and competency to stand trial. These psycholegal relationships are

DOI: 10.4324/9781003385028-29

addressed in Part V. A number of my own cases are presented, including illustrative cases of bipolar, dissociative, and neurocognitive disorders.

REFERENCES

American Psychiatric Association. (2022). *Diagnostic and Statistical Manual of Mental Disorders. Fifth edition. Text revision.* Washington, D.C.: American Psychiatric Association.

World Health Organization. (2015). *International Classification of Diseases. Tenth revision. Clinical modification. (ICD-10-CM.)* https://icd10cmtool.cdc.gov/?fy=FY2023.

25   Neurodevelopmental disorders

Neurodevelopmental disorders include intellectual developmental disorder (IDD) and autism spectrum disorders (ASD). Persons who have these disorders typically show poor judgment, concrete thinking, and low levels of interpersonal skill. They may lack the flexibility and adaptability that would demonstrate sufficient capacities for initiative and volition. When they enter the justice system, these features may interfere with their competency to stand trial and criminal responsibility.

INTELLECTUAL DEVELOPMENTAL DISORDER (IDD)

Research suggests that persons who have IDD may be over-represented in the criminal justice system (McCarthy et al., 2016). They may be at greater risk of violent offending, sexual offending, and sexual victimization (Fogden et al. 2016).

Persons who have IDD lack judgment and impulse control. They are easily persuaded by others to do things that go against their better interests, like participating in sexual activity or crime. Several reasons for this can be identified. Persons who have IDD typically:

1 *Lack the intellectual skills necessary for sound judgment.* They may lack the ability to predict the consequences of behavior. They may lack the memory skills needed to remember past events and incorporate those memories into their current decision-making processes. When a malefactor suggests to them that they participate in a crime, they may not perceive that this is likely to get them into trouble, even if it is something that has gotten them into trouble in the past.
2 *Lack employment and leisure interests.* This gives them a lot of unoccupied time with which to get into trouble.
3 *Do not have a well-articulated plan for their future.* When a malefactor suggests a crime, it does not conflict with a plan of their own, because they do not have one. People who have a plan for their lives – perhaps

DOI: 10.4324/9781003385028-30

involving school, career, and family – are more likely to resist antisocial influences, because time spent in the justice system is not consistent with their life plan. When no such plan exists, individuals are more easily persuaded to participate in crime.

4 *Are isolated and socially needy.* When someone pretends to be their friend, they may be seduced into following their suggestions.

In my own practice, I have observed two scenarios that repeatedly get people with IDD into trouble with the law.

The first pattern is known as the "fall guy." In practice it works like this. Crews that are engaged in crimes – such as robberies and burglaries – seek out people with IDD in their neighborhoods and extended families and then "groom" them to make them useful during the commission of crimes. When the crew "cases" the scene of their next crime, they plan an escape route for themselves and also take note of the avenue that the police are most likely to use, if the police arrive during the commission of the crime. The person with IDD is given something incriminating to hold – like a weapon, a drug, or a piece of stolen merchandise – and is placed in a location where the police are likely to see them. The more intelligent members of the crew know that the police are less likely to continue searching for suspects once they have already made an arrest. (The de facto role of the police is to apprehend defendants who can be linked to particular crimes.) In this way, persons who have IDD are held responsible for the crimes of their more intelligent associates, and they are processed into our jails, courts, and prisons.

A second pattern that frequently gets persons with IDD into trouble with the law is related to their sexual behavior. Persons who have IDD are deficient in their intellectual abilities and adaptive behaviors, but typically they have normal sex drives. What they lack is sound judgment, social skills, impulse control, and the level of desirability that would attract appropriate sex partners. They tend to be socially isolated. Potential partners do not find them attractive or seek them out. Persons who have IDD may get into trouble by having sexual relations with children, the elderly, or other people with disabilities. While their actions may appear to be predatory, often they are related to their social isolation, impulsivity, lack of judgment, poor social skills, and low desirability.

IDD and competency to stand trial

Intellectual limitations and lack of communication skills may render defendants who have IDD incompetent to stand trial (IST; see Chapter 10). Almost 60 percent of defendants with IDD have been found incompetent to stand trial (Everington & Dunn, 1995). IDD is a lifelong condition, and defendants may be unlikely to achieve competency (Mossman, 2007). However, Samuel and Michals (2011) found that 33 to 50 percent of defendants with IDD ultimately attained competency through a competency restoration program.

Another competency restoration program ("the Slater Method") that was designed specifically for defendants who have low levels of intelligence was field-tested at the Eleanor Slater Hospital in Cranston, Rhode Island. Results with subjects who had either IDD or borderline intellectual functioning (BIF) were encouraging, in that 61.1 percent attained competency, which compared favorably with the results of traditional treatment (16.7 percent; Wall & Christopher, 2012).

AUTISM SPECTRUM DISORDER (ASD; F84.0)

Public attention was drawn to a possible link between violence and autism spectrum disorder (ASD) in 2012, when Adam Lanza, a 20-year-old man with ASD, shot and killed twenty-six people at the Sandy Hook Elementary School in Newtown, Connecticut. Similar events involving young men with ASD occurred at Isla Vista, California, in 2014, when Elliot Rodger (age 22) killed six people and wounded fourteen others, and at Umpqua Community College in Roseburg, Oregon, in 2015, when Chris Harper-Mercer (age 26) shot and killed nine people and wounded nine others. Questions regarding a possible link between ASD and crime deserve careful study.

The literature on crime and ASD consists of case reports and group studies (often with small numbers of subjects) that have employed various strategies, including (a) identifying the frequency with which persons who have ASD commit crimes and (b) identifying the prevalence of ASD in offender populations to see if persons with ASD are over-represented in these populations. Several review articles have been published.

Rutten et al. (2017) systematically reviewed the literature and identified twelve studies, five of which reported the prevalence of delinquency in people who have ASD and seven of which reported the prevalence of ASD in forensic populations. The five studies (N = 1,672) reporting on the prevalence of delinquency in persons with ASD found this to be lower than the rate of delinquency in the general population, although a Danish study (Mouridsen et al., 2008; N = 313) found a tendency to commit arson. In the seven studies (N = 4,107) of offender populations, the prevalence of ASD was found to be rather high, which was not surprising given that some of these were clinical samples, including residents of a forensic hospital and defendants who were referred for mental health evaluations. The authors were not able to conclude that individuals with ASD are overly represented in the criminal justice system.

Del Pozzo et al. (2018) found mixed results in studies of crimes and ASD, and summarized:

> when the quality and inclusiveness of the evidence, and nature of samples are taken into consideration, the studies showing a link between ASD and violent behavior are fewer and, to our minds, less convincing than those demonstrating no link. (p. 55)

Melvin et al. (2020) summarized as follows:

> The proposed proclivity for criminal behaviours suggested in the early literature on Autism Spectrum Disorders (ASD) has not been confirmed.

Crimes committed by persons with ASD have included arson (e.g., Everall & Lecouteur, 1990; Radley & Shaherbano, 2011); threats (Faccini, 2010); sex offenses (e.g., Higgs & Carter, 2015; Kohn et al., 1998; Murphy, 2010); assault (e.g., Bjørkly, 2009; Woodbury-Smith et al., 2006); and homicide (e.g., Mukaddes & Topcu, 2006; Sabuncuoglu et al., 2015). The offense committed most frequently by persons with ASD is physical assault (Del Pozzo et al., 2018). Physical assaults by persons with ASD are equally likely to occur against strangers or non-strangers like family members or caregivers, and equally likely to occur against one individual or against a group of people at the same time (Bjørkly, 2009).

Most people who have ASD are law-abiding citizens. In fact, they may have an overactive sense of right and wrong that makes them unlikely to commit crimes (Tantam, 2000). Large-sample surveys, in fact, have found that people with ASD are less likely to break the law than matched counterparts (Howlin, 2004; Woodbury-Smith et al., 2006).

In the search for a possible relationship between ASD and crime, significant third variables must be identified and their contribution to the problem must be appreciated. Van Buitenen et al. (2021) reported a Dutch sample of offenders with ASD (N = 394) and found high levels of features known to be associated with violence, including high levels of suggestibility, high comorbidity with substance use disorders (39.8 percent), high comorbidity with psychotic disorders (31.7 percent), and a history of childhood trauma including victimization. Those authors suggested that it was these features and not ASD itself that contributed to their crimes. They wrote,

> One could argue that violent offending in individuals with ASD is a result of the known risk associated with their comorbid disorders rather than their ASD. (p. 186)

Similarly, Kawakami et al. (2012) found a history of childhood adversity associated with criminal behavior among individuals with ASD. Del Pozzo et al. (2018) wrote:

> We conclude that, on the whole, while research findings are mixed, they lend support to the assertion that ASD does not cause violence, and indicate that when violent behavior occurs in people with ASD, it is the result of third variables including poor parental control, family environment, criminality, bullying, or psychiatric comorbidity (e.g., psychosis), that go undetected or untreated ... We conclude that while there are particular circumstances under which the risk for violent behavior is increased in people with ASD, ASD per se are not a significant risk factor for violent behavior. (p. 53)

Indeed, high levels of comorbidity have been identified. A Swedish study of 9-year-old children found that comorbidity is the rule rather the exception. Only 4 percent did not have a co-occurring psychiatric disorder, and more than half (50.3 percent) had four or more coexisting psychiatric disorders (Lundström et al., 2014).

While there may be no overall relationship between ASD and crime, certain features of ASD have been identified that may be relevant in the evaluation of individuals who have committed crimes. For example, persons with ASD:

- may have deficits in empathy that contribute to antisocial behavior (Chen et al., 2003; Katz & Zemishlany, 2006; Kristiansson & Sörman, 2008; Murrie et al., 2002); for example, Murrie et al. (2002) reported a series of four violent sex offenders with ASD who were "genuinely unaware of the harm they caused their victims" (p. 66)
- may have limited theory of mind, which can cause them to behave impulsively with no regard for the thoughts or feelings of others, to miss or misinterpret social or emotional cues, and to fail to appreciate the implications their own behavior has regarding others (Frith, 1991; Hippler et al., 2010; Søndenaa et al., 2014)
- may have deficits in emotional regulation and moral reasoning that lead to violence (Lerner et al., 2012)
- may lack communication skills and have interpersonal difficulties that get them into trouble with the law (Barry-Walsh & Mullen, 2004)
- may have interests and behaviors that are unusual, repetitive, circumscribed, and may be sexual and illegal (Aral et al., 2018; Faccini, 2010;

Woodbury-Smith et al., 2010) – these features (plus a low level of social skill) are common among child pornographers, and in fact ASD has been used as a defense in the trials of several child pornographers (Steel, 2016)

- may misinterpret the intentions, feelings, and social cues of others, which may lead to aggression and unwanted sexual advances (Cooper et al., 1993; 't Hart-Kerkhoff et al., 2009; Kohn et al., 1998)
- may be overly sensitive and have difficulty recognizing facial cues, which has been implicated in cases of homicide (Schwartz-Watts, 2005)
- may have difficulty coping with change and stress, which can trigger impulsive, uncontrolled conduct (Hippler et al., 2010)
- may lack coping skills and be prone to rumination, which can increase risk of interpersonal violence (Murphy, 2013)
- may be highly suggestible and overly compliant when other people suggest criminal activity (van Buitenen et al., 2021; Del Pozzo et al., 2018; Im, 2016; Långström et al., 2009; Mouridsen, 2012)
- may have social impairments, restricted interests, difficulty perceiving non-verbal cues, and ritualistic behaviors that can lead to frustration, anxiety, confusion, and loss of control and may be associated with increased risk of violence (Bjørkly, 2002; Howlin, 1998).

Im (2016) hypothesized:

Individuals with ASD may possess sensitized prefrontal-cortical-limbic networks that are overloaded in the face of trauma, leading to unchecked limbic output that produces violent behavior, and/or cognitive dysfunction (including deficits in theory of mind, central coherence, and executive function) that impacts trauma processing in ways that portend violence. (p. 184)

Im believed that, while his hypothesis has "case-based support," further study is needed to confirm that trauma increases risk of violence among persons with ASD and to explore the underlying mechanisms.

Over 1,000 genes have been identified that contribute to ASD (David et al., 2016; Lichtenstein et al., 2010). Twin studies have demonstrated significant genetic overlap with disorders that are believed to contribute to the risk of violence, namely, attention-deficit hyperactivity disorder (ADHD), conduct disorder (CD), and schizophrenia (Carroll & Owen, 2009; Craddock & Owen, 2010; Kerekes et al., 2014; Lichtenstein et al., 2010; Lundström et al., 2014; Ronald et al., 2008). In a large archival study of 5,739 individuals with ASD, it appeared at first as if ASD was associated with risk of violence (relative risk = 1.39), but once ADHD and CD were controlled statistically, the relative risk of violence among persons with ASD fell significantly to 0.85 (Heeramun et al., 2017).

Late diagnosis and lack of supervision have been implicated in crimes that might have been prevented (Chesterman & Rutter, 1993; Dein & Woodbury-Smith, 2010; Milton et al., 2002; Murphy, 2010; Tiffin et al., 2007), suggesting that early identification and proper supervision may help to prevent crime.

Certain features of ASD may raise important questions about a defendant's competency to stand trial and criminal responsibility (Mayes, 2003). Defendants who have ASD may lack the capacity to cooperate with an attorney, in which case they may be incompetent to stand trial (see Chapter 10). Cognitive limitations also may render them incompetent to stand trial. Many individuals with ASD also have IDD (American Psychiatric Association, 2022, p. 67). The UCLA-University of Utah study of 483 Utah residents with ASD found that 66 percent scored below 70 on standardized IQ tests (Ritvo et al., 1989).

Persons with ASD may show deficits in moral reasoning, which raises questions about their criminal responsibility (Grant et al., 2018; Katz & Zemishlany, 2006; Silva & Haskins, 2006). Their inability to predict the social outcomes of their behavior may raise questions about mens rea, specifically their capacity to do things *purposely* and *knowingly*.

Persons with ASD who are incarcerated are likely to have significant difficulty adjusting to prison life (Robertson & McGillivray, 2015; Vinter et al., 2020) and difficulty responding to treatment. Higgs and Carter (2015) pointed out limitations of traditional therapy for persons with ASD:

> group based interventions require participants to carry out introspection, sharing personal information and interacting in a group, all activities that an individual with ASD will invariably find challenging. (p. 112)

Melvin et al. (2020) called sex offenders with ASD "the hardest group to treat, that changes the least." A number of authors have observed that sex offenders with ASD are difficult to treat because of cognitive rigidity, narrow interests, social naïveté, weak central coherence, limited perspective-taking, egocentricity, sexual deviance, antisocial tendencies, and deficits in empathy, communication, and social interaction. Their thoughts may perseverate on deviant fantasies. Narrow interests may include excessive masturbation and paraphilias (Barry-Walsh & Mullen, 2004; Dein & Woodbury-Smith, 2010; Higgs & Carter, 2015; Melvin et al., 2020; Milton et al., 2002; Murphy, 2010).

For further information on contemporary viewpoints on ASD and crime, readers are referred to the book edited by Tyler and Sheeran (2022).

ATTENTION-DEFICIT/HYPERACTIVITY DISORDER (ADHD)

The links between ADHD, CD, and delinquency in juveniles are well established (Biederman et al., 2008; Foley et al., 1996; Satterfield & Schell, 1997).

Comorbidities with other disorders are high. About one fourth of the children and adolescents who have the combined presentation (i.e., both attention-deficit and hyperactivity) also have CD. Most children and adolescents who have disruptive mood regulation disorder also meet the diagnostic criteria for ADHD. Personality disorders, substance use disorders, and intermittent explosive disorder also are more common among persons who have ADHD (American Psychiatric Association, 2022, p. 75).

In a review of eighteen prospective studies, with a total of 5,501 subjects, Storebø and Simonsen (2016) found that ADHD – with and without comorbid CD – was a strong predictor of antisocial personality disorder. Thirteen cross-sectional/retrospective studies with a total of 2,451 subjects suggested that comorbid ADHD and CD may be a subtype of ADHD, and that impulsivity and callous/unemotional traits in these subjects predict the development of antisocial personality disorder.

The presence of ADHD is not likely to contribute to a judicial finding of insanity or incompetency to stand trial. However, it may contribute to assessments of impulse control, predictions of recidivism, and determinations of likelihood of rehabilitation, which are important components of juvenile sentencing (see Chapter 15) and transfer of juveniles to adult court (see Chapter 11).

REFERENCES

American Psychiatric Association. (2022). *Diagnostic and Statistical Manual of Mental Disorders. Fifth edition. Text revision.* Washington, D.C.: American Psychiatric Association.

Aral, A., Nur Say, G., & Usta, M. B. (2018). Distinguishing circumscribed behavior in an adolescent with Asperger syndrome from a pedophilic act: A case report. *Journal of Psychiatry and Neurological Studies, 31*, 102–106. doi:10.5350/dajpn2018310111.

Barry-Walsh, J. B., & Mullen, P. E. (2004). Forensic aspects of Asperger's syndrome. *Journal of Forensic Psychiatry & Psychology, 15*(1), 96–107. doi:10.1080/14789940310001638628.a.

Biederman, J., Petty, C. R., Dolan, C., Hughes, S., Mick, E., Monuteaux, M. C., & Faraone, S. V. (2008). The long-term longitudinal course of oppositional defiant disorder and conduct disorder in ADHD boys: Findings from a controlled 10-year prospective longitudinal follow-up study. *Psychological Medicine, 38*(7), 1027–1036. doi:10.1017/S0033291707002668.

Bjørkly, S. (2002). Psychotic symptoms and violence toward others – a literature review of some preliminary findings: Part 1. Delusions. *Aggression and Violent Behavior, 7*(6), 617–631. doi:10.1016/S1359-1789(01)00049-0.

Bjørkly, S. (2009). Risk and dynamics of violence in Asperger's syndrome: A systematic review of the literature. *Aggression and Violent Behavior*, 14(5), 306–312. doi:10.1016/j.avb.2009.04.003.

Carroll, L. S., & Owen, M. J. (2009). Genetic overlap between autism, schizophrenia and bipolar disorder. *Genome Medicine*, 1(10), 102. doi:10.1186/gm102.

Chen, P. S., Chen, S. J., Yang, Y. K., Yeh, T. L., Chen, C. C., & Lo, H. Y. (2003). Asperger's disorder: A case report of repeated stealing and the collecting behaviours of an adolescent patient. *Acta Psychiatrica Scandinavica*, 107(1), 73–76. doi:10.1034/j.1600-0447.2003.01354.x.

Chesterman, P., & Rutter, S. C. (1993). Case report: Asperger's syndrome and sexual offending. *Journal of Forensic Psychiatry*, 4, 555–562. doi:10.1080/095 85189308408222.

Cooper, S. A., Mohamed, W. N., Collacott, R.A. (1993). Possible Asperger's syndrome in a mentally handicapped transvestite offender. *Journal of Intellectual Disability Research*, 37(2), 189–194. doi:10.1111/j.1365-2788. 1993.tb00587.x.

Craddock, N., & Owen, M. J. (2010). The Kraepelinian dichotomy – going, going … but still not gone. *British Journal of Psychiatry*, 196(2), 92–95. doi:10.1192/ bjp.bp.109.073429.

David, M. M., Enard, D., Ozturk, A., Daniels, J., Jung, J.-Y., Diaz-Beltran, L., & Wall, D. P. (2016). Comorbid analysis of genes associated with autism spectrum disorders reveals differential evolutionary constraints. *PLoS one*, 11(7), e0157937. doi:10.1371/journal.pone.0157937.

Dein, K., & Woodbury-Smith, L. (2010). Asperger syndrome and criminal behaviour. *Advances in Psychiatric Treatment*, 16, 112–131. doi:10.1192/APT.BP. 107.005082.

Del Pozzo, J., Roché, M. W., & Silverstein, S. M. (2018). Violent behavior in autism spectrum disorders: Who's at risk? *Aggression and Violent Behavior*, 39, 53–60. doi:10.1016/j.avb.2018.01.007.

Everall, I. P., & Lecouteur, A. (1990). Firesetting in an adolescent boy with Asperger's syndrome. *British Journal of Psychiatry*, 157(2), 284–287. doi:10. 1192/bjp.157.2.284.

Everington, C., & Dunn, C. (1995). A second validation study of the Competence Assessment for Standing Trial for Defendants with Mental Retardation (CAST-MR). *Criminal Justice and Behavior*, 22(1), 44–59. doi:10.1177/0093854895 022001004.

Faccini, L. (2010). The man who howled wolf: Diagnostic and treatment considerations for a person with ASD and impersonal repetitive fire, bomb and presidential threats. *American Journal of Forensic Psychiatry*, 31(4), 47–68.

Fogden, B. C., Thomas, S. D. M., Daffern, M., & Ogloff, J. R. P. (2016). Crime and victimisation in people with intellectual disability: A case linkage study. *BMC Psychiatry*, 16(170), 1–9. doi:10.1186/s12888-016-0869-7.

Foley, H. A., Carlton, C. O., & Howell, R. J. (1996). The relationship of attention deficit hyperactivity disorder and conduct disorder to juvenile delinquency: Legal implications. *Bulletin of the American Academy of Psychiatry and the Law*, 24(3), 333–345. PMID: 8889133.

Frith, U. (1991). Asperger and his syndrome. In U. Frith (Ed.). *Autism and Asperger syndrome* (pp. 1–36). Cambridge: Cambridge University Press.

Grant, T., Furlano, R., Hall, L., & Kelley, E. (2018). Criminal responsibility in autism spectrum disorder: A critical review examining empathy and moral reasoning. *Canadian Psychology, 59*(1), 65–75. doi:10.1037/cap0000124.

't Hart-Kerkhoff, L. A., Jansen, L. M., Doreleijers, T. A., Vermeiren, R., Minderaa, R. B., & Hartman, C. A. (2009). Autism spectrum disorder symptoms in juvenile suspects of sex offenses. *Journal of Clinical Psychiatry, 70*(2), 266–272. doi:10.4088/jcp.08m04635.

Heeramun, R., Magnusson, C., Gumpert, C. H., Granath, S., Lundberg, M., Dalman, C., & Rai, D. (2017). Autism and convictions for violent crimes: Population-based cohort study in Sweden. *Journal of the American Academy of Child and Adolescent Psychiatry, 56*(6), 491–497. doi:10.1016/j.jaac.2017.03.011.

Higgs, T., & Carter, A. J. (2015). Autism spectrum disorder and sexual offending: Responsivity in forensic interventions. *Aggression and Violent Behavior, 22*, 112–119. doi:10.1016/j.avb.2015.04.003.

Hippler, K., Viding, E., Klicpera, C., & Happé, F. (2010). Brief report: No increase in criminal convictions in Hans Asperger's original cohort. *Journal of Autism and Developmental Disorders, 40*(6), 774–780. doi:10.1007/s10803-009-0917-y.

Howlin, P. (1998). Practitioner review: Psychological and educational treatments for autism. *Journal of Child Psychology and Psychiatry, 39*(3), 307–322. PMID: 9670087.

Howlin, P. (2004). Psychiatric disturbances in adulthood. In P. Howlin (Ed.). *Autism and Asperger syndrome: Preparing for adulthood* (pp. 271–299). London: Routledge.

Im, D. S. (2016). Trauma as a contributor to violence in autism spectrum disorder. *Journal of the American Academy of Psychiatry and the Law, 44*(2), 184–192. PMID: 27236173.

Katz, N., & Zemishlany, Z. (2006). Criminal responsibility in Asperger's syndrome. *Israeli Journal of Psychiatry and Related Sciences, 43*(3), 166–173. PMID: 17294982.

Kawakami, C., Ohnishi, M., Sugiyama, T., Someki, F., Nakamura, K., & Tsujii, M. (2012). The risk factors for criminal behaviour in high-functioning autism spectrum disorders (HFASDs): A comparison of childhood adversities between individuals with HFASDs who exhibit criminal behaviour and those with HFASD and no criminal histories. *Research in Autism Spectrum Disorders, 6*(2), 949–957. doi:10.1016/j.rasd.2011.12.005.

Kerekes, N., Lundström, S., Chang, Z., Tajnia, A., Jern, P., Lichtenstein, P., Nilsson, T., & Anckarsäter, H. (2014). Oppositional defiant- and conduct disorder-like problems: neurodevelopmental predictors and genetic background in boys and girls, in a nationwide twin study. *PeerJ, 2*, e359. doi:10.7717/peerj.359.

Kohn, Y., Fahum, T., Ratzoni, G., & Apter, A. (1998). Aggression and sexual offense in Asperger's syndrome. *Israeli Journal of Psychiatry and Related Sciences, 35*(4), 293–299.

Kristiansson, M., & Sörman, K. (2008). Autism spectrum disorders – legal and forensic psychiatric aspects and reflections. *Clinical Neuropsychiatry*, 5(1), 55–61. Available at www.clinicalneuropsychiatry.org/download/no-1-february-2008-autism-spectrum-disorders-legal-and-forensic-psychiatric-aspects-and-reflections/.

Långström, N., Grann, M., Ruchkin, V., Sjöstedt, G., & Fazel, S. (2009). Risk factors for violent offending in autism spectrum disorder: A national study of hospitalized individuals. *Journal of Interpersonal Violence*, 24(8), 1358–1370. doi:10.1177/0886260508322195.

Lerner, M., Haque, O., Northrup, E., Lawer, L., & Bursztajin, H. (2012). Emerging perspectives on adolescents and young adults with high functioning autism spectrum disorders, violence and criminal law. *Journal of the American Academy of Psychiatry and Law*, 40(2), 177–190. PMID: 22635288.

Lichtenstein, P., Carlstrom, E., Rastam, M., Gillberg, C., & Anckarsatar, H. (2010). The genetics of autism spectrum disorders and related neuropsychiatric disorders in childhood. *American Journal of Psychiatry*, 167(11), 1357–1363. doi:10.1176/appi.ajp.2010.10020223.

Lundström, S., Reichenberg, A., Melke, J., Rastam, M., Kerekes, N., Lichtenstein, P., Gillberg, C., & Anckrasater, H. (2014). Autism spectrum disorders and coexisting disorders in a nationwide Swedish twin study. *Journal of Child Psychology and Psychiatry*, 56(6), 702–710. doi:10.1111/jcpp.12329.

Mayes, T. (2003). Persons with autism and criminal justice: Core concepts and leading cases. *Journal of Positive Behavioral Interventions*, 5(2), 92–100. doi:10.1177/10983007030050020401.

McCarthy, J., Chaplin, E., Underwood, L., Forrester, A., Hayward, H., Sabet, J., Young, S., Asherson, P., Mills, R., & Murphy, D. (2016). Characteristics of prisoners with neurodevelopmental disorders and difficulties. *Journal of Intellectual Disability Research*, 60(3), 201–206. doi:10.1111/jir.12237.

Melvin, C. L., Langdon, P. E., & Murphy, G. H. (2020). "They're the hardest group to treat, that changes the least." Adapted sex offender treatment programmes for individuals with Autism Spectrum Disorders: Clinician views and experiences. *Research in Developmental Disabilities*, 105. doi:10.1016/j.ridd.2020.103721.

Milton, J., Duggan, C., Latham, A., Egan, V., & Tantam, D. (2002). Case history of co-morbid Asperger's syndrome and paraphilic behaviour. *Medicine, Science and the Law*, 42(3), 237–244. doi:10.1177/002580240204200308.

Mossman, D. (2007). Predicting restorability of incompetent criminal defendants. *Journal of the American Academy of Psychiatry and the Law*, 35(1), 34–43. Available at https://jaapl.org/content/jaapl/35/1/34.full.pdf.

Mouridsen, S. E. (2012). Current status of research on autism spectrum disorders and offending. *Research in Autism Spectrum Disorders*, 6(1), 79–86. doi:10.1016/j.rasd.2011.09.003.

Mouridsen, S. E., Rich, B., Isager, T., & Nedergaard, N. J. (2008). Pervasive developmental disorders and criminal behaviour: A case control study. *International Journal of Offender Therapy*, 52(2), 196–205. doi:10.1177/0306624X07302056.

Mukaddes, N. M., & Topcu, Z. (2006). Case report: Homicide by a 10-year-old girl with autistic disorder. *Journal of Autism and Developmental Disorders*, *36*(4), 471–474. doi:10.1007/s10803-006-0087-0.

Murphy, D. (2010). Extreme violence in a man with an autistic spectrum disorder: Assessment and treatment within high-security psychiatric care. *Journal of Forensic Psychiatry and Psychology*, *21*(3), 462–477. doi:10.1080/14789940903426885.

Murphy, D. (2013). Risk assessment of offenders with an autism spectrum disorder. *Journal of Intellectual Disabilities and Offending Behaviour*, *4*(1–2), 33–41. doi:10.1108/JIDOB-02-2013-0004.

Murrie, D. C., Warren, J. I., Kristiansson, M., & Dietz, P. E. (2002). Asperger's syndrome in forensic settings. *International Journal of Forensic Mental Health*, *1*, 59–70. doi:10.1080/14999013.2002.10471161.

Radley J., & Shaherbano, Z. (2011). Asperger syndrome and arson: A case study. *Advances in Mental Health & Intellectual Disabilities*, *5*, 32–36. doi:10.1108/20441281111187171.

Ritvo, E. R., Freeman, B. J., Pingree, C., Mason-Brothers, A., Jorde, L., Jenson, W. R., McMahon, W. M., Petersen, P. B., Mo, A., & Ritvo, A. (1989). The UCLA-University of Utah epidemiologic survey of autism: Prevalence. *American Journal of Psychiatry*, *146*(2), 194–199. doi:10.1176/ajp.146.2.194.

Robertson, C. E., & McGillivray, J. A. (2015). Autism behind bars: A review of the research literature and discussion of key issues. *Journal of Forensic Psychiatry and Psychology*, *26*(6), 719–736. doi:10.1080/14789949.2015.1062994.

Ronald, A., Simonoff, E., Kuntsi, J., Asherson, P., & Plomin, R. (2008). Evidence for overlapping genetic influences on autistic and ADHD behaviours in a community twin sample. *Journal of Child Psychology and Psychiatry, and Allied Disciplines*, *49*(5), 535–542. doi:10.1111/j.1469-7610.2007.01857.x.

Rutten, A. X., Vermeiren, R. R. J. M., & Nieuwenhuizen, C. V. (2017). Autism in adult and juvenile delinquents: A literature review. *Child and Adolescent Psychiatry and Mental Health*, *11*, 45–57. doi:10.1186/s13034-017-0181-4.

Sabuncuoglu, O., Irmak, Y. I., Demir, N. U., Murat, D., Tumba, C., & Yilmaz, Y. (2015). Sibling death after being thrown from window by brother with autism: Defenestration, an emerging high-risk behavior. *Case Reports in Psychiatry*, Article ID 463694, 1–3. doi:10.1155/2015/463694.

Samuel, S., & Michals, T. (2011). Competency restoration. In E. Y. Drogin, F. M. Dattilio, R. L. Sadoff, & T. G. Gutheil (Eds.) *Handbook of forensic assessment: Psychological and psychiatric perspectives* (pp. 79–96). Hoboken, NJ: Wiley. doi:10.1002/9781118093399.ch4.

Satterfield, J. H., & Schell, A. J. (1997). A prospective study of hyperactive boys with conduct problems and normal boys: Adolescent and adult criminality. *Journal of the American Academy of Child and Adolescent Psychiatry*, *36*(12), 1726–1735. doi:10.1097/00004583-199712000-00021.

Schwartz-Watts, D. M. (2005). Asperger's disorder and murder. *Journal of the American Academy of Psychiatry and the Law*, *33*(3), 390–393. PMID: 16186206.

Silva, J. A., & Haskins, B. G. (2006). Asperger's disorder and murder. *Journal of the American Academy of Psychiatry and the Law*, *34*(1), 133–134. PMID: 16585258.

Søndenaa, E., Helverschou, S. B., Steindal, K., Rasmussen, K., Nilson, B., & Nøttestad, J. A. (2014). Violence and sexual offending behavior in people with autism spectrum disorder who have undergone a psychiatric forensic examination. *Psychological Reports*, 115(1), 32–43. doi:10.2466/16.15.PR0.115c16z5.

Steel, C. (2016). The Asperger's defense in digital child pornography investigations. *Psychiatry, Psychology, and Law*, 23(3), 473–482. doi:10.1080/13218719.2015.1080150.

Storebø, O. J., & Simonsen, E. (2016). The association between ADHD and antisocial personality disorder (ASPD): A review. *Journal of Attention Disorders*, 20(10), 815–824. doi:10.1177/1087054713512150.

Tantam, D. (2000). Adolescence and adulthood of individuals with Asperger syndrome. *Asperger Syndrome*, 13, 367–399.

Tiffin, P., Shah, P., & le Couteur, A. (2007). Diagnosing pervasive developmental disorders in a forensic mental health setting. *British Journal of Forensic Practice*, 9(3), 31–40. doi:10.1108/14636646200700018.

Tyler, N. & Sheeran, A. (2022). *Working with autistic people in the criminal justice and forensic mental health systems: A handbook for practitioners*. London: Routledge. doi:10.4324/9781003036722.

van Buitenen, N., Meijers, J., van den Berg, C. J. W., & Harte, J. M. (2021). Risk factors of violent offending in mentally ill prisoners with autism spectrum disorders. *Journal of Psychiatric Research*, 143, 183–188. doi:10.1016/j.jpsychires.2021.09.010.

Vinter, L. P., Dillon, G., & Winder, B. (2020). "People don't like you when you're different": Exploring the prison experiences of autistic individuals. *Psychology, Crime & Law*. doi:10.1080/1068316X.2020.1781119.

Wall, B. W., & Christopher, P. P. (2012). A training program for defendants with intellectual disabilities who are found incompetent to stand trial. *Journal of the American Academy of Psychiatry and the Law*, 40(3), 366–373. https://jaapl.org/content/jaapl/40/3/366.full.pdf.

Woodbury-Smith, M. R., Clare, I. C. H., Holland, A. J., & Kearns, A. (2006). High functioning autistic spectrum disorders, offending and other law-breaking: Findings from a community sample. *Journal of Forensic Psychiatry & Psychology*, 17(1), 108–120. doi:10.1080/14789940600589464.

Woodbury-Smith, M., Clare, I. C. H., Holland, A. J., Watson, P. C., Bambrick, M., Kearns, A., & Staufenberg, E. (2010). Circumscribed interests and offenders with autism spectrum disorders: A case–control study. *Journal of Forensic Psychiatry and Psychology*, 21, 366–377. doi:10.1080/14789940903426877.

26   Schizophrenia spectrum and other psychotic disorders

Persons who have disorders on the schizophrenia spectrum may have symptoms in one or more of five domains: delusions, hallucinations, disorganized thought and speech, grossly disorganized or abnormal motor behavior, and negative symptoms (American Psychiatric Association, 2022, pp. 101–103). The so-called "positive symptoms" of psychosis (namely, hallucinations and delusions) are "positive" in the sense that they add something to the person that is not normally found in people who do not have this disorder – they sense things that are not real, and/or they have beliefs that are not based in reality. The negative symptoms of psychosis are "negative" in the sense that the person lacks certain qualities that are ordinarily found in persons who do not have the disorder – namely, normal levels of cognition, emotion, goal-directed behavior, and/or social interaction. People who have schizophrenia may show little emotion. They may show little interest in socializing with other people. They may lack ambition or interests. They may be capable of sitting alone quietly for long periods of time without giving any indication of what they are thinking.

THE POSITIVE SYMPTOMS OF SCHIZOPHRENIA: HALLUCINATIONS AND DELUSIONS

People who do not have psychotic disorders typically perceive their internal experiences like fear and desire in terms of feelings, thoughts, and wishes. They know that they "own" these experiences in the sense that they know they belong to them. Persons who have psychotic disorders, on the other hand, may not "own" their fears and desires but may experience them as hallucinations or delusions – that is, as things that belong to other people or other entities, for example, voices talking to them (auditory hallucinations) or imaginary malicious intent in other people (paranoid delusions).

DOI: 10.4324/9781003385028-31

Positive symptoms like hallucinations and delusions create a world of unreality that may render a defendant incapable of understanding the world as the rest of us perceive it.

Hallucinations

Lim et al. (2016) identified 14 sensory modalities in which people can hallucinate:

- visual
- auditory
- olfactory
- gustatory
- exteroceptive
- interoceptive
- proprioceptive
- kinesthetic
- vestibular
- cenesthetic
- pain
- sexual
- temperature
- temporal.

Lim et al. reported a Dutch sample of 750 persons with schizophrenia and found that 80 percent had a history of hallucination, comprising 27 percent who had hallucinated in only one sensory modality and 53 percent who had hallucinated in more than one modality. That is to say, hallucination in more than one sensory modality is the norm for persons with schizophrenia.

The type of hallucination that most often leads a person with schizophrenia into legal difficulties is the auditory hallucination, and especially the command auditory hallucination, in which the person hears a voice telling them what to do. The defendant who experiences a command auditory hallucination may lose their ability to control their own behavior (i.e., volitional incapacity; see Chapter 19). This person also may think that obeying the voice is the right thing to do, in which case they may lose their ability to tell right from wrong (i.e., moral incapacity).

Persons who have schizophrenia and who experience command auditory hallucinations usually can resist these commands. When they do surrender to the commands and commit crimes, a forensic mental health professional may be called upon to explain why this defendant – who ordinarily can resist their command hallucinations – failed to control themselves and obeyed a command at this moment in time.

Case study #13: Annie – homicide in response to a command auditory hallucination

Annie was my patient on the forensic ward of a state mental hospital. Her husband had been sitting in their living room watching television when Annie came up behind him with a kitchen knife and killed him by stabbing him in the neck. She was responding to a voice that told her to do this.

Annie was 43 years of age and she had a long history of schizophrenia that was poorly controlled. For twenty years she had been a patient at the local community mental health center. Medication had been prescribed, but she did not cooperate in taking it. She commonly experienced command auditory hallucinations, but she had always been able to resist them in the past (as do most people who have command auditory hallucinations). In order to understand her behavior on the night of the homicide, I had to find out if anything had been different about that night. I learned that, on the night that Annie killed her husband, she had discovered that he was unfaithful to her. She was overwhelmed with rage and unable to resist the voice that told her to kill him. My opinion was that Annie was insane at the time of the crime. She had a serious mental illness, and her moral reasoning and self-control had been lost due to her illness and her immediate circumstances.

Delusional beliefs

There is an old saying that people build castles in the air, and people who have psychotic disorders move in. Many cases of insanity (including many of the landmark cases reviewed in Part IV) involve delusional beliefs.

Delusional beliefs are not as rare as we might like them to be. The DSM-5-TR (American Psychiatric Association, 2022, p. 107) estimates that the lifetime prevalence of delusional disorder (F22) is 0.2 percent of the population, and the lifetime prevalence of schizophrenia (F20.9; a condition in which many but not all patients experience delusional beliefs) is between 0.3 and 0.7 percent (p. 116). If the lifetime prevalence of delusional beliefs is 0.5 percent, and if you know 100 people, then the probability is 39.4 percent that you know someone who has, did have, or will have a delusional belief. If you have been a forensic mental health professional for any length of time, then the probability that you have seen someone with a delusional belief is almost certainly around 100 percent.

Case study #14: Betty – a stalker

Betty was my patient when I worked at a suburban mental health clinic. She was court-ordered into outpatient psychotherapy when she was convicted of stalking. Her diagnosis was schizophrenia.

Betty was 34 years of age. She lived alone and was socially isolated. When she was in her twenties she had married a cisgender man, but the marriage lasted only two years and it ended in divorce. She had no children.

Betty was a stocky woman of average height. She was biologically female and she identified herself as a cisgender and heterosexual woman. She wore no makeup. Her hair was closely cropped. She wore loose-fitting clothes traditionally made for men: men's trousers, shirts, jackets, and boots. She had been a sanitation worker in the past, but she left that job and she was receiving disability income due to her severe mental illness.

Betty denied having a mental illness and she resisted treatment. Like most people who have delusions, she was certain that her interpretation of reality was correct and that everybody else was wrong. She was convinced that the judge, district attorney, victim, and anybody else who thought she had committed a crime was wrong. People who are that suspicious and that inflexible in their thinking typically do not interact well with a psychotherapist. She was not good about keeping appointments. She refused to take medication. When she did come to my office, she was frankly paranoid. My office was in a two-story building with a drop ceiling and an attic. Betty was certain that there were people in the attic, watching her and listening to her as we spoke. Betty insisted that she had not stalked the victim but that the victim had stalked her.

The victim of her stalking was an attractive and well-dressed younger woman who lived in the same neighborhood. Betty told me that every time she saw this young woman she felt a "thump" in her vagina. Betty believed that this woman was able to enter her (Betty's) body through a paranormal process and make her vagina "thump." Betty accosted the woman in public, walking up to her and demanding that she stop entering her body. The first time Betty did this, the victim ignored her. The second time Betty accosted the woman in public, she called the police. Betty was arrested and was found guilty of stalking.

From a psychodynamic point of view, paranoia is the projection of an unacceptable impulse. The person who is the object of paranoia is misperceived as harboring the impulse that (a) belongs to the patient, (b) the patient finds unacceptable, and (c) the patient cannot admit to themselves. Betty was not able to accept her own sexual impulses toward this woman. She denied them and projected them onto the victim. Betty did not "own" her own desires and physical sensations. In Betty's mind, the victim was responsible for everything, even for the sensations in her own body.

During our time in therapy, Betty avoided the victim and she stayed out of further trouble with the law. She made no progress in therapy and her mental illness did not improve.

DELUSIONAL BELIEFS CAN BE DISTINGUISHED FROM EXTREME BELIEFS

Reality is a shared, subjective, social construct, and the distinction between delusional and non-delusional beliefs is partly related to whether anyone else shares that belief. Please consider two examples from some of the world's largest religions. The belief that we have an invisible soul that returns to earth after death – perhaps in the form of an animal – would seem like an unusual idea to many people, but it is shared by half the world's population. The idea that our invisible soul carries a stain left behind by two ancestors who lived in a garden would be an unusual belief to many people, but it is shared by about 30 percent of the world's population. If only one person held these beliefs, we might consider that person to be delusional, but because these beliefs are shared by many, are codified in authoritative literature, and are taught in families and in educational programs, we cannot consider them to be anything other than normal beliefs. The due diligence of a forensic mental health professional may involve finding out whether an unusual belief is shared by anybody in the defendant's social group.

Mark Cunningham (2018) developed a structured professional judgment (SPJ) for discerning whether unusual beliefs are delusional: the Model of Analysis for Differentiating Delusional Disorder from the Radicalization of Extreme Beliefs–17 Factor (MADDD-or-Rad-17). Cunningham's model is based on seven primary areas of analysis:

- belief content
- belief style
- subjective distress and social dysfunction associated with the belief

- social influences in belief formation, maintenance, and behavior
- social inclusion (i.e., whether the defendant is integrated and productive in their community)
- prodromal factors (i.e., indicators of emerging psychosis)
- behavioral or action factors (i.e., disturbances that accompany acting on the belief).

Within each of these seven areas, Cunningham identified features for analysis, yielding a total of seventeen factors:

- idiosyncrasy
- improbability
- grandiosity
- rigid adherence to belief despite disconfirming evidence
- suspension of critical judgment
- preoccupation with the belief
- distress and functional impairment associated with the belief
- extent to which the beliefs have constituted a social difficulty
- interaction with a community of like believers
- social motivators (i.e., the extent to which the belief arises and/or continues in a social context of like believers)
- social facilitation/tangible support
- social inclusion
- prodromal symptomatology
- willingness to act on the belief
- compulsion to act on the belief
- rigid moral distinctions in acting on the belief
- psychological disorganization associated with the belief.

Let us apply the MADDD-or-Rad-17 to the case of Betty – who believed that another woman was entering her body – as an exercise in distinguishing extreme belief from delusion. Betty's beliefs were odd, idiosyncratic, and improbable. They were grandiose in the sense that she believed the younger woman desired a sexual experience with her, and not vice versa. Betty was unable to think critically about her experience. Her behavior was ego-syntonic and not distressful to her – she blamed other people – but it had gotten her into trouble with the law. She was socially isolated. There was no community of like believers. Her schizophrenia was manifested by multiple symptoms (like believing there were people in my ceiling). Betty clearly was experiencing delusional thoughts, and the MADDD-or-Rad-17 is useful in distinguishing delusion from extreme belief.

DISORGANIZED THOUGHT AND SPEECH, GROSSLY DISORGANIZED OR ABNORMAL MOTOR BEHAVIOR, AND NEGATIVE SYMPTOMS OF SCHIZOPHRENIA

These symptoms of schizophrenia are less likely than the positive symptoms to be associated with intentional crime. They may, however, be useful in understanding a crime and in negating mens rea by demonstrating lack of knowledge and purpose. They may help to explain a defendant's reckless or negligent behavior. Disorganization can help to explain reckless and preposterous actions. Negative symptoms may help to explain failure to take appropriate action in a situation that required action (i.e., negligence).

REFERENCES

American Psychiatric Association. (2022). *Diagnostic and Statistical Manual of Mental Disorders. Fifth edition. Text revision.* Washington, D.C.: American Psychiatric Association.

Cunningham, M. D. (2018). Differentiating delusional disorder from the radicalization of extreme beliefs: A 17-factor model. *Journal of Threat Assessment and Management*, 5(3), 137–154. doi:10.1037/tam0000106.

Lim, A., Hoek, H. W., Deen, M. L., & Blom, J. D. (2016). Prevalence and classification of hallucinations in multiple sensory modalities in schizophrenia spectrum disorders. *Schizophrenia Research*, 176(2–3), 493–499. doi:10.1016/j.schres.2016.06.010.

27   Bipolar and related disorders

Mental health professionals recognize four moods in persons who have bipolar disorder: depressed, irritable, elevated, and expansive. Mild variations of these moods may be familiar to everyone. In persons who have bipolar disorder, the variations in these moods can be extreme. Depressed moods can be so severe that the person cannot go to work, cannot interact with others, and cannot leave the house or get out of bed. Irritable moods can be so severe that they lead to acts of violence.

People in an elevated mood feel better than good. Self-esteem is inflated. Everything is wonderful. They may feel extraordinarily self-confident and may show signs of grandiosity. They feel like they are floating on a cloud and they can do no wrong.

Expansive mood involves increased goal-directed activity and increased capacity for social interaction. The person may talk excessively and tirelessly to multiple persons. They may be "the life of the party." They may be hypersexual and have frequent encounters with one or more sex partners. They may be capable of working long hours for days at a time with very little need for sleep. They may, for example, be capable of making numerous cold calls for days at a time. Not infrequently, expansive moods help people find success in business, sales, politics, the military, the arts, or government. However, moments of irritability and poor judgment can unravel all that they have achieved, as can spells of profoundly depressed mood during which they are unable to function.

A patient of mine who has bipolar disorder showed expansive mood and poor judgment one day when she was sitting in a traffic jam at a busy intersection. In her mind, the right thing for her to do was to get out of her car, walk into the middle of the intersection, and start directing traffic, and she proceeded to do so.

The mood swings of bipolar disorder may include depressed, manic, and hypomanic episodes. Manic episodes involve "abnormally and persistently elevated, expansive, or irritable mood and abnormally and persistently increased activity or energy, lasting at least 1 week … (or any duration if

DOI: 10.4324/9781003385028-32

hospitalization is necessary)." Hypomanic episodes may be shorter in duration but last at least four consecutive days (American Psychiatric Association, 2022, p. 140).

People who have bipolar disorder may be capable of such remarkably poor judgment that they destroy their health, finances, and legal status, as well as the lives of others (Fovet et al., 2015). The loss of judgment in bipolar disorder can be so profound that people who have this disorder are advised to let a trusted person manage their finances through a power of attorney so that they do not destroy their future when they go into a manic phase. Manic episodes also are especially pernicious, because irritated and expansive moods can lead to a variety of violent and non-violent crimes. Some individuals are prone to outbursts of rage and aggression. There is a pressured quality to their behavior that reduces their capacity for self-control. Manic episodes may in fact be the mental disorder that is most commonly found in cases of volitional incapacity (Giorgi-Guarnieri et al., 2002; Vitacco & Packer, 2004). (See Chapter 19 for a discussion of volitional incapacity.)

People who have bipolar disorder may continue to behave somewhat irrationally between episodes. They may continue to show deficits in executive functioning and verbal memory between episodes (i.e., during the "euthymic phase"; Srivastava et al., 2019; Volkert et al., 2016).

Case study #15: Morris – a patient with bipolar disorder

The first patient I saw who had bipolar disorder remains for me the prototype of what this disorder is like and how it can affect a person and their family.

I interviewed Morris while I was working on the psychiatric ward of a Midwestern veterans' hospital. He was 47 years old and, until recently, had owned a successful jewelry business.

A few weeks before our interview, Morris had switched from his normal, euthymic mood into a manic episode. He sold his business, used cash to buy a large quantity of loose diamonds, and left his home. When his sisters finally located him, he was living in a motel room in Florida with two prostitutes. His sisters persuaded him to return home and accept admission to the hospital.

I first met Morris at his intake interview. He was very depressed and looked miserable. He slumped deeply in his chair. He had no energy. He made no eye contact. He barely opened his eyes, and when he did he looked only at the floor. His speech was slow and he barely spoke above a whisper. Medical staff informed us that he had a large stool impaction. The treatment team began the standard intake interview, but Morris was too depressed and fatigued to endure the interview. After only a few minutes, he asked if he could return to his bed, and he was allowed to do so. He stayed in bed for the rest of day.

The next time I saw Morris was a few days later. He was like a different person. He was energetic and talkative. His words and movements were rapid. He walked briskly and waved his arms in large gestures. His speech was loud and fast. There was an eager, intense quality to his eye contact. His mood was expansive and elevated and he had a wide grin on his face. Medical staff informed us that his stool impaction was gone.

This was in 1974, when mental patients were kept in psychiatric hospitals sometimes for decades at a time, before the sweeping reforms of deinstitutionalization. Morris was housed on a ward along with several dozen men who were severely regressed due to psychotic disorders. Some of these men had been hospitalized for more than thirty years. Morris had a host of impractical ideas for ways to organize these severely regressed men into group activities. Staff nicknamed him the "Mayor of Ward C." (Gratefully, nicknaming patients is largely a thing of the past. In many correctional settings, nicknaming patients by staff is expressly forbidden and that rule is strictly enforced.)

To my knowledge Morris did not face any criminal charges. Under a slightly different set of circumstances he might have faced charges for solicitation and claims related to breach of fiduciary duty, in which case his severe bipolar disorder could have been taken into consideration.

REFERENCES

American Psychiatric Association. (2022). *Diagnostic and Statistical Manual of Mental Disorders. Fifth edition. Text revision.* Washington, D.C.: American Psychiatric Association.

Fovet, T., Geoffroy, P. A., Vaiva, G., Adins, C., Thomas, P., & Amad, A. (2015). Individuals with bipolar disorder and their relationship with the criminal justice system: A critical review. *Psychiatric Services, 66*(4), 348–353. doi:10.1176/APPI.PS.201400104

Giorgi-Guarnieri, D., Janofsky, J., Keram, E., Lawsky, S., Merideth, P., Mossman, D., Schwartz-Watts, D., Scott, C., Thompson, J., Jr., & Zonana, H. (2002). AAPL practice guideline for forensic psychiatric evaluation of defendants raising the insanity defense. *Journal of the American Academy of Psychiatry and the Law, 30*(2 Suppl): S3–S40. PMID 12099305.

Srivastava, C., Bhardwaj, A., Sharma, M., & Kumar S. (2019). Cognitive deficits in euthymic patients with bipolar disorder: State or trait marker? *Journal of Nervous and Mental Diseases*, 207(2), 100–105. doi.org/10.1097/NMD.0000000000000920.

Vitacco, M. J., & Packer, I. K. (2004). Mania and insanity: An analysis of legal standards and recommendations for clinical practice. *Journal of Forensic Psychology Practice*, 4(3), 83–95. doi:10.1300/J158v04n03_06.

Volkert, J., Schiele, M. A., Kazmaier, J., Glaser, F., Zierhut, K. C., Kopf, J., Kittel-Schneider, S., & Reif, A. (2016). Cognitive deficits in bipolar disorder: From acute episode to remission. *European Archives of Psychiatry and Clinical Neuroscience*, 266(3), 225–237. doi:10.1007/s00406-015-0657-2.

28 Depressive disorders

Depressive disorders are very common in our society, but they are not ordinarily involved in the prelude to a crime. It is more typical for the externalized, energized, non-depressed, and disinhibited individual to present the greater risk to public safety and not the internalized, fatigued, withdrawn, and inhibited person who has a depressive disorder. Symptoms of depression – including social withdrawal, reduced energy, and reduced motivation – are more likely to inhibit acting out rather than precipitate it.

Sleep deprivation and inability to concentrate can help explain episodes of poor judgment. Depressive disorders can include periods of inaction and low motivation that can help explain lack of purpose and lack of knowledge. Depressive disorders may sometimes help explain the failure to take appropriate action that can result in crimes of negligence; an example of this is presented below in Case study #16. The presence of a depressive disorder at the time of an offense may help to argue for mitigation.

Competency to stand trial may be affected by inability to concentrate and loss of interest in life. A case involving the latter was presented in Chapter 10 (Case study #4).

Depression and risk of suicide is very common among persons who have been arrested and incarcerated. Suicide in prisons occurs at two to five times the rate of suicide in the general population, varying significantly with race. In the five-year period of 2015–2019, the prison suicide rate for Whites was 93 per 100,000, for Hispanics was 26 per 100,000, and for Blacks was 18 per 100,000 (Carson, 2021). Contrast that with the suicide rate in the general population in 2020: 16.9 for Whites, 7.5 for Hispanics, and 7.8 for Blacks (Ehlman et al., 2022). This represents a fivefold increase for Whites, a threefold increase for Hispanics, and a twofold increase for Blacks.

Sometimes an adult kills a family member before committing suicide. A suicidal parent may kill a child rather than leave the child parentless (as occurred in the case of Leslie deVeau, discussed in Chapter 22). Another case of homicide and suicide is presented below in Case study #17.

DOI: 10.4324/9781003385028-33

Case study #16: Joan – a crime of negligence

Joan was my patient when I worked at a mental health clinic in a suburban community. She had been severely depressed for years. Her depression was linked to a long and sad history of many personal losses and trauma. Often she did not leave her house, and many days she got out of bed only to eat, bathe, and use the bathroom.

Joan had attempted suicide several times. None of our interventions provided any significant relief. A number of antidepressant medications were tried and then discontinued due to side effects. She refused to participate in group therapy or in an intensive outpatient program. Her therapy with me consisted of one weekly visit, which during COVID-19 was conducted by telephone, which meant that she did not have to leave her house. She received disability benefits for depression, which was a sufficient amount of income, because she shared a rented house with two roommates. Her roommates did the grocery shopping and ran errands. Joan was too depressed even to look at her mail.

Unfortunately for Joan, she was eligible for jury duty. A citizen in her age bracket cannot go without opening their mail and stay out of trouble with the law. She received a summons for jury duty, was not aware of it, and did not reply. In her state, failure to report for jury duty is considered contempt of court and can be punished with a fine of up to $1,000 and up to five days in jail. At her request, I wrote a letter to the court, explaining that she had failed to report for jury duty because of mental illness. This may have resolved the matter, because no charges were filed.

Case study #17: Colonel Smith – a murder-suicide

During an early part of my career, I was a military officer and provided mental health consultation to all medical services including orthopedics. While I was stationed on a small island in the Caribbean, an orthopedic surgeon consulted me about a patient, a colonel who had suffered a leg injury. The surgeon was concerned because the colonel was complaining of insomnia and was showing signs of psychomotor retardation and inability to concentrate.

In addition to having a leg injury, the colonel had recently been passed over for promotion to general. It was the third time he had been passed over for general, which meant that he had to retire from military service. He would never be a general.

The surgeon debated over whether to refer the colonel for mental health services. Symptoms like insomnia, psychomotor retardation, and inability to concentrate are non-specific symptoms that can be caused by a great many medical and psychological illnesses. Ultimately, he chose to refer the colonel to neurology instead of mental health. Perhaps he was concerned about the stigma attached to a mental health referral. Several weeks later, the colonel took his shotgun and killed his wife, their 16-year-old son, and himself.

Leg injuries are very often depressing. The person with a leg injury typically cannot exercise and cannot do many of the things they enjoy. Often they gain weight and lose physical attractiveness. Exercise, recreation, and physical attractiveness are important to maintaining a good mood.

As I reflect back on Colonel Smith, I wish that I had been more assertive about getting that referral from the surgeon. Perhaps it would have made a difference. I no longer have any contact with the surgeon, and I do not know whether the death of Colonel Smith is one of the things that he, too, regrets in his retirement.

REFERENCES

Carson, E. A. (2021). Suicide in local jails and state and federal prisons, 2000–2019 – statistical tables. Bureau of Justice Statistics. Publication Series: Mortality in Local Jails and State Prisons. Retrieved 10/20/2022 from https://bjs.ojp.gov/library/publications/suicide-local-jails-and-state-and-federal-prisons-2000-2019-statistical-tables.

Ehlman, D. C., Yard, E., Stone, D. M., Jones, C. M., & Mack, K. A. (2022). Changes in suicide rates – United States, 2019 and 2020. *Morbidity and Mortality Weekly Report, 71*, 306–312. Retrieved 10/20/2022 from 10.15585/mmwr.mm7108a5external.

29 Trauma- and stressor-related disorders

Persons who have suffered stress and trauma in their homes, neighborhoods, schools, workplaces, or in combat may develop trauma- and stress-related disorders. They are likely to see the world as a dangerous place where they have to take extraordinary measures to protect themselves. The home environment which for many people is a source of comfort and nurturance is for many others a scene of violence and shame. These individuals carry the dual burdens of trauma and conditioning: suffering the effects of trauma and learning by imitation that violence is an acceptable solution to life's problems. Many victims of trauma also suffer brain injuries, in which case they are triply burdened.

Symptoms like anger, recklessness, self-destruction, sleeplessness, concentration problems, and exaggerated startle response can add to the burden carried by these individuals and may predispose them toward violence and loss of judgment.

Trauma- and stressor-related disorders can affect human behavior in at least two ways that are pertinent to crime and criminal defense. First, acute stress disorder (F43.0) and post-traumatic stress disorder (F43.10) can involve moments of dissociation during which people lose contact with their environment and lose control over their behavior (American Psychiatric Association, 2022). The functional limitations that apply to the dissociative disorders (see Chapter 30) apply equally well to the dissociative moments that can occur in acute stress disorder and post-traumatic stress disorder.

Second, trauma including severe child abuse can result in an angry and vengeful orientation toward society that leads to antisocial behavior. This situation is aggravated when social service agencies fail to respond appropriately to reports of child abuse. These features are illustrated in the case of Mitchell Sims, which is presented below.

The diagnosis of post-traumatic stress disorder is not often used in the insanity defense, but it can be useful in mitigation (Jovanović et al., 2015).

DOI: 10.4324/9781003385028-34

Case study #18: Mitchell Carlton Sims – the "Domino Pizza Killer"

Mitchell Carlton Sims was convicted of the murders of three Domino Pizza employees. He has the death penalty in two states – California and South Carolina. During his childhood, he was the victim of some of the most pervasive physical and sexual abuse that I have encountered. He is one of the many individuals I met in prison who had no opportunity to have a normal life.

Sims was born in Fort Knox, Kentucky. He was the victim of relentless verbal, physical, and sexual abuse throughout his childhood and teenage years, perpetrated by his stepfather. His stepfather struck him repeatedly in the head with his fist; beat him frequently on his back, legs, and buttocks, to the point of drawing blood; and repeatedly forced him to participate in sexual acts by threatening to beat him. These sex acts included mutual oral sex with his stepfather; mutual fondling and oral sex with his little sister (three years his junior – beginning when his sister was 8 years old and continuing until Sims left the home at age 17); and, on one occasion, sexual relations with his mother.

His history of childhood sexual abuse induced lasting feelings of shame, anger, and low self-esteem. Being forced into inappropriate sexual relations by your own father figure destroys the bonds of nurturance and protection that are supposed to exist in the father-son relationship. Having sexual relations with your own mother tears away the bonds of authority and nurturance that are supposed to exist in the mother-son relationship.

On one occasion during Sims' childhood, the police were called to the home, and they removed him briefly, but he received no help from social services and he was returned home without further intervention.

Sims' stepfather introduced him to alcohol, marijuana, and "speed," beginning around age 6 or 7. By age 13 or 14, Sims was drinking heavily. Hard liquor was easy for him to get because his friend's father owned a liquor store. Sims brought a bottle of liquor to school every day. He could drink a pint to a fifth in one day. "I would drink until I passed out," he said. He had alcohol blackouts. He was arrested as a juvenile for public drunkenness.

When Sims could not get alcohol, he would sniff glue, beginning at age 14. He estimated that he sniffed glue 100 times. In his teenage years, he experimented with cocaine and a variety of pills.

Sims suffered numerous minor head injuries in accidents, fights, and sports. He has a scar above his right eye that is so old and so deep that it looks like a wrinkle. He does not know how he got it. His left hand and arm are relatively uncoordinated, which would be consistent with an injury to the right frontal lobe of the brain.

Sims did well in school until the ninth grade, when he began to drink heavily. He dropped out of school in the eleventh grade, passed the GED examination, and joined the Army. At that time, his drugs of choice were LSD, vodka, and beer. In the Army he fell in love with a married woman and seized upon a bizarre plot to separate her from her husband – he had an accomplice shoot him in the arm, and then he accused her husband. The plot was revealed and, after two years of military service, Sims was given a bad conduct discharge. He was sentenced to one year of hard labor at Fort Leavenworth. This unusual crime revealed several themes about Sims: his remarkably poor judgment, his tendency toward self-destruction, his willingness to think of violence as a solution to problems, and his overwhelming dependence on romantic love.

Once he was released from prison he worked at grocery stores in North Carolina and Virginia. He was a good worker and was promoted to manager. Then he was fired for setting off firecrackers in a store after hours. This was a low point emotionally. He already suffered chronic depression in relation to his history of child abuse, then he got a bad conduct discharge, and now he had failed in the world of civilian employment.

Sims married in his early twenties but having spent his childhood in an abusive and highly sexualized environment he was not a good candidate for marriage. He was desperate for an attachment, but he felt unworthy of a good relationship, and he did not know how to make his marriage work. He overvalued sexuality, and finding new sex partners became his priority. He threatened a prostitute in a bar with a gun and was arrested. When at the age of 25 he met Ruby Padgett (age 20) – a former prostitute and a victim of childhood abuse herself – he found his sexual match. Ruby liked to be hit and slapped during the sex act, he reported. She wanted the sex act to resemble a rape. From the time they met in South Carolina until they were arrested four months later in Las Vegas, Nevada, they had a spree of sex, alcohol, drugs, robbery, and murder.

Sims and Padgett gave opposite accounts of who was the dominant partner in their relationship. Padgett would try to defend herself at her trial by claiming that Sims had forced her to participate in armed robbery and murder. According to Sims, Padgett was the one in control. He described her as being controlling and manipulative. She withheld sex in order to convince him to do things. "I wanted to do things to please her," he said. He feared losing her, and he had a desperate fear of abandonment.

Shortly after they met, Sims left his wife, and he and Padgett moved in together, renting a trailer in a city 100 miles away. He found part-time work as a driver for Domino's Pizza. When his truck broke down, he was unable to work. Ruby threatened to leave. Sims felt like a failure again, and he was desperate. They had no money, no groceries, no propane to heat their trailer, and the rent was due. Sims sold his blood to get money for food.

Eighteen months before the first murder, while Sims was working as a part-time driver, somebody robbed the Domino's Pizza store where he worked. Sims was not involved in that robbery, but he began to think of ways he could rob Domino's. He planned a robbery with Ruby, including the time and method, but then he did not go through with it, for which she gave him a verbal lashing. Then, when he finally decided to go through with the robbery, he told himself, "You can't chicken out this time. You can't go back to her again and tell her that you didn't do it."

On December 3, 1985, Sims drove to the Domino's Pizza store in Hanahan, South Carolina. Two men were working in the office. He robbed them at gunpoint and shot them both with a .25 caliber pistol. One man died at the scene. The other man lived a few days, despite having four bullet wounds to his head and neck. He lived long enough to drive to the police station and tell the police that his killer was Mitchell Sims.

Sims and Ruby fled to Glendale, California, where they checked into a motel and ordered a pizza. When the 21-year-old driver arrived, they overpowered him, took his money, bound him, stuffed a washcloth in his mouth, put a pillowcase over his head, and drowned him in the bathtub. They wiped every surface of the room with a wet towel. Sims went to the driver's store and robbed it of $2,000. A customer came into the store during the robbery, suspected that a crime was in progress, and called the police. The police found two men bound in the refrigerator, with nooses around their necks stretched so tight that they had to stand on their toes to keep from strangling.

Sims and Padgett fled to Las Vegas, where they were apprehended on Christmas Day, 1985. Sims was condemned to death in California. A photograph of the bound corpse in the motel bathtub was particularly persuasive to the jury. Then he was extradited to

South Carolina, where he was condemned to death for the two murders he had committed there.

Ruby Padgett tried to defend herself by saying that Sims had forced her to participate in these crimes. The prosecution pointed out that, after these murders, Padgett had spent a holiday with Sims in Las Vegas, spending the money they had obtained from these crimes. Expert opinion was obtained that Padgett had battered woman syndrome. For reasons unknown to me, this opinion was not used at her trial. (Battered women typically do not take advantage of opportunities to flee, as they are too frightened to escape because it would only aggravate their batterer. They believe that their batterer would track them down and be angrier than they were before, so it is better not to leave.) Padgett was found guilty of murder and armed robbery, and she was sentenced to life without the possibility of parole (LWOP). She currently is a resident of the California Department of Corrections and Rehabilitation.

I testified at Sims' appeal in the State of California. He has post-traumatic stress disorder from the many years of physical and sexual abuse during his childhood and adolescence. He suffers chronic anxiety, depression, and feelings of self-hatred. He has recurrent nightmares about the abuse that he suffered. Since childhood, he has suffered recurrent, involuntary, intrusive, and distressing thoughts and images of the abuse. When he reads a news story or hears a news report about child abuse, he is reminded of his own abuse history, and he is intensely distressed. He finds it hard to talk about the abuse and he avoids doing so. He tries to push the memories away. He does not remember everything that happened and he does not want to remember. He feels detached and estranged from people. He finds it hard to stay asleep and he sleeps only three or four hours at a time. He is irritable in the mornings. He complains of poor memory and finds it hard to concentrate most of the time.

In prison, he suffered daily panic attacks for several years. These were characterized by a pounding heart, a choking sensation, and fears that he was dying or losing his mind. His EKG was taken on three or four occasions, and these were negative.

During our interviews, Sims looked sad and discouraged. His eyes filled with tears when he spoke about his past. I noticed trembling and a relative lack of coordination in his left arm, which would be consistent with an injury to the right cerebral hemisphere (and might be related to the deep scar on his right forehead).

Sims' motivation for these crimes must be understood within the context of severe child abuse and his feelings of desperation in response to threatened abandonment. At the time of these offenses, Sims was trying desperately to hold onto his relationship with Ruby Padgett, who was threatening to leave him because he had no money. He was intoxicated much of the time and his judgment was impaired. He was willing to do anything, even armed robbery and murder, to get money and hold onto her.

Post-traumatic stress disorder helps to explain his violent orientation toward others. Severe and persistent child abuse had caused posttraumatic stress disorder with fears of abandonment and an angry, antisocial orientation toward his victims. His emotional neediness helps to explain his robberies that were motivated by his need for money and his need to hold onto Ruby, but it does not explain the sadistic elements involved in the Glendale crimes.

Mitigation testimony did not sway the appeals court judge in California who affirmed the death penalty. Sims had hoped to stay in South Carolina, where his family could visit him, but instead he was transferred to California. He now resides on death row at San Quentin State Prison.

Case study #19: Alfonse – a violent man with amnesia for severe childhood sexual abuse

I include the case of Alfonse in order to illustrate some of the difficulties that may be encountered in conducting forensic mental health evaluations. He serves as a reminder that the victims of severe childhood abuse may repress their histories of abuse so thoroughly that these memories do not enter their consciousness.

Alfonse was accused of armed robbery and aggravated assault. He was 32 years old, unmarried, and had no children. He had grown up in a rural part of the state and he had not done well in school. Psychological testing indicated borderline intellectual functioning (ICD-10-CM code R41.83); that is, a low level of IQ not quite in the range of intellectual developmental disability (see Chapter 25).

Bail had not been granted and Alfonse was in jail awaiting trial. Our interviews took place in the inner recesses of a county jail, in a small room with a table and two chairs.

Alfonse's speech was fluent, but his understanding of words was idiosyncratic. Our interviews were difficult – not only did I have to ask him the right questions, but I had to make sure that he understood my words in the manner I intended them, and very often he did not. Personality testing with verbal tests like the MMPI was not possible, because his understanding of words was idiosyncratic. The words I spoke and the words on the tests were familiar to him (he had heard and seen them before), but his understanding was oblique, based on occasional usages, connotations, and personal associations that did not match my own understanding of those words. I attributed his unique understanding of words to a combination of borderline intellectual functioning and a subtle form of language disorder (F80.2) that affected his verbal comprehension. Also, Alfonse had been raised in a culture that was very different from my own. Even though we lived in the same state, I could not rule out the possibility that cultural factors had contributed to his unusual understanding of language.

I ask every patient a series of questions about their mental health. This includes any history of mental health treatment, hallucination, paranoia, suicide attempts, and child abuse. Alfonse denied all these markers of mental illness. Despite his verbal difficulties with the interview, I was able to establish that his disorders were not psychotic or autistic in nature, and that his level of intelligence – while considerably below average – was not in the range of intellectual developmental disorder (IDD). I did not find any evidence of a major mental illness that might be the basis for an insanity defense. I concluded that he was able to cooperate with his attorney and competent to stand trial as long as his attorney took the time to make sure that Alfonse understood their verbal communications. I did not see any other form of mental illness – that is, until I spoke with his older sister.

I routinely contact family members for their point of view when I conduct a forensic evaluation. In the case of Alfonse, his older sister was eager to speak with me. She told me that Alfonse had been the victim of severe sexual abuse perpetrated by multiple family members from the time he was very young. Alfonse had denied this. I interviewed him again and asked him again about sexual abuse during childhood, and he again denied it. I was in the position of having to decide whether I believed Alfonse or his sister. Under normal circumstances, a defendant is the best informant about their own life, but in this case I concluded that his sister was the more credible informant. I did not believe that Alfonse was consciously lying in order to protect his reputation and the reputation of his family. He answered my questions and denied any history of child abuse in a blunt and uncomplicated manner that suggested he believed what he was telling me and that he had repressed thoroughly all memories of sexual abuse during childhood.

I passed this information along to his attorney. The presence of a trauma-related disorder did not interfere with Alfonse's competency to stand trial or with his criminal responsibility, but it might be used in mitigation.

I include the case of Alfonse here as a caution to readers that childhood abuse can be so traumatic that the victim does not remember it. Forensic examiners may find themselves in the position of believing a collateral informant over the information provided by the defendant themselves. (Unfortunately, I have no follow-up information on Alfonse and I do not know the outcome of his trial.)

REFERENCES

American Psychiatric Association. (2022). *Diagnostic and Statistical Manual of Mental Disorders. Fifth edition. Text revision.* Washington, D.C.: American Psychiatric Association.

Jovanović, A. A., Dunjić, B. D., & Milovanović, S. D. (2015). Forensic aspects of posttraumatic stress disorder. In C. Martin, V. Preedy, & V. Patel (Eds.) *Comprehensive guide to post-traumatic stress disorder* (pp. 77–96). London: Springer Nature. doi:10.1007/978-3-319-08613-2_93-1.

30   Dissociative disorders

"Dissociation" can be defined as the separation of two mental processes that normally go together. For example, people usually remember the things that they do. When people do things but do not remember them, this may be the condition known as dissociative amnesia (F44.0). Amnesia is a relatively mild form of dissociation. Other dissociations can be so profound that entire personalities are walled off and unaware of each other, as can occur in dissociative identity disorder (DID; F44.81).

The element of crime known as mens rea (see Chapters 7 and 8) includes such factors as knowledge, purpose, and consciousness. Serious questions about responsibility arise when a crime is committed in a state of divided consciousness.

DISSOCIATIVE AMNESIA (F44.0)

Memory is not perfect, and people forget things. Forgetting is usually an entirely normal phenomenon. Normal factors that influence forgetting include fatigue and old age. Pathological factors that influence forgetting include intoxication, brain disorders, and dissociation.

In dissociative amnesia, autobiographical information is lost that is usually of a traumatic or stressful nature. Usually the person forgets a specific event, group of events, or aspects of a specific event. In some cases they may show global forgetting of their identity and history.

Defendants often claim that they do not remember the crime. While this may at times be related to dissociative amnesia, many of these claims are probably malingered, as defendants seek to conceal evidence and evade responsibility. A survey by Rubenzer (2018, p. 129) indicated that 14.6 percent of defendants examined for competency to stand trial feigned amnesia for the offense.

Mangiulli et al. (2022) recently reviewed 128 alleged cases of dissociative amnesia reported in peer-reviewed journals from 2000 to 2020 and found little evidence to support the existence of this disorder. Most of

DOI: 10.4324/9781003385028-35

those authors failed to rule out ordinary forgetting and malingering. Mangiulli et al. urged clinicians and researchers to be more critical in their investigations of alleged dissociative amnesia.

DISSOCIATIVE IDENTITY DISORDER (F44.81)

In dissociative identity disorder (DID), a person's "parts" or "alters" are separate personalities that may have varying levels of awareness of each other. Good epidemiological data on DID appear to be lacking. Statistics reported by the American Psychological Association (2022, p. 333) suggest that the condition occurs in 1.1 to 1.5 percent of the population, but these estimates are based on samples that are so limited they might not generalize to the rest of the population. My own experience in treating and evaluating persons with this disorder suggests that the prevalence is well below 1 percent.

DID can include some of the most extraordinary somatic and cognitive expressions found in any form of mental illness. Goleman (1988) reported the case of a boy who was allergic to orange juice in one identity but was not allergic in another. Josef Breuer's famous case Anna O. – one of the first cases in the history of psychoanalysis – had two identities from December 1881 to June 1882: one lived in the present and the other thought it was 365 days earlier (Breuer & Freud, 1895/2000, referenced in Ellenberger, 1970, p. 482).

The diagnosis of DID rarely appears in the insanity defense. A survey by Steadman et al. (1993) of eight states and 7,689 insanity defense cases from the late 1970s to early 1980s found the diagnosis of DID in only fifteen cases, and seven of those were in one state (Ohio; referenced in Appelbaum & Greer, 1994).

DID can appear at any age, but it often has its roots in childhood. People who have DID often had traumatic childhoods, which they survived by dissociating. A person who has DID may have an angry and destructive alter who holds on to the rage left by childhood trauma. This angry alter may be capable of committing acts of violence. When an alter commits a crime, the courts are faced with a unique dilemma – in no other condition can one identity commit a crime, and then a separate identity goes on trial. The dilemma for the courts is to decide whether to hold the alter to the local standards of insanity, or to accept that this is a person with a serious mental disorder who must be considered insane. Courts have resolved this dilemma in both directions, as explained below.

Also, defendants may try to malinger this disorder, in which case a forensic mental health professional can assist the trier of fact by determining whether a defendant is malingering or does in fact have this disorder.

Chapter 22 discussed how forty-seven of the fifty-two jurisdictions in the United States have laws that define insanity as some combination of cognitive, moral, and volitional incapacities. When the court chooses to enforce the local definition of insanity with a defendant who has DID, the forensic mental health expert can assist the trier of fact by determining (1) which alter was manifest, and (2) whether that alter demonstrated one of the three incapacities at the moment of the offense. This is the legal formula that was used to convict defendant Norma Roman of possession of heroin with intent to distribute in *Commonwealth v. Roman* (1993). Her argument – that her alternate personality was a drug dealer but her host personality was not – did not prevail at her trial. (Indeed, it is difficult to imagine that the insanity defense could prevail in the crime of drug dealing, because this is a crime that involves a lot of skill in planning, preparation, transaction, concealment, and interpersonal negotiation. It is a crime where the motivation is likely to be an uncomplicated case of financial gain, and where the incentive to malinger is powerful.)

In *Ohio v. Grimsley* (1982), the defense argued that the "primary personality (Robin)" should not be held accountable for the drunk driving of the secondary personality (Jennifer). The court rejected this argument and decided that the issue of responsibility was based on "the personality then controlling her behavior" (*Ohio v. Grimsley*, 1982, at 268).

The opposite conclusion – that a person who has DID has a severe mental illness and should be considered insane regardless of the incapacities of an alter – was advocated in a law journal by Saks (1992) and then was adopted by a federal court of appeals in *United States v. Denny-Shaffer* (1993).

United States v. Denny-Shaffer (Tenth Cir., 1993)

Bridget Denny-Shaffer had been a victim of physical and sexual abuse during her childhood. She worked as a labor-and-delivery nurse and stole a baby from a hospital nursery in New Mexico, crossed state lines, and took the baby to Minnesota. Two expert witnesses testified at her trial: one for the prosecution and one for the defense. Both experts agreed that Denny-Shaffer had "multiple personality disorder" (as it was known before the label changed in 1994 with the publication of the DSM-IV). Both experts testified that the identities who kidnaped the baby were alternate personalities and not her host personality. The prosecution witness, Mary Alice Conroy, Ph.D., ABPP, of the Federal Correctional Institution in Lexington, Kentucky, testified that these alters did not experience either cognitive or moral incapacities (which are the standards for insanity in federal crimes; see 18 U.S.C. § 17(a)). She testified that "Each of the personalities taken alone knew, or was very capable of knowing, what she was doing and of making moral judgments" (*United States v. Denny-Shaffer*, at 1008)

The defense expert lacked forensic expertise and had no opinion regarding the cognitive and moral incapacities of the alters (at 1008). Because Denny-Shaffer could not demonstrate that her alters had cognitive or moral incapacities, the trial judge found no evidence for her claim of insanity and refused to instruct the jury regarding insanity (at 1012). Because insanity was her only defense, Denny-Shaffer then waived her right to a jury determination. The judge found her guilty of kidnaping and sentenced her to 5 years and 3 months in prison.

A three-judge panel disagreed with the trial judge's decision. This panel found that the evidence of insanity was sufficient to warrant consideration by a jury, and they voided her conviction. This panel (a) accepted that Ms. Denny-Shaffer had a severe mental illness; (b) noted the long, legal tradition of making exceptions for people who have severe mental illness; and (c) found it meaningful that her host personality was not aware of her behavior at the time of the offense and was not able to judge the wrongfulness of her actions (at 1013).

The prosecution's expert, Dr. Conroy, stated the dilemma in her report as follows:

A final opinion of the criminal responsibility of Bridget Denny-Shaffer is a matter for the trier of fact to determine exactly how the standard will be applied in this case. In the application of the standard provided by law, a Multiple Personality Disorder is unique. If the standard is taken to mean that all alters, or at least the host personality, must be fully aware of the nature, quality, and wrongfulness of an act, then Bridget Denny-Shaffer was not responsible at the time of the instant offense. Such an application would probably mean that no one suffering from Multiple Personality Disorder could be held responsible for anything unless all alters were co-conscious at all times, regardless of their mental status otherwise. Such is almost never the case.

If, on the other hand, a Multiple Personality Disorder is viewed as a single individual with varying personality components and not divided as though he or she were a group of separate people, the issue changes. In such a case, the question would be whether, at the time of the instant offense, the personality in control suffered from a mental disease or defect such as to be unable to understand the nature, quality, and wrongfulness of their acts. If this is the appropriate application of the standard, then, in my professional opinion, at the time of the instant offense, Bridget Denny-Shaffer did suffer from a significant mental illness, but it was not such to render her unable to understand the nature, quality, and wrongfulness of her acts. (*United States v. Denny-Shaffer*, at fn. 7)

The three-judge panel, in footnote 7, reminded the court that it was beyond the scope of an expert witness to offer an opinion on the ultimate issue of insanity, as specified in Rule 704(b), which was part of the Insanity Defense Reform Act of 1984 (see Chapter 22).

The panel quoted the decision in *United States v. Ryan* (1931), that

[a] literal application of a statute which would lead to absurd consequences is to be avoided whenever a reasonable application can be given which is consistent with the legislative purpose. (*United States v. Ryan*, at 175)

The panel found the trial judge's decision to be too "restrictive" (*United States v. Denny-Shaffer*, at 1014), remanded her case for a new trial, and directed that her next jury be instructed regarding the insanity defense (at 1021). This second trial did not take place. Denny-Shaffer pleaded guilty on March 4, 1994, and was sentenced to 3 years and 10 months in prison (which was essentially time served plus one year), to be followed by 5 years of supervised release. She served another 6 months in prison and was released on September 23, 1994 (Willis, 2016).

Case study #20: Françoise – a girl with dissociative identity disorder

The most remarkable case of DID I have encountered in my own practice was that of a 15-year-old girl, who was my patient during my years as a military officer and whom I first reported in *Family Process* (Venn, 1984).

Françoise was my patient while I was stationed on a small island in the Atlantic Ocean, far from the U.S. mainland. She had been on the island for six months when her mother and stepfather brought her to the military hospital on a Sunday morning when I was officer-of-the-day. Her mother had married an enlisted man the year before, and Françoise suddenly found herself in an unfamiliar environment. She was unaccustomed to the life of a military dependant, which included the isolation and privation of overseas duty on a small island far from home.

Françoise was born in Ohio and she was the elder of two sisters. Her parents had separated and divorced when she was 13 years old. She lived with her mother, but emotionally she remained loyal to her father. Her mother took a job in law enforcement. One evening a bullet was fired through their kitchen window. During the weeks of divorce proceedings, Françoise had five or six episodes of visual hallucination, each lasting up to 20 seconds, in which she saw her mother shot through the head and lying in a pool of blood. During one of these hallucinations, Françoise burst out screaming in school. (For Françoise, who lived with her mother but remained emotionally loyal to her father, this hallucination was a perfect synthesis of fear for her mother's safety and wish-fulfillment of rage against her mother for abandoning her father. Visual hallucinations can some-times indicate an incipient psychosis, but there was no other indication of psychosis in Françoise's behavior.) Also, around this time Françoise experienced a series of vivid nightmares, set during the frontier days of America, in which a French woman and her baby were killed by Native Americans, who set fire to their cabin.

A year after the divorce, her mother married a young non-commissioned officer, five years her junior. This man had never married before and he had no experience with children. Suddenly he had a new wife, two teenage daughters, and shortly afterward an overseas tour of duty. Françoise did not get along with her stepfather and they quarreled frequently. She became an angry and truculent girl who did not help out around the house and spent long hours in front of the mirror preening over her makeup and long hair.

The family was relocated to the island less than a year into the marriage. The adjustment expected of Françoise was enormous. She was separated from everything she knew, including the father she loved. She was enrolled in a new school in a foreign country, and she was forced to live in a small house on a military base with a stepfather she did not like. Any one of these adjustments would have been difficult enough, but all of them at once overwhelmed her and her fragile mental health.

Françoise had never before been a military dependant and her peers at the high school did not accept her. She had four or five "fainting spells" at school, during which both legs became numb and paralyzed. Each time, she was taken to the hospital in an ambulance. Medical tests were negative. Six months into the tour of duty, her alternate personality emerged.

On a Friday night, the high school held a dance, and the girls of the French Club hosted a kissing booth. Françoise was an avid student of French language and culture. Her biological father was French and had an unmistakably French surname. She had studied French in school since the fourth grade. While living in Ohio, they had visited the historical district of Marietta and it had made a great impression on her. (Marietta was founded in 1788 and was named for Queen Marie Antoinette, in gratitude for French assistance during the American Revolution.)

The other girls of the French Club abandoned Françoise at the kissing booth that Friday night. She sat there alone and received only four customers the entire night. On Saturday night, she drank a glass of absinthe and went for a walk with her younger sister and a girlfriend. Françoise's mother described this friend as being "very aggressive with boys." The three girls met two boys and went to a secluded park full of large trees. The other two girls paired off with the boys. The "aggressive" girl rudely told Françoise to go away. Françoise climbed into a large tree and stayed there. (Her younger sister was developing sexually more quickly than she was. Françoise, in the space of two days, had been abandoned by her peers in the French Club *and* by her sister and friend in the park.)

Françoise had to be helped down from the tree. She was stuporous and had to be taken home in a taxi and carried into the house. She did not respond to her name. She did not recognize her family. Whereas previously she had spoken English with an Ohio accent, she now spoke French and spoke English with a French accent. She said that her name was Jeanne Marie Thérèsa Le Grand Ducourtieux, that she was 17 years old, and that she lived in Marietta, Ohio. She said that her parents had emigrated from Nice to Montreal, where she was born, and that she had emigrated to Marietta with her husband, her brother, and her infant daughter, Dori Marie. Jeanne gave a detailed family history, including imaginary people, places, and events. Imaginary people were named and their personalities were described. She thought it was the early 1800s. She said that her baby had been killed by Native Americans, who set fire to their cabin. She had thought that her brother was pulling her from the fire, but when she opened her eyes it was not her brother and she was in a foreign country surrounded by strangers. Her main concern was to join her husband in Marietta, Ohio. (Had this occurred on the mainland, she might have engaged in the purposeful but irrational travel that is sometimes characteristic of people who have dissociative disorders.)

On Sunday morning, her symptoms had not abated. The family took her to see their pastor and then took her to the hospital where I was on duty. I interviewed her together with her parents. I could see that she had dissociated, but her symptoms were so unusual that I also considered the possibility of malingering. As part of a clinical interview, I conduct a routine mental status examination. Her concentration (serial sevens), recent memory, and abstract thinking (proverbs) were intact. Her parents had told her where she was and what year it was, and she repeated this information to me, but she thought she was supposed to be in Marietta, Ohio, in the early nineteenth century. I examined her orientation and fund of information by asking her questions from history, geography, and the Christian liturgical year. She knew that Easter is a movable feast. She knew the presidents from Washington to Jefferson only. When I asked her which state lies across the river from Marietta, she said, "Virginia." I provoked her a little, because I was skeptical and I was trying to rule out malingering, and I said, "Everybody knows that West Virginia is across the river from Marietta." She maintained flatly that Virginia lies across the river from Marietta and that she had never heard of West Virginia. (Only later did I remember that West Virginia did not become a state until 1863, when it broke away from the Confederacy. Jeanne's orientation to time, person, and place were consistent with someone who was living during the Jefferson administration, 1801–1809. Note that Thomas Jefferson was ambassador to France from 1784 to 1789, during which time the city of Marietta was founded.)

Françoise looked tense and her affect was constricted. Her mother looked upset. The most distressed person in the room was her stepfather, who wept, clawed at the air with his fingers, and cried out, "I want my daughter back!" (Indeed, of the three people in the room, her stepfather had the most to lose, in terms of what this situation could mean for his military career.) Françoise's facial expression was blank except for brief, hostile glances at her parents that actually made her stepfather feel relieved. He laughed and said, "There is a trace of my old Françoise."

Jeanne (the new personality) had no memory or awareness of Françoise. The first clinical interview lasted two hours, during which the identity of Jeanne held fast. She never changed her story or lost her French accent. I did not admit her to the hospital, because she was not a danger to herself or others, and a hospital admission would have separated her from her family, may have solidified a "sick role," and probably would have made the situation worse. I advised the family to take her home and return for daily outpatient appointments. I also asked them to take her to the school on Monday morning, to see if she might surrender the Jeanne identity. They did, and she did not. The family had a short interview with the vice principal, during which she maintained the Jeanne identity, and then they returned home.

During the next several days, Jeanne demonstrated that she was a very different girl than Françoise. Whereas Françoise had worn blue jeans and T-shirts, Jeanne rejected this clothing and said that it made no sense to her. Jeanne made her own clothing: a simple bonnet from a sheet of white cloth and a long skirt from a calico print. Jeanne cut and sewed these garments herself. Françoise had never sewn anything and in fact she had proved to be incompetent even at sewing buttons on straight.

Françoise had spent long hours in front of a mirror primping her long hair and makeup. She always applied makeup carefully, wore her long, wavy hair over her shoulders, and wore her blouses open at the throat. Jeanne, on the other hand, was modest, even prudish, in her dress and grooming. She wore no makeup, pulled her hair back tightly, and buttoned her blouse to the collar and pinned it with a brooch. Jeanne was polite and well-mannered and spoke only when spoken to, in contrast to the insolent and argumentative teenager that Françoise had become.

Whereas Françoise had been interested in art and guitar, Jeanne showed no interest in these activities and preferred doing household chores. She cooked, sewed, and cleaned house.

Jeanne ate foods that Françoise despised: hot cereal and raw onions. Whereas Françoise had shown no interest or talent in cooking, Jeanne offered to cook for the family in exchange for her room and board (showing an awareness of fiscal duty that Françoise had not). Jeanne cooked a ham and French pastry (Napoleons) to the family's amazement. Jeanne did not understand modern appliances. She was frightened by the noisy vacuum cleaner and she offered to beat the rugs. She also was frightened by cars, trucks, and jet noise. (She consented to ride in a car to the hospital, school, and church.) She was confused by ham in a can, mashed potatoes in a box, and starch in a spray can. In the kitchen she did not understand modern appliances and used a wooden spoon and a stoneware bowl, calling these "the only sensible" utensils in their kitchen. She offered to cook a ham and asked, "Where is the smokehouse?" She asked for a potato to boil so she could starch her bonnet, and she was surprised when her mother gave her a spray can. Later she offered to dust and she asked for "the feathers." When her mother produced another spray can, she asked, "Do you dust with starch?"

The identity of Jeanne was not entirely consistent, and several lacunae appeared. Jeanne was not able to explain where she learned English or how she came to be wearing Françoise's necklace. She looked perplexed when she was asked these questions. She did not know the year of her birth, and she could never specify exactly what year she thought it was. On the fifth day, she referred to pillow stuffing as "foam." (This was the only time she used a word that was not consistent with Jeanne's fund of information.) According to a

French translator, Jeanne did not speak with the "sweet" accent of southern France, from which she claimed heritage, but with the guttural accent of northern France which Françoise had learned in school. (Her French teachers in the United States had studied in Paris and Alsace.)

I continued to check for malingering, and at times I took a skeptical and provocative approach. On Monday, the third day of the fugue, her mother grew tired of my skeptical approach and she began to resent it. She decided to befriend Jeanne. She quit resisting the alter personality and she accepted Jeanne as a real person. She made a pact with Jeanne that she would help her get to Marietta if Jeanne would help her get her daughter back. Jeanne relaxed physically after they made this agreement. By the fifth day, the mother's acceptance of Jeanne had ripened into affection. She wrote in her diary, "How often do we get the opportunity to get into a person's subconscious and really get to know them? I am gaining a better understanding of my daughter. She really is a beautiful, caring person, and so talented." Her mother wrote that Jeanne was "better adjusted" than Françoise. Jeanne could "cook, sew, clean, care for herself, plan her future. She is very self-sufficient." As her mother became more accepting of Jeanne, the girl continued to relax physically and she became more talkative.

On the morning of the sixth day, Jeanne reported to her mother a dream that paralleled Françoise's behavior in the park. In the dream, a girl was with some friends who deserted her. The girl climbed into a tree and wished she were somewhere else. She said, "I am going to leave this place. I don't know how, but I will, and I'm not going to come back until I have healed the hurt and until people realize I have feelings. I am not a nobody, a marionette on a stage." In Françoise's dream, the girl's anger mounted until she grew "dizzy and light-headed." The girl in the dream then remembered a dream of her own about a woman in a cabin fire, and she thought, "Take my place and let me go away for a while to rest until they can all understand. You can make them understand. You can help me. Please let me change." She could feel the heat of the flames, and she felt someone pull her away from the fire. Jeanne related this dream to her mother, and said cryptically, "There is one more dream to go and Françoise will be back." Later that day, a friend suggested that they take Jeanne to the tree where the fugue began. Sitting under the tree, Jeanne entered a stuporous, twilight state, and she awakened as Françoise. Her first reaction was shock at the clothing she was wearing: the simple bonnet and long skirt. She thought they were playing a joke on her, and she hurried home to change.

Françoise had no memory of Jeanne. She could not account for the last six days and thought it was still Saturday. Her mother had been growing fond of Jeanne and reported feeling disappointment at the return of Françoise.

At my next meeting with the family, Françoise did not know who I was. When shown the clothing she had made, she reacted with disbelief and said she could never sew a stitch. She was seen for follow-up sessions biweekly for eight months. The Jeanne identity did not reappear, and her amnesia for the event persisted. She was a remarkably good hypnotic subject, capable of a wide range of hypnotic phenomena. She obtained a perfect score on the Stanford Hypnotic Clinical Scale (Hilgard & Hilgard, 1975), suggesting an extreme level of hypnotic susceptibility. Hypnosis was used in her follow-up therapy for relaxation and ego-strengthening, but not for exploration, because Françoise made it clear that she wanted to put the entire incident behind her.

Françoise had one more "fainting spell" three weeks after she returned to school. This time, in consultation with mental health staff, she was not removed to the hospital but was kept at school by the nurse. Further spells did not occur.

Had these events occurred in the contiguous U.S. and not on a small island, and not under the close supervision of her family, Françoise may have traveled to Marietta, which is what she thought she needed to do. Purposeful but irrational travel sometimes occurs among persons who have dissociative disorders. (The ICD-CM-10 continues to recognize the diagnosis of dissociative fugue: F44.1. This diagnosis was omitted from the DSM-5; American Psychiatric Association, 2013.)

Whereas Françoise had been a sullen and depressed teenager who rejected her current circumstances and longed for reunion with her divorced father, the alternate identity of Jeanne had been a polite, willing, and helpful worker around the house. Jeanne had found a way to experiment with roles that were unfamiliar to Françoise but which might become necessary to her in the near future. As her mother grew to appreciate and even prefer this new identity, the girl was placed in a paradoxical situation, and it was only a matter of time before she returned to her original identity.

This episode of DID was remarkable for many reasons. It involved a total shift of interests, attitudes, language, culture, and orientation to time, person, and place. The episode was accompanied by dreams and trance-like states as she entered and exited the alternate personality. The episode was like a waking dream that lasted for six days. It expressed symbolically her profound attachment to her biological father. It reinforced for me, as her therapist, the effect that divorce can have on a child and the depth of commitment that a child may have for a parent who was left behind.

Françoise did not face any criminal charges. Under a different set of circumstances, she might have faced charges for disturbing the peace (for example, if a police officer and not a taxi driver had been summoned to the park that night), and for the status offenses of underage drinking and runaway (if she had obeyed her impulse to travel to Marietta). If sanity had been an issue, I would have argued that Françoise was not guilty by reason of insanity (except for underage drinking, which was done by her host personality before the dissociative episode). I would have argued that her behavior demonstrated all three incapacities of insanity: cognitive, moral, and volitional. She had not perceived reality and had not known who she was (cognitive incapacity). She felt compelled to travel to Ohio (volitional incapacity), and she would have thought that traveling to Ohio was the right thing to do (moral incapacity).

REFERENCES

American Psychiatric Association. (2013). *Diagnostic and Statistical Manual of Mental Disorders. Fifth edition.* Arlington, VA: American Psychiatric Publishing.

American Psychiatric Association. (2022). *Diagnostic and Statistical Manual of Mental Disorders. Fifth edition. Text revision.* Washington, D.C.: American Psychiatric Association.

Appelbaum, P. S., & Greer, A. (1994). Who's on trial? Multiple personalities and the insanity defense. *Psychiatric Services*, 45(10), 965–966. doi:10.1176/PS.45.10.965.

Breuer, J., & Freud, S. (1895/2000). *Studies on hysteria.* New York: Basic Books.

Commonwealth v. Roman, 606 NE 2d 1333 (Massachusetts, 1993).

Ellenberger, H. F. (1970). *The discovery of the unconscious: The history and evolution of dynamic psychiatry.* New York: Basic Books.

Goleman, D. (June 28, 1988). Probing the enigma of multiple personality. New York Times, Section C, p. 1. Retrieved 11/27/2022 from www.nytimes.com/1988/06/28/science/probing-the-enigma-of-multiple-personality.html.

Hilgard, E. R., & Hilgard, J. R. (1975). *Hypnosis in the relief of pain.* Los Altos, CA: Kaufmann.

Mangiulli, I., Otgaar, H., Jelicic, M., & Merckelbach, H. (2022). A critical review of case studies on dissociative amnesia. *Clinical Psychological Science*, 10(2), 191–211. doi:10.1177/21677026211018194.

Ohio v. Grimsley, 3 Ohio App. 3d 265, 444 NE2d 1071 (1982).

Rubenzer, S. (2018). *Assessing negative response bias in competency to stand trial evaluations*. Oxford: Oxford University Press.

Saks, E. R. (1992). Multiple personality disorder and criminal responsibility. *Southern California Interdisciplinary Law Journal*, *10*(2), 185–204. https://gould.usc.edu/why/students/orgs/ilj/assets/docs/10-2%20Saks_Article.pdf.

Steadman, H. J., McGreevy, M. A., Morrissey J. P., Callahan, L., Robbins, P. C., & Cirincione, C. (1993). *Before and after Hinckley: Evaluating insanity defense reform*. New York: Guilford.

United States v. Denny-Shaffer, 2 F3d 999 (Tenth Cir., 1993).

United States v. Ryan, 284 U.S. 167, 52 S. Ct. 65, 76 L.Ed. 224 (1931).

Venn, J. (1984). Family etiology and remission in a case of psychogenic fugue. *Family Process*, *23*, 429–435 doi:10.1111/j.1545-5300.1984.00429.x.

Willis, D. (2016). Twenty-five years after hospital kidnapping, twins look back. *Las Cruces Sun-News*. Retrieved 12/21/2022 from www.lcsun-news.com/story/news/2016/05/29/twenty-five-years-after-hospital-kidnapping-twins-look-back/85141450/.

31   Disruptive, impulse-control, and conduct disorders

The category known as "disruptive, impulse-control, and conduct disorders" embraces a set of disorders that occur among both children and adults. These disorders are characterized by behaviors that violate the rights of others. Persons who have these disorders are often in conflict with social norms and authority figures. They constitute a large percentage of the adult and juvenile defendants in our courts, prisons, and probation offices. Washburn et al. (2008) administered version 2.3 of the Diagnostic Interview Schedule for Children to 1,715 juvenile detainees in Chicago, Illinois, and found that 46 percent had conduct disorder and 20 percent had oppositional defiant disorder (F91.3).

These are externalizing disorders that are associated with disinhibition and negative emotion and are negatively correlated with constraint and agreeableness. These disorders are highly comorbid with each other and frequently comorbid with substance use disorders (American Psychiatric Association, 2022, pp. 521–522).

The combination of conduct disorder and attention-deficit/hyperactivity disorder in juveniles is especially pernicious and predicts the development of antisocial personality disorder (F60.2) in adulthood. (This research is reviewed in Chapter 25.)

Antisocial personality disorder (F60.2) has the distinction of being coded twice in the DSM-5-TR – both as a disruptive behavior disorder and as a personality disorder. Adults who have antisocial personality disorder constitute a large portion of the men and women in our courts, prisons, and probation offices (see Chapter 34).

The DSM-5-TR recognizes two types of "self-control" problems: (1) poorly controlled emotions (e.g., the temper outbursts of intermittent explosive disorder, F63.81); and (2) poorly controlled behaviors, which may or may not involve poorly controlled emotions. (Consider the callous indifference and cold, constricted emotion of conduct disorder.) Oppositional defiant disorder represents an "intermediate" type of disorder

DOI: 10.4324/9781003385028-36

with an even balance between negative emotions (like anger and irritation) and oppositional behaviors (like defiance and argument).

Persons with intermittent explosive disorder are subject to temper outbursts that are out of proportion to the stressors that provoke them. These outbursts are not premeditated. They are sudden and spontaneous, can involve verbal aggression and physical assault, and are not instrumental (i.e., they are not performed in order to obtain an objective, such as money, power, or intimidation). Lack of premeditation raises the possibility that these assaults are committed without knowledge or purpose (i.e., they may lack mens rea; see Chapters 7 and 8).

Persons who have impulse control disorders like kleptomania (F63.2) and pyromania (F63.1) experience a cycle of tension before the act, followed by a sense of pleasure, gratification, or relief during the commission of the act. Their ability to control their own behavior is questionable.

Numerous studies have demonstrated that the brains of children with conduct problems differ from the brains of normal controls. Neuroimaging has found that children with conduct problems have less gray matter in the amygdala, frontal, temporal, and insular regions of the brain (Rogers & De Brito, 2016; Sebastian et al., 2016; Sterzer et al., 2007). These brain areas subserve important behavioral functions like empathy and decision making. For example, Sterzer et al. (2007) found a relationship between empathy and the volume of gray matter in the anterior insula.

Were we to adopt a purely mechanistic view of brain-behavior relationships, we might conclude that these studies indicate that brain deficits cause these behavior problems. However, let us remember that these studies are correlational in nature and that cause-and-effect relationships regarding the brain and behavior are not likely to be solved with simple formulae. The brain is not a simple machine (as was discussed briefly in Chapter 7). A more balanced point of view might argue that the children who have these brain abnormalities carry an extra burden in terms of their thoughts and emotions – a burden that is not shared by their peers. While their unusual brains may not excuse their behavior, they do suggest that they carry an extra burden in terms of conforming their conduct to the requirements of the law.

REFERENCES

American Psychiatric Association. (2022). *Diagnostic and Statistical Manual of Mental Disorders. Fifth edition. Text Revision.* Washington, D.C.: American Psychiatric Association.

Rogers, J. C., & De Brito, S. A. (2016). Cortical and subcortical gray matter volume in youths with conduct problems: A meta-analysis. *Journal of the American Medical Association Psychiatry*, 73(1), 64–72. doi:10.1001/jamapsychiatry.2015.2423.

Sebastian, C. L., De Brito, S. A., McCrory, E. J., Hyde, Z. H., Lockwood, P. L., Cecil, C. A., & Viding, E. (2016). Grey matter volumes in children with conduct problems and varying levels of callous-unemotional traits. *Journal of Abnormal Child Psychology, 44*(4), 639–649. doi:10.1007/s10802-015-0073-0.

Sterzer, P., Stadler, C., Poustka, F., & Kleinschmidt, A. (2007). A structural neural deficit in adolescents with conduct disorder and its association with lack of empathy. *Neuroimage, 37*(1), 335–342. doi:10.1016/j.neuroimage.2007.04.043.

Washburn, J., Teplin, L., Voss, L., Simon, C., Abram, K., & McClelland, G. (2008). Psychiatric disorders among detained youths: A comparison of youths processed in juvenile court and adult criminal court. *Psychiatric Services, 59*(9), 965–973. doi:10.1176/appi.ps.59.9.965.

32   Substance-related and addictive disorders

The multifaceted relationship between substance use and crime pervades our society and permeates our criminal justice and correctional systems. Not only are the possession, sale, and manufacture of certain drugs illegal, but certain drugs are associated with acts of aggression, and an abundance of property crime and violent crime – including theft, burglary, robbery, and murder – is motivated by a defendant's need to sustain a drug habit. In 2006, Miller et al. estimated the annual economic burden of violent crime involving drugs and alcohol in the United States at more than $120 billion. The Office of National Drug Control Policy (2011), using data from 2007, estimated the total cost of illegal drug use in the United States at $193 billion: $120 billion in lost productivity, $11 billion in health care costs, and $61 billion in criminal justice costs.

Substance use and crime are so intertwined in our society that DeMatteo et al. wrote in 2015 that "[It] is arguably a false dichotomy to talk about individuals who commit crimes and those who use substances as being separate populations" (p. 325).

More than 80 percent of offenders in the United States are involved with substance use, which includes those who were arrested for a substance-related offense, those who were intoxicated at the time of the offense, crimes committed to support a drug habit, and offenders who have a history of serious substance abuse (National Center on Addiction and Substance Abuse, 2010). In a sample of ten urban sites, more than 60 percent of adults arrested tested positive for at least one illegal drug at the time of their arrest. In half of those sites (Chicago; Minneapolis; New York; Portland, Oregon; and Sacramento), more than 70 percent of arrestees tested positive for at least one illegal drug (Office of National Drug Control Policy, 2012).

Drugs that are associated with acts of aggression include alcohol, anabolic steroids, cocaine, amphetamines, sedatives, opiates, and hallucinogens. Drugs can precipitate aggression by altering the neurotransmitters dopamine, norepinephrine, gamma-aminobutyric acid (GABA), and serotonin

DOI: 10.4324/9781003385028-37

(Anderson & Bokor, 2012). (Brain research like this has influenced some writers to predict that eventually a neurochemistry of "brain states" will replace the common-law hypotheses of "mental states" that currently dominates criminal justice – for example, in the doctrine of mens rea. This hypothesis was discussed briefly in Chapter 7.)

The relationship between substance use and violence is one of the best established and most thoroughly researched topics in the field of mental health, with literally thousands of studies in print. A person who is under the influence of an intoxicating substance is prone to impulsive behavior, is less able to exercise good judgment, and is susceptible to persuasion by others. The relationship between substance use and violence is so robust that substance use serves as a valuable component in predicting future violence in risk assessment instruments like the VRAG-R and HCR-20 (see Chapter 12).

A meta-meta-analysis by Duke et al. (2018) of thirty-two previous meta-analyses – comprising thousands of studies conducted between 1985 and 2014 – found that the connection between substance use and violence has an overall effect size of almost half a standard deviation ($d. = 0.45$). Male gender and psychotic illness increased the effect size that already existed between substance use and violence.

Methamphetamine in particular has been linked to acts of violence (Foulds et al. 2020). Alcohol may not necessarily incline a person to violence (Pernanen, 1991). Research has investigated the conditions under which alcohol may or may not contribute to violence. Studies by Gustafson (1993, 1994) suggest that drinkers do not respond with violence unless they are provoked, and they do not respond with violence if other means of communication are available to them.

JUDICIAL AND FOLK PSYCHOLOGICAL DECISIONS REGARDING SUBSTANCE USE AND CRIME

Judicial decisions regarding intoxication and crime were reviewed in Chapter 8. The landmark in this series is the U.S. Supreme Court decision in *Montana v. Egelhoff* (1996) – a murder trial in which the court upheld the Montana law adhering to the common-law principle that a voluntarily intoxicated person is just as culpable as a non-intoxicated person.

Although voluntary intoxication may not negate mens rea, defendants may find that voluntary intoxication is useful as mitigation, in order to obtain a reduced sentence or a conviction for a lesser crime.

In cases of addiction, we may question just how voluntary an intoxication might be. The burden of addiction may compromise an agent's free will. Addictions are highly stigmatized in our society. Folk psychological attitudes toward people who have addictions are generally negative, but these attitudes may vary with one's personal and family experience and with one's judgments about the addict's genetic burden. The person who has a strong genetic load toward alcoholism has less room in which to exercise their free will and decide whether or not they will drink. A defendant who is addicted to alcohol and has a strong family history of alcoholism may be judged less harshly than someone who does not carry the same genetic burden. Not all persons who have a strong genetic load go on to become alcoholics, but, for a person who has that genetic burden and is actively drinking, the decision about whether to take another drink may be about as voluntary as deciding whether to have blue or brown eyes.

Attitudes toward addiction may also vary with the stage of the disorder. The adolescent who takes their first drink may be judged less harshly than the young adult who drinks heavily and is on the cusp of alcoholism, who likewise may be judged less harshly than the chronic alcoholic who has destroyed their health, employment, finances, marriage, family, and legal status. These in turn may be judged more harshly than the chronic alcoholic who drank heavily for decades and now suffers permanent brain damage (see the case of settled insanity in Chapter 8).

People (including jurors) tend to act on suppositions that are based on their own experience. Jurors who have little experience with addictions may be reluctant to believe that there are people who have no control over their drinking and drug use. Nevertheless, triers of fact can sometimes be persuaded through mitigation testimony.

In twelve-step programs like Alcoholics Anonymous, the first step is admitting that you are powerless – that is, admitting that the substance is more powerful than you are, and that you have no control over whether or not you will use it. The addict who believes they can control their own substance use is in denial and has not taken the first step. By the same reasoning, a society who believes that addicts can control their own substance use may be in denial about the nature of this disorder.

Case study #21: Henry – methamphetamine use and attempted murder

Every prisoner is an individual, to be sure, but some stand out as being unlikely candidates for the correctional environment and better suited to the mental health system. One such prisoner on my caseload was Henry, and the questions that were raised by his incarceration continue to disturb me.

Henry was my patient in the general population of a medium security yard of a prison where he was serving a long sentence for attempted murder. He was an unusual prisoner. He kept to himself and never made eye contact. His affect was inappropriate and "silly." Whenever I spoke to him, he grinned and looked at the floor. He gave short, direct answers to fact-related questions, but he never volunteered any information, never elaborated on his answers, never initiated a topic or conversation, and never told anybody what he was thinking. Whenever I tried to find out what he was thinking, he would go mute. He never told his lawyers or anybody else what he was thinking on the day of his crime or why he stabbed a total stranger three times in the back.

At the age of 28, Henry was unemployed and was living with his parents in an apartment in a large urban community. He was a regular user of methamphetamine. Close to their apartment was a construction site. Henry stood on the sidewalk outside the construction site for hours and stared at the men working there. He did this for three consecutive days. On the third day, he took out a knife, walked up behind one of the construction workers, and stabbed him three times in the back. He had no prior relationship with this man. They were complete strangers to each other.

After the stabbing, Henry went home, packed a few belongings, and fled. He was apprehended a short time later. The fact that he fled indicates that he knew he was in trouble, and this would have made it harder for him to argue either moral or volitional incapacity, although he may have lacked capacity at the moment of the crime and then found it again by the time he got home. We will never know what he was thinking, because he never told anybody. He did not tell me and he did not tell his lawyers at the time of his trial.

If not for Henry's drug use, he might have been a candidate for the insanity defense, which might have been good for him, because then he may have gone to a hospital and not to a prison. But, because Henry was intoxicated at the time of his crime, his lawyers had no interest in pursuing an insanity defense. The case of Henry continues to trouble me, because his crime was pointless and bizarre, and because Henry probably has a mental illness on the schizophrenia spectrum. His specific diagnosis cannot be ascertained, because he never tells anybody what he is thinking, which is probably related to a high degree of suspiciousness, which is probably a feature of his mental disorder.

Henry's tragedy has several dimensions. One is the fact that substance abuse in his community is commonplace. Henry lives in a state where an estimated 321,000 people used methamphetamine in the past year (Substance Abuse and Mental Health Services Administration, 2022).

Most probably he is in prison and not in the mental health system because he was intoxicated at the time of his offense, but intoxication is common in his community. His crime was inexplicable, but drug use in his community is quite ordinary. His drug of choice is one that is known to potentiate violence (Foulds et al., 2020). It is likely that he used methamphetamine to self-medicate a serious mental illness in a community where drug use is common but participation in the mental health system is stigmatized. Finally, Henry's dependence on methamphetamine raises the question of just how voluntary his intoxication may have been.

Henry's behavior during the crime was purposeful but bizarre. We may assume that he knew what he was doing and knew that it was wrong, as evidenced by the fact that he fled from his home immediately after the stabbing. His behavior suggests that he had sufficient knowledge and purpose to have mens rea, but his crime was bizarre and suggests insanity. People almost always act with knowledge and purpose – even when they are insane. What makes a defendant insane is not that they lacked knowledge or purpose, but that their knowledge and purpose were insane.

REFERENCES

Anderson, P. D., & Bokor, G. (2012). Forensic aspects of drug-induced violence. *Journal of Pharmacy Practice*, 25(1), 41–49. doi:10.1177/0897190011431150.

DeMatteo, D., Filone, S., & Davis, J. (2015). Substance use and crime. In B. L. Cutler, & P. A. Zapf (Eds.) *APA handbook of forensic psychology. Volume 1: Individual and situational influences in criminal and civil contexts* (pp. 325–349). Washington, D.C.: American Psychological Association.

Duke, A. A., Smith, K., Oberleitner, L. M. S., Westphal, A., & McKee, S. A. (2018). Alcohol, drugs, and violence: A meta-meta-analysis. *Psychology of Violence*, 8(2), 238–249. doi:10.1037/vio0000106.

Foulds, J. A., Boden, J. M., McKetin, R., & Newton-Howes, G. (2020). Methamphetamine use and violence: Findings from a longitudinal birth cohort. *Drug and Alcohol Dependence*, 207, 107826. doi:10.1016/j.drugalcdep.2019.107826.

Gustafson, R. (1993). What do experimental paradigms tell us about alcohol-related aggressive responding? *Journal of Studies on Alcohol, Supplement, 11*, 20–29. doi:10.15288/jsas.1993.s11.20.

Gustafson, R. (1994). Alcohol and aggression. *Journal of Offender Rehabilitation*, 21(3–4), 41–80. doi:10.1300/J076v21n03_04.

Miller, T. R., Levy, D. T., Cohen, M. A., & Cox, K. L. C. (2006). Costs of alcohol and drug-involved crime. *Prevention Science*, 7(4), 333–342. doi:10.1007/s11121-006-0041-6168455.

Montana v. Egelhoff, 518 U.S. 37 (1996).

National Center on Addiction and Substance Abuse. (2010). *Behind bars II: Substance abuse and America's prison population*. New York: Author.

Office of National Drug Control Policy. (2011). *How illicit drug use affects business and the economy*. Washington, D.C.: Author.

Office of National Drug Control Policy. (2012). *2011 annual report: Arrestee drug abuse monitoring program II*. Washington, D.C.: Author.

Pernanen, K. (1991). *Alcohol in human violence*. New York: Guilford Press.

Substance Abuse and Mental Health Services Administration. (2022). 2019–2020 National Surveys on Drug Use and Health. Retrieved 10/13/2022 from www.samhsa.gov/data/sites/default/files/reports/rpt35344/2020NSDUHsaeTotals01102022/NSDUHsaeTotals2020.pdf.

33   Neurocognitive disorders

People who have brain injuries and brain disorders may have difficulties with mood, cognition, and judgment that interfere with their abilities to perceive reality, control their conduct, and obey the requirements of the law. Factors like emotional dysregulation and problems with reasoning and executive functioning can make it difficult for them to plan and regulate their activities. Cognitive difficulties can include a lack of ability to incorporate feedback, which means that people do not learn from their mistakes, which can lead to crime and recidivism.

Authors including Blair (2007) and Raine (2013) have drawn attention to the significance of the limbic system and prefrontal cortex in regulating emotional behavior and inhibiting violence. Unfortunately, the ventral and medial surfaces of the prefrontal cortex are uniquely susceptible to damage because they rest against rough surfaces of the skull and can be bruised or torn from blows to the head or from the inertial forces involved in falls and motor vehicle collisions. Damage to these areas of the brain can lead to a downward spiral of increased aggression and further brain injury.

The brain is susceptible to a wide variety of clinical conditions, including vascular disorders, many of which increase with advanced age. An elderly person who begins to commit crimes in old age may be suspected of having a brain disorder.

Case study #22: Harold – a senior citizen with a grudge

Harold was no stranger to civil protest. At the age of 61, he staged a sit-in that lasted several hours at a public health clinic that had denied him treatment (because he was not eligible to receive treatment at that clinic – in other words, not only was Harold prone to civil protest but also to disordered thinking and poor judgment). At the age of 64, he shackled himself to a chair in protest at a county council meeting.

DOI: 10.4324/9781003385028-38

Harold had the misfortune of owning a farm that lay close to Interstate 95 during the height of the crack cocaine epidemic of the 1980s. This was a time when large-scale drug operations smuggled raw cocaine by boat into Florida (a state with 1,350 miles of coastline: too large an area for law enforcement to monitor effectively). Raw cocaine was driven north on Interstate 95 to makeshift laboratories in the rural southeast, where it was processed into crack cocaine and then shipped to the big cities up north.

Harold's farm lay several miles down a county dirt road. His nearest neighbor lived a mile farther down. The many luxury vehicles that drove up and down the road day in, day out were out of place, and Harold was certain that he knew what was going on at the next farmhouse. He was certain that it was being used as a crack cocaine factory.

Harold reported his suspicions to the local police, but he could not interest them in his problem. The police already knew Harold for his public protests, his displays of temper, and his disordered thinking. Harold gave the police an ultimatum: They had ten days to fix the problem. When the ten days were up and nothing happened, Harold – who was dedicated to solving the drug crisis alone if he had to – hitched his plow to his tractor and plowed up a swath of the dirt road, making it impassable. This only got him in trouble with the law. He was arrested for malicious injury to county property. The charge was dropped through the efforts of the public defender, but Harold was not appeased. He later told the press, "This wasn't going to keep me from getting back at them. I didn't know what I was going to do yet, but I knew I was going to have my revenge."

Harold, who at the time was 67 years of age, told his wife nothing about his plans. He sent her to visit relatives in a city eighty miles away. He bought a dual wheel truck and fitted the truck bed with two 250-gallon drums. He put truck tires around the drums so they wouldn't roll. He filled the drums with 500 gallons of gasoline. He also put into his truck a bulletproof vest, a gas mask, two shotguns (including an automatic 12-gauge shotgun), and a five-shot .30-06 rifle.

The County had just spent $2 million building a new, state-of-the-art law enforcement center with a jail and a sally port. Harold crashed his truck through the sally port. He expected to die and he expected to take "dozens, maybe even hundreds of people," along with him. He got out of the truck, opened both drums, and let the gasoline run out. He soaked a torch made of rags in the gasoline, walked around to the front of the truck, lit the torch with a match, and threw it into the gasoline. He expected an explosion that would kill him and everyone else who was there. However, the gasoline caught fire and did not explode. He started a gun battle with the police that lasted twenty minutes. Four police officers were wounded. Harold was shot six times. He was firing his automatic 12-gauge shotgun when a bullet cut off his thumb. "With my thumb gone, I couldn't hold onto the gun," he said. He put the gun down, stepped out from cover, and lay down on the grass.

Harold was taken to a hospital, where he was treated for his injuries. A leg was removed due to multiple gunshot wounds. Medical examination revealed atrial fibrillation, which can affect cognition in two ways: through variations in blood flow to the brain (known as transient ischemic attacks or TIAs), and through small strokes that are caused by emboli cast into the bloodstream. A pacemaker was installed. Once Harold was medically stable, he was transferred to the state forensic hospital, where he became my patient. I administered a battery of neuropsychological tests that showed significant deficits in a number of cognitive functions. Harold was found incompetent to stand trial and he was kept at the hospital for nine years, after which he was found competent and he proceeded to trial.

Harold pleaded guilty but mentally ill (GBMI), which in his state is the equivalent of volitional incapacity (see Chapter 19), to assault with intent to kill, two counts of assault and battery with intent to kill, second-degree arson, and possession of a firearm during the commission of a violent crime. The judge accepted his plea of GBMI and placed him on probation. The judge said,

> These are horrible crimes, but he was mentally ill due to an organic mental disorder. He knew what he was doing, but he could not control himself because of his disorder. The psychiatrist has stated that he is no longer a threat to anyone or to himself. Thank goodness for the progress of modern medicine!

Harold in his old age had cerebral pathology in relation to atrial fibrillation. He had multiple neurocognitive deficits and he demonstrated poor judgment, low impulse control, irritated mood, a rigid sense of right and wrong, and a big grudge against law enforcement. He justified to himself that his crimes had been necessary and were the right thing to do. A defense of not guilty by reason of insanity due to moral incapacity might have been feasible, but most defenses of moral incapacity are based on delusions, and Harold was not delusional. His defense was based on poor judgment in relation to neurocognitive deficits. He pleaded volitional incapacity, and this plea was accepted by the judge.

When Harold was interviewed by a local newspaper, he told the reporter that he did not regret his behavior. He said, "You got to stand up for yourself. If people don't stand up for their rights, they ain't nobody." Harold died at home at the age of 80.

Case study #23: Peter – an injured combat veteran of the Iraq War

Peter returned from combat in Iraq with posttraumatic stress disorder and a penetrating head wound. An improvised explosive device (IED) had sent small bits of metal through the air, and one of them had pierced his skull.

I was serving as a consultant to a military hospital when Peter became my patient. He was still on active duty. Upon his release from the hospital, he was re-assigned as a drill instructor in basic training. However, he was not well-suited to this kind of work. He was subject to violent fits of temper, and he gained a reputation for being too rough with his trainees. Peter was removed from his position as a drill instructor after he slammed a young trainee to the ground for not doing what he was told. He did not face a court-martial, but under a slightly different set of circumstances he might have gone on trial for assault. He was re-assigned to a desk job and was ordered into psychotherapy.

At home, he had become verbally and physically abusive to his wife, and she had left him.

Peter was my patient for several months before I moved to another state. When I last saw him, he was hanging on: living alone, controlling his temper, and holding onto his assignment and his career.

The angry outbursts that are typical of post-traumatic stress disorder, potentiated by the emotional disinhibition resulting from a brain injury, can lead to life-altering events that an individual must cope with for years to come.

REFERENCES

Blair, R. J. R. (2007). The amygdala and ventromedial prefrontal cortex in morality and psychopathy. *Trends in Cognitive Sciences, 11*, 387–392. doi:10.1016/j.tics.2007.07.003.

Raine, A. (2013). *The anatomy of violence: The biological roots of crime.* New York: Random House.

34   Personality disorders

The personality disorders are a varied collection of "enduring patterns of inner experience and behavior" (American Psychiatric Association, 2022, p. 733). The disorders in this category are quite varied and in many cases have little in common with each other. Some of the personality disorders tend to be associated with crime, but many are not. Some are internalized, inhibitory disorders that reduce the likelihood of an individual's participation in crime. These include schizoid personality disorder (F60.1) in Cluster A, avoidant personality disorder (F60.6) in Cluster C, and obsessive-compulsive personality disorder (F60.5) also in Cluster C. Persons who have these disorders rarely get in trouble with the law. On those occasions when they are accused of acts of negligence, their disorders may help to explain those moments when they failed to take suitable actions.

In my own experience, the personality disorders that are most likely to be involved in criminal behavior are paranoid personality disorder (F60.0) and schizotypal personality disorder (F21) in Cluster A; antisocial personality disorder (F60.2), borderline personality disorder (F60.3), and narcissistic personality disorder (F60.81), all in Cluster B; and dependent personality disorder (F60.7) in Cluster C. For some of these disorders, epidemiologists have collected data on their prevalence in prisons, and this research is reviewed here.

CLUSTER A PERSONALITY DISORDERS

Persons who have Cluster A personality disorders "often appear odd or eccentric" (American Psychiatric Association, 2022, p. 734).

Paranoid personality disorder (F60.0)

Persons who have paranoid personality disorder (F60.0) have abnormal ideas and strained interpersonal relationships. They are suspicious of others and subject to distortions of thought. When they commit a crime, it

DOI: 10.4324/9781003385028-39

may be due to poor interpersonal relationships and suspiciousness of others, as may occur in cases of stalking and assault.

Schizotypal personality disorder (F21)

Schizotypal personality disorder (F21) has the distinction of being coded twice in the DSM-5-TR – both as a personality disorder and on the schizophrenia spectrum. Persons who have schizotypal personality disorder are subject to delusional beliefs and other distortions of thought that also characterize other people with disorders on the schizophrenia spectrum. A person with schizotypal personality disorder may, for example, have a delusional belief that results in moral incapacity.

CLUSTER B PERSONALITY DISORDERS

Persons who have Cluster B personality disorders are often "dramatic, emotional, or erratic" (American Psychiatric Association, 2022, p. 734). These are features that tend to create interpersonal difficulties and may predispose them to criminal behavior.

Antisocial personality disorder (ASPD; F60.2)

Adults who have antisocial personality disorder (ASPD) constitute a large portion of the men and women in our courts, prisons, and probation offices. Their combination of irritability, impulsivity, indifference to others, and disregard for social norms predisposes them to conflict with the law. A collection of sixty-two surveys from twelve countries indicated that 47 percent of the men and 21 percent of the women in prison had antisocial personality disorder (Fazel & Danesh, 2002).

People often confuse ASPD with psychopathy, but these are two separate concepts that come from two different intellectual traditions. Psychopathy is not a diagnosis in the DSM. The concept of psychopathy comes not from the American Psychiatric Association but from a separate tradition that includes the early work by psychiatrist Hervey Cleckley (1941/1988) of Augusta, Georgia. (For more information about the nature of psychopathy, please see the work of Robert Hare of the University of British Columbia, reviewed in Chapter 12.) The DSM-5-TR diagnosis of antisocial personality disorder relies on seven factors that include a combination of external behaviors (crime, deception, and violence), internal factors (impulsivity, irritability, and lack of remorse), and lifestyle factors (irresponsibility). The concept of psychopathy includes these as well as a number of other, similar, internal, external, affective, and interpersonal factors, including need for stimulation and "criminal versatility" (i.e., variety of criminal endeavors).

Assessment with the PCL-R (a test that measures psychopathy; see Chapter 12) of 5,408 male prisoners at fifteen institutions in the U.S. and Canada found that 16 percent exceeded the preferred cut score of 30 and above (Hare, 2003, pp. 30, 164). Because 47 percent of male prisoners have antisocial personality disorder (Fazel & Danesh, 2002), but only 16 percent of male prisoners meet the PCL-R criteria for psychopathy, it has been suggested that the prisoners who have psychopathy are "the worst of the worst."

Brain research has identified certain abnormalities among persons with psychopathy (see reviews by Hare, 2003; Kiehl & Sinnot-Armstrong, 2013; and Patrick, 2006). Damasio (1994) theorized that the ventromedial frontal cortex plays an important role in psychopathy and other forms of disinhibition. He wrote,

> One might say, metaphorically, that reason and emotion "intersect" in the ventromedial frontal cortices, and that they also intersect in the amygdala. (p. 70)
>
> I would like to propose that there is a particular region in the human brain where the systems concerned with emotion/feeling, attention, and working memory intersect so intimately that they constitute the energy source of both external action (movement) and internal action (thought, animation, reasoning). This fountainhead region is the anterior cingulate cortex. (p. 71)

Theories like these have led some authors to predict that eventually a science of "brain states" will replace the theory of "mental states" that has dominated the law since the invention of mens rea and the insanity defense. (But the brain is not a simple machine, and the improbability of this hypothesis was addressed briefly in Chapter 7.)

Borderline personality disorder (BPD; F60.3)

Persons with borderline personality disorder (BPD) are subject to mood swings. Their relationships with other people tend to be unstable. They can be impulsive and violent, often in response to fear of abandonment. When they commit acts of violence, typically these occur within their own homes and are directed against intimate partners or other people who are known to them (Sarkar, 2019); that is, their acts of violence tend not to be instrumental or predatory in nature but rather are woven into a complex, intimate relationship characterized by an unstable attachment. Their acts of violence typically are intended to keep the attached person close to them, but usually have the opposite effect of driving that person away.

People with BPD are over-represented in the prison population. Whereas the prevalence of BPD in the general population is estimated to be around 2.7 percent (American Psychiatric Association, 2022, p. 755), the epidemiological studies reviewed by Sansone and Sansone (2009) indicate that the prevalence in prisons is as high as 25 to 50 percent. BPD among prisoners tends to be associated with a history of childhood sexual abuse, impulsive and violent crime, comorbid antisocial traits, and incarceration for domestic violence.

In psychodynamic terms, adults who have BPD probably had unstable attachments as children and experienced psychological trauma during the crucial months of individuation and separation from their mothers, resulting in unstable patterns of attachment as adults (see Mahler et al., 1975/2008).

Narcissistic personality disorder (NPD; F60.81)

People who have narcissistic personality disorder (NPD) are absorbed in self-love and have little regard for the well-being of others. They may be capable of committing a variety of crimes that are related to their sense of entitlement, lack of boundaries, and indifference toward others. They often have a sense of grandiosity that is characterized by boldness, aggression, and exploitation of others (Dickinson & Pincus, 2003; Mitra & Fluyau, 2022; Pincus et al., 2009).

In terms of psychodynamics and psychological traumatology, it is likely that individuals with narcissistic personality disorder were traumatized as children and therefore are fixated at childhood levels of narcissism. This means that their self-love is actually a cover-up for deep-seated feelings of helplessness and inadequacy. Although they often make life more difficult for others, and as long as we can protect ourselves from their malfeasance, they are more to be pitied than hated or feared.

Criminal behavior (regardless of a defendant's diagnosis) often reflects a narcissistic sense of entitlement and lack of personal boundaries. In property crimes, defendants behave as if a victim's possessions belong to them. In sex crimes, defendants behave as if the victim's body belongs to them. In homicide, even the victim's life belongs to them. Many criminals have narcissistic tendencies and feel free to do with another person's body, life, or property as they see fit. In defendants with narcissistic personality disorder, these tendencies are even more pronounced.

CLUSTER C PERSONALITY DISORDERS

Persons who have Cluster C personality disorders "often appear anxious or fearful" (American Psychiatric Association, 2022, p. 734). People with dependent personality disorder (F60.7) experience a powerful sense of attachment that can sometimes turn to violence when that relationship is threatened. The processes by which love relationships can become violent have been delineated by Meloy (2002, 2006). In contrast to the narcissistic and antisocial personalities of Cluster B, these defendants commit acts of violence, not out of indifference to others, but out of frustrated love.

REFERENCES

American Psychiatric Association. (2022). *Diagnostic and Statistical Manual of Mental Disorders. Fifth edition. Text revision.* Washington, D.C.: American Psychiatric Association.

Cleckley, H. (1941/1988). *The mask of sanity. Fifth edition.* St. Louis: Mosby.

Damasio, A. R. (1994). *Descartes' error: Emotion, reason and the human brain.* New York: Grosset/Putnam.

Dickinson, K. A., & Pincus, A. L. (2003). Interpersonal analysis of grandiose and vulnerable narcissism. *Journal of Personality Disorders, 17*(3), 188–207. doi:10.1521/pedi.17.3.188.22146.

Fazel, S., & Danesh, J. (2002). Serious mental disorder in 23,000 prisoners: A systematic review of 62 surveys. *Lancet, 16*(359), 545–550. doi:10.1016/S0140-6736(02)07740-1.

Hare, R. D. (2003). *The Hare Psychopathy Checklist – Revised. Second edition.* Toronto: Multi-Health Systems.

Kiehl, K., & Sinnot-Armstrong, W. (Eds.) (2013). *Handbook on psychopathy and law.* New York: Oxford University Press.

Mahler, M. S., Pine, F., & Bergman, A. (1975/2008). *The psychological birth of the human infant: Symbiosis and individuation.* New York: Basic Books.

Meloy, J. R. (2002). *Violent attachments.* Lanham, MD: Rowman & Littlefield.

Meloy, J. R. (2006). *The scientific pursuit of stalking.* San Diego, CA: Specialized Training Services.

Mitra, P., & Fluyau, D. (updated May 1, 2022). *Narcissistic personality disorder.* In StatPearls [Internet], Treasure Island, FL: StatPearls Publishing; 2022 Jan–. www.ncbi.nlm.nih.gov/books/NBK556001/.

Patrick, C. J. (2006). Back to the future: Cleckley as a guide to the next generation of psychopathy research. In C. J. Patrick (Ed.) *Handbook of psychopathy* (pp. 605–617). New York: Guilford Press.

Pincus, A. L., Ansell, E. B., Pimentel, C. A., Cain, N. M., Wright, A. G. C., & Levy, K. N. (2009). Initial construction and validation of the Pathological Narcissism Inventory. *Psychological Assessment, 21*(3), 365–379. doi:10.1037/a0016530.

Sansone, R. A., & Sansone, L. A. (2009). Borderline personality and criminality. *Psychiatry (Edgmont)* 6(10), 16–20. PMID: 20011575; PMCID: PMC2790397.

Sarkar, J. (December 2019). Borderline personality disorder and violence. *Australasian Psychiatry, 27*(6), 578–580. doi:10.1177/1039856219878644.

35 Paraphilic disorders

People who have paraphilic disorders sometimes violate the boundaries of others, at which point their abnormal behaviors become illegal. This is true of the voyeuristic (F65.3), exhibitionistic (F65.2), frotteuristic (F65.81), sexual sadism (F65.52), and pedophilic (F65.4) disorders (APA, 2022).

Persons who have paraphilic disorders typically report a cycle of desire that is characterized by mounting tension followed by release of tension as the act is performed and completed. They typically know that the behavior is criminal, and they know the consequences of being caught, but their capacity for volitional control is questionable. They may be unable to resist their own impulses. Efforts at self-control may only increase their mounting tension and anxiety, which further indicates a lack of volitional control.

Their reaction to their own behavior is complex, both enjoying it and being repulsed by it at the same time. An example is Mr. X, the fetishistic baker's assistant reported by Krafft-Ebing (1886/1926):

A baker's assistant, aged thirty-two, single, previously of good repute, was discovered stealing a handkerchief. In sincere remorse, he confessed that he had stolen from eighty to ninety such handkerchiefs. He cared only for handkerchiefs, and indeed, only for those belonging to young women attractive to him. In his outward appearance the culprit presented nothing peculiar. He dressed himself with much taste. His conduct was peculiar, anxious, depressed, and unmanly, and he often lapsed into whining and tears. Lack of self-reliance, weakness of comprehension, and slowness of perception and reflection were notice-able ... He lived in good circumstances; never had a severe illness; was well-developed. In relating his history, he showed weakness of memory and lack of clearness ... His anxious, uncertain state of mind gave rise to a suspicion of onanism. The culprit confessed that he had been given to this practice excessively since his nineteenth year. For some years, as

DOI: 10.4324/9781003385028-40

a result of this vice, he had suffered with depression, lassitude, trembling of his limbs, pain in the back, and disinclination for work. Frequently a depressed, anxious state of mind came over him, in which he avoided people. He had exaggerated, fantastic notions about the results of sexual intercourse with women, and could not bring himself to indulge in it. Of late, however, he had thought of marriage. With great remorse and in a weak-minded way, he now confessed that six months ago, while in a crowd, he became violently excited sexually at the sight of a pretty young girl, and was compelled to crowd up against her. He felt an impulse to compensate himself for the want of a more complete satisfaction of his sexual excitement, by stealing her handkerchief. Thereafter, as soon as he came near attractive females, with violent sexual excitement, palpitation of the heart, erection and *impetus coeundi,* the impulse would seize him to crowd up against them and *faute de mieux,* steal their handkerchiefs. Although the consciousness of his criminal act never left him for a moment, he was unable to resist the impulse. During the act he was uneasy, which was in part due to his inordinate sexual impulse, and partly to the fear of detection.

Ten years later Mr. X was arrested again. Krafft-Ebing reported:

On searching his house, 446 ladies' handkerchiefs were found. He stated that he had already burned two bundles of them. In the course of the examination, it was further shown that X had been punished with imprisonment for fourteen days in 1883 for stealing twenty-seven handkerchiefs, and again with imprisonment for three weeks in 1886 for a similar crime ... X had married in 1879, and embarked in an independent business, and in 1881 he made an assignment. Soon after that his wife, who could not live with him, and with whom he did not perform his marital duty (denied by X), demanded a divorce. Thereafter he lived as assistant baker to his brother. He complained bitterly of an impulse for ladies' handkerchiefs, but when an opportunity offered, unfortunately, he could not resist it. In the act he experienced a feeling of delight, and felt as if someone were forcing him to it. Sometimes he could restrain himself, but when the lady was pleasing to him he yielded to the first impulse. He would be wet with sweat, partly from fear of detection, and partly on account of the impulse to perform the act. He said he had been sexually excited by the sight of handkerchiefs belonging to women since puberty. He could not recall the exact circumstances of this fetishistic association. The sexual excitement occasioned by the sight of a lady with a handkerchief hanging out of her pocket had constantly increased. This had repeatedly caused erection, but never ejaculation. After his twenty-first year, he said, he had inclination to normal sexual indulgence, and had coitus without difficulty without ideas of handkerchiefs. With increasing fetishism, the appropriation of handkerchiefs had afforded him much more satisfaction than coitus. The appropriation of the handkerchief of a lady attractive to him was the same as intercourse with her would have been. In the act he had true orgasm.

If he could not gain possession of the handkerchief he desired, he would become painfully excited, tremble and sweat all over. He kept separate the handkerchiefs of ladies particularly pleasing to him, and revelled in the sight of them, taking great pleasure in it. The odour of them also gave him great delight, though he states that it was really the odour peculiar to the linen, and not the perfume, which excited him sensually. He had masturbated but very seldom.

X complained of no physical ailments except occasional headache and vertigo. He greatly regretted his misfortune, his abnormal impulse – the evil spirit that impelled him to such criminal acts. He has but one wish: that someone might help him. (Krafft-Ebing, 1886/1926, pp. 255–258)

The persistence of this man's behavior for over a decade, despite repeated arrests and incarcerations, suggests his inability to control this behavior.

REFERENCE

Krafft-Ebing, R. V. (1886/1926). *Psychopathia sexualis.* New York: Physicians and Surgeons Book Company.

36 Mental disorders less commonly associated with crime

ANXIETY DISORDERS

Anxiety is an internalized reaction that is more likely to inhibit rather than precipitate acting out. It is not the nervous, internalized individual who presents the greater risk to public safety, but rather the worry-free, externalized, disinhibited, and careless individual who presents the greater risk. Feelings of anxiety can overwhelm a person and can lead to irrational behaviors or to inaction. Failure to take appropriate action due to an anxiety disorder can help explain crimes of negligence. The presence of an anxiety disorder also can be used to argue for mitigation.

People who have anxiety disorders are likely to experience cognitive deficits, including deficits in memory and attention (Ferreri et al., 2011). These deficits may be severe enough to interfere with competency to stand trial until the defendant can be stabilized and competency can be restored.

OBSESSIVE-COMPULSIVE AND RELATED DISORDERS

Persons with obsessive-compulsive and related disorders can be so rigid and inflexible in their behavior that they lack the capacity to conform their conduct to the requirements of the law. Adapting to the ever-changing circumstances of life demands flexibility in decision making from moment to moment.

Failure to take appropriate action due to an obsessive-compulsive disorder can help to explain crimes of negligence. The presence of an obsessive-compulsive disorder also can be used in mitigation, when the disorder has relevance for the crime and/or the sentence.

Like the anxiety disorders discussed above, obsessive-compulsive and related disorders are internalized reactions that typically inhibit rather than potentiate crime. It is the disinhibited, externalized, and careless individual who presents the greater risk to public safety and not the careful, cautious, meticulous person who has an obsessive-compulsive disorder.

DOI: 10.4324/9781003385028-41

SLEEPWALKING (F51.3)

Sleepwalking is fairly common. Estimates of lifetime prevalence have ranged from 6.9 to 29.2 percent, and estimates of past-year prevalence for adults have ranged from 1.5 to 3.6 percent (American Psychiatric Association, 2022, p. 454). If the past-year prevalence is 3 percent, and you know 100 adults, then the probability that you know somebody who has had a sleepwalking episode in the past year is 95 percent.

Sleepwalking may be relevant to forensic evaluation in the defense known as "automatism" (see Chapter 8). Automatism indicates a lack of mens rea, because the defendant was not conscious at the time of the crime and therefore was not in possession of the requisite knowledge and purpose. Mens rea is a conscious phenomenon, and the defendant who is not conscious at the time of a crime does not have mens rea.

REFERENCES

American Psychiatric Association. (2022). *Diagnostic and Statistical Manual of Mental Disorders. Fifth edition. Text revision.* Washington, D.C.: American Psychiatric Association.

Ferreri, F., Lapp, L. K., & Peretti, C. S. (2011). Current research on cognitive aspects of anxiety disorders. *Current Opinion in Psychiatry, 24*, 49–54. doi:10.1097/YCO.0b013e32833f5585.

Epilogue
The future of forensic mental health

One subtext of this book, as mentioned in the Preface, has been to approach the study of criminal justice as a history of how society treats the powerless. This includes indigents, defendants, prisoners, juveniles, people with mental illness, people with intellectual developmental disorder, people afflicted with substance use disorders, and our racial, political, and sexual minorities. These are people who often lack the social, financial, and personal resources to participate fully in our political and economic systems. Many of them are quite helpless. How we treat them is a measure of our value as human beings and our value as a society.

Preserving the life and liberty of a person with a mental disorder who is in trouble with the law has never been an easy task, and it has gotten harder. The political opponents of the insanity defense have succeeded in whittling it down in state and federal legislatures until the defense of volitional incapacity remains in only seventeen states, and four states have done away with the insanity defense altogether. The U.S. Supreme Court made it clear in *Kahler v. Kansas* (2020; see Chapter 24) that Americans who have severe mental illness do not have a constitutional right to the insanity defense. More specifically, cognitive incapacity (which is rare) can be part of a mens rea defense (see Chapters 7 and 8), but if a defendant with a severe mental illness cannot tell right from wrong (moral incapacity), or if they are not able to control their own behavior (volitional capacity), then they are not entitled to the insanity defense.

Given their victory in *Kahler*, it is not likely that any of the four abolitionist states – Idaho, Kansas, Montana, and Utah – will reinstate the insanity defense any time soon. It is more likely that the abolitionist movement will spread to other jurisdictions, possibly beginning with the other four states – Louisiana, Mississippi, Nevada, and Washington – who abolished the insanity defense during the twentieth century (only to have it reinstated by their state supreme courts). The fact that this has not yet happened may be related to a lack of recent high-profile cases. High-profile cases like *People v. White* (1981; see Chapter 21) and *United States v.*

DOI: 10.4324/9781003385028-42

Hinckley (1981; see Chapter 22) have had the effect of shrinking the insanity defense. Changes to the laws – such as those that occurred (1) in Michigan in 1975 when two cases prompted that state to create the first verdict of guilty but mentally ill; (2) in California after Dan White assassinated Mayor George Moscone and Supervisor Harvey Milk in 1978; and (3) after John Hinckley, Jr., shot President Ronald Reagan in 1981 – have directed persons who have severe mental illness and committed acts of violence into prisons instead of hospitals. The laws of the four abolitionist states give them the option of sending defendants with severe mental illness to hospitals instead of prisons, but they send them with felony convictions and not civil commitments, which means that, even if their illness goes into remission (as it did with John Hinckley, Jr.), they must serve their entire term. Mental illness fluctuates and it can be treated. People can get better. Hinckley, as terrible as his crime was, has overcome his illness and is living independently in his community.

Regardless of what the opponents of the insanity defense may think about moral and volitional incapacities, history and experience show that they are real. It is predictable that defendants who have severe mental illnesses along with moral and volitional incapacities will continue to appear in our courtrooms, whether our legislatures choose to recognize them or not. There is an old riddle attributed to Abraham Lincoln: "If you call a tail a leg, how many legs does a dog have?" The answer is four, because a tail is *not* a leg.

The "due process" era of Chief Justice Earl Warren (see Chapter 1) has passed. Recent decisions by the U.S. Supreme Court (1) have allowed the states to abolish the insanity defense (*Kahler v. Kansas,* 2020; see Chapter 24); (2) have permitted courts to sentence juveniles to life in prison without the possibility of parole without arriving at a separate finding of incorrigibility (*Jones v. Mississippi,* 2021; see Chapter 15); and (3) have allowed police interrogators to omit the *Miranda* warnings (see *Miranda v. Arizona,* 1966) and not risk civil liability (*Vega v. Tekoh,* 2022; see Chapter 9). These recent decisions by the U.S. Supreme Court have eroded the rights of all citizens who get in trouble with the law, and not just those who have mental illness.

One potential hazard of having a supermajority on the high court is that writs of certiorari will not be granted to cases that interest only the minority. The U.S. Supreme Court grants certiorari according to the "rule of four," and three justices alone cannot grant a writ of certiorari. Although the possibility exists that the supermajority may deny certiorari to cases that involve the civil liberties of defendants, what has happened instead is that cases involving the civil rights of defendants continue to be heard, and the court has been a cutting floor where those civil liberties have disappeared.

Another disturbing trend in the administration of criminal justice has been the rising number of plea bargains (see Chapter 4). The frequency of plea bargains approaches 100 percent, and the frequency of trials approaches zero. Trials are expensive, time-consuming, and labor-intensive affairs. Prosecutors can insulate their budgets by bringing as few cases to trial as possible. They can achieve this by inflating charges – for example, by charging a defendant with murder when the facts better fit the crime of manslaughter – and frightening defendants (even innocent ones) into pleading guilty to a lesser offense. Juries are notoriously harsh, and defendants may try to avoid them at any cost. In terms of forensic mental health assessment, evaluations of "competency to stand trial" are better conceptualized as "competency to plea bargain" in most cases. In the eyes of the U.S. Supreme Court, these two competencies do not differ from each other (see *Godinez v. Moran*, 1993).

In terms of verdicts and sentences, intellectual developmental disorder (IDD; see Chapter 17) in murder trials (in capital cases and in the plea of guilty but with intellectual disability; see Chapter 4) is the only mental disorder that has not been parsed into sets of discrete functions (with the possible exception of dissociative identity disorder [DID] in federal courts; see *United States v. Denny-Shaffer* (1993), discussed in Chapter 30). For all other mental disorders (e.g., schizophrenia, bipolar disorder, and DID in the state of Ohio – see *Ohio v. Grimsley* (1982), discussed in Chapter 30), not only must a defendant demonstrate that they have the disorder, but they must demonstrate how the unique features of their disorder satisfy the relevant psycholegal categories (e.g., the rational and factual understanding of competency to stand trial, or the three incapacities of insanity). This exception may be due to the fact that IDD is such a globally debilitating condition. Whatever the reason, IDD is a rare exception in the law, where a defendant need only demonstrate that they have the disorder in order for the proper judicial remedies to be applied. Developments in the law generally proceed by creating new distinctions and not blurring them (with exceptions like *Godinez v. Moran,* discussed above). Although I would hate to see life grow harder for people with IDD, we might anticipate a future prosecutor who tries to divide IDD into its relevant psycholegal functions by arguing that it is not enough to demonstrate that a defendant has IDD, but also requiring the defendant to demonstrate that features of IDD like concrete thinking and susceptibility to peer pressure were relevant to their behavior during the commission of the crime.

At this time, there is widespread concern about the quality of mental health services that are available in our courts and prisons. Our hope is that the level of professionalism will improve. This involves improved training, improved application of professional standards like the "Specialty Guidelines for Forensic Psychologists" (SGFP; American Psychological Association, 2013; reproduced here as Appendix A), and Board certification. The certifying body for forensic psychology in the United States is the American Board of Forensic Psychology (ABFP), created in 1977 under the leadership of its first president, Dr. Florence Kaslow, and later incorporated into the boards of professional psychology that operate under the auspices of the American Psychological Association. The ABFP currently has 340 members. That is fewer than seven per state. The bulk of forensic work is not being done by ABFP-certified psychologists, but by the thousands of mental health professionals who do not have ABFP certification. This situation is not likely to change. ABFP-certified psychologists are useful in individual cases and in providing training, consultation, and leadership, but we are too few in number to do a large portion of the work. It does not seem likely that ABFP membership will increase greatly in the future. Board certification is a daunting process, requiring many long hours of effort and preparation, and the examination has a pass rate of only 30 percent, which means that 70 percent of candidates have nothing to show at the end of that long process but the ignominy of having failed an examination, and this does not look good during voir dire. The psychologist who seeks Board certification assumes this risk. Lack of professionalism among practitioners is not the only threat to the quality of forensic mental health services. Criminals and juvenile delinquents are not highly valued members of our society, and funds are not always available to hire sufficient staff.

As the field of forensic mental health has matured, a variety of psychometric tests have emerged that assess psycholegal questions like comprehension of rights, competency to stand trial, criminal responsibility, risk of recidivism, amenability to treatment, malingering, and sophistication and maturity. Some of the most widely used tests are reviewed in this book. These are objective methods that were developed in the second half of the twentieth century to replace the subjective judgments of mental health professionals and to improve our scientific credibility. Efforts to improve these tests will no doubt continue. This will include the creation of new tests, improvements on existing tests, improved training of forensic practitioners so they can appreciate the quantitative and qualitative aspects of these tests, and the extension of tests into new areas and additional segments of the population. For example, risk assessment methods like the PCL-R and VRAG began with studies of adult white male offenders, but as the decades passed these instruments were extended for use with other populations, including women, juveniles, and racial minorities. This research into the subgroups of our society is essential if our methods are to have credibility when they are applied to these segments of our population. Research of this type can be expected to continue.

In conclusion, mental health professionals have a unique role to play in our criminal and juvenile justice systems. We have abundant opportunities to contribute meaningfully to the due process of law. For a mental health professional to participate fully in these processes, it would help if they understood the basic concepts of law. This includes due process, the admissibility of expert testimony, the standards of evidence, the goals of sentencing, the four levels of mens rea, the varieties of pleas and verdicts, and the three incapacities of insanity. This book attempts to provide the reader with fundamental knowledge in these areas. My underlying belief is that the complete forensic mental health professional is someone who understands (a) the nature of mental illness in its psychological, sociological, biological, and cultural dimensions; (b) the therapies; (c) psychometric testing and its mathematics; (d) enough about the law to function as an expert witness; and (e) the history of this wide-ranging field. My purpose in writing this book has been to introduce the reader to these ideas. My hope is that the book will do its part to prepare mental health professionals – and the attorneys who examine us – to participate more meaningfully in our criminal and juvenile justice processes.

REFERENCES

American Psychological Association. (2013). Specialty guidelines for forensic psychologists. *American Psychologist*, 68(1), 7–19. doi:10.1037/a0029889.

Godinez v. Moran, 509 U.S. 389 (1993).

Jones v. Mississippi, 593 U.S. ____, 141 S. Ct. 1307 (2021).

Kahler v. Kansas, 589 U.S. ____, 140 S. Ct. 1021 (2020).

Miranda v. Arizona, 384 U.S. 436 (1966).

Ohio v. Grimsley, 3 Ohio App. 3d 265, 444 NE2d 1071 (1982).

People v. White, 117 Cal. App. 3d 270, 172 Cal. Rptr. 612 (California, 1981).

United States v. Denny-Shaffer, 2 F3d 999 (10th Cir., 1993).

United States v. Hinckley, 525 F. Supp. 1342 (D.D.C. 1981).

Vega v. Tekoh, 597 U.S. ____, 142 S. Ct. 2095 (2022).

Glossary

actus reus Literally, "guilty act." The action involved in the commission of a crime. "[The] forbidden conduct," in the words of the Model Penal Code (q.v.), Section 1.13(9)(a). Actus reus is distinct from mens rea (q.v.)

affirmative defense A defense that admits the defendant committed the actus reus but argues that there were extenuating circumstances that render the defendant not guilty of a crime. The defendant who makes an affirmative defense says, basically, "Yes, I did it, but there was a reason for it, so it is not a crime." Examples of affirmative defense include insanity, duress, and self-defense.

American Law Institute (ALI) A non-profit organization created in 1923 by a group of law professors, lawyers, and judges who wanted to improve American justice by eliminating some of the uncertainties and unnecessary complexities that plagued it. The ALI proceeded in drafting the Model Penal Code (MPC, q.v.) according to "the principle of legality." (See Chapter 7.)

area under the curve (AUC) The area between the receiver operating characteristic curve (q.v.) and the midline. Used to evaluate the ability of people or tests to make accurate predictions. Originally developed with radar operators during World War II and now applied to the results of psychometric tests, including tests that predict future violence. (See also signal detection theory, q.v.) AUC measures the relationship between a continuous variable (e.g., scores on a test) and a dichotomous variable (e.g., safe or dangerous). AUC values range from 0.50 (no better than chance) to 1.00 (perfect accuracy). The closer the AUC is to 1.00, the more accurate is the test. Qualitative evaluations of AUC values have been suggested as follows (see Appendix O):

small effect: AUC = 0.56 to 0.63

moderate effect: AUC = 0.64 to 0.70

large effect: AUC = 0.71 to 1.00.

arraignment   A legal procedure that takes place early in the course of the proceedings against a defendant, at which a defendant is informed of the charge against them and enters a plea. In most situations, the arraignment follows an indictment (q.v.). Bail may be set at an arraignment.

bench trial   A trial in which a judge serves as the trier of fact (q.v.).

capacity   Defined in *Clark v. Arizona* (2006, fn. 7), as "the ability to form a certain state of mind or motive, understand or evaluate one's actions, or control them."

capital offense   An offense that warrants the death penalty.

case law   Law created by judges (i.e., the judicial branch of government) in the process of resolving disputes. Distinguished from statutory law (q.v.) and regulation (q.v.) Case law comprises judicial interpretations of statutory laws and regulations.

certiorari   Literally "to be informed of," refers to the process by which the U.S. Supreme Court decides whether or not it will hear a case. When a petitioner submits a request for a writ of certiorari, they are asking the Court to hear their case. When the Court issues a writ of certiorari, it has agreed to hear the case. Writs of certiorari are issued according to the "rule of four." If four of the nine Supreme Court justices agree that a case should be heard, then the case goes forward. The Court operates according to a principle of "ripeness" in deciding which cases to hear. That is, when an issue has gained sufficient attention – for example, when a number of lower courts have addressed an issue that needs clarifying – then the U.S. Supreme Court may grant certiorari and issue a ruling. (For an illustration of "ripeness," see the discussion of *Daubert vs. Merrell Dow Pharmaceuticals, Inc.*, 1993, in Chapter 3.)

classical test theory   One of several theories for evaluating the meaning of test scores (See Lord & Novick, 1968; Novick, 1966). (Alternative theories regarding the interpretation of test scores are item response theory and generalizability theory. See Appendix O.)

cognitive incapacity   A form of insanity in which a defendant does not know the nature of their action.

command auditory hallucination   Hearing a voice that tells you what to do. Often accompanied by a delusional belief. May be a symptom of a schizophrenia spectrum disorder. Most of the people who have command auditory hallucinations are able to resist the commands and do not obey them.

common law   In the United States, the phrase "common law" refers to all of the case law (q.v.) and statutory law (q.v.) of England and the colonies until the time of the American Revolution. English common law was created largely by judges and jurists who were involved in the resolution of disputes, using a large set of traditional legal principles that stretched back into antiquity and included particularly the ancient, unwritten laws of England. The era of English common law can be dated roughly from the time of the Norman invasion in 1066 until the late nineteenth century, by which time most laws were being passed by legislators instead of being created by judges in the resolution of disputes. English common law therefore spanned roughly eight centuries and produced a number of highly influential texts. The four great scholars of English common law were Henry de Bracton (c. 1210–c. 1268), Edward Coke (1552–1634), Matthew Hale (1609–1676), and Sir William Blackstone (1723–1780). English common law has always been highly influential in U.S. court decisions. (A partial exception is the state of Louisiana, which uses English common law in criminal procedures but whose civil procedures embrace elements of French and Spanish law.)

compatibilism   The philosophical theory of human behavior that free will and determinism are compatible with each other (i.e., they both exist at the same time). Compatibilists do not believe in the existence of agent-causal free will, i.e., that human beings are capable of making decisions that are independent of the deterministic forces that pervade our lives. Most professional philosophers are compatibilists. To a compatibilist, a criminal defendant is morally responsible for their behavior even if they were not exercising agent-causal free will at the time, because agent-causal free will does not exist. A compatibilist philosophy is possible when you define "free will" in a manner that makes it possible, as did Thomas Hobbes (1588–1679), who defined freedom as the absence of constraints, and David Hume (1711–1776), who defined free will as a perception and, to paraphrase, as "doing what you want to do." This is a compatibilist definition of free will, because a person can be controlled by deterministic forces and still be doing what they want to do.

correlation coefficient   A statistic measuring the strength of the relationship between two variables. Correlation coefficients range from -1.00, which represents a perfect negative relationship, to $+1.00$, which represents a perfect positive relationship. A value of 0 designates that no relationship exists between the two variables. The farther the value is from 0, the stronger the relationship. Many methods have been devised to calculate the correlation coefficient, and many of these methods are suitable to particular functions, like the use of Cohen's kappa coefficient (k; Cohen, 1968), which is used to measure interrater reliability (q.v.). Correlation coefficients have been designated by the letter "r" since the time of Sir Francis Galton (Galton, 1877, p. 532).

delusion   A false belief. A delusional belief may be a symptom of a schizophrenia spectrum disorder. Delusions are often present in cases of moral incapacity (q.v.).

deterministic   Not free. Caused by forces that lie outside the control of agent-causal free will, including internal forces like biological and psychological pressures, and external forces like social, political, economic, religious, and military pressures.

dissociation   A separation or splitting of mental states that normally hold together. Dissociation can be a normal ego-defense mechanism, although in some cases it is pathological. The most common example is amnesia, which is a separation of memory from action. Memory and action are usually cohesive. We usually remember the things we do. When we do not remember the things we do, it could be normal forgetting or it could be the dissociated state known as amnesia. Other forms of dissociation include derealization and depersonalization (which involve the separation of one's sense of self from its usual sensory inputs, so that the world about you and even your own actions seem unreal to you) and the creation of alternative personalities such as occurs in fugue states and dissociative identity disorder. Psychopathological conditions that can include dissociations are the psychoses, the dissociative disorders, anxiety disorders, and trauma- and stressor-related disorders like post-traumatic stress disorder. In non-pathological conditions, dissociative states can be effective ego-defense mechanisms.

duress   A situation in which one person forces another person to do something illegal. The person who perpetrates duress may be guilty of a crime. The person who is the victim of duress may be exonerated.

elements of a crime   The aspects of a crime that must be proved by the prosecution in order to sustain a conviction. Section 1.13(9) of the Model Penal Code (q.v.) lists five elements of a crime:

1 "the forbidden conduct" (i.e., actus reus)
2 the required kind of culpability (i.e., mens rea)
3 any factor that negates an excuse or justification for such conduct
4 any factor that negates a defense under the statute of limitations
5 any factor that establishes jurisdiction or venue.

Motive (q.v.) or causation is the reason for a crime, but motive is not an element of a crime: i.e., it is not something that a prosecutor must establish in order to obtain a conviction.

error   A word that has multiple definitions in an applied science like psychology. Observed scores (q.v.) differ from true scores (q.v.), which is a form of error. Interrater reliabilities (q.v.) and test-retest reliabilities (q.v.) are always less than perfect, which is a form of error. For a further discussion of error and the sources of error, see Appendix O. The concept of error became important to expert testimony when the U.S. Supreme Court decision in *Daubert v. Merrell Dow Pharmaceuticals, Inc.* (1993) listed "known or potential error rate" as the third of five factors that trial judges can use to determine the admissibility of expert testimony.

expansive mood   A period of increased goal-directed activity and increased social interaction. Expansive mood can involve high levels of energy, self-confidence, reduced need for sleep, capacity for working long hours, and capacity for multiple interpersonal relationships. Persons in an expansive mood may talk excessively and tirelessly to multiple persons. They may be hypersexual and have an unusual number of sexual relations with one or more partners.

folk psychology   The set of beliefs about human behavior and the causes of human behavior that are adopted by persons who are untrained in psychology, including most jurors.

fundamental attribution error   The tendency of people to overemphasize the role of character and underemphasize the role of situations and environments when making judgments about the causes of a person's behavior (see Ross, 1977). The chilling possibility exists that much of the criminal law of the past 6,000 years can be attributed to fundamental attribution error.

grand jury   A group of citizens who are summoned for duty, are sworn in under oath, are instructed by a judge, and hear the prosecution present its evidence against a defendant. If the grand jury believes the prosecution has sufficient evidence to proceed with a trial (i.e., "probable cause"), it returns a "bill of indictment." In common parlance, the defendant is then "bound over" for trial. If the grand jury does not believe the prosecution has sufficient evidence to proceed to trial, it issues a "no bill." The size of a grand jury varies from one jurisdiction to another, but they contain more than the fourteen members (twelve jurors and two alternates) of a jury who will hear a trial (known as a "petit jury"). Hence the name "grand jury."

hallucination   A perception of something that does not exist. Contrast "hallucination" with "pseudohallucination" (q.v.).

hypnagogic   Related to the period of time during which a person is falling asleep.

hypnopompic   Related to the period of time during which a person is waking from sleep. Hallucinations (q.v.) during the hypnopompic period are not unusual and do not necessarily indicate the presence of a mental illness.

incapacity   Lack of capacity (q.v.). *Clark v. Arizona* (2006) defined "insanity" in terms of three incapacities – cognitive, moral, and volitional incapacities.

indictment   A decision by a grand jury (q.v.) that a prosecutor has sufficient evidence (i.e., "probable cause") to proceed with a trial against a defendant. An indictment is followed by an arraignment (q.v.).

insanity defense   An affirmative defense in which a defendant argues that no crime was committed because they had an exculpatory mental illness at the time. American courts recognize four varieties of insanity defense (depending on the jurisdiction): cognitive incapacity, moral incapacity, volitional incapacity, and the product test. See the discussion in Chapter 19; see also *Clark v. Arizona* (2006).

intent   "the state of mind with which the act is done or omitted" (Black et al., 1990, p. 810). Intent may include a defendant's goal or plan. Intent is the defendant's goal toward the victim at the moment of the crime. Intent is inferred from behavior. Intent is also known as "goal" or "purpose."

interrater reliability   A measurement of the reliability of psychometric tests that is obtained by having two independent raters give the same test to the same set of subjects and then calculating the degree of correspondence as a correlation coefficient.

intuition   A form of knowledge that is independent of the four other modes of human knowledge; namely, sensory perception (either conscious or unconscious), logic, scientific method, and divine inspiration. Familiar intuitions include the existence of free will and the existence of a human soul. Intuition is different from imagination. An intuition is about something that is assumed (i.e., assumed by the intuitor) to exist and not to be imaginary. Sensory perception, logic, and the scientific method are public events in the sense that they can be shared, discussed, interpreted, and agreed upon between people in a way that the private phenomena of intuition cannot.

irresistible impulse   A concept originating in Scottish common law that was an early version of the concept of volitional incapacity (q.v.). Irresistible impulse (or volitional capacity) constitutes a third prong of the insanity defense when it is added to the cognitive and moral incapacities identified in the M'Naghten Rule (q.v.).

knowledge Awareness of information. The relevant level of mens rea is called "knowingly" (see Chapter 7).

malice A mental state of intent (q.v.) to do harm without sufficient justification. Used in the definition of "murder" as "malice aforethought," i.e., the intentional development of a plan to do harm without sufficient justification.

mens rea Literally, "guilty mind." The mental state involved in the commission of a crime. The Model Penal Code (MPC) (q.v.) of the American Law Institute (ALI) recognizes four levels of mens rea: purposely, knowingly, recklessly, and negligently (see Chapters 7 and 8).

M'Naghten Rule The definition of insanity in English law, embracing the concepts of cognitive incapacity (q.v.) and moral incapacity (q.v.). The M'Naghten Rule is based upon the jury instructions given by Lord Chief Justice Tindal in the 1843 murder trial of Daniel M'Naghten:

[The] question to be determined is, whether at the time the act in question was committed, the prisoner had or had not the use of his understanding, so as to know that he was doing a wrong or wicked act … To establish a defence on the ground of insanity, it must clearly be proved that, at the time of the committing of the act, the party accused was labouring under such a defect of reason, from disease of the mind, as not to know the nature and quality of the act he was doing; or if he did know it, that he did not know he was doing what was wrong. (*Regina v. M'Naghten* (1843, at 722)

Model Penal Code (MPC) A sample set of laws written by the American Law Institute (q.v.) that was intended to serve as an exemplar for laws in all American jurisdictions. First published in 1953 and then revised in 1962, 1985, and 2017, the MPC was written with the hope of improving American justice by eliminating some of its uncertainties and unnecessary complexities (see Chapter 7).

moral incapacity A form of insanity in which the defendant was unable to distinguish right from wrong. Moral incapacity exists when an agent believes they are doing the right thing and does not perceive that their action is wrong.

motive "What prompts a person to act, or fail to act" (Black, 1990, p. 810). The reason for or cause of a crime. The inner drive or desire that prompts a defendant to act. Motives that we commonly infer in criminal behavior include emotional and motivational states like rage, lust, fear, envy, greed, revenge, and expediency.

negligence   One of the four levels of mens rea (q.v.) identified in the Model Penal Code (q.v.). Related to a state of nonawareness. Negligence exists when the defendant did not know something they should have known. Defined by Morse (1984, p. 38) as "culpable nonawareness of substantial and unjustifiable risk."

observed score   The score that a person gets on a test. In classical test theory (Lord & Novick, 1968; Novick, 1966), the observed score differs from the true score (q.v.) according to the equation:

$$O = T + E$$

where the observed score (O) is a combination of a true score (T) plus error (E).

pseudohallucination   A misperception. A misinterpretation of a perception of something real (as opposed to a "hallucination," q.v.). Pseudohallucinations can be relevant to the defense of cognitive incapacity (q.v.). For example, Thomas Erskine used a historic illustration in the trial of James Hadfield – the example of someone who commits homicide, believing he is killing a "brute animal" and not a human being (see Chapter 20).

purpose   A behavior is purposeful when it is done with intent (q.v.) The highest of the four levels of mens rea (q.v.) identified in the Model Penal Code (q.v.), entailing the highest level of moral responsibility.

reasonable   A word that is commonly found in the law, but whose definition tends to be tautological, e.g., a "reasonable action" is something that a "reasonable person" would do.

"reasonable degree of professional certainty"   A phrase that is sometimes heard in courts regarding expert testimony. By using this phrase, an expert witness asserts that they believe what they are saying is true, and they believe that other experts in their field would reach the same conclusion. Sometimes the profession is identified, as in "a reasonable degree of medical certainty" or "a reasonable degree of psychological certainty." A definition of the phrase is tautological (as is true of all standards regarding "reasonableness"). A reasonable degree of professional certainty is the degree of certainty that a reasonable professional would hold. It is not a fanciful, whimsical, or imaginary certainty (as if an attorney would retain an expert to say something fanciful, whimsical, or imaginary!). The use of this phrase has been discouraged by certain courts and by the U.S. Department of Justice (see Chapter 3).

receiver operating characteristic (ROC) curve   A statistical method for evaluating the ability of people or tests to make accurate predictions. Originally developed with radar operators during World War II and now applied to psychometric tests, e.g., tests that predict future violence. The ROC curve measures the relationship between a continuous variable (e.g., the scores on a test) and a dichotomous variable (e.g., safe vs. violent). The ROC curve is created when the test's sensitivity is plotted on the vertical axis and the false positive rate (which equals 1 minus specificity) is plotted on the horizontal axis. The curve that results represents all possible cut scores. (See Figure O.1 for an illustration of an ROC curve. See also area under the curve (AUC) and signal detection theory in this Glossary.)

recklessness   Unjustifiable indulgence in risky behavior. One of the four levels of mens rea (q.v.) identified in the Model Penal Code (q.v.). Defined by Morse (1984, p. 38) as "awareness of substantial and unjustifiable risk."

regulation   Rules that are created by the executive branch of government (i.e., the departments and agencies that report to the president, governors, and cabinets) in order to ensure uniform implementation of law. Distinguished from case law (q.v.) and statutory law (q.v.). Regulations do not have the force of law, but can be influential when decisions are made in court. Federal regulations are published first in the Federal Register, which is published five days a week, and then are arranged by subject in the Code of Federal Regulations.

sentence   A hardship or loss that is imposed by an authority upon a defendant because of a crime.

signal detection theory   The statistical theory for evaluating the ability of people or tests to make accurate predictions, embracing concepts of area under the curve (AUC; q.v.) and receiver operating characteristic (q.v.). Originally developed with radar operators during World War II, and now applied to the results of psychometric tests, including tests that predict future violence.

Star Chamber   A room that formerly existed in the royal Palace of Westminster (until that room was removed in 1806). Named for the ceiling which was decorated with representations of stars. During the reigns of Tudor and Stuart monarchs, this room was used to make judicial decisions outside of public scrutiny. These secret processes were violations of due process and were abolished by the Habeas Corpus Act of 1640. The term "Star Chamber" has come to refer to any abuse of judicial power that is conducted in secret.

status offense   A behavior that is illegal only because of the young age of the offender. Examples are truancy, runaway, and underage drinking. Adults are free to leave home, quit attending school, or have a drink, but juveniles are not allowed these liberties because of their age.

statutory law   Law passed by the legislature. Distinguished from case law (q.v.) and regulation (q.v.).

test-retest reliability   A measurement of the reliability of psychometric tests that is obtained by giving the same test to the same set of subjects at two different points in time, and then calculating the degree of correspondence as a correlation coefficient.

trier of fact   The person or persons who will hear the testimony presented in court and will determine the facts of the case, e.g., whether a defendant is guilty as charged. In the case of a jury trial, the trier of fact is the jury. When no jury is involved, the trier of fact is the judge (see bench trial, q.v.).

trier of law   The person who presides over a trial and interprets questions of law for the trier of fact (q.v.). In a jury trial, the trier of law is the judge, whose role includes interpreting the law for the jury.

true score   In classical test theory (Lord & Novick, 1968; Novick, 1966), the true score is the score that a person would get on a test if there were no such thing as error. The true score is a mathematical abstraction, because some degree of error is inevitable on psychometric tests. (See the definition of "observed score.") Error can be estimated by calculating the reliability of a test, which gives us a basis for estimating the true score in terms of confidence intervals (see Appendix O).

volition   The capacity of an agent to make individual, independent decisions that direct their own behavior.

volitional incapacity   The form of insanity in which a defendant lacked the capacity to conform their conduct to the requirements of the law. Volitional incapacity as a form of insanity defense (q.v.) is recognized in only seventeen states (see Chapters 19 and 22).

REFERENCES

Black, H. C., with Nolan, J. R., & Nolan-Healey, J. M. (1990). *Black's law dictionary. Sixth edition.* St. Paul, MN: West Publishing Company.

Clark v. Arizona, 548 U.S. 735 (2006).

Cohen, J. (1968). Weighed kappa: Nominal scale agreement with provision for scaled disagreement or partial credit. *Psychological Bulletin, 70*(4), 213–220. doi:10.1037/h0026256.

Daubert v. Merrell Dow Pharmaceuticals, Inc., 509 U.S. 579 (1993).

Galton, F. (April 5–19, 1877). Typical laws of heredity. *Nature,* 15 (388, 389, 390); 492–495, 512–514, 532–533. doi:10.1038/015492a0.

Lord, F. M., & Novick, M. R. (1968). *Statistical theories of mental test scores.* Reading, MA: Addison-Welsley Publishing Company.

Morse, S. J. (1984). Undiminished confusion in diminished capacity. *Journal of Criminal Law and Criminology*, 75(1), 1–55. doi:10.2307/1143205.

Novick, M.R. (1966). The axioms and principal results of classical test theory. *Journal of Mathematical Psychology*, (3)1, 1–18. doi:10.1016/0022-2496(66)90002-2.

Regina v. M'Naghten, 10 Clark & Fin. 200, 8 Eng. Rep. 718 (1843).

Ross, L. (1977). The intuitive psychologist and his shortcomings: Distortions in the attribution process. In L. Berkowitz (Ed.) *Advances in experimental social psychology. Volume 10.* (pp. 173–220). New York: Academic Press.

Index

Note to readers: The page locators in **bold** refer to tables and the page locators in *italics* refer to figures.

Printed in the USA
CPSIA information can be obtained
at www.ICGtesting.com
LVHW010932270124
770126LV00009B/1037